VMWARE ESX SERVER
IN THE ENTERPRISE

VMWARE ESX SERVER IN THE ENTERPRISE

PLANNING AND SECURING VIRTUALIZATION SERVERS

EDWARD L. HALETKY

PRENTICE
HALL

Upper Saddle River, NJ • Boston • Indianapolis • San Francisco

New York • Toronto • Montreal • London • Munich • Paris • Madrid

Cape Town • Sydney • Tokyo • Singapore • Mexico City

Many of the designations used by manufacturers and sellers to distinguish their products are claimed as trademarks. Where those designations appear in this book, and the publisher was aware of a trademark claim, the designations have been printed with initial capital letters or in all capitals.

The author and publisher have taken care in the preparation of this book, but make no expressed or implied warranty of any kind and assume no responsibility for errors or omissions. No liability is assumed for incidental or consequential damages in connection with or arising out of the use of the information or programs contained herein.

The publisher offers excellent discounts on this book when ordered in quantity for bulk purchases or special sales, which may include electronic versions and/or custom covers and content particular to your business, training goals, marketing focus, and branding interests. For more information, please contact:

> U.S. Corporate and Government Sales
> (800) 382-3419
> corpsales@pearsontechgroup.com

For sales outside the United States please contact:

> International Sales
> international@pearsoned.com

Library of Congress Cataloging-in-Publication Data:

Haletky, Edward.
  VMware ESX server in the enterprise : designing and securing virtualization servers / Edward Haletky.— 1st ed.
     p. cm.
  Includes bibliographical references.
  ISBN 0-13-230207-1 (pbk. : alk. paper) 1. VMware. 2. Virtual computer systems. 3. Operating systems (Computers) I. Title.
  QA76.9.V5H35 2007
  005.4'3—dc22
                            2007044443

ISBN-13: 978-0-13-230207-4
ISBN-10: 0-13-230207-1

Text printed in the United States on recycled paper at R. R. Donnelley in Crawfordsville, Indiana.
Fourth Printing, July 2008

Editor-in-Chief
Karen Gettman

Acquisitions Editor
Jessica Goldstein

Senior Development Editor
Chris Zahn

Managing Editor
Gina Kanouse

Project Editor
Andy Beaster

Copy Editor
Keith Cline

Indexer
Erika Millen

Publishing Coordinator
Romny French

Cover Designer
Chuti Prasertsith

Composition and Proofreading
Fastpages

This Book Is Safari Enabled

Safari BOOKS ONLINE ENABLED
The Safari® Enabled icon on the cover of your favorite technology book means the book is available through Safari Bookshelf. When you buy this book, you get free access to the online edition for 45 days.

Safari Bookshelf is an electronic reference library that lets you easily search thousands of technical books, find code samples, download chapters, and access technical information whenever and wherever you need it.

To gain 45-day Safari Enabled access to this book:

- Go to http://www.prenhallprofessional.com/safarienabled
- Complete the brief registration form
- Enter the coupon code 4BA2-YYDB-7R37-E4BV-6Q29

If you have difficulty registering on Safari Bookshelf or accessing the online edition, please e-mail customer-service@safaribooksonline.com.

Visit us on the Web: www.prenhallprofessional.com

To my wife, whom I thank for her support and understanding.

Table of Contents

Acknowledgments

I would like to acknowledge my original coauthors: Paul and Sumithra. Although they were not able to complete the work, I am very thankful for their early assistance and insights into the world of virtualization. I would also like to thank my reviewers; they provided great feedback. I would like to also thank Bob, once a manager, who was the person who started me on this journey by asking one day 'Have you ever heard of this VMware stuff?' I had. This book is the result of many a discussion I had with customers and my extended team members, who took a little extra work so that I could concentrate on virtualization. I want to thank Greg from the Hewlett-Packard Storage team for his help and insights into SCSI Reservation Conflicts. Last but not least, I would like to acknowledge my editors. Thank you one and all.

About the Author

Edward L. Haletky graduated from Purdue University with a degree in aeronautical and astronautical engineering. Since then, he has worked programming graphics and other lower-level libraries on various UNIX platforms. Edward recently left Hewlett-Packard, where he worked on the Virtualization, Linux, and High-Performance Technical Computing teams. He owns AstroArch Consulting, Inc., providing virtualization, security, and network consulting and development. Edward is very active (rated Virtuoso by his peers) on the VMware discussion forums providing answers to security and configuration questions.

Preface

How often have you heard this kind of marketing hype around the use of ESX Server and its compatriots, GSX Server and VMware Workstation?

ESX Server from VMware is hot, Hot, HOT!

The latest version of ESX Server does everything for you!

A Virtualization Utopia!

VMware is the Bomb!

VMware ESX, specifically its latest incarnation, Virtual Infrastructure 3, does offer amazing functionality with virtualization, dynamic resource load balancing, and failover. However, you still need to hire a consultant to come in to share the mysteries of choosing hardware, good candidates for virtualization, choosing installation methods, installing, configuring, using, and even migrating machines. It is time for a reference that goes over all this information in simple language and detail so that readers with different backgrounds can begin to use this extremely powerful tool.

Therefore, this book explains and comments on VMware ESX Server versions 2.5.x and 3.0. I have endeavored to put together a "soup to nuts" description of the best practices for ESX Server that can also be applied in general to the other tools available in the Virtual Infrastructure family inside and outside of VMware. To this end, I use real-world examples wherever possible and do not limit the discussions to just those products developed by VMware, but instead expand the discussion to virtualization tools developed by Vizioncore, Hewlett-Packard (HP), and other third parties. Given that I worked for HP, I use HP hardware and tools to show the functionality we are discussing, yet everything herein translates to other hardware just as easily. Although things are named differently between HP and their competitors, the functionality of the hardware and hardware tools is roughly the same. I have endeavored to present all the methods available to achieve best practices, including the use of graphical and command-line tools.

As you read, keep in mind the big picture that virtualization provides: better utilization of hardware and resource sharing. In many ways, virtualization takes us back to the days of yore when developers had to do more with a lot less than we have available now. Remember the Commodore 64 and its predecessors, where we thought 64KB of memory was huge? Now we are back in a realm where we have to make do with fewer resources than perhaps desired. By keeping the big picture in mind, we can make the necessary choices that create a strong and viable virtual environment. Because we are doing more with less, this thought must be in the back of our mind as we move forward and helps to explain many of the concerns raised within this tome.

As you will discover, I believe there is quite a bit of knowledge to acquire and numerous decisions to make before you even insert a CD-ROM to begin the installation. How these questions are answered will guide the installation, as you need to first understand the capabilities and limitations of the ESX environment, and the application mix to be placed in the environment. Keeping in mind the big picture and your application mix is a good idea as you read through each chapter of this book.

Who Should Read this Book?

This book delves into many aspects of virtualization and is designed for the beginning administrator as well as the advanced administrator.

How Is this Book Organized?

Here is, in brief, a listing of what each chapter brings to the table.

Chapter 1: System Considerations

By endeavoring to bring you "soup to nuts" coverage, we start at the beginning of all projects: the requirements. These requirements will quickly move into discussions of hardware and capabilities of hardware required by ESX Server, as is often the case when I talk to customers. This section is critical, because understanding your hardware limitations and capabilities will point you to a direction that you can take to design your virtual datacenter and infrastructure. As a simple example, picture the idea of whether you will need to run 23 servers on a set of blades. Understanding hardware capabilities will let you pick and choose the appropriate blades for your use and how many blades should make up the set. In addition, understanding your storage and virtual machine (VM) requirements can lead you down different paths for management, configuration, and installation. Checklists that lead to each chapter come out of this discussion. In particular, look for discussions on cache capabilities, the best practice for networking, mutual exclusiveness when dealing with storage area networks (SANs), hardware requirements for backup and disaster recovery, and a checklist when comparing hardware. This chapter is a good place to start when you need to find out where else in the book to go look for coverage of an issue.

Chapter 2: Version Comparison

Before we launch down the installation paths and further discussion, best practices, and explorations into ESX, it is time to take time out and discuss the differences between ESX version 3.x.x and ESX version 2.5.x. This chapter opens with a broad stroke of the brush and clearly states that they *are* different. Okay, everyone knows that, but the chapter then delves into the major and minor differences that are highlighted in further chapters of the book. This chapter creates another guide to the book similar to the hardware guide that will lead you down different paths as you review the differences. The chapter covers installation differences, VM differences, and management differences. Once these are clearly laid out and explained, the details are left to the individual chapters that follow. Why is this not before the hardware chapter? Because hardware may change, but the software running on it definitely has with ESX 3, so this chapter treats the hardware as relatively static when compared to the major differences between ESX version 3 and ESX version 2.

Chapter 3: Installation

After delving into hardware considerations and ESX version differences, we head down the installation path, but before this happens, there is another checklist that helps us to best plan the installation. Just doing an install will get ESX running for perhaps a test environment, but the best practices will fall out from planning your installation. You would not take off in a plane without running down the preflight checklist. ESX server is very similar, and it is easy to get into trouble. As an example, we had one customer that decided on an installation without first understanding the functionality required for clustering VMs together. This need to cluster the machines led to a major change and resulted in the reinstallation of all ESX servers in many different locations. A little planning would have alleviated all the rework. The goal is to make the readers aware of these gotchas before they bite. After a review of planning, the chapter moves on to various installations and discusses where paths diverge and why they would. As an example, installing boot from SAN is quite a bit different from a simple installation, at least in the setup, and due to this there is a discussion of the setup of the hardware prior to installation for each installation path. When the installations are completed, there is post-configuration and special considerations when using different SANs or multiple SANs. Limitations on VMFS with respect to sizing a LUN, spanning a LUN, and even the choice of a standard disk size could be a pretty major concern. This chapter even delves into the vendor and Linux software that could be added after ESX Server is fully installed and why you would or would not want to do add it. Also this chapter suggests noting the divergent paths so that you can better install and configure ESX Server. When it comes to the additional software, this chapter leads you to other chapters that discuss the usage details in depth. And last, this chapter covers some of the aspects of automated deployment of ESX Servers and the tools needed to accomplish this task.

Chapter 4: Auditing, Monitoring, and Securing

Because the preceding chapter discussed additional software, it is now time to discuss even more software to install that aids in the auditing, monitoring, and securing of ESX server. This chapter approaches ESX from the perspective of security, and out of that will come better tools for monitoring and auditing your server for failures and possible issues. There is nothing like having to read through several thousands of lines of errors just to determine a problem started. Using good monitoring tools will simplify this task and even enable better software support. That is indeed a bonus! Yet knowing when a problem occurred is only part of monitoring and auditing; you also need to know who did the deed and where they did it, and hopefully why. This leads to auditing. More and more government intervention (Sarbanes-Oxley) requires better auditing of what is happening and even when. This chapter launches into automating this as much as possible. Why would I need to sit and read log files when the simple application can e-mail me when there is a problem? How do I get these tools to page me or even self-repair? I suggest you take special note of how these concepts, tools, and implementations fit with your overall auditing, monitoring, and security requirements. Also, note how security works inside ESX, because this is an extremely different view of the world, generally distinct from normal systems.

Chapter 5: Storage with ESX

There are many issues dealing with SANs within ESX. There are simple ones from "is my SAN supported" and "why not" to more complex ones such as "will this SAN, switch, Fibre Channel host bus adapter provide the functionality I desire?" Because SANs are generally required to share VMs between ESX Servers, we discuss them in depth. This chapter lets you in on the not-so-good and the good things about each SAN and what the best practices are for use, support, and configuration. Also discussed in this chapter are network-attached storage (NAS) and iSCSI support within ESX. With SANs, there is good, bad, and the downright ugly. For example, if you do not have the proper firmware version on some SANs, things can get downright ugly very quickly! Although the chapter does not discuss the configuration of your SAN for use outside of ESX, it does discuss presentation in general terms and how to get the most out of hardware and, to a certain extent, software multipath capabilities. This chapter suggests you pay close attention to how SAN and NAS interoperate with ESX Server.

Chapter 6: Effects on Operation

Before proceeding to the other aspects of ESX, including the creation of a VM, it is important to review some operational constraints associated with the management of ESX and the running of VMs. Operation issues directly affect VMs. These issues are as basic as maintaining lists of IPs and netmasks, when to schedule services to run through the complexities imposed when using remote storage devices, and its impact on how and when certain virtualization tasks can take place.

Chapter 7: Networking

This chapter discusses the networking possibilities within ESX Server and the requirements placed upon the external environment if any. A good example is mentioned under the hardware discussion, where we discuss hardware redundancy with respect to networking. In ESX Server terms, this discussion is all about network interface card (NIC) teaming, or in more general terms, the bonding of multiple NICs into one bigger pipe for the purpose of increasing bandwidth and failover. However, the checklist is not limited to just the hardware but also includes the application of best practices for the creation of various virtual switches (vSwitches) within ESX Server, what network interfaces are virtualized, and when to use one over the other, as well as any network lag considerations. It also includes the pitfalls related to debugging problems related to the network. The flexibility of networking inside ESX server implies that the system and network administrators also have to be flexible, as the best practices dictated by a network switch company may lead to major performance problems when applied to ESX Server. Out of this chapter comes a list of changes that may need to be applied to the networking infrastructure, with the necessary data to back up these practices so that discussions with network administrators do not lead toward one-sided conversations. Using real-world examples, this chapter runs through a series of procedures that can be applied to common problems in setting up networking within ESX Server.

Chapters 8 and 9: Configuring ESX from a Host Connection, and Configuring ESX from a Virtual Center or Host

These chapters tie it all together; we have installed, configured, and attached storage to our ESX Server. Now what? Well, we need to manage our ESX Server. There are three primary ways to manage an ESX Server: the use of the management user interface (MUI), which is a web-based client; the use of Virtual Center (VC), which is a .NET client; and the use of the command-line interface (CLI); as well as variations on these provided by HP and third parties. These chapters delve into configuration and use of these interfaces. Out of these chapters will come tools that can be used as part of a scripted installation of an ESX server, as mentioned in Chapter 3.

Chapter 10: Virtual Machines

This chapter goes into the usage of the management interfaces as I address real-world examples of planning installations. This chapter discusses making and storing images of your installation media, where to place VM configuration files, choosing your installation size, and how dynamic disks, logical volume manager, and minimized installs affect that size. Also, this chapter launches into a discussion of the various swap files available to ESX and when each is used and why. In essence, the chapter discusses everything you need to know before you start installing VMs. Once that is discussed, it is possible to launch into installation of VMs using all the standard interfaces. We install Windows, Linux, and NetWare VMs, pointing out where things diverge on the creation of a VM and what has to be done post install. This chapter looks at specific solutions to VM problems posed to us by customers: the use of eDirectory, private labs, firewalls, clusters, growing Virtual Machine File Systems (VMFSs), and other customer issues. This chapter is an opportunity to see how VMs are created and how VMs differ from one another and why. Also, the solutions shown are those from real-world customers, and they should guide you down your installation paths.

Chapter 11: Dynamic Resource Load Balancing

Because monitoring is so important, it is covered once more with an eye toward dynamic resource load balancing (DRLB) and utilization goals. The chapter discusses the use of various performance-monitoring tools that will add to your understanding of how to balance resources across multiple ESX Servers. Whereas some tools perform DRLB, still others report the important aspects for the administrator to apply changes by hand. With the advent of DRLB, there needs to be a clear understanding of what is looked at by such tools. This chapter gives you that understanding by reviewing hardware-utilization data, usage data, and performance data presented by various tools. Then, after this data is understood, the chapter shows you the best practices for the application of the data using VMotion, ESX Server clustering techniques, and how to apply alarms to various monitoring tools to give you a heads up when something needs to happen either by hand or has happened dynamically. I suggest paying close attention to the makeup of DLRB to understand the limitations of all the tools.

Chapter 12: Disaster Recovery and Backup

A subset of DLRB can apply to disaster recovery (DR). DR is a huge subject, so it is limited to just the ESX Server and its environment that lends itself well to redundancy and in so doing aids in DR planning. But, before you plan, you need to understand the limitations of the technology and tools. DR planning on ESX is not more difficult than a plan for a single physical machine. The use of a VM actually makes things easier if the VM is set up properly. A key component of DR is the making of safe, secure, and proper backups of the VMs and system. What to backup and when is a critical concern that fits into your current backup directives, which may not apply directly to ESX Server and which could be made faster. The chapter presents several real-world examples around backup and DR, including the use of redundant systems, how this is affected by ESX and VM clusters, the use of locally attached tape, the use of network storage, and some helpful scripts to make it all work. In addition, this chapter discusses some third-party tools available to make your backup and restoration tasks simpler. The key to DR is a good plan, and the checklist in this chapter will aid in developing a plan that encompasses ESX Server and can be applied to all the Virtual Infrastructure products. Some solutions require more hardware (spare disks, perhaps other SANS), more software (Vizioncore's ESXRanger, Power Management, and so on), and almost all of them require time to complete.

Epilogue: The Future of Virtualization

After all this, the book concludes with a discussion of the future of ESX Server.

Appendixes

Appendix A, "Security Scripts," presents a shell script that can be used to increase the security of an ESX Server. Appendix B, "ESX Version 3 Text Installation," presents the ESX text installation and Appendix C, "ESX Version 3 Graphical Installation," presents the ESX installation through the graphical interface.

References

This element suggests possible further reading.

Reading...

Please sit down in your favorite comfy chair, with a cup of your favorite hot drink, and prepare to enjoy the chapters in this book. Read it from cover to cover, or use as it a reference. The best practices of ESX Server sprinkled throughout the book will entice and enlighten, and spark further conversation and possibly well-considered changes to your current environments.

Chapter 1

System Considerations

The design and architecture of a VMware ESX Server environment depends on a few different considerations, ranging from the types of applications and operating systems to virtualize, to how many physical machines are desired to virtualize, to upon what hardware to place the virtual environments. Quite quickly, any discussion about the virtual infrastructure soon evolves to a discussion of the hardware to use in the environment. Experience shows that, before designing a virtual datacenter, it's important to understand what makes a good virtual machine host and the limitations of current hardware platforms. In this chapter, customer examples illustrate various architectures based on limitations and desired results. These examples are not exhaustive, just a good introduction to understand the impact of various hardware choices on the design of the virtual infrastructure. An understanding of potential hardware use will increase the chance of virtualization success. The architecture potentially derived from this understanding will benefit not just a single ESX Server, but also the tens or hundred that may be deployed throughout a single or multiple datacenters. Therefore, the goal here is to develop a basis for enterprisewide ESX Server deployment. The first step is to understand the hardware involved.

As an example, a customer wanted a 20:1 compression ratio for virtualization of their low-utilization machines. However, they also had networking goals to compress their network requirements at the same time. The other limiting factor was the hardware they could choose, because they were limited to a certain set, with the adapters precisely limited. The specifications stated that with the hardware they could do what they wanted to do, so they proceeded down that path. However, what the hardware specification states is not necessarily the best practice for ESX, and this led to quite a bit of hardship as they worked through the issues with their chosen environment. They could have alleviated certain hardships early on with a better understanding of the impact of ESX on the various pieces of hardware and that hardware's impact on ESX. (Whereas most, if not all, of the diagrams and notes use Hewlett-Packard hardware, these are just examples; similar hardware is available from Dell, IBM, Sun, and many other vendors.)

Basic Hardware Considerations

An understanding of basic hardware aspects and their impact on ESX can greatly increase your chances of virtualization success. To begin, let's look at the components that make up modern systems.

When designing for the enterprise, one of the key considerations is the processor to use, specifically the type, cache available, and memory configurations; all these factors affect how ESX works in major ways. The wrong choices may make the system seem sluggish and will reduce the number of virtual machines (VMs) that can run, so it is best to pay close attention to the processor and system architecture when designing the virtual environment.

Before picking any hardware, always refer to the VMware Hardware Compatibility Lists (HCLs), which you can find as four volumes at www.vmware.com/support/pubs/vi_pubs.html:

- ESX Server 3.x Systems Compatibility Guide
- ESX Server 3.x I/O Compatibility Guide
- ESX Server 3.x Storage/SAN Compatibility Guide
- ESX Server 3.x Backup Software Compatibility Guide

Processor Considerations

Processor family, which is not a huge consideration in the scheme of things, is a consideration when picking multiple machines for the enterprise because the different types of processor architectures impact the availability of ESX features. Specifically, mismatched processor types will prevent the use of VMotion. VMotion allows for the movement of a running VM from host to host by using a specialized network connection. VMotion momentarily freezes a VM while it copies the memory and register footprint of the VM from host to host. Afterward, the VM on the old host is shut down cleanly, and the new one will start. If everything works appropriately, the VM does not notice anything but a slight hiccup that can be absorbed with no issues. However, because VMotion copies the register and memory footprint from host to host, the processor architecture and chipset in use needs to match. It is not possible without proper masking of processor features to

VMotion from a Xeon to an AMD processor or from a single-core processor to a dual-core processor, even if it is the same family of processor that was introduced in ESX version 2.5.2. If the Virtual Machine to be moved is a 64 bit VM, then the processors must match exactly as there is no method available to mask processor features. Therefore the processor architecture and chipset (or the instruction set) is extremely important, and because this can change from generation to generation of the machines, it is best to introduce two machines into the virtual enterprise at the same time to ensure VMotion actually works. When introducing new hardware into the mix of ESX hosts, test to confirm that VMotion will work.

Best Practice

Standardize on a single processor and chipset architecture. If this is not possible because of the age of existing machines, test to ensure VMotion still works, or introduce hosts in pairs to guarantee successful VMotion. Different firmware revisions can also affect VMotion functionality.

Ensure that all the processor speed or stepping parameters in a system match, too.

Note that many companies support mismatched processor speeds or stepping in a system. ESX would really rather have all the processors at the same speed and stepping. In the case where the stepping for a processor is different, each vendor provides different instructions for processor placement. For example, Hewlett-Packard (HP) will require that the slowest processor be in the first processor slot and all the others in any remaining slots. To alleviate any type of issue, it is a best practice that the processor speeds or stepping match within the system.

Before proceeding to the next phase, a brief comment on dual-core (DC) versus single-core (SC) processors is warranted. ESX Server does not differentiate in its licensing scheme between DC and SC processors, so the difference between them becomes a matter of cost versus performance gain of the processors. The DC processor will handle more VMs than an SC but also cost more and has support only in the later releases of ESX. In some cases, it is possible to start with SC processors and make the first upgrade of the ESX Servers to be DC processors in their effort to protect the hardware investment. If performance is the issue, DC is the way to go. Nevertheless, for now, the choice is a balance of cost versus performance. Due to current shared-cached mechanisms for DC, an eight-core or four-processor server has the same processing power as if there were seven physical processors, and once shared cache goes away there is a good chance the efficiency of the DC will match that of a true eight-way machine.

Cache Considerations

Unlike matching processor architectures and chipsets, it is not important to match the L2 Cache between multiple hosts. A mismatch will not prevent VMotion from working. However, L2 Cache is most likely to be more important when it comes to performance because it controls how often main memory is accessed. The larger the L2 Cache, the better an ESX Server will run. Consider Figure 1.1 in terms of VMs being a complete process and the access path of memory. Although ESX tries to limit memory usage as much as possible, with 40 VMs this is just not possible, so the L2 Cache plays a significant part in how VMs perform.

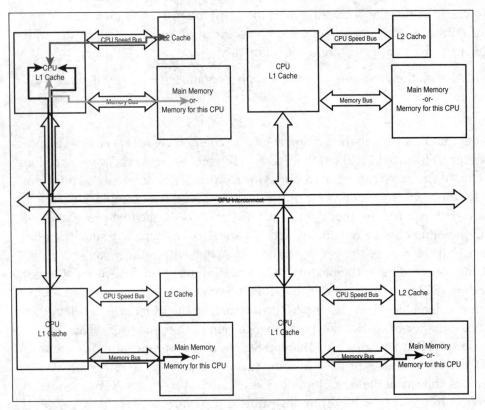

Figure 1.1 Memory access paths

As more VMs are added to a host of the same operating system (OS) type and version, ESX will start to share code segments between VMs. Code segments are the instructions that make up the OS within the VM and *not* the data segments that contain the VM's memory. Code-segment sharing between VMs does not violate any VM's security, because the code never changes, and if it does, code-segment sharing is no longer available for the VMs. That aside, let's look at Figure 1.1 again. When a processor needs to ask the system for memory, it first goes to the L1 Cache (up to a megabyte usually) and sees whether the memory region requested is already on the processor die. This action is extremely fast, and although different for most processors, we can assume it is an instruction or two (measured in nanoseconds). However, if the memory region is not in the L1 Cache, the next step is to go to the L2 Cache, which is generally off the die, over an extremely fast channel (green arrow) usually running at processor speeds. However, this takes even more time and instructions than L1 Cache access, and adds to the overall time to access memory. If the memory region you desire is not in L2 Cache, it is in main memory (yellow arrow) somewhere, and must be accessed and loaded into L2 Cache so that the processor can access the memory, which takes another order of magnitude of time to access. Usually, a cache line is copied from main memory, which is the desired memory region and some of the adjacent data, to speed up future memory access. When we are dealing with non-uniform memory access (NUMA) architecture, because is the case with AMD processors, there is yet another step to memory access if the memory necessary is sitting on a processor board elsewhere in the system. The farther away it is, the slower the access time (red and black arrows), and this access over the CPU inter-connect will add another order of magnitude to the memory access time, which in processor time can be rather slow.

Okay, but what does this mean in real times? Assuming that we are using a 3.06GHz processor, the times could be as follows:

- L1 Cache, one cycle (~0.33ns)
- L2 Cache, two cycles, the first one to get a cache miss from L1 Cache and another to access L2 Cache (~0.66ns), which runs at CPU speeds (green arrow)
- Main memory is running at 333MHz, which is an order of magnitude slower than L2 Cache (~3.0ns access time) (yellow arrow)
- Access to main memory on another processor board (NUMA) is an order of magnitude slower than accessing main memory on the same processor board (~30–45ns access time, depending on distance) (red or black arrow)

This implies that large L2 Cache sizes will benefit the system more than small L2 Cache sizes; so, the larger the better, so that the processor has access to larger chunks of contiguous memory, because the memory to be swapped in will be on the larger size and this will benefit the performance of the VMs. This discussion does not state that NUMA-based architectures are inherently slower than regular-style architectures, because most NUMA-based architectures running ESX Server do not need to go out to other processor boards very often to gain access to their memory.

Best Practice
Invest in the largest amount of L2 Cache available for your chosen architecture.

Memory Considerations

After L2 Cache comes the speed of the memory, as the preceding bulleted list suggests. Higher-speed memory is suggested, and lots of it! The quantity of memory and the number of processors govern how many VMs can run simultaneously without overcommitting this vital resource. In many cases, the highest-speed memory often comes with a lower memory penalty. An example of this is the HP DL585, which can host 32GB of the highest-speed memory, yet it can host 64GB of the lower-speed memory. So, obviously, there are trade-offs in the number of VMs and how you populate memory, but generally the best practice is high-speed and a high quantity. Consider that the maximum number of vCPUs per core is eight. On a 4-processor box, that could be 32 VMs. If each of these VMs is 1GB, we need 33GB of memory to run the VMs. Why 33GB? Because 33GB gives both the console OS (COS, the service console) and the VMkernel up to 1GB of memory to run the VMs. Because 33GB of memory is a weird number for most computers these days, we would need to overcommit memory. When we start overcommitting memory in this way, the performance of ESX can degrade. In this case, it might be better to move to 64GB of memory instead. However, that same box with DC processors can, theoretically, run up to 64 VMs, which implies that we take the VM load to the logical conclusion, and we are once more overcommitting memory. However, eight VMs per processor is a theoretical limit, and it's hard to achieve. (It is not possible to run VMs with more vCPUs than available physical cores, but there is still a theoretical limit of eight vCPUs per core.) There are rumors that it has been done. Unfortunately, that pushes the machine to its limits and is not recommended. Recommended memory utilization differs significantly for each configuration.

Best Practice

High-speed memory and lots of it! However, be aware of the possible trade-offs involved in choosing the highest-speed memory. More VMs may necessitate the use of slightly slower memory.

What is the recommended memory configuration? This subject is covered when we cover VMs in detail, because it really pertains to this question; but, the strong recommendation is to put in the maximum memory the hardware will support that is not above the 64GB limit set by ESX (because overcommitting memory creates too much of a performance hit and should only be done in extreme circumstances). However, this is a pretty major cost-benefit solution because redundancy needs to be considered with any implementation of ESX; it is therefore beneficial to cut down on the per-machine memory requirements to afford redundant systems.

I/O Card Considerations

The next consideration is which I/O cards are supported. Unlike other operating systems, there is a finite list of supported I/O cards. There are limitations on the redundant array of inexpensive drives (RAID) arrays, Small Computer System Interface (SCSI) adapters for external devices including tape libraries, network interface cards (NICs), and Fibre Channel host bus adapters. Although the list changes frequently, it boils down to a few types of supported devices limited by the set of device drivers that are a part of ESX. Table 1.1 covers the devices and the associated drivers.

Table 1.1

Devices and Drivers			
Device Type	**Device Driver Vendor**	**Device Driver Name**	**Notes**
Network	Broadcom	bcm5700	
	Broadcom	bcm5721	
	Intel	e1000	Quad-port MT is supported on ESX >= 2.5.2
	Intel	e100	
	Nvidia	forcedeth	ESX >= 3.0.2 only
	3Com	3c90x	ESX <= 2.5.x only
	AceNIC	Acenic	ESX <= 2.5.x only

continues...

Table 1.1   continued

Devices and Drivers			
Device Type	**Device Driver Vendor**	**Device Driver Name**	**Notes**
Fibre Channel	Emulex	Lpfcdd	Dual/single ports
	Qlogic	qla2x00	Dual/single ports
SCSI	Adaptec	aic7xxx	Supported for external devices
	Adaptec	aic79xx	Supported for external devices
	Adaptec	adp94xx	Supported for external devices
	LSI Logic	ncr53c8xx	ESX <= 2.5.x only
	LSI Logic	sym53c8xx	ESX <= 2.5.x only
	LSI Logic	mptscsi	
RAID array	Adaptec	dpt_i2o	ESX <= 2.5.x only
	HP	cpqarray	External SCSI is for disk arrays only. ESX <= 2.5.x only
	HP	cciss	External SCSI for disk arrays only
	Dell	aacraid	
	Dell	megaraid	
	IBM/Adaptec	ips	
	IBM/Adaptec	aacraid	
	Intel	gdth	ESX <= v2.5.x only
	LSI	megaraid	
	Mylex	DAC960	
iSCSI	Qlogic 4010	qla4010	ESX v3 only

If the driver in question supports a device, in most cases it will work in ESX. However, if the device requires a modern device driver, do not expect it to be part of ESX, because ESX by its very nature does not support the most current devices. ESX is designed to be stable, and that often precludes modern devices. For example, Serial Advanced Technology Attachment (SATA) devices are not a part of ESX version 2.5, yet are a part of ESX version 3.5 (soon to be available). Another missing device that is commonly requested is the TCP Offload Engine NIC (TOE cards), and the jury is still out on the benefit given the network sharing design of ESX. As noted in the table, various SCSI adapters have limitations. A key limitation is that an Adaptec card is required for external tape drives or libraries and that any other type of card is usable with external disk arrays.

Best Practice Regarding I/O Cards

If the card you desire to use is *not* on the HCL, do not use it. The HCL is definitive from a support perspective. Although a vendor may produce a card and self-check it, if it is not on the HCL VMware will not support the configuration.

Table 1.1 refers particularly to those devices that the VMkernel can access, and not necessarily the devices that the COS installs for ESX versions earlier than 3.0. There are quite a few devices for which the COS has a driver, but the VMs cannot use them. Two examples of this come to mind, the first are NICs not listed in Table 1.1 but that actually have a COS driver; Kingston or old Digital NICs fall into this category. The second example is the IDE driver. It is possible to install the COS onto an Intelligent Drive Electronics (IDE) drive for versions of ESX earlier than version 3, or SATA/IDE drives for ESX version 3. However, these devices cannot host a Virtual Machine File System (VMFS), so a storage area network (SAN) or external storage is necessary to hold the VM disk files and any VMkernel swap files for each VM.

For ESX to run, it needs at a minimum two NICs (yes, it is possible to use one NIC, but this is never a recommendation for production servers) and one SCSI storage device. One NIC is for the service console and the other for the VMs. Although it is possible to share these so that only one NIC is required, VMware does not recommend this except in extreme cases (and it leads to possible performance and security issues). The best practice for ESX is to provide redundancy for everything so that all your VMs stay running even if network or a Fibre Channel path is lost. To do this, there needs to be some considerations around network and Fibre configurations and perhaps more I/O devices. The minimum best practice for network card configuration is four ports, the first for the SC, the second and third teamed together for the VMs (to provide redundancy), and the fourth for VMotion via the VMkernel interface on its own private network. For full redundancy and performance, six NIC ports are recommended with the extra NICs being assigned to the service console and VMotion. If another network is available to the VMs, either use 802.1q virtual LAN (VLAN) tagging or add a pair of NIC ports for redundancy. Add in a pair of Fibre Channel adapters and you gain failover for your SAN fabric. If there is a need for a tape library, pick an Adaptec SCSI adapter to gain access to this all-important backup device.

Best Practice

Four NIC ports for performance, security, and redundancy and two Fibre Channel ports for redundancy are the best practice for ESX versions earlier than version 3. For ESX version 3, six NIC ports are recommended for performance, security, and redundancy.

If adding more networks for use by the VMs, either use 802.1q VLAN tagging to run over the existing pair of NICs associated with the VMs or add a new pair of NICs for the VMs.

When using iSCSI with ESX version 3, add another NIC port to the service console for performance, security, and redundancy.

When using Network File System (NFS) via network-attached storage (NAS) with ESX version 3, add another pair of NIC ports to give performance and redundancy.

If you are using locally attached tape drives or libraries, use an Adaptec SCSI adapter. No other adapter will work properly. However, the best practice for tape drives or libraries is to use a remote archive server.

For ESX version 3, iSCSI and NAS support is available, and this differs distinctly from the method by which it is set up for ESX version 2.5.x and earlier. iSCSI and NFS-based NAS are accessed using their own network connection assigned to the VMkernel similar to the way VMotion works or how a standard VMFS-3 is accessed via Fibre. Although NAS and iSCSI access can share bandwidth with other networks, keeping them separate could be better for performance. The iSCSI VMkernel device must share the subnet as the COS for authentication reasons, regardless of whether Challenge Handshake Authentication Protocol (CHAP) is enabled, although an NFS-based NAS would be on its own network. Before ESX version 3, an NFS-based NAS was available only via the COS, and iSCSI was not available when those earlier versions were released. Chapter 8, "Configuring ESX from a Host Connection," discusses this new networking possibility in detail.

Disk Drive Space Considerations

The next item to discuss is what is required for drive space. In essence, the disk subsystem assigned to the system needs to be big enough to contain the COS and

ESX. The swap file for the COS, storage space for the virtual swap file (used to overcommit memory in ESX), VM disk files, local ISO images, and backups of the Virtual Machine Disk Format (VMDK) files for disaster-recovery reasons. If Fibre Channel or iSCSI is available, it is obvious that you should offload the VM disk files to these systems. When we are booting from a SAN we have to share the Fibre Channel adapter between the service console and ESX for ESX earlier than version 3.0. The sharing of the Fibre Channel adapter ports is not a best practice and is offered as a matter of convenience and not really suggested for use. (Boot from a SAN is covered fully in Chapter 3, "Installation"). Putting temporary storage (COS swap) onto expensive SAN or iSCSI storage is also not a best practice; the recommendation is that there be some form of local disk space to host the OS and the COS swap files. It is a requirement for VMotion in ESX version 3 that the per-VM VMkernel swap live on the remote storage device. The general recommendation is roughly 72GB in a RAID 1 or mirrored configuration for the operating system and its necessary file systems, and for local storage of ISO files and other items as necessary.

For ESX versions earlier than version 3, the VMkernel swap file space should be twice the amount of memory in the machine. However, if twice the amount of memory in the machine is greater than 64GB, another VMkernel swap file should be used. Each VMkernel swap file should live on its own VMFS. VMs could live on a VMFS created larger than 64GB, and then a few VMs could live with the virtual swap files. However, if there will be no VMs on these VMFS partitions, the partitions could be exactly 64GB and use RAID 0 or unprotected RAID storage. The caveat in this case is if you lose a drive for this RAID device, it's possible the ESX Server will no longer be able to overcommit memory and those VMs currently overcommitted will fail. Use the fastest RAID level and place the virtual swap file on a VMFS on its own RAID set. It is also possible to place the VMkernel swap with the operating system on the recommended RAID 1 device. RAID 5 is really a waste for the VMkernel swap. RAID 1 or the VMFS partition containing the VMkernel swap file for ESX versions earlier than version 3 is the best choice.

For ESX version 3, there is no need to have a single VMkernel swap file. These are now included independently with each VM.

Any VMFS that contains VMs should use a RAID 5 configuration for the best protection of data. Chapter 12, "Disaster Recovery and Backup," covers the disk configuration in much more detail as it investigates the needs of the local disk from a disaster-recovery (DR) point of view. The general DR point of view is to have enough local space to run critical VMs from the host without the need for a SAN or iSCSI device.

Best Practice for Disk

Have as much local disk as possible to hold VMkernel swap files (twice memory for low-memory systems and equal to memory for the larger-memory systems) for ESX versions earlier than version 3.

Have as much local disk necessary to hold the OS, local ISO images, local back-ups of critical VMs, and perhaps some local VMs.

Basic Hardware Considerations Summary

Table 1.2 conveniently summarizes the hardware considerations discussed in this section.

Table 1.2

Best Practices for Hardware

Item	ESX Version 3	ESX Versions Earlier Than Version 3	Chapter to Visit for More Information
Fibre Ports	Two 2GB	Two 2GB	Chapter 5

Network Ports	Six 1GB
	  Two for COS
	  Two for VMs
	  Two for VMotion
		Four 1GB
		  One for COS
		  Two for VMs
		  One for VMotion
			Chapter 8

Local disks	SCSI RAID Enough to keep a copy of the most important VMs	SCSI RAID Enough to keep a copy of the most important VMs and local vSwap file	
iSCSI	Two 1GB network ports via VMkernel or iSCSI HBA	N/A	Chapter 8
SAN	Enterprise class	Enterprise class	Chapter 5
Tape	Remote	Remote	Chapter 11
NFS-based NAS	Two 1GB network ports via VMkernel	Via COS	Chapter 8
Memory	Up to 64GB	Up to 64GB	

Networks	Three or four
	  Admin/iSCSI network
	  VM network
	  VMotion network
	  VMkernel network
		Three
		  Admin network
		  VM network
		  VMotion network
			Chapter 8

Specific Hardware Considerations

Now we need to look at the hardware currently available and decide how to best use it to meet the best practices listed previously. All hardware will have some issues to consider, and applying the comments from the first section of this chapter will help show the good, bad, and ugly about the possible hardware currently used as a virtual infrastructure node. The primary goal is to help the reader understand the necessary design choices when choosing various forms of hardware for an enterprise-level ESX Server farm. Note that the number of VMs mentioned are based on an average machine that does not do very much network, disk, or other I/O and has average processor utilization. This number varies too much based on the utilization of the current infrastructure, and these numbers are a measure of what each server is capable of and are not intended as maximums or minimums. A proper analysis will yield the best use of your ESX Servers and is part of the design for any virtual infrastructure.

Blade Server Systems

Because blade systems (see Figure 1.2) virtualize hardware, it is a logical choice for ESX, which further virtualizes a blade investment by running more servers on each blade. However, there are some serious design considerations when choosing blades. The majority of these considerations are in the realm of port density and availability of storage. Keep in mind our desire to have at least four NICs, two Fibre Channel ports, and local disk: Many blades do not have these basic requirements. Take, for example, the IBM HS20. This blade has two on-board NICs and two Fibre Channel ports. Although there is plenty of Fibre Channel, there is a dearth of NICs in this configuration. That is not to say that the HS20 is not used, but the trade-off in its use is either lack of redundancy, or security, and performance trade-offs. Other blades have similar trade-offs, too. Another example is the HP BL3 p blade. Although it has enough NIC ports, the two Fibre Channel ports share the same port on the fabric, which in essence removes Fibre redundancy from the picture. On top of that restriction, the BL3 p uses an IDE/ATA drive and not a SCSI drive, which implies that a SAN or iSCSI server is also required to run VMs. There are also no Peripheral Component Interconnect (PCI) slots in most blades, which makes it impossible to add in an additional NIC, Fibre, or SCSI adapter. In addition to the possible redundancy issue, there is a limitation on the amount of memory that you can put into a blade. With a blade, there is no PCI card redundancy because all NIC and Fibre ports are part of the system or some form of dual-port mezzanine card. If more than one network will be available to the VMs, 802.1q VLAN tagging would be the recommendation, because there is no way to add more NIC ports and splitting the NIC team for the VMs would remove redundancy. Even with these trade-offs, blades make very nice commonly used ESX Servers. It is common for two processor blades to run between four and ten VMs. This limitation depends on the amount of memory available. On four-processor blades, where you can add quite bit more memory, the loads can approach those of comparable nonblade systems.

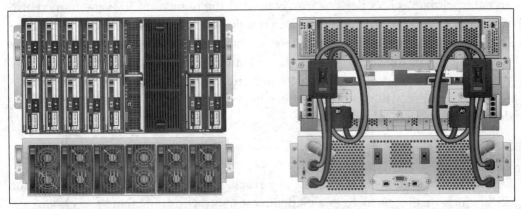

Figure 1.2 Front and back of blade enclosure
Visio templates for image courtesy of Hewlett-Packard.

Best Practice with Blades
Pick blades that offer full NIC and Fibre redundancy.

1U Server Systems

The next device of interest is the 1U server (see Figure 1.3), which offers in most cases two on-board NICs, generally no on-board Fibre, perhaps two PCI slots, and perhaps two to four SCSI/SAS disks. This is perfect for adding a quad-port NIC and a dual-port Fibre controller; but if you need a SCSI card for a local tape device, which is sometimes necessary but never recommended, there is no chance to put one in unless there is a way to get more on-board NIC or Fibre ports. In addition to the need to add more hardware into these units, there is a chance that PCI card redundancy would be lost, too. Consider the HP DL360 as a possible ESX Server, which is a 1U device with two SCSI or SATA drives, two on-board NICs, and possibly a mezzanine Fibre Channel adapter. In this case, if we were using

ESX version 2.5.x or earlier, we would need to only choose SCSI drives, and for any version, we would want to add at least a quad-port NIC card to get to the six NICs that make up the best practice and gain more redundancy for ESX version 3. In some cases, there is a SCSI port on the back of the device, so access to a disk array will increase space dramatically, yet often driver deficiencies affect its usage with tape devices.

Figure 1.3 1U server front and back
Visio templates for image courtesy of Hewlett-Packard.

In the case of SAN redundancy, if there were no mezzanine Fibre Channel adapter, the second PCI slot would host a dual-port Fibre Channel adapter, which would round out and fill all available slots. With the advent of quad-port NIC support, adding an additional pair of NIC ports for another network requires the replacement of the additional dual-port NIC with the new PCI card. There are, once again, a fair number of trade-offs when choosing this platform, and its low quantity of memory implies fewer VMs per server, perhaps in the four to ten range of VMs, depending on the quantity of memory and size of disk in the box. With slightly more capability than blades, the 1U box makes a good backup server, but can be a workhorse when needed.

Best Practice for 1U Boxes
Pick a box that has on-board Fibre Channel adapters so that there are free slots for more network and any other necessary I/O cards. Also, choose large disk drives when possible. There should be at least two on-board network ports. Add quad-port network and dual-port Fibre Channel cards as necessary to get port density.

2U Server Systems

The next server considered is the 2U server (see Figure 1.4), similar to the HP DL380. This type of server usually has two on-board Ethernet ports, perhaps one on-board Fibre Channel port, and usually an external SCSI port for use with external drive arrays. In addition to all this, there are at least three PCI slots, up to six

SCSI drives, and at least twice as much memory than a 1U machine. The extra PCI slot adds quite a bit of functionality, because it either can host an Adaptec SCSI card to support a local tape drive or library, which is sometimes necessary but never recommended, or it can host more network capability. At the bare minimum, at least two more NIC ports are required and perhaps a dual-port Fibre Channel adapter if there is not a pair of ports already in the server. Because this class of server can host six SCSI disks, they can be loaded up with more than 1TB of space, which makes the 2U server an excellent stand-alone ESX Server. Introduce dual-core processors and this box has the power to run many VMs. The major limitation on this class of server is the possible lack of network card space and the memory constraint. Even with these limitations, it is a superb class of server and provides all the necessary components to make an excellent ESX Server.

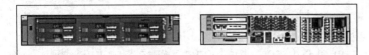

Figure 1.4 Front and back of 2U server
Visio templates for image courtesy of Hewlett-Packard.

Pairing a 2U server with a small tape library to become an office in a box that ships to a remote location does not require a SAN or another form of remote storage because it has plenty of local disk space, to which another disk array connects easily. Nevertheless, the 2U has the same characteristics as a 1U box in many cases. Is the extra memory and PCI slot very important? It can be, and depending on the type of server, there might be a need for a dual or quad-port NIC, dual-port host bus adapter (HBA), and a SCSI adapter for a tape library. The extra slot, extra memory, and lots of local disk make this class of server an extremely good workhorse for ESX. It is possible to run between 6 and 24 VMs on these types of servers depending on available memory and whether DC processors are in use.

Best Practice for 2U Servers

Pick a server that has at least two on-board NIC ports, two on-board Fibre Channel ports, plenty of disk, and as much memory as possible. Add a quad-port network card to gain port density and, if necessary, two single-port Fibre Channel adapters add more redundancy

Large Server-Class Systems

The next discussion combines multiple classes of servers (see Figure 1.5). The class combines the 4, 8, and 16 processor machines. Independent of the processor count, all these servers have many of the same hardware features. Generally, they have four SCSI drives, at least six PCI slots, two on-board NICs, RAID memory, and very large memory footprints ranging from 32GB to 128GB. The RAID memory is just one technology that allows for the replacement of various components while the machine is still running, which can alleviate hardware-based downtime unless it's one of the critical components. RAID memory is extremely nice to have, but it is just a fraction of the total memory in the server and does not count as available memory to the server. For example, it is possible to put a full 80GB of memory into an HP DL760, but the OS will only see 64GB of memory. The missing 16GB becomes the RAID memory pool, which comes into use only if there is a bad memory stick discovered by the hardware. Generally, the larger machines have fewer disks than the 2U servers do, but it makes up for that by having an abundance of PCI buses and slots enabling multiple Fibre Channel adapters and dual-port NICs for the highest level of redundancy. In these servers, the multiple Fibre Channel ports suggested by the general best practice would each be placed on different PCI buses, as would the NIC cards to get better performance and redundancy in PCI cards, SAN fabric, and networking. These types of servers can host a huge number of VMs. The minimum number of VMs is usually in the range of 20, but it can grow to as high as 50 depending on processor count, utilization, and load.

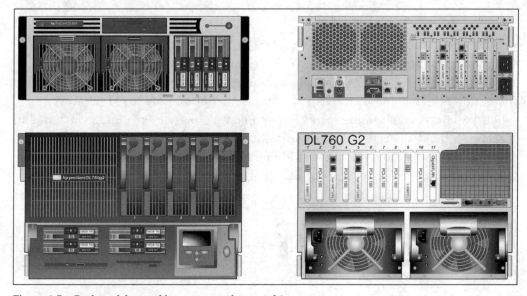

Figure 1.5 Back and front of large server-class machines
Visio templates for image courtesy of Hewlett-Packard.

The Effects of External Storage

There are many different external storage devices, ranging from simple external drives, to disk arrays, shared disk arrays, active/passive SAN, active/active SAN, SCSI tape drives, to libraries, Fibre-attached tape libraries.... The list is endless actually, but we will be looking at the most common devices in use today and those most likely to be used in the future. We shall start with the simplest device and move on to the more complex devices. As we did with servers, this discussion points out the limitations or benefits in the technology so that all the facts are available when starting or modifying virtual infrastructure architecture.

For local disks, it is strongly recommended that you use SCSI/SAS RAID devices; although IDE is supported for running ESX, it does not have the capability to host a VMFS, so some form of external storage will be required. ESX version 3 supports local SATA devices, but they share the same limitations as IDE. In addition, if you are running any form of shared disk cluster, such as Microsoft Cluster servers, a local VMFS is required for the boot drives, yet remote storage is required for all shared volumes using raw disk maps. If one is not available, the shared disk cluster will fail with major locking issues.

> **Best Practice for Local Disks**
> Use SCSI or SAS disks.

Outside of local disks, the external disk tray or disk array (see Figure 1.6) is a common attachment and usually does not require more hardware outside of the disk array and the proper SCSI cable. However, like stand-alone servers, the local disk array does not enable the use of VMotion to hot migrate a VM. However, when VMotion is not required, this is a simple way to get more storage attached to a server. If the disk array is a SATA array, it is probably better to go to SCSI instead, because although you can add more space into SATA, SCSI is much faster and is supported on all versions of ESX.

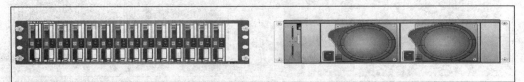

Figure 1.6   Front and back of an external disk array
Visio templates for image courtesy of Hewlett-Packard.

The next type of device is the shared disk array (see Figure 1.7), which has its own controllers and can be attached to a pair of servers instead of only one. The on-board controller allows logical unit numbers (LUNs) to be carved out and to be presented to the appropriate server or shared among the servers. It is possible to use this type of device to share only VMFS-formatted LUNs between at most four ESX hosts because that is generally the limit on how many SCSI interfaces that are available on each shared disk array. It is a very inexpensive way to create multi-machine redundancy. However, using this method limits the cluster of ESX Servers to exactly the number of SCSI ports that are available, and limits the methods for accessing raw LUNs from within VMs.

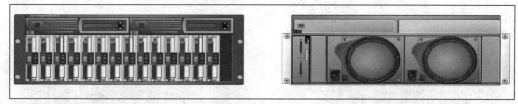

Figure 1.7 Front and back of a shared SCSI array
Visio templates for image courtesy of Hewlett-Packard.

Best Practice for Local Storage
Use local or locally attached SCSI-based storage systems.

A SAN is one of the devices that will allow VMotion to be used and generally comes in an entry-level (see Figure 1.8) and enterprise-level (see Figure 1.9) styles. Each has its uses with ESX and all allow the sharing of data between multiple ESX hosts, which is the prime ingredient for the use of VMotion. SAN information is covered in detail in Chapter 5, "Storage with ESX."

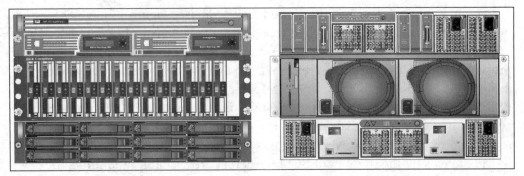

Figure 1.8   Front and back of an entry-level SAN with SATA drives
Visio templates for image courtesy of Hewlett-Packard.

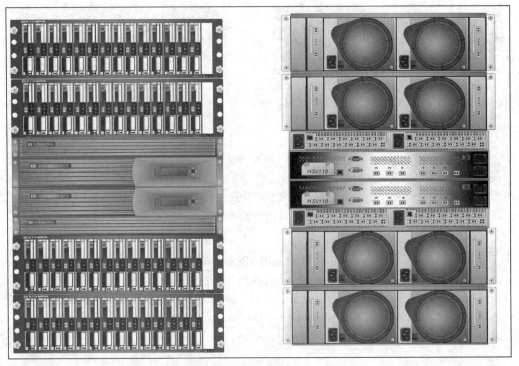

Figure 1.9   Front and back of an enterprise-level SAN
Visio templates for image courtesy of Hewlett-Packard.

Although SATA drives are not supported for ESX earlier than version 3.5, when directly attached to a host unless a SCSI to SATA bridge adapter is in use, they are supported if part of a SAN (refer to Figure 1.8). However, they are slower than using SCSI drives, so they may not be a good choice for primary VMDK storage, but would make a good temporary backup location; the best solution is to avoid non-SCSI drives as much as possible. Although the entry-level SAN is very good for small installations, enterprise-class installations really require an enterprise-level SAN (refer to Figure 1.9). The enterprise-level SAN provides a higher degree of redundancy, storage, and flexibility for ESX than an entry-level version. Both have their place in possible architectures. For example, if you are deploying ESX to a small office with a pair of servers, it is less expensive to deploy using an entry-level SAN than a full-sized enterprise-class SAN.

Best Practice for SAN Storage

Use SCSI-based SAN storage systems. For small installations, entry-level systems may be best; however, for anything else, it is best to use enterprise SAN systems for increased redundancy.

The last entry in the storage realm is that of NAS devices (see Figure 1.10), which present file systems using various protocols including Network File System (NFS), Internet SCSI (iSCSI), and Common Internet File System (CIFS). Of particular interest is the iSCSI protocol, which is SCSI over Internet Protocol (IP). This protocol is not supported as a storage location for virtual machine disk files in ESX versions earlier than 3.0, but support is available for later versions. With NAS, there is no need for Fibre Channel adapters, only more NICs to support the iSCSI and NFS protocols while providing redundancy. In general, iSCSI and NAS run slightly more slowly than Fibre Channel when looking at the raw speeds networking currently available.

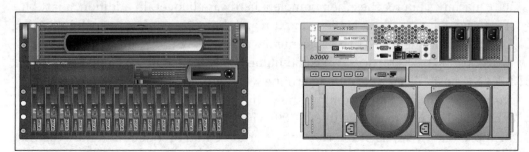

Figure 1.10 NAS device
Visio templates for image courtesy of Hewlett-Packard.

> **Best Practice for iSCSI**
> NAS or iSCSI are not supported on versions earlier than ESX version 3.0; do not use this device until an upgrade is available. Also, have enough COS NIC ports to provide redundancy and bandwidth.

Examples

Now it is time to review what customers have done in relation to the comments in the previous sections. The following six examples are from real customers, not from our imagination. The solutions proposed use the best practices previously discussed and a little imagination.

Example 1: Existing Datacenter

A customer was in the midst of a hardware-upgrade cycle and decided to pursue alternatives to purchasing quite a bit of hardware; the customer wanted to avoid buying 300+ systems at a high cost. They decided to pursue ESX Server. Furthermore, the customer conducted an exhaustive internal process to determine the need to upgrade the 300+ systems and believes all of them could be migrated to ESX, because they meet or exceed the documented constraints. Their existing machine mix includes several newer machines from the last machine refresh (around 20), but is primarily made up of machines that are at least 2 to 3 generations old, running on processors no faster than 900MHz. The new ones range from 1.4GHz to 3.06GHz 2U machines (see Figure 1.4). The customer would also like to either make use of their existing hardware somehow or purchase very few machines to make up the necessary difference, because the price for ESX to run 300+ machines approaches their complete hardware budget. In addition, a last bit of information was also provided, and it really throws a monkey wrench into a good solution: They have five datacenters with their own SAN infrastructure.

Following best practices, we could immediately state that we could use the 3.06GHz hosts. Then we could determine whether there were enough to run everything. However, this example shows the need for something even more fundamental than just hardware to run 300+ virtual machines. It shows the need for an appropriate analysis of the running environment to first determine whether the 300+ servers are good candidates for migration, followed by a determination of which servers are best fit to be the hosts of the 300+ VMs. The tool used most often to perform this analysis is the AOG Capacity Planner. This tool will gather up various utilization and performance numbers for each server over a one- to two-month period. This information is then used to determine which servers make good candidates to run as VMs.

Best Practice
Use a capacity planner or something similar to get utilization and performance information about servers.

When the assessment is finished, you can better judge which machines could be migrated and which could not be. Luckily, the customer had a strict "one application per machine" rule, which was enforced, and which removes possible application conflicts and migration concerns. With the details released about their current infrastructure, it was possible to determine that the necessary hardware was already in use and could be reused with minor hardware upgrades. Each machine would require dual-port NIC and Fibre Channel cards and an increase in memory and local disk space. To run the number of VMs required and to enable the use of VMotion, all machines were paired up at each site at the very least, with a further recommendation to purchase another machine per site (because there were no more hosts to reuse) at the earliest convenience so that they could alleviate possible machine failures in the future. To perform the first migrations, some seed units would be borrowed from the manufacturer and LUNs carved from their own SANs allowing migration from physical to virtual using the seed units. Then the physical host would be converted to an ESX Server and the just-migrated VM VMotioned off the borrowed seed host. This host would be sent to the other sites as their seed unit when the time came to migrate the hosts at the next datacenter. This initial plan would be revised once the capacity planner was run and analyzed.

Example 2: Office in a Box

One of the author's earliest questions was from a company that wanted to use ESX to condense hundreds of remote locations into one easy-to-use and -administer package of a single host running ESX with the remote office servers running as VMs. Because the remote offices currently used outdated hardware, this customer also felt that he should use ESX because it would provide better remote management capability. The customer also believed that the hardware should be upgraded at these remote offices all over the world. Their goal was to ship a box to the remote location, have it plugged in, powered up, and then remotely manage the server. If there were a machine failure of some sort, they would ship out a new box. The concern the customer had was the initial configuration of the box and how to perform backups appropriately.

One of the very first questions we ask the customer is whether they will be using Microsoft Clusters now or in the future of their ESX deployment. When we first started the discussions, they claimed this was never going to be the case. Just in case, we made sure that they set up their six-drive dual-processor machines with a full complement of memory and disks, an extra dual-port Ethernet card, an external tape device via an Adaptec card (see Figure 1.11), and enough file system space for a possible shared system. We discussed a SAN and the use of VMotion, but the customer thought that this would be overkill for their remote offices. For their datacenter, this was a necessity, but not for a remote office.

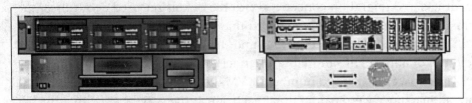

Figure 1.11 Office in a box server with tape library
Visio templates for image courtesy of Hewlett-Packard.

However, the best-laid plan was implemented incorrectly, and a year after the initial confirmation of the customer's design, they needed to implement Microsoft Clustering as a cluster in a box. Because of this oversight, the customer had to reinstall all the ESX Servers to allocate a small shared-mode VMFS. They had to reinstall their machines, but first they set up their operating system disk as a RAID 1, making using of hardware mirroring between disks 1 and 2, leaving the last four disks to make a RAID 5 + 1 spare configuration of 146GB disks. The smaller disks met their VM load quite nicely. On the RAID 5 LUN, they created two file systems, one for the VMFS for the public (nonclustered) VMs and a smaller partition for the shared data drives for the cluster.

Although using a single partition for the two distinct VMFSs is not generally recommended because of LUN-locking considerations, it can be and has been done in a single host environment, as we are discussing. If an entry-level SAN (refer to Figure 1.8) were used, another host would have been added, and the multiple partition approach would *not* be a best practice due to the nature of SCSI reservations, which are further discussed in Chapter 5. However, in a single-host configuration, SCSI reservations are less of a concern, so use of multiple partitions on the same LUN is not going against any best practices. Ideally, it would be proper to have three LUNs: RAID 1 for the OS and RAID 5 for both necessary VMFSs. However, three LUNs would require at least eight disks, and a disk array would have been necessary, increasing the expense for not much gain, because the VMs in question are small in number and size.

Example 3: The Latest and Greatest

One of our opportunities dealt with the need for the customer to use the latest and greatest hardware with ESX Server and in doing so to plan for the next release of the OS at the same time. The customer decided to go with a full blade enclosure using dual CPU blades with no disk, and many TOE cards so that they could boot their ESX Servers via iSCSI from a NAS (see Figure 1.12). The customer also required an easier and automated way to deploy their ESX Servers.

This presented several challenges up front. The first challenge was that the next release of the OS was not ready at the time, and the HCL for the current release *and* the first release of the next version of ESX showed that some of their desired options would *not* be implemented. So, to use ESX, the hardware mix needed to be changed for ESX version 2.5 and for version 3.0. The customer therefore traded in the TOE cards for Fibre cards or blanks. They also realized that iSCSI and NAS receive limited support in the first release of ESX version 3.0. Therefore, they also needed to get access to local disks to implement their desired virtualization.

The main concern here is that the customer wanting the latest and greatest instead got a mixed bag of goodies that were not compatible with the current release, and the prelist of the HCL for the next release did not list their desired hardware either. In essence, if it is not on the HCL now, most likely it will not be on the list in the future; if you can get a prerelease HCL, this can be verified. In essence, this customer had to change their plans based on the release schedules, and it made for quite a few headaches for the customer and required a redesign to get started, including the use of on-board SCSI drives and the use of a SAN. In essence, always check the HCL on the VMware website before purchasing anything.

As for the deployment of ESX, the on-board remote management cards and the multiple methods to deploy ESX made life much easier. Because these concepts are covered elsewhere, we do not go into a lot of detail. ESX provides its own method for scripted installations just for blades. Many vendors also provide mechanisms to script the installations of operating systems onto their blades. The key to scripted installations is adding in all the extra bits often required that are outside of ESX, including hardware agents and other necessary software.

Example 4: The SAN

Our fourth example is a customer who brought in consulting to do a bake-off between competing products using vendor-supplied small SANs. Eventually, the customer made a choice and implemented the results of the bake-off in their production environment that used a completely different SAN that had some significant differences in functionality. Although this information was available during the bake-off, it was pretty much a footnote. This in turn led to issues with how they were implementing ESX in production that had to be reengineered. What made this customer unique is that they wanted to get ESX 3.0 style functionality while using ESX 2.5. Although a noble goal, it leads to setting up 2.5 in a mode that does not follow best practices but that is supportable. The customer wanted to store all VM data on the SAN, including the VM configuration and log files. The customer wrote up their desire and wanted confirmation that this was a supportable option.

The architecture decided upon called for each ESX Server to mount a home directory from the SAN so that VM configuration files could be stored on the SAN, and because the VMFS was already on the SAN, everything related to a VM would be stored on the SAN using two distinctly different file systems. To enable the multiple SAN-based file systems, it is necessary to share the Fibre Channel Adapters between the COS and the VMs for ESX versions before 3.0. The sharing of the Fibre Channel adapters is not a best practice and often causes problems. To limit issues, it is best to have one file system per LUN. Because the customer wanted to have the configuration files available to each possible server, the customer created multiple Linux ext3 file systems sharing the same LUN. This also does not follow the best practice of one file system per LUN. However, they did not mix file system types, so there are no Linux file systems sharing a portion of a LUN with VMFS. This is a good thing because both the VMkernel and the Linux kernel can lock a LUN separately when Fibre Channel adapters are shared, and this will cause SCSI reservations and other SCSI issues. We discuss these issues in Chapter 5.

Even though this customer uses several functions that do not follow best practices, this example is here to point out that although best practices exist, they do not define what is supported or even capable with ESX. We confirmed their architecture was supportable, but also pointed out the best practices and possible problems. Many of the items that were not best practices with ESX versions earlier than 3.0 are now a part of ESX version 3.0. From this example, ESX version 3.0 incorporates the storage of VM configuration and disk files on a VMFS, instead of needing to use multiple file systems and possibly problematic configurations. Understanding the limitations of ESX will aid in the use of ESX with various hardware.

Example 5: Secure Environment

It is increasingly common for ESX to be placed into secure environments as long as the security specialist understands how ESX works and why it is safe to do so. However, in this case, the security specialist assumed that because the VMs share the same air they are therefore at risk. Although we could prove it was not the case, the design of the secure environment had to work within this limitation. The initial hardware was two dual-CPU machines and a small SAN that would later be removed when they proved everything worked and their large corporate SANs took over. The customer also wanted secure data not to be visible to anyone but the people in the teams using the information.

This presented several concerns. The first is that the administrators of the ESX box must also be part of the secure teams, have the proper corporate clearances, or be given an exception, because anyone with administrator access to an ESX Server also has access to all the VMDKs available on the ESX Server. Chapter 4, "Auditing, Monitoring, and Securing," goes into securing your ESX environment in quite a bit of detail, but suffice to say, virtualization has its own issues. Because the customer wanted to secure their data completely, it is important to keep the service console, VMotion, and the VM networks all on their own secure networks, too. Why should we secure VMotion and everything? Because VMotion will pass the memory footprint of the server across an Ethernet cable and, combined with access to the service console, will give a hacker everything a VM is doing. If not properly secured, this is quite a frightening situation.

Whereas the company had a rule governing use of SANs to present secure data LUNs, they had no such policy concerning ESX. In essence, it was important to create an architecture that kept all the secure VMs to their own set of ESX Servers and place on another set of ESX Servers those things not belonging to the secure environment. This kept all the networking separated by external firewalls and kept the data from being accessed by those not part of the secure team. If a new secure environment were necessary, another pair of ESX Servers (so we can VMotion VMs) would be added with their own firewall.

The preceding could have easily been performed on a single ESX Server, yet require the administrators to have the proper corporate clearances to be allowed to manipulate secured files. Given this and the appropriate network configuration inside ESX, it is possible to create many different secure environments within a single ESX host, including access to other secure machines external to ESX. However, this customer did not choose this option.

Example 6: Disaster Recovery

We were asked to do a DR plan for a customer that had two datacenters in close proximity to each other. The customer wanted a duplicate set of everything at each site so that they could run remotely if necessary. This is not an uncommon desire, because they in effect wanted a hot site implementation. Their current ESX Server load was two dual-CPU hosts at each location, two distinctly different SANs, and some slightly different operational procedures. The currently light load on each ESX Server would eventually grow until new machines were placed in the environment.

Due to the disparate SAN environments, it was impossible to create a SAN copy of the data because the SANs spoke different languages. Therefore, a hardware solution to the problem was out of the question. This in turn led to political issues that had to be ironed out. Once allowed to proceed, the decision was made to create backups using some other mechanism and physically copy the VMs from site to site using some form of automated script. Although there are plenty of tools that already do this, ESX comes equipped with the necessary script to make backups of VMs while they are still running, so in essence a hot copy can be made by ESX with a bit of scripting. Tie this to a local tape drive (which the customer also wanted to place into the mix) and a powerful local and remote backup solution emerges.

Various other approaches were discussed, but unfortunately, they would not work. A key idea was to use VMotion, but the distances involved implied the VMs would be shipped over a very long yet dedicated wire from site to site, which would put the memory footprints of the VMs at risk. Earlier versions of ESX solve this issue by not allowing VMotion to work through a gateway and router. ESX version 3 on the other hand allows VMotion to work through a router and gateway. Another possibility was the use of an offsite backup repository, but that would make restoration slower.

A plan was devised that made the best use of the resources, including remote backups, backup to tape, and storage of tapes offsite. In essence, everything was thought about, including the requirement for a third site in case the impossible regional disaster hit. Little did we know....

The DR plan that was implemented made restoration much easier when the natural disaster hit. What could have taken weeks to restore took just days because the customer had DR backups of the virtual disk files for every VM on the system. These types of backups happen through the COS and should be considered as part of any deployment of ESX. A backup through the VMs, which is the traditional method to back up servers, requires other data-restoration techniques that take much longer than a backup and restore of a single file.

Hardware Checklist

Now that we have been through a few of the concepts related to the hardware and the individual limitations of various machines listed, we can devise a simple hardware checklist (see Table 1.3) that, if followed, will create a system that follows best practices.

Table 1.3

Hardware Checklist		
Hardware	**Best Practice**	**Comments**
Network adapters (discussed further in Chapter 8)	Two gigabit ports for service console	Two gigabit ports could be used for ESX version 3.0 with load balancing and failover, but for ESX version 2.5.x or earlier a watchdog is necessary.
	Two gigabit ports for VMotion	ESX 2.5.x: Two gigabit ports could be used, but the second port is purely for failover.
	Two gigabit ports per network available to the VMs	More than two gigabit ports in a team can cause switching issues. 802.1q VLAN tagging is also available.
	Two gigabit or more ports for NAS	ESX version 3.0 only. Two gigabit ports provide failover and bandwidth.
		ESX version 3.0 only. NFS is the only supported NAS protocol. CIFS is not supported.
iSCSI	Two gigabit ports for iSCSI either in the form of gigabit NICs or an iSCSI HBA	ESX version 3.0 only. Support for boot from iSCSI required an iSCSI HBA. An iSCSI HBA is a specialized TCP Offload Engine NIC.

continues...

Table 1.3   continued

Hardware Checklist		
Hardware	**Best Practice**	**Comments**
Fibre Channel adapters (discussed further in Chapter 5)	Two 2GbE (Gigabit Ethernet) ports	This will provide failover and some multipath functionality with active-active style of SANs.
	Two 4GbE ports	In the future, 4GbE Fibre Channel ports will be supported.
Tape drives or libraries	Adaptec SCSI card	Internal and external tape drives or libraries require an Adaptec SCSI card to be of use.
CPU	Match CPUs within a host	
	Match CPUs between hosts	Required for VMotion.
Disk (discussed further in Chapter 12)	Minimum a 72GB RAID 1 for OS	
	Minimum a 2xMemory RAID 0 for virtual swap	If 2xMemory is 64Gb or less, only one RAID 0 is necessary. If 2xMemory is 128GB, two 64GB RAID 0 disk is necessary. ESX <= 2.5.x only.
	RAID 5 for local VMFS	This is mainly for DR purposes, or if you do not have SAN or iSCSI storage available.

Extra Hardware Considerations

All versions of ESX support connections from the VirtualCenter Management Server, and for ESX version 3 there is the license server and the VMware Consolidated Backup (VCB) proxy server. Because these tools are used to manage or interact with the ESX datacenter it might be necessary to consider the need for specialized hardware to run them and the databases to which they connect. Although many administrators run VirtualCenter within a VM, others never run it from a VM.

Best Practices for Virtual Infrastructure non-ESX Servers

VCB proxy server must run from a physical server because the LUNs attached to the ESX Servers must be presented to the VCB proxy server.

VirtualCenter Management Server can run from a VM, but the best practice is to use a physical server.

VMware License Server should always run on a physical server. It does not need to be a large machine. It is a good idea to keep it with the VirtualCenter Management Server.

Database Server, used by VirtualCenter, should reside on a SQL clustered set of servers. One node of the cluster could be a VM for backup functionality.

Conclusion

There is quite a bit to consider from the hardware perspective when considering a virtualization server farm. Although we touch on networking, storage, and disaster recovery in this chapter, it should be noted that how the hardware plays out depends on the load, utilization goals, compression ratios desired, and the performance gains of new hardware (which were not discussed). The recommendations in this chapter are suggestions of places to start the hardware design of a virtualization server farm. Chapter 2, "Version Comparison," delves into the details of and differences between ESX version 3.0 and earlier versions to help you better understand the impact of hardware on ESX. Understanding these differences will aid you in coming up with a successful design of a virtual environment.

Chapter 2

Version Comparison

VMware started with a "please try this, it is cool, and tell us what to fix" version of VMware Workstation. Soon after that, VMware Workstation version 2 came out, and the world of computing changed. When version 4 of VMware Workstation came out, more and more people started to use the product, and soon after came the server versions GSX and ESX. With ESX, another change to computing took place, and *virtualization* has become the buzzword and driving force behind many datacenter choices.

VMware produces four major products with varying capabilities and functionality. The products form a triangle where VMware Workstation is at the bottom with the broadest ranges of functionality and capability. It is here that VMware tries out new ideas and concepts, making it the leading edge of virtualization technology. The second tier is VMware ACE and VMware Player, which play VMs that already exist and provide many of the capabilities of VMware Workstation but without the capability to make changes. The third tier of the triangle is GSX and VMware Server, which could be said to be VMware Workstation on steroids as it is a middle ground between VMware Workstation and ESX, providing VM Server-style functionality while running upon another operating system: Windows or Linux. The pinnacle tier is ESX, which is its own operating system and the version comparison covered within this chapter.

The VMware Infrastructure product consists of Workstation, ACE, GSX, and ESX. The VMware Administration product is composed of VMware Virtual Center Server (VC), VMware High Availability (HA), Distributed Resource Scheduling (DRS), SAN, iSCSI, and NAS, and VMotion. The last product suite is VMware Tools, which is composed of the VMware Converter the new Physical to Virtual (P2V) and VMware Consolidated Backup (VCB).

ESX version 3 and ESX version 2.5.x differ in many ways, and some of them revolve around what Administration products are available to each, and others around how the functionality of the earlier version was implemented inside the new version. ESX version 3 appears very different from ESX version 2.5.x in many ways. There are changes in just about every subsystem, and all for the better. This is the release of ESX that brings many of the VMware Workstation five cutting-edge technologies into the server environment, including the new virtual hardware and disk file format and functionality (including snapshot).

Because so many subsystems have had modifications and enhancements, they need to be broken out in more detail. It is easy to say it is a new operating system, but in essence ESX version 3 is an enhancement to ESX version 2.5.3 that simplifies administration and increases functionality, incorporating common customer-requested improvements.

The version comparison of ESX in this chapter looks at the following:

- The VMkernel (the nuts and bolts of the virtualization hypervisor)
- The boot process and tools of the console operating system (COS) or service console
- The changes to virtual networking (vNetwork)
- New and different VMFS data stores, virtual resource capabilities
- Backup methods
- Licensing methods
- Virtual hardware functionality
- VM management
- Server and VM security
- Installation differences
- VMware Certified Professional changes

VMkernel Differences

The heart of ESX is the VMkernel, and future enhancements all stem from improvements to this all-important subsystem. The new VMkernel supports new and different guest operating systems and upgrades to support the latest COS version and driver interactions. The VMkernel looks similar to a Linux kernel, but it is not a Linux kernel. However, it does have some similarities. The most interesting similarity is the way modules are loaded, and the list of supported modules has changed drastically. Table 2.1 shows the standard modules loaded by each version of ESX for a Proliant server. The table will differ for each vendor's hardware in minor aspects, but it should be noted that for ESX version 3 some new modules are hardware independent.

Table 2.1

Module Version Differences for Proliant Hardware		
ESX Vversion 2.5.x	**ESX Vversion 3.0**	**Comments**
vmklinux	vmklinux	Linux interface
nfshaper	nfshaper	NFS
aic7xxx	aic7xxx	Adaptec SCSI HBA for local tape device
e1000 | e100 | bcm5700	e1000 | e100 | tg3 | forcedeth	Intel, and Broadcom, and Nvidia pNIC drivers
lpfcdd_2xx | qla2[23]00_xxx	lpfcdd_7xx | qla2300_7xx | qla4010	Emulex and Qlogic FC-HBA
cpqarray | cciss | ips | aic...	cciss | ips | aic...	RAID HBA
bond	bond	vSwitch bonding
	vmkapimod	VMkernel API module
	vmfs2	VMFS-2
	vmfs3	VMFS-3
	nfsclient	VMkernel NFS client
	iscsi_mod	VMkernel iSCSI support
nfshaper		vSwitch traffic shaper
migration	migration	VMkernel VMotion
	fsaux	VMFS utilities

The default modules have changed greatly, and some things have gone out the door. ESX version 3 is more modular, which enables the capability to add devices without requiring a recompile of the VMkernel. One of the key enhancements is the addition of separate modules for the VMFS versions and vmkapimod, which provides the application programming interface (API) for interacting with the VMkernel for purposes of management. The added modules enhance the capabilities of ESX and enable third parties to create management tools similar to the Virtual Infrastructure Client (VIC).

One major change to the VMkernel is the ability to mask off processor capabilities on a per-VM basis. This allows for better integration of disparate processors into the mix. For example, it is possible to set bitmasks to allow the VMotion of a VM from an SC Xeon to a DC AMD processor. However, this useful feature is currently only available for 32-bit VMs.

Some modules disappeared from ESX version 3; and if these devices are required, upgrading to ESX version 3 will not be possible. Table 2.2 lists the missing devices. The developers of ESX version 3 preferred to stabilize on modern hardware, and much of the older hardware is obsolete.

Table 2.2

Obsolete Devices	
Driver	**Device**
cpqarray	Compaq SmartArray devices earlier than the SmartArray 5300
gdth	GDT SCSI disk array controller
3c990	3Com EtherLink 10/100 PCI NIC with 3XP Processor
acenic	AceNIC/3C985/GA620 Gigabit Ethernet
ncr53c8xx	NCR53C SCSI
sym53c8xx	SYM53C SCSI
dpt_i20	Adaptec I20 RAID Driver
nfshaper	Traffic Shaper

In addition to the driver changes, ESX version 3 now loads differently. Before, the VMkernel would load after the COS kernel loaded as a service startup, but that has also changed. The VMkernel now loads much earlier in the process so that the COS VM can be fully created. Although the change is not huge, it is significant because the COS is now a VM independent of the VMkernel, which reduces resource contention.

Another significant change to ESX version 3 is the lack of a need to divvy up the PCI devices between the VMkernel (and the VMs) and the service console (or the COS). ESX version 3 does this automatically now on installation, and it is no longer necessary to perform any such divvying up for all devices. It is possible, however, to query HBA devices using the `vmkpcidivy` command, but it is not possible to use this command to change them.

The last and probably the most significant change to the VMkernel is the opening up of the VMkernel to more than just the VMotion network. Now there can be a multitude of physical NICs (pNICs) associated with the VMkernel for purposes of NFS, iSCSI, and VMotion. The VMkernel has its own network access, so it is no longer dependent upon what the COS has available yet presents its own problems with network creation and usage. Support for NFS via a NAS directly in the VMkernel alleviates bottlenecks on the COS and provides different storage options for VM files, including disk files. In addition, the VMkernel now can access iSCSI and NFS targets for placement of VMDKs files for use with ESX. The iSCSI target can have its own network interfaces within the VMkernel, thereby alleviating any form of bottleneck possibly caused by going through the COS for this information. All access to data stores (VMFS and otherwise) used by the VMkernel is now independent of the COS. Although the COS can still read and write these files, it is no longer the gatekeeper to the VMkernel. A complete discussion of the data store types appears later in this chapter.

Console Operating System/Service Console

There are two major differences between ESX version 3 and earlier releases related to the COS: the version and the tools available.

Version Differences

Simply put, the COS has been upgraded from being based on a variant of Red Hat version 7.2 to being based on a variant of Red Hat Enterprise Linux Server version 3.0 Update 6 (RHEL3-ES). However, ESX is in no way a complete distribution of Linux. Technically, it is not Linux at all, because the VMkernel is what is interacting with the hardware and the COS is running within a VM. Legally, the VMkernel is not Linux either, as it proprietary. Although the COS is a variant of Linux, it is just a management appliance and not the operating system of ESX.

Even with the change in COS version, the rule that "no Red Hat updates should be used" has been changed. All updates to the COS should come only from VMware. This is crucial. Consider the following: ESX consists of a single CD-ROM, whereas the official version of RHEL3-ES takes up four CD-ROMs. Therefore, they are not the same and should never be considered the same. For RHEL3-ES, the method to configure any part of the system is to use the supplied redhat-config- scripts. These are not a part of ESX. Instead, there are a series of esxcfg- scripts that do not map one to one to the original Red Hat scripts.

The esxcfg- scripts, however, outlined in a later chapter, do map pretty well to the new management tool: Virtual Infrastructure Client 2.0 (VIC). This allows for either the client to be used to configure an ESX Server or the VIC to be used. The VIC replaces the management user interface (MUI) presented by ESX versions earlier than version 3.0. Although there continues to be a web-based interface, it does not present a method to configure the ESX Server or a way to create VMs.

ESX has a kernel that is proprietary and modified from the stock RHEL3-ES kernel and therefore cannot be Linux. The modifications to the stock kernel allow the VMkernel and the COS kernel to cohabitate, by redirecting PCI devices via kernel command-line arguments to be either presented directly to the COS or to the VMkernel. The difference here between ESX version 3 and earlier versions is that there is no longer any control over how devices are assigned and presented to the VMkernel or COS. This is automated so that most, if not all, devices are presented and managed through the VMkernel. However, the COS in ESX version 3 only sees devices presented or passed through from the VMkernel and does not interact directly with the hardware unless using a pass through device.

In ESX versions earlier than version 3, the VMkernel would load after the COS had fully booted, and the VMkernel would usurp all the PCI devices set to be controlled by the kernel options. In ESX version 3, this has changed. The VMkernel loads first now, and then the rest of the COS. The COS is now running within a specialized VM with more privileges than a standard VM. Table 2.3 lists the boot steps for ESX versions 2.5.x and earlier versions and how ESX version 3 is related to the older boot method.

Table 2.3

ESX Server Boot Steps		
ESX 2.5.x	**ESX version 3.0**	**Comments**
LILO	GRUB	Boot Loader (bootstrap process that loads the kernel).
kernel-2.4-9vmnix	kernel-2.4.21-37.0.2vmnix	Loaded by the boot loader.
N/A	VMkernel	VMkernel is loaded from the RAM disk associated with the kernel during the first phase of the kernel boot.
Linux devices	VMkernel devices	Devices loaded from the RAM disk associated with the kernel during the first phase of the kernel boot.
Second-phase kernel load	Second-phase kernel loaded	The second phase of the kernel is loaded into the administrative VM created when the VMkernel was loaded and becomes the kernel for the COS.
init	init	Process that loads all other processes and which is started by the second phase of the kernel boot.
S00vmkstart	S00vmkstart	S00 represents the first set of user mode programs to run. S00vmstart ensures that there is no other VMkernel process running; if there is, the VMkernel process is halted.
N/A	S01vmware	S01 represents the second level of user mode programs to run on boot. In this case, the VMkernel network and storage modules are started.

ESX 2.5.x	ESX version 3.0	Comments
N/A	S09firewall	S09 represents the tenth level of user mode programs to run on boot. In this case, the ESX firewall is started using `esxcfg-firewall`.
S10network	S10network	S10 represents the eleventh level of user mode programs to run on boot. In this case, the COS network is started.
S12syslog	S12syslog	S12 represents the thirteenth level of user mode programs to run on boot. In this case, the logging daemon syslog is started.
N/A	S55vmware-late	S55 represents the fifty-sixth level of user mode programs to run on boot. In this case, the NAS and iSCSI VMkernel devices are initialized using `esxcfg-nas` and `esxcfg-swiscsi` tools.
S56xinetd	S56xinetd	S56 represents the fifty-seventh level of user mode programs to run on boot. In this case, the Internet super-daemon `xinetd` is started. The `vmware-authd` server is now running inside the COS.
N/A	S85vmware-webAccess	S85 represents the eighty-sixth level of user mode programs to run on boot. In this case, the web-based MUI is started.
N/A	S90pegasus	S90 is the ninety-first level of user mode programs to run on boot. The OpenPegasus Common Interface Model/Web Based Enterprise Management Server used for managing the ESX Server.
S90vmware	N/A	S90 is the ninety-first level of user mode programs to run on boot. The VMkernel starts here, and VMkernel devices are loaded after the VMkernel usurps PCI devices; in addition, the `vmware-serverd`, and `vmware-authd` processes start.
S91httpd.vmware	N/A	S91 represents the ninety-second level of user mode program to run on boot. The MUI is now running.
N/A	S97vmware-vmkauthd	S97 represents the ninety-eighth level of user mode programs to run on boot. The VMkernel authorization server is initialized inside the VMkernel.
N/A	S98mgmt-vmware	S98 represents the ninety-ninth level of user mode programs to run on boot. The VMware host agent is now running. The host agent replaces the `vmware-serverd` server.
Login enabled	Login enabled	After the startup processes are run, the system is fully operational and login is enabled on the console.

Tool Differences

In addition to all the boot changes and OS changes, the ESX-specific commands have changed, forcing many custom scripts to need some form of rewriting. Many of the older commands are available but do completely different things now. Table 2.4 shows the ESX 2.5.x-specific commands and how they have changed in ESX version 3.

Table 2.4

ESX 2.5.3 COS Commands Functionality in ESX Version 3	
ESX Command	**ESX Version 3 Functionality**
vmware-cmd	Very similar to earlier versions, but because the VM configuration files have changed, what this command returns is now different.
vmkpcidivy	Functionality to divvy the PCI devices not available and now only able to query VM HBA data.
vmsnap.pl	Not functional. Specifies to use VMware Consolidated Backup (VCB).
vmsnap_all	Not functional. Specifies to use VCB.
vmres.pl	Not functional. Specifies to use VCB.
vmkfstools	Modified to only manipulate file systems, run file system checks. Virtual swap file functionality is no longer available.
vmkmultipath	No longer available, use `esxcfg-mpath`.
vm-support	Different output.
vmkload_mod	This command has not changed.

Another major change to the COS is the use of the vmxnet_console module and the creation of a vSwitch specifically for the COS. In the past, vmxnet_console was considered a necessary evil. Now the vmxnet_console device driver is used to tie the COS directly into a vSwitch specifically for the service console and only the service console. Although this might seem to inherit all the problems that the previous vmxnet_console driver had, it does not. The two major reasons for this are the improvements to the driver itself and the fact that the COS is its own VM, albeit a special VM. The `esxcfg-vswif` command will allow the modification of this vSwitch port from the COS command line. With the introduction of the COS vSwitch, the eth0 device is no longer used as the default Ethernet device; instead, the vswif0 device is used.

The last but most interesting aspect of the COS is that if the COS crashes, it's possible that the whole ESX Server will not crash. There is a good chance that the VMs will stay running. A case in point, a server received an NMI (nonmaskable interrupt) on the COS, but because it's its own VM, the COS VM died, but the rest of the server stayed running. This is an extremely nice improvement, allowing for better handling of error conditions that can occur within the COS. Because the COS is no longer running, the only option in this situation is to cleanly shut down each VM by using Remote Desktop–style tools. Any access via the VIC, ESX web tools, or anything related to the COS will not work, including VMotion.

Virtual Networking

In addition to the creation of the service console virtual switch (vSwitch), the vSwitch in general has changed greatly. There is an additional load-balancing method called port ID, which is now the default. The vSwitch will now load balance based on the source switch port ID where the data entered the vSwitch from the VM. In the past the default behavior was to load balance based on the source Media Access Control (MAC) address of the VM. The older functionality has not been removed. Load balancing is still only applied to outgoing packets. However, after the communication has been established, the network path used remains the same.

In addition to the changes to load balancing, there are now nonmanual ways to set up beacon monitoring, data link layer security policies, 802.3ad, and the other load-balancing methods. The ESX version 2.5.x requirement was to modify files by hand. The changes improve the overall management of vSwitches considerably. In addition, vSwitches are now defaulted to 56-port unmanaged switches with the same limitations as before with regard to spanning tree. However, the number of ports can be set to one of the following values 8, 24, 56, 120, 248, 504, or 1,016. A vSwitch is considered to be unmanaged because there is no way to set up port-by-port configurations on the vSwitch.

In addition to being able to set the size of a vSwitch, it is possible to set the failover order for a vSwitch and its pNICs and the recovery behavior when bringing a failed pNIC back into service. The failover policy is either to return to the original pNIC or to continue using the existing pNIC. The new behavior is called *rolling*, where rolling will use the existing pNIC until it also fails and another pNIC is brought online.

In the past, the data link layer (Layer 2) security policies were set on each VM individually, but now they are set on the vSwitch/port group in question. All VMs attached to the vSwitch now inherit the vSwitch security policy with regard to promiscuous mode, forged transmits, and MAC address-change acceptance. The method by which traffic shaping is changed for a vSwitch has also been modified and simplified.

Another change to the vSwitch is the creation of port groups. In the past, it was possible to create a set of port groups for *any* vSwitch. The devices without pNICs look like individual vSwitches with different VLANs. It is possible to connect up to a vSwitch, port groups, and VMs to add up to the number of ports associated with a vSwitch. Still, it is not yet possible to layer vSwitches. With the addition of the VMkernel networks for NAS and iSCSI devices, it is now extremely important to add in routes and Domain Name System (DNS) servers for all service console and VMkernel vSwitches. There is only one default route and DNS server per network stack. The service console is one stack, and the VMkernel is the other. Each VMkernel stack has a default route and gateway yet shares the same DNS server.

By in large, the major change to vSwitches is the management tool used to create them, either graphically or via the ESX command line. The VIC contains an extremely nice graphical tool that shows network representations, including which VMs are currently associated with which VLANs and vSwitches. It is much easier to see the effect on a VM by a vSwitch change.

Table 2.5 summarizes the virtual network functional differences between ESX 2.5.x and ESX 3.

Table 2.5

Virtual Network Functional Comparison		
vNetwork Functionality	**ESX v2.5.x**	**ESX v3**
Logical ports	Fixed 32 ports	Settable to 8, 24, 56, 120, 248, 504, or 1,016 ports
Port groups	Many per vSwitch	Many per vSwitch
802.1q	Supported	Supported
802.3ad	Supported	Supported
NIC teaming	Supported	Supported
Source port ID load balancing	N/A	Supported
Source MAC address load balancing	Supported	Supported
Source IP address load balancing	Supported	Supported
GUI-settable standby pNICs	N/A	Supported
Rolling mode for standby pNICs	N/A	Supported
VMotion through router/gateway	N/A	Supported
Beacon monitoring	Supported	Supported

Data Stores

One of the most important changes is the addition of data stores to ESX. In the past, they were referred to as VMFS-based LUNs shared either off a local SCSI/RAID adapter or off a SAN. Now a data store refers to anywhere the VMkernel can store data. This can be a SAN, NFS-based NAS device, or an iSCSI device. While a VMDK performs better on a VMFS file system, which still requires some form of SCSI interface, either through the FC HBA (Fibre Channel host bus adapter), local SCSI/RAID controller, or off an iSCSI target, NFS is also a target requiring a specialized form of VMDK called a 2 GB Sparse file. So the NFS target, while available to the VMkernel, is a good place for ISO images. In general, the configuration file is in the same place as the VMDK, although that is not a requirement. In no way, however, is the VM configuration and log data stored on the COS, unless of course the COS shares an NFS-based file system with the VMkernel, which we would not recommend. With ESX version 3, the VMkernel can no longer directly access any COS file system.

The introduction of iSCSI and NFS over NAS increases ESX version 3's capabilities immensely and enables non-SAN-based ESX solutions. In addition to all these enhancements, the VMFS has also been enhanced to be a true file system. No longer flat, the new file system, VMFS-3, can have directories, which allows for the storage of an entire VM, including configuration (VMX) files, in a single directory. ESX version 2.5 users who wanted to store VM configuration files on the SAN had to share the FC HBA (which is definitely not recommended). The placement of the VMX files on the SAN allows a LUN-to-LUN copy to back up the entire VM. In addition, it is possible to use an NFS-based NAS solution to store all the necessary ISO images for VMs, VM files, and any configuration files. It is, however, still impossible to put a nonexported VMDK onto an NFS-based NAS. NFS-based NAS requires a VMkernel vSwitch to use as the network path to access because the VMkernel no longer shares access to the COS file systems. At this time, it is not possible to use a CIFS share. You can only use an NFS share. It is possible to mount a CIFS share onto any Linux system and then share it out to the VMkernel using NFS. Unlike NFS, the iSCSI data store can host VMFS or any other supported file system, which in most cases will be VMFS-3. iSCSI requires a VMkernel vSwitch to use, and the iSCSI server must also be visible to the COS or reside on the COS subnet. In this case, it is important to create a VMkernel port on the COS vSwitch specifically for iSCSI. The implications of this are addressed in the security chapter, too. There will be more on these vSwitches in Chapter 8, "Configuring ESX from a Host Connection."

The new VMFS-3 file system supports up to 2TB LUNs. In addition, ESX version 3 supports up to 256 LUNs versus the 128 available on earlier versions of ESX.

Table 2.6 presents a summary of the data sort options by ESX version.

Table 2.6

Data Store Functional Comparison		
Data Store Functionality	**ESX v2.5.x**	**ESX v3**
VMFS on SAN	Supported	Supported
VMFS on iSCSI	N/A	Supported using iSCSI Initiator within COS or via iSCSI HBA. Requires the VMkernel device and COS must participate in the iSCSI network.
NFS	N/A	Supported for 2GB sparse files only, which is the old-style Workstation, GSX, or template file formats.
VMFS-1	R/O	R/O.
VMFS-2	R/W	R/O.
VMFS-3	N/A	R/W.
LUN size	2TB	2TB.
LUN count	128	256 (but only 128 at a time).
Default Disk.MaxLUN setting	8	128.
Access to COS file systems	Full access	Limited to just /vmimages.
COS access to data stores	Supported	Supported.

Virtual Resources

ESX version 3 does not introduce any new virtual resources into ESX. The basic four still exist: CPU, memory, network, and storage. However, what ESX version 3 does add are two important concepts. The first is the concept of resource pools. A resource pool is a set of resources on one or more ESX Servers for use by a set of VMs. A resource pool is defined by how much of the CPU, memory, network, and storage is awarded to the set of VMs within the pool.

When a resource pool spans more than one ESX Server, an ESX Server cluster is necessary. To create this is relatively simple from a VIC perspective. However, under the hood quite a bit is going on in ESX version 3. ESX version 3 uses the Legato Automated Availability Management (Legato AAM) suite to manage the shared resource pools and ESX Server cluster failover. In the new terminology, the shared resource pools are Distributed Resource Scheduling (DRS), while a cluster of more than one ESX Server is VMware High Availability (HA). The DRS and HA tools will perform many tasks that for ESX version 2.5 were only performed by hand or by a specialized and proprietary script. Those tasks involve the balancing of VMs across multiple hosts and the restarting of VMs on another ESX Server when a host crashes.

The management of virtual resources using DRS balances VMs across multiple ESX Servers either automatically or by hand using notifications. The same holds true for HA. You can set how interactive you want things to be or how automatic. If you create a VM in a resource pool, for example, the DRS tool could place the initial VM on a server other than the one you have targeted. DRS uses VMotion technology to balance the resources across multiple nodes, while HA uses a series of watchdogs to monitor the availability of a host and, if necessary, start the VM up on one of the other hosts in the ESX cluster.

For ESX versions earlier than ESX version 3, several tools provided warning behavior, but they required quite a bit of scripting. The first was the HP Virtual Machine Manager (VMM), which could automatically LiveMotion (VMotion) VMs from host to host depending on CPU utilization. It was also possible to use VC or VMM to determine whether a VM was alive and, if it was not, force a startup of a VM on another ESX Server. Once more, for ESX versions prior to ESX version 3, this required quite a bit of scripting. VMware had a tool at one time called the Poor Man's Cluster to perform limited HA capability, but that is no longer available. DRS and HA are some of the more exciting changes to ESX, because they create hands-off recovery and VM load-balancing mechanisms.

Table 2.7 provides a comparison of the how the versions support virtual resources.

Table 2.7

Virtual Resource Functional Comparison		
Functionality	**ESX v2.5.x**	**ESX v3**
CPU	Supported	Supported
Memory	Supported	Supported
Disk	Supported	Supported
Network	Supported	Supported
Resource pools	N/A	Based on CPU/memory resources utilization only
Clusters	N/A	Supported
Distributed resource scheduling	Extremely limited via HPSIM Virtual Machine Manager plug-in	Based on CPU/memory resource utilization only, requiring an ESX cluster
High availability	By Hand/Poor Man's Cluster	Full Support via Legato Automated Availability Management requiring an ESX cluster

Backup Differences

ESX versions earlier than version 3 used either VM-based backup mechanisms or VMDK-based backup mechanisms, and the same holds true with ESX version 3. However, ESX version 3 introduced the snapshot capability. The snapshot allows for the creation of a memory and disk image that will hold a snapshot in time of the running VM. To do this, snapshot uses the traditional REDO mode mechanism with a predisk copy communication with the VMware Tools running in the VM to quiesce the VMDK and to ensure that the disk is not active. The quiescent disk and memory can then be copied fully, producing a snapshot in time of the running VM. When the snapshot is completed, the REDO log is once more committed.

Snapshot ability is a great asset because it now works with a new VMware tool called Consolidated Backup (VCB). VCB uses a specialized machine to act as a proxy server for backup purposes. The proxy server would communicate with the ESX Servers and create snapshots and then allow the mounting of the snapshots to the proxy server so that they can then be backed up using one tool. The snapshots could then be backed up either at the file level of the full disk level. VCB reduces licensing costs for backup agents per VM, centralizes backup, and offloads the backup function from the actual ESX Server, thereby reducing the CPU and storage overhead associated with backups from the ESX Server.

This has been a major want-list item for VMware's customers and has some very exciting possibilities.

Table 2.8 summarizes the backup functions by ESX version.

Table 2.8

Backup Functional Comparison		
Functionality	ESX v2.5.x	ESX v3
vmsnap.pl	Supported	Deprecated
Snapshots	N/A	Supported
VMware consolidated backup	N/A	Supported
vRanger	Supported	Supported
VMM	Supported	Supported
LUN mirroring	Supported only by SAN appliance	Supported only by data store appliance

Licensing Differences

ESX versions earlier than version 3 had four licenses (ESX Server, VMotion Agent, Virtual Center Agent, and Virtual SMP) and a license for the VC server. ESX version 3 introduces a host of new licenses. The same four exist, but there is now the VMFS-3 license required for SAN and iSCSI access. There is also the DRS and HA licenses. But there are also different licensing bundles. The Virtual Infrastructure License bundle comprising the original four no longer exists; instead, there are license levels and the option to buy à la carte.

The first bundle is the startup bundle that includes ESX Server, and no restrictions on memory or storage capabilities.

The second bundle is the foundation bundle that includes virtual SMP, no restrictions on memory or storage capabilities, and VMFS-3 licensing. The VMotion license can be used with this bundle or the next.

The third bundle is the enterprise bundle and includes VCB, VMotion, DRS, and HA licenses into the mix.

And finally, VirtualCenter Management Server is once more its own license bundle and is added to any of the three.

The previous licensing mechanism was to use license keys that the ESX and VC products would load locally into ESX or load into the VC for each product's usage. ESX version 3 still allows local license keys; however, the full effects of enterprise-class products are only available when a License Server and VC are used. The License Server and keys are now using the MacroVision License Manager (LM) and keys generated for the LM tools. The change in licensing mechanisms implies that instead of typing in a license key by hand, you either point the license server to a downloaded file or use a host-based license file. As of Patch 2 for the VMware License Server, it is possible to use multiple server license files as long as they all reside in the same directory on the License Server.

All VMware Virtual Infrastructure licensing is done per socket, not per core, with the exception of the VirtualCenter Management Server license.

Table 2.9 provides a rundown of the licensing differences between ESX versions 2.5.x and 3.

Table 2.9

Licensing Functional Comparison		
Functionality	ESX v2.5.x	ESX v3
ESX	Separate or with VI bundle	Starter, foundation, enterprise
VMotion	Separate or with VI bundle	Separate, foundation, enterprise
VirtualCenter Management Server	Separate	Licensed separately
HA	N/A	Separate or enterprise
DRS	N/A	Separate or enterprise
VCB	N/A	Separate or enterprise
SAN	Part of ESX License	Separate, foundation, enterprise
iSCSI	N/A	Separate, foundation
NFS	N/A	Starter, foundation, enterprise
vSMP	Separate	Separate
VMware Converter	N/A	Partially free or separate purchase for full functionality; Full functionality free with enterprise; however, if you own P2V Assistant or VirtualCenter Management Server, you are entitled to VMware Converter Enterprise
Host-based license	Supported	Supported
Server-based license	N/A	Supported via MacroVision LM tools

VMware Certified Professional

The VMware Certified Professional (VCP) exam has been updated for ESX version 3, and there is a new exam prepared to gain the VCP for ESX version 3. Any previous VCP will still exist, *but* will not apply to ESX version 3. Another change to the VCP is the requirement to take at least one VMware ESX version 3 course. Any ESX version 2 VCP can take the VCP for version 3 without first having to sit a class. However, if you fail the VCP for ESX version 3 exam, to retake the exam you must first take the full four-day VMware ESX version 3 course.

The passing grade for the VCP is 70%; to be a VMware Certified Instructor, the passing grade is 85%.

Virtual Hardware

The VM hardware in use for ESX version 3 does not differ much from that available for ESX version 2.5.x and earlier versions. USB devices are still not available for use. What ESX version 3 does bring to the party is enhanced drivers for the PCNET32 network (or vlance) adapter and for all other virtualized devices. There has been no introduction of new devices, just new functionality. There is a change in how to choose network devices. Before the administrator had to select the PCNET32 (vlance) device or the vmxnet device from the settings for the VM. Now all it takes is to install the proper driver in the VM. Each VM now supports one, two, or four virtual CPUs (vCPUs), and up to 16GB of memory. There is now support for 64-bit guest operating systems when using 64-bit hardware.

New functionality also includes snapshots and the management of snapshots discussed earlier. Because snapshots are associated with each VM, the snapshot manager is part of the tools for a given VM. In addition, there is better handling of raw device maps (RDMs) and overcommitted memory. Virtual RDMs are still pointers within the VMFS metadata to a system LUN off a SAN or iSCSI, but they now have new filenames, so they are immediately noticeable. There is now a -rdm in the filename. For overcommitted memory, ESX versions earlier than version 3 used a centralized VMkernel swap file (vSWP). However, with ESX version 3, there is a vSWP per VM, and it is stored in the same directory as all the files for the VM, not a central location. Nor is there a way to change the file size except to increase or decrease the amount of memory associated with a VM.

Snapshots introduce different disk modes to the VM, too. No longer are there just the four modes, but a completely new mode that allows snapshots to occur. Once snapshots are disabled, the original four modes are available. However, this also disables the availability of VCB for the VM in question, and once more the standard backup mechanisms are required. In addition to the external changes, the enhanced VMware Tools work with snapshots.

In essence, the virtual hardware has surpassed the level of VMware Workstation version 5.5, but it still does not support USB devices. The VMs created on at least VMware Workstation 5.5 will run on ESX version 3 without modification, but not the reverse.

Another change to the virtual hardware is the support for N+1 Microsoft Clustering. There is no longer a two-VM limit to the number of nodes in a Microsoft cluster. The full eight nodes can now be configured. However, to do this requires the boot drive for each node of the cluster to reside on local SCSI VMFS-3 storage. When using the traditional two-node Microsoft cluster, the boot drive for each node of the cluster can reside on any available VMFS-3.

The location of all files associated with a VM in its own directory on a VMFS is a major and desired change to ESX. This enhances the management of the VM, and because the directory structure is enforced using the VIC and other tools, it creates one way to manage the VMs.

Another minor, but relatively important change is the fact that it is now possible to mount a local ISO, CD-ROM, or floppy image to be used by a VM. That means that the client VIC machine can host the ISO, CD-ROM, or floppy image and that it is no longer necessary to go into a server room just to flip a CD-ROM.

It is also possible to hot-add SCSI drives direct to a running VM. If your VM needs more disk space, it is now easily added without bringing down the system.

Table 2.10 summarizes the virtual hardware comparison between versions 2.5.x and 3 of ESX.

Table 2.10

Virtual Hardware Functional Comparison		
Functionality	ESX v2.5.x	ESX v3
vCPU	1 or 2	1, 2, or 4
USB	No	No
MSCS	2 nodes	Up to 8 nodes
Configuration File Location	In /home	With VMDK
Memory	3.6 GB	16GB
SCSI HBA	LSI|BUSLogic	LSI|BUSLogic
vNIC	Selectable pcnet32 or vmxnet	Flexible
64-Bit Guests	No	Only on 64-bit hardware
vHardware Level	< Workstation 5.5	>= Workstation 5.5
Snapshots	N/A	Supported
vSWP	Global	With VMDK

Virtual Machine and Server Management

Another major change to ESX version 3 is that of the integrated tools available to manage VMs and ESX. The command line is always available and is no longer independent of VIC 2.0, which is now downloadable to any Windows machine from any ESX Server, and is the primary tool for managing ESX. Just about everything the VIC can configure is also configurable from the ESX Server command line. The exception items are those requiring a VC server such as DRS, HA, and VMotion. However, there is no more confusion between command line, MUI and VC, because the VIC is not only the management client for the ESX Server. It is also the client for VC. The VIC updates itself when there are command lines. If the update does not happen fast enough, there is the capability to refresh any VIC screen.

The VC web access is the same as the ESX Server web access for ESX version 3. The web access provides the capability to control the VMs but not the capability to configure or manage the ESX Server. In addition to the new web access system, there is the new remote console, which uses a web-based plug-in to display the VM console as opposed to a separately installed program as was the case for earlier versions.

It is also easier to create VMs of all the supported operating systems, because the VIC will automatically prepare the virtual hardware just by selecting the OS type involved. In the past, there was some jiggling with virtual SCSI adapters associated with various operating systems. This has now been changed.

To make VMotion easier, the CD-ROM and floppy devices are both unconnected at first. In addition, after a migration the CD-ROM and floppy devices are left disconnected, so there is no need to be concerned about this when it comes time to VMotion.

Table 2.11 summarizes the virtual management differences across versions.

Table 2.11

Virtual Management Functional Comparison		
Functionality	ESX v2.5.x	ESX v3
MUI	Supported, independent of VC	Supported for access to VMs *only*
Command line (CLI)	Supported, independent of VC	Supported, integrated with VIC
VC	Supported, independent of MUI and CLI	Supported, integrated with CLI and MUI
VM creation	64-git and 2.6 kernel versions of Linux require custom VM creation modes	No special requirements for 2.6 kernels; in addition, virtual floppy image for Windows XP SCSI driver now a part of ESX install

Security Differences

The security difference between ESX version 3 and earlier releases is night and day. The primary change is the implementation of an iptables-based firewall for ESX version 3. This change alone makes the newest version of ESX an improvement over earlier versions; but because there are now more vSwitches required, the physical security of ESX becomes the predominant concern.

The security differences between versions are summarized in Table 2.12.

Table 2.12

Security Functional Comparison		
Functionality	ESX v2.5.x	ESX v3
iptables	On media not installed by default	Installed and configured
Data link layer security	With VM	On vSwitch and vSwitch portgroups

Installation Differences

There are minor differences between ESX version 2.5.x and 3 in the installation or upgrade routines. Although the install can work on unsupported SCSI or RAID hardware, the boot of ESX will generally fail. So it is important to use a supported SCSI or RAID adapter. It is possible to upgrade various versions of ESX earlier than version 3, and that list is fully available in Chapter 3, "Installation." Not all versions of ESX support this upgrade however.

There are two noticeable differences between the upgrade routine for ESX version 3 and that of earlier versions. The first is that there is no longer a request for a license key because that is handled by the VIC. The second is the automated disk layout. VMware has placed the log files on their own disk partition, thereby limiting the disk full errors that were prevalent with ESX versions earlier than version 3. Another significant improvement in the ESX 3 install routine is that you can now choose your initial COS NIC rather than be forced to let ESX choose the first NIC it finds on the PCI bus and then have to somewhat painfully change it later.

ESX versions earlier than version 3 install on and run from any disk media supported by Red Hat Linux version 7.2. With ESX version 3, however, although it is possible to install onto disk media supported by RHEL3-ES, is it not possible to run from anything but one of the supported SCSI/RAID devices. However, a VMFS will *not* be available when booting ESX from IDE or SATA (supported with version 3.5) until a supported data store is available.

Conclusion

This chapter provided a review of the major differences between VMware ESX versions 2.5x and 3 and serves as a starting point from which to plan an upgrade. Major differences were pointed out in each of the sections. However, the biggest ones are the following:

- The way ESX boots, which removes possible resource contention
- The addition of the VMkernel vNetwork
- Use of NFS and iSCSI as VM data stores; resource pools and clustering
- VMware Consolidated Backup
- A real firewall
- Integrated management methods
- New licensing methods
- VMs with four vCPUs and 16GB of memory while making networking easier

The following chapters go into ESX version 3 in detail.

Chapter 3

Installation

Installing or upgrading ESX Server software can take about 20 minutes depending on the hardware involved. However, it takes a lot longer to plan the steps we need to take before we start installing. With proper planning, we can avoid the costly mistake of finding out much later we did not really want to boot from the SAN or that the file system size for root or VM images is too small and end up reinstalling and starting all over again. See the section "Example 2: Office in a Box," in Chapter 1, "System Considerations," for a case where starting over again was necessary. We also do not want to find out after the fact that the hardware we have on hand is not compatible with the software and is unsupported. In this chapter, we go through a checklist of all the information you need to make the right decisions for installing the ESX Server software in your environment. For information about ESX hardware issues, see Chapter 1.

When you install or upgrade an ESX Server, you can quickly install more ESX Servers that share similar configurations using a scripted installation. Using the tool provided by the ESX Server, a script file is created, and this can then be used to install other ESX Servers. The resulting script file is used to kick-start other ESX Servers unattended. See the end of this chapter for detailed information about how to perform a scripted installation.

Table 3.1 lists the general information necessary before the installation or upgrade of an ESX Server takes place. Most of these items are mere reminders of tasks that may be completed by others in an organization, but they are still very important to gather nonetheless.

Table 3.1

Installation Checklist

Step #	Step Short Description	Additional Decision or Information Needed	Dependency
1	Read the release notes.		
2	Read all relevant documentation.	This includes the ESX Installation Guide.	
3	Is the hardware configuration supported?		See Chapter 2
4	Is the hardware functioning correctly?		Vendor diagnostics
5	Is the firmware at least at minimum supported levels?		Vendor information
6	Is the system BIOS correctly set?		Vendor information
7	Boot disk location	Local SAN iSCSI	iSCSI is supported by ESX version 3, using very specific hardware only
8	VMware ESX server licenses		ESX version 3 License Server
9	VM License and installation materials		
10	Service console network information	Static IP address Hostname (FQDN) Network mask Gateway address DNS information	
11	VMkernel network information (iSCSI, VMotion, and possible NFS [NAS] vSwitches)	Static IP address Hostname (FQDN) Network mask Gateway address DNS information	Chapter 10
12	Memory allocated to service console		
13	VMkernel swap size		ESX 2.5.x only
14	PCI device allocation: console, VM, or shared	Memory SCSI storage controller Ethernet controller Fibre Channel device	ESX 2.5.x only
15	Number of virtual network switches		Chapter 10
16	Virtual network switch label name(s)		Chapter 10
17	File system layout		
18	Configure the server and the FC-HBA to boot from the SAN.	Or disconnect if not using boot from SAN.	Chapter 6
19	ESX Server installation		
20	Connecting to MUI for the first time.		
21	Additional software packages to install		

Step #	Step Short Description	Additional Decision or Information Needed	Dependency
22	Guest operating system software		
23	Guest operating system licenses		
24	Network information for each guest operating system	IP address Hostname (FQDN) Network mask Gateway address DNS information	Chapter 10
25	Location of License Server and VC Server	IP address	

Upgrade Steps

In an upgrade of ESX Server from ESX versions earlier than ESX version 3, you have some additional up-front considerations. Review Chapter 2, "Version Comparison," in detail and pay close attention to the unsupported hardware. If you must upgrade hardware to move to ESX version 3, a reinstallation may be required. Generally, an installation is necessary if there is a wholesale replacement of a boot RAID or SCSI controller. However, before you upgrade anything this is one important question to ask:

Are you satisfied with your backup?

This is such a simple question, but often it is overlooked. Although upgrades are possible, it is not recommended to perform an upgrade, as explained later in this chapter. An upgrade to ESX version 3 would leave behind several rather large files (the global vSwap file) and other bits of configuration information. However, the upgrade is supported if the proper version of ESX version 2.x.x is in use. Although the full list will be part of the ESX upgrade documentation from VMware, here is a short list of upgradeable versions of ESX:

- ESX Server version 2.1.1
- ESX Server version 2.1.2
- ESX Server version 2.1.3
- ESX Server version 2.2
- ESX Server version 2.5.1
- ESX Server version 2.5.2
- ESX Server version 2.5.3
- ESX Server version 2.5.4

The steps for an upgrade are similar to the steps for an install, with some minor differences. For example, the file system placements and allocations will not be changed. If the system is a "boot from SAN" configuration, be sure that the only LUNs mounted are the boot volume and necessary VMFS volumes. All other LUNs should not be seen by the ESX Server—specifically, ext3 type file systems other than the boot LUN.

Consider the following: Red Hat does not recommend an upgrade when moving from major release to major release of their operating system. Because the pre-upgrade COS is running Red Hat version 7.2 and the post-upgrade COS will be running Red Hat version 3.0 Enterprise Server Update 6, the Red Hat recommendation is to reinstall and restore any important bits as necessary. However, as you learned in Chapter 2, ESX is *not* Linux, so this recommendation needs to be considered, but is not necessary to obey. Reinstallation is generally better, but the decision is in your hands.

If the desired path is to reinstall, it is strongly recommended that the complete ESX Server be backed up to a remote location on either tape or disk. At the very least, back up all VM configuration files and data, located in /home/vmware, /root/vmware, or any other VM configuration location. When the author reinstalled an existing ESX Server that had the default installation recommended herein for ESX 2.5.x, all he did was copy the VM configuration (VMX) files in /home/vmware/VMNAME to a remote machine. In addition, disable all remote SAN connections so that the installation has no chance to affect the VMFS LUNs. The specific pre-upgrade steps are covered in the following sections.

Step 1: Back Up ESX

Be sure to answer the following question: Are you satisfied with your backup? Are all the specialized system changes in the COS saved somewhere? Are the VM configuration files saved? Is everything in /vmimages saved? What about copies of all the VMs? In effect, you are asking this question: "Are all the little changes made to the ESX Server stored somewhere safe?" Consider backing up the contents of the /etc and /home directories at the very least for all the little configuration changes.

Step 2: Read the Release Notes

Read the Release Notes to find out whether any features or special instructions match your desired installation and hardware. The Release Notes will mention newly added features, resolved and known issues, bug fixes, security alerts, and necessary workarounds for various installation issues. Release Notes are available for each version of ESX at the VMware website: www.vmware.com/support/pubs/vi_pubs.html.

Step 3: Perform a Pre-Upgrade Test

Part of the ESX version 3 ISO, CD-ROM, or tar gzip image of ESX version 3 is a pre-upgrade test tool that enables you to determine whether an upgrade is possible on the existing version of ESX. It is recommended to run this test. Assuming that the ISO image or CD-ROM is mounted onto /mnt/cdrom, the following can be performed to run the pre-upgrade test:

```
# cd /mnt/cdrom/scripts
# ./preupgrade.pl
Checking existing VMs...
Checking VM versions...
Checking for repeatable resume...
Checking disk space...
Done. You may now upgrade the system.
```

Step 4: Prepare Your ESX Server

Follow these steps to prepare your ESX Server for upgrade, assuming the pre-upgrade test has been passed. If the upgrade test was not passed, move to the installation steps:

1. Once more, are you satisfied with your server backup?
2. Are there any VMs in suspended state? Resume the guest OS, shut it down, and power off the VM.
3. Are there any disks in undoable mode? Shut down the guest OS, commit or discard the changes, and power down the VM.
4. Did the shutdown of the guest OS and powering down of the VMs go cleanly?
5. Are all .vmdk and .vmx files backed up?
6. Make a list of all the VMs, or capture the list from the MUI via some form of graphical capture tool. This information is also in the file /etc/vmware/vm-list.
7. Write down the virtual network configuration, or capture the list from the MUI via some form of graphical capture tool. This information is also available in the files /etc/vmware/hwconfig and /etc/vmware/netmap.conf.
8. Write down existing storage configuration information, or capture this information from the Storage Management pages of the MUI. This

information is also available in the output of the `vmkmultipath -q` command and the file `/etc/vmware/hwconfig`.

9. What third-party applications are running on your current ESX Server? Will they work under ESX 3.0? Specifically, any hardware or backup agents should be reviewed. In most cases, these agents or tools will need to be de-installed prior to the upgrade. For HP Insight Manager agents, definitely de-install these prior to an upgrade. At this time, it is a good idea to make sure that any agent configurations are recorded or saved to a remote location.

10. Make a copy of the password file and any other user-specific information.

Remember the upgrade process is irreversible! *So, are you comfortable with your backup?*

Now proceed to the normal installation steps covered in the next section; there is a decision point about upgrades presented in that section.

Installation Steps

The installation steps are just a little more involved than the backup steps, of course. However, they begin simply enough.

Step 1: Read the Release Notes

Read the Release Notes to find out whether any features or special instructions match your desired installation and hardware. The Release Notes will mention newly added features, resolved and known issues, bug fixes, security alerts, and necessary workarounds for various installation issues. Release Notes are available for each version of ESX at the VMware website: www.vmware.com/support/pubs/vi_pubs.html.

Step 2: Read All Relevant Documentation

Read the relevant installation documentation for ESX. Although it is extremely easy to install ESX, reading through the procedure once will prepare you for all the possible contingencies for a chosen installation path.

Step 3: Is Support Available for the Hardware Configuration?

Verify and understand your hardware configuration per Chapter 2.

Step 4: Verify the Hardware

Verify the hardware on which ESX will be installed. Specifically, run any hardware diagnostic tools available from the hardware vendor to test all subsystems for failures and deficiencies. Because ESX will stress any hardware past any normal operational point, be sure that all components are in working order. For example, normally a Windows-based operating system installation barely uses resources, whereas ESX makes use of *all* available resources. Use the memtest86 program to stress test memory before ESX is put into production on a server. Memtest86, from www.memtest86.org, will run multiple types of memory tests in a repetitive fashion to determine whether there are bad sticks somewhere in the system. Use of hardware diagnostics such as the SmartStart tools from HP, or similar tools for other hardware types, will determine whether there are also any failures in memory or other subsystems. This step can save time and frustration later.

Best Practice for Hardware

Run memory tests for at least 48 hours; for some hardware, 72 hours is best.

Verify that memory is balanced across CPU sockets for AMD-based NUMA machines.

Be sure the system has been verified; ESX taxes hardware more than any other OS and will find hardware issues other operating systems will not.

Step 5: Are the Firmware Levels at Least Minimally Supported?

Verify that the firmware versions on each ESX Server host are at the appropriate levels; in most cases, this implies the latest level of firmware, but in some cases this could be a not-so-recent level. While verifying the firmware versions on each ESX host, take the extra time to also verify the firmware versions on all switches, Fibre, or network (and on SANs or other attached storage devices). This is the most important step and the most often ignored step of the installation, and it can cause the most dramatic of failures. As an example, a customer had a constant ESX failure related to a SAN rebooting periodically, which in effect knocked it offline while the storage processor rebooted. The firmware revision of the SAN was several iterations below the minimum required level for a SAN connected to an ESX Server. After this item was fixed the problems went away. In some cases, the minimum required firmware for your storage, systems, switches, and I/O cards will not be listed in the ESX installation guide or HCLs; in this case, contact the hardware vendor for the information.

Best Practice for Hardware Firmware Versions

Use the most current firmware for all hardware connected to or associated with an ESX Server unless otherwise specified by VMware or the hardware vendor.

Ensure the firmware versions for all hardware connected to or associated with ESX are at the proper levels.

Step 6: Is the System and Peripheral BIOS correctly set?

Verify that the BIOS settings are correct for the systems and peripherals to be used. This is another often-overlooked installation step. Some system hardware requires that various BIOS settings be set properly for ESX to run properly. If the BIOS is not set properly, the ESX Server will crash or experience mysterious problems. For example, on some HP Xeon-based hardware, the BIOS needs to have the MPS Table Mode set to Full Table APIC. If this does not occur, when the systems are fully loaded with PCI cards, IRQs are not assigned properly, and either PCI cards do not get registered or the devices show up with unexpected and quite incorrect settings. Cases in point are NICs, which often show up in unchangeable half-duplex modes.

Best Practice for System BIOS

For multicore systems, node Interleaving should be disabled (this enables NUMA) for significant performance gains.

Be sure the add-in (Fibre Channel, SCSI, network, and so on) hardware BIOS settings are set properly.

Be sure the system BIOS settings are set properly so that ESX runs properly and does not mysteriously crash.

Step 7: Where Do You Want the Boot Disk Located?

Decide how to boot your server. A typical installation is to install the OS on a server's internal disk or on a disk directly attached to the server. However, some of the FC HBAs have enhanced configurable BIOS that support booting from a storage device attached to a SAN or even from iSCSI. However, booting from SAN or iSCSI has some limitations and unique benefits over a traditional installation.

Installing to boot from SAN or iSCSI should occur when the ESX Server host system is diskless or has no usable local storage devices. In these cases, the system could be a diskless blade or some other server that has multiple paths to a SAN. Installing to boot from SAN or iSCSI will also allow the cloning of an ESX Server by copying the system LUN to another LUN on a SAN or iSCSI server. This form of ESX Server deployment may not actually save time over other forms of ESX Server deployments. In addition, booting from SAN or iSCSI creates the capability to make an ESX Server independent of the actual hardware. If the hardware goes bad, just point the new ESX Server to the existing LUNs and reboot from an already installed LUN, thereby increasing possible DR capabilities. However, this also causes other problems, because now the ESX Server in question depends entirely on the Fibre or network fabric. So, part of the decision needs to be based on what part of the ESX Server infrastructure has the lowest mean time to failure: SAN, iSCSI, or local disks.

Installing to boot from SAN or iSCSI should not occur if shared disk clusters, such as Microsoft Clustering and Red Hat clusters, would be in use, raw disk maps are required, or when there is a need for a raw SCSI device mapped from the ESX Server host to a VM. In addition, booting from SAN on ESX versions earlier than version 3 requires the sharing of the FC HBA between the service console and the VMs, which will cause increased contention in the SCSI subsystem when communicating to the SAN. Booting from SAN or iSCSI can also increase the complexity of an ESX Server configuration, because now the replacement server needs the FC HBAs properly configured. SAN connections to a machine must be via switch fabric and not an arbitrated loop connection. Any IDE or non-SCSI local drives must be disabled to perform the installation. One ESX Server must only see each boot LUN at a time by masking, zoning, or presentation. In some cases, use of a SAN or iSCSI server is slightly more expensive than one based on a local disk, but that depends on the type of SAN or iSCSI server and drives used.

Step 8: VMware ESX Server License

Register the Virtual Infrastructure license keys to receive the individual licenses for the ESX Server, VMotion, Virtual SMP, and the VC Agent. Without the ESX

Server license, you will not be able to complete the configuration of the ESX Server or create and launch VMs. For ESX version 3, there are new licenses and license management tools. The differences between ESX version 3 and earlier versions regarding licensing are documented in Chapter 2. Be sure to have the appropriate license file or license management software running. However, it is not necessary to have the license management software running prior to installation, just prior to configuration. For ESX version 3, VMware ships out a code that is used to retrieve your licenses. To do this, you must have a login on the VMware site. Select the Account link and then Manage Product Licenses, from there you can download the appropriate license files.

Step 9: VM License and Installation Materials

Determine the location of any license and installation materials necessary to install the actual VMs. Although not particularly a part of an ESX Server install, these will be necessary to install any VMs. In some cases, the delay in finding the necessary license and installation materials for the VMs has delayed the implementation of ESX.

Step 10: Service Console Network Information

Acquire all network information required to install ESX properly. No ESX Server should boot from DHCP in an enterprise environment. If a DHCP server disappears for too long, and a lease expires, the ESX Server will suddenly lose access from its service console, which implies the ESX Server can no longer be managed remotely. If this happens, the only solution is to use either a remote or local console to fix the network problem. On ESX version 3, there is a possibility that there is no stable MAC address from which to base the Dynamic Host Configuration Protocol (DHCP) address for the server. Therefore, do not use DHCP. It is best to have ready the network addresses, netmasks, gateways, and DNS servers for the installation. Also, include addresses for the service console, the VMkernel to support VMotion, and access to various NFS or iSCSI data stores for ESX version 3.

Step 11: Memory Allocated to the Service Console

Determine how many VMs will run on this ESX Server. A VM has access to the physical host's hardware resources such as CPU, memory, disk, and network and there is a little bit of the CM within the COS to handle the management of the Virtual Machine. Therefore, it is important to pick the proper size of memory for the service console before installation. Note that each ESX Server can host up to

128 vCPUs and up to 200 registered VMs. However, it is not possible to run 200 VMs at the same time.

Because changing the service console memory configuration requires a reboot, it is best to determine the appropriate value ahead of time. For ESX versions earlier than version 3, it is possible to set the COS memory from the installation screens. However, with version 3, the only way to set the memory configuration for the COS VM is after installation. The maximum COS memory setting is 800MBs. The author generally runs agents and increases the amount to this limit.

Best Practice for Service Console Memory Allocation

If running third-party agents within the service console, increase the amount of memory assigned.

Increase memory assigned to the service console to prevent the service console from swapping.

Step 12: VMkernel Swap Size (ESX Versions Earlier Than Version 3 Only)

Determine the size of the VMkernel swap file to create, which in turn dictates the size of the local VMFS to create and a part of the necessary local disk space. Because local vSwap can be only 64GB in size, multiple files might need to be created based on the number of VMs to be used with the ESX Server. The vSwap file comes into play only when an ESX overcommits the memory usage of a system. vSwap is usually 2x physical memory, but if memory is to never be overcommitted, vSwap could be the size of memory. It can never be less than the size of memory.

In addition, determine the location of the vSwap files. It is best to use the local storage disk for the swap file that is used by the COS and the vSwap file that is used by the VMs. Even when booting from the SAN, it is better to have local storage for swap and vSwap. If the ESX Server's local disk controller is non-SCSI based, it will not be able to create a VMFS partition on it. Therefore, on these systems you have no choice but to put the vSwap on the SAN.

To create the 200 registered VMs mentioned previously, it is necessary to set up enough vSwap files to allow memory overcommitment for the memory size required by all 200 VMs. As an example, in the author's lab, there is an ESX Server with 50+ VMs on it representing all supported versions of guest operating systems available. Although there is only 6GB of memory on this system, there are enough vSwap files to accommodate all the registered VMs.

Step 13: PCI Device Allocations

For ESX versions earlier than version 3 determine whether each PCI device is dedicated to the console, dedicated to the VM, or shared between the two. In general, the installation steps will pick what will go where, giving you a chance to modify this information during the installation. SCSI disk controllers are usually shared between the service console and the VMs. However, if the SCSI disk controller is to be used with a local tape device, it is often required that you not share this with the VMs, unless the desire is for a VM to control the local tape device. Ethernet controllers are automatically divvyed between the service console and the VMs, but can also be shared between the two. This is explained in Chapter 8, "Configuring ESX from a Host Connection," because it has to happen after installation. Assign Fibre Channel controllers to the VMs except in the "boot from SAN" situation and other rare cases.

For ESX version 3, it is also possible to assign PCI devices, but that is an advanced function that must occur after installation and is not covered here.

Step 14: File System Layouts

Determine the file system layout to use for the ESX Server, where the file systems will live, and how much space to allocate for each. Often, customers have created ESX Servers without paying too much attention to the file system layout and have had to reinstall the OS when they find out later that there is not enough room to create a local VMFS, VM images directory in which to store ISO images, or create backups of the VMs.

The automatic partition option (default for ESX version 2.x) creates five partitions: root, boot, swap, vmkcore, and VMFS. Because the /var partition is where the log files get stored in the /var/log directory, there is a chance that these log files might grow to fill up the root partition. If the root partition gets full, it often results in unpredictable behavior such as the inability to connect to the service console, connect to the management user interface (MUI), create, or manipulate a VM. It might even corrupt critical files. To this end, Table 3.2 and Table 3.3 define disk partition and file system layouts for each version of ESX. For ESX version 3, the /var/log partition already exists.

The major difference between ESX version 3 and earlier versions is that there is no longer a need for local space for the VM configuration files and logs, because these are stored on the VMFS-3 file systems. Also, the ESX version 3 boot disk requirements have shrunk considerably.

Table 3.2

File System Layout Recommendations for Version 3 Only

LUN	Mount Point	Partition Size	Partition Type	Use
OS RAID 1 (minimum 146GB[1])	/boot	100MB	ext3	Store Linux and VMware kernel images
		1GB	swap	Service console swap (2x desired service console memory up to 2GB)
	/	4GB	ext3	Root
	/var/log	4GB	ext3	Log files
	/tmp	4GB	ext3	Store temporary files
	/var	4GB	ext3	Core files and other variable files, system initialization images for scripted install
	/vmimages	12GB or grow to fill LUN	ext3	ISO/floppy images to use with install
VMFS RAID 5 (minimum 146GB[1])		100MB	vmkcore	Core dump (VMkernel)
		Grow to fill LUN	VMFS-3	VM directories
				VM templates
				Used for MSCS drive C: virtual disks or for disaster recovery of failed remote storage
Up to 256 VMFS RAID 5 LUNs off SAN/iSCSI/ NFS		# of VMs per LUN * size of VMs	VMFS-3	VM directories
				VM templates

[1] *More about LUN sizes for business continuity/disaster recovery in Chapter 12, "Disaster Recovery and Backup."*

Table 3.3

File System Layout Recommendations for Versions Earlier Than Version 3 Only

LUN	Mount Point	Partition Size	Partition Type	Use
OS RAID 1	/boot	100MB	ext3	Store Linux and VMware kernel images
		1GB	Swap	Service console swap (2x desired service console memory up to 2GB)
	/	2GB	ext3	Root
	/home	4GB	ext3	User directories, VM configuration, and log files
	/var	4GB	ext3	Log files, system initialization images for scripted install

continues...

Table 3.3   continued

File System Layout Recommendations for Versions Earlier Than Version 3 Only

LUN	Mount Point	Partition Size	Partition Type	Use
	/tmp	1GB	Ext3	Store temporary files
	/vmimages	Grow to fill LUN	Ext3	ISO images, default backup directory (vmsnap.pl uses this)
VMFS RAID 5 or RAID 0 for vSwap		100MB Grow to Fill LUN	Vmkcore VMFS-2	Core dump (VMkernel) vSwap
Up to 128 VMFS RAID 5 LUNs off SAN		# of VMs per LUN * size of VMs	VMFS-2	Virtual disks vSwap files VM Suspend files VM templates

---

Best Practice for File System Layout

/boot, /, and swap must be primary partitions. The tools should automatically assign these to primary partitions, but always double check.

Do not let the root system get full! Keep the location of the VM configuration and log files, var, tmp, and VM images (for ESX versions earlier than version 3) on separate partitions.

Step 15: Configure the Server and the FC HBA to Boot from SAN or Boot from iSCSI

This is a decision point. All of Step 15 reviews how to set up booting from SAN or iSCSI for all versions of ESX. If booting from SAN or iSCSI is desired, continue through this step. However, if a traditional installation is desired, skip to the next step.

If booting from SAN or iSCSI is the desired boot method for the ESX Server, configure the server and FC HBA appropriately. To configure a server to boot from SAN, a few adjustments are necessary to the system BIOS to specify the boot order so that the SAN or iSCSI device is seen first in the boot order for the server. In addition to boot order adjustments, any IDE controllers need to be disabled.

For example, to configure an HP Proliant or blade server for boot from SAN, enter the server BIOS by pressing F9 at the appropriate prompt to start the

ROM-based Setup Utility (RBSU), resulting in what is shown in Figure 3.1. After entering the RBSU, the first step in setting up boot from SAN is to change the boot order, making the Fibre Channel HBA (FC HBA) the first boot controller by selecting the Boot Controller Order menu option. From the Boot Controller Order screen, select the appropriate line to move the primary FC HBA to be the first controller, as shown in Figure 3.2.

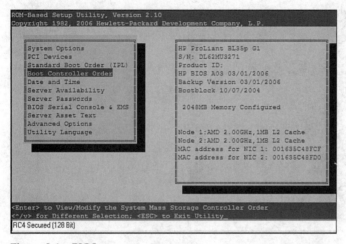

Figure 3.1 BIOS

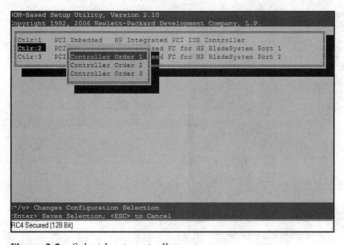

Figure 3.2 Select boot controller

The next step is to return to the main RBSU screen (refer to Figure 3.1) and head down a new path to disable any IDE controller for an IDE non-SCSI disk-based system. On a Proliant Blade BL3x Server, this can be found under Advanced Options, which has an IDE Controller item (see Figure 3.3). Select the IDE Controller item and change its state to Disabled (see Figure 3.4). If the blade or server in question does not have an IDE disk controller, skip this step.

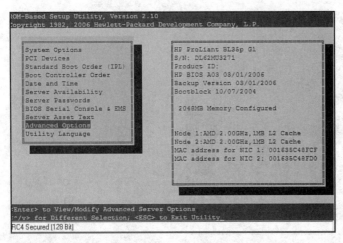

Figure 3.3 Advanced options

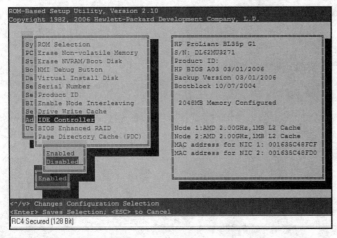

Figure 3.4 Disable IDE controller

Exit the RBSU and boot the system until the FC HBA BIOS is accessible and configured for boot from SAN or iSCSI.

The FC HBA has its own configuration for boot from SAN that depends on the controller being used. The main goal of these BIOS changes is to configure the HBA to recognize the SAN or NAS LUN presented as the boot LUN for the ESX Server.

The next major step in the process for boot from SAN, or even iSCSI, is to enable the FC HBA device BIOS that allows the FC HBA to see boot disks hanging off the SAN or NAS. If the FC HBA BIOS is disabled, the SAN disks are not accessible as boot devices.

Setting Up the Emulex HBAs

After configuring the system BIOS to change the boot order, reboot the server and monitor the POST power-on messages for the following phrase:

```
Press <Alt E> to GO TO Emulex BIOS Utility
```

Just prior to this message, there is a list of the World Wide Numbers (WWNs) for all the FC HBA ports installed in the system. Record the WWN to perform the proper SAN zoning and presentation. When the message appears, press the Alt and E keys simultaneously to enter the Emulex BIOS Utility, as shown in Figure 3.5.

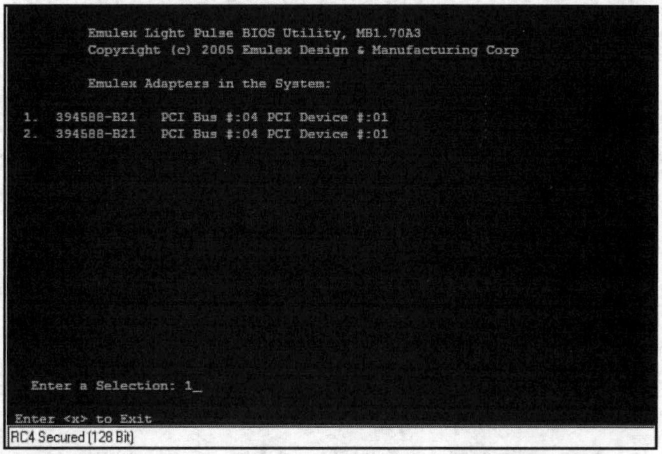

Figure 3.5 Emulex BIOS Utility

After selecting the first FC HBA, which is the primary FC HBA port or card, at the Enter a Selection prompt proceed to Option 2, Configure This Adapter's Parameters, with the results shown by Figure 3.6.

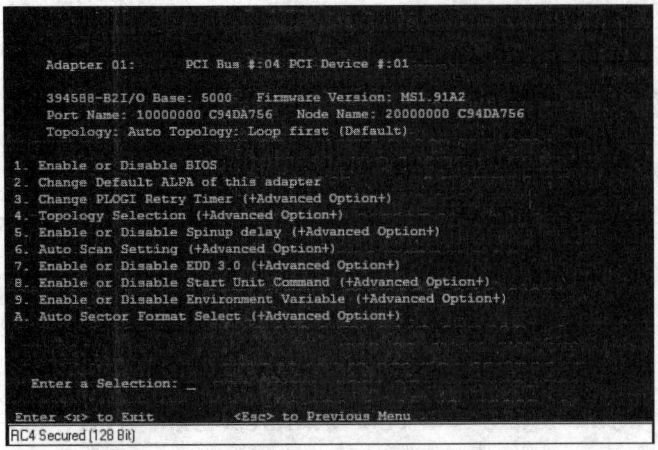

```
    Adapter 01:        PCI Bus #:04 PCI Device #:01

    394588-B2I/O Base: 5000   Firmware Version: MS1.91A2
    Port Name: 10000000 C94DA756   Node Name: 20000000 C94DA756
    Topology: Auto Topology: Loop first (Default)

1. Enable or Disable BIOS
2. Change Default ALPA of this adapter
3. Change PLOGI Retry Timer (+Advanced Option+)
4. Topology Selection (+Advanced Option+)
5. Enable or Disable Spinup delay (+Advanced Option+)
6. Auto Scan Setting (+Advanced Option+)
7. Enable or Disable EDD 3.0 (+Advanced Option+)
8. Enable or Disable Start Unit Command (+Advanced Option+)
9. Enable or Disable Environment Variable (+Advanced Option+)
A. Auto Sector Format Select (+Advanced Option+)


    Enter a Selection: _

Enter <x> to Exit          <Esc> to Previous Menu
RC4 Secured (128 Bit)
```

Figure 3.6   Emulex Configure This Adapter

As stated, there is a need to set up the BIOS for the FC HBA to allow it to see drives as bootable volumes. You do that by selecting Option 1, Enable or Disable BIOS and then pressing 1 to enable the BIOS. After enabling the BIOS, the next step is to set the topology of the Fibre network to be point to point. The topology tells the FC HBA how to view the Fibre network, and because there is a one-to-one mapping between the FC HBA port and the boot LUN, the topology is set to point to point. To do this, choose Option 4, Topology Selection, (+Advanced Option+), and select Point to Point. After you have made these selections, the BIOS can be exited and the server rebooted.

However, the system is still not fully configured, because the boot devices have not been defined. The boot device will be presented by the SAN and zoned by the switches to the primary FC HBAs WWN recorded earlier. After the presentation and zoning is completed, the device must be chosen as a boot device. So once more, enter the Emulex BIOS Utility and select the first FC HBA, which is the primary FC HBA to which everything has been presented and zoned. Now select Option 1, Enable or Disable BIOS, and modify the list of saved boot devices. As shown in Figure 3.7, set up the primary and secondary boot paths for the listed devices. Each FC HBA has at least one port listed. Each port has an associated World Wide Port Number (WWPN). Because it is recommended to have two FC HBA ports per ESX Server, there will be two WWPNs, whose last two digits are unique. The unique last two digits are used to pick which port is to be used as the primary and secondary boot path. Choose 1 to pick the primary boot path, and when prompted, enter the hexadecimal LUN ID of the LUN defined as the boot disk. Of all LUNs associated with the ESX Server, the lowest-valued LUN is the boot disk, with the exception of LUN ID 0, which is often the controlling LUN. If LUN ID 0 is present, do not select it as a boot LUN.

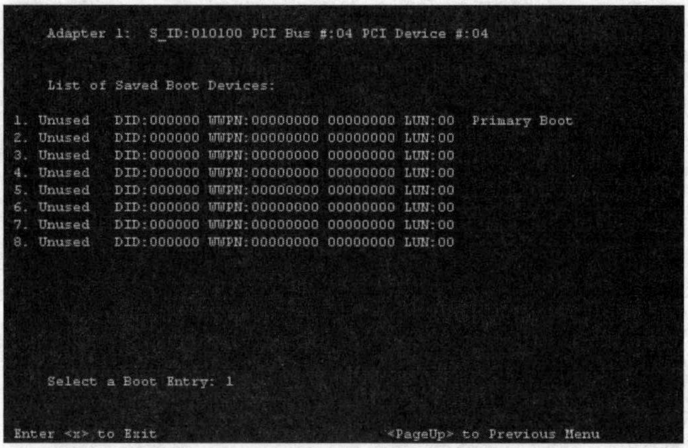

Figure 3.7 Emulex saved boot devices

After the saved boot devices have been set up, select option 01 representing the WWPN that is the boot device, as shown in Figure 3.8, to tell the system which WWPN is to be booted. Once more, exit the Emulex BIOS and reboot the server. Now the Emulex FC HBA is ready to boot from the SAN and to be installed

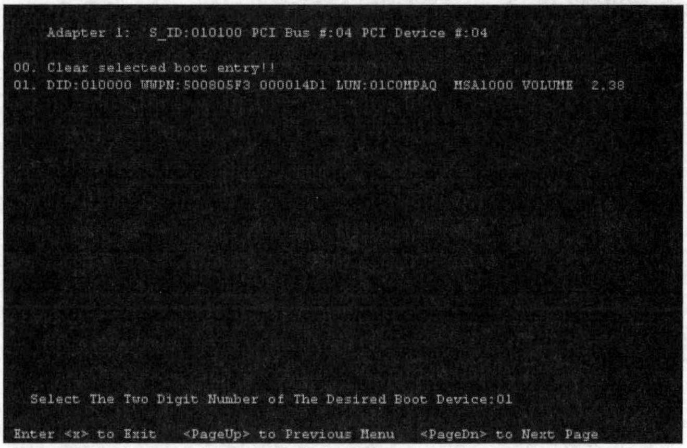

Figure 3.8 Emulex Select Boot Device

Setting Up QLogic FC HBAs

Similar to Emulex FC HBAs, Qlogic FC HBAs need to have their BIOS enabled and the boot LUN specified. Unlike Emulex, however, the topology does not need to be set to boot from the SAN, nor is there a reboot in the middle of the configuration. After configuring the system BIOS to change the boot order, reboot the server and monitor the POST power-on messages for the following phrase:

```
Press <CTRL-Q> for Fast!UTIL
```

When the phrase appears, press Ctrl+Q to enter the Qlogic BIOS to configure it for boot from SAN. When you are in the BIOS, the Select Host Adapter menu will appear listing all available Qlogic FC HBAs. The first in the list will be the primary FC HBA port. Select it as the device from which to boot per Figure 3.9.

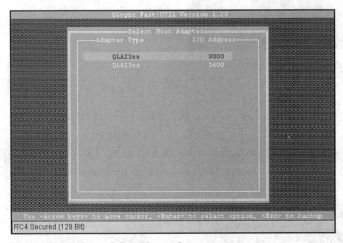

Figure 3.9   Qlogic Select Host Adapter

After selecting the host adapter to manipulate the Fast!UTIL, options will be displayed with an opportunity to select the Configuration Settings option. Under the Host Adapter Configuration Settings menu, select the Host Adapter Settings Menu item to enable the BIOS per Figure 3.10.

After returning to the Configuration Settings menu, select the Selectable Boot Settings menu option to set the enabled primary boot LUN, as shown in Figure 3.11. The display will show the primary boot port name and LUN. Be sure to select the proper LUN. Some installations require more than one LUN, because LUN 0 could be the controlling LUN. Do not select the controlling LUN.

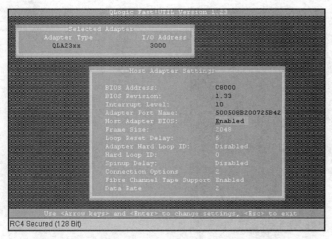

Figure 3.10   Qlogic Select Host Adapter Settings

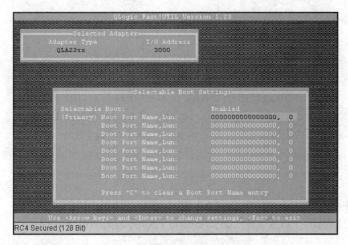

Figure 3.11   Qlogic Selectable Boot Settings

Select the primary boot port name and LUN, and a new menu will appear to enable you to select the Fibre Channel device associated with the SAN from which to boot and then the specific LUN, which will become the boot LUN, as shown in Figure 3.12.

Save all the changes to configure the Qlogic device for boot from SAN and reboot the server to complete the installation.

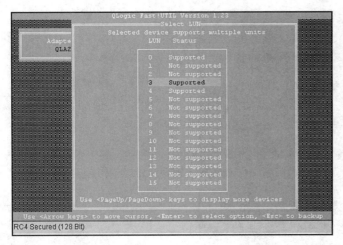

Figure 3.12   Qlogic Select LUN

ESX Version 3

Now that boot from SAN has been configured, the installation of ESX can continue. Granted, there are also some gotchas with boot from SAN for ESX versions earlier than version 3. The primary concern goes away, and that is the contention between the service console and the VMkernel. ESX version 3 no longer suffers from this problem. In addition to Boot from SAN, ESX version 3 offers the capability to boot from iSCSI.

Set Up Boot from iSCSI

It is not currently supported to boot ESX from iSCSI. However, when it does become available, the Qlogic QLA4010 TCP Offload Engine (TOE) controller will be necessary.

Step 16: Start ESX Server Installations

If you are not planning to boot from SAN, disconnect the system from the SAN or iSCSI server. A disconnect from remote storage could be as simple as the removal of the cables or accomplished by taking the ESX Server out of the zoning or presentation of LUNs. Having SANs connected during installation, except in the case of boot from SAN, can adversely affect the boot of the ESX Server when the installation is completed. In addition, this prevents erasure of the SAN disks, even accidentally, by the installation. It is not necessary to disconnect the SAN from the server, but be aware that the installation will show all presented disks, and even a slight slip up could destroy existing SAN volume data.

Start the system installation by either using a remote console device with virtual CD-ROM capability similar to the HP ILO device or insert the ESX Server CD-ROM into the disk tray of the ESX Server. The installation proceeds using the decisions made in the first 14 steps of the installation. At this point, the ESX Server will boot, and two types of installations can be performed: If the installation is over the HP ILO or similar type of device, it is recommended to use the text-based installation; all other installations can use the graphical install. In addition to choosing graphical over text, there is a need to apply the boot from SAN decision and either choose the Boot from SAN option or not when performing an install. Figure 3.13 displays the primary boot screen for ESX version 3, and Figure 3.14 displays the primary boot screen for ESX version 2. As you can see, the screens differ quite a bit.

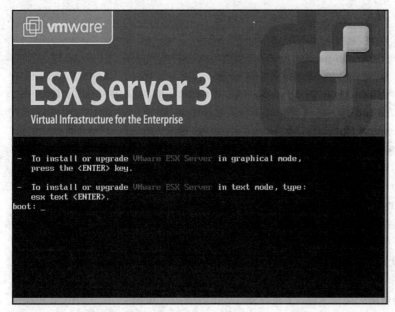

Figure 3.13   ESX version 3 primary boot screen

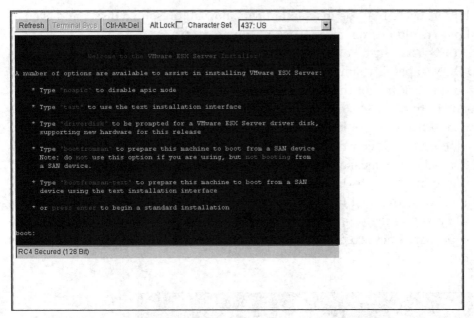

Figure 3.14 ESX version 2.5.x primary boot screen

However, they are the starting point for any installation and offer the choices on how to proceed. Appendix B (text install) and Appendix C (graphical install) will provides screen shots for the complete ESX version 3 installations; however, the goal here is not to repeat every other ESX book that runs through an installation in painful detail. Everything listed before this section of the chapter is to list out any necessary prework that will make the installation go smoothly so that installations do not need to be repeated. The reason for this focus is that we have discovered that many customers do not follow the guidelines and end up reinstalling to fix issues with disk space that can be avoided with careful planning. The post-steps listed after this step assist in completing the installation.

When the installation begins, you must address certain critical sections. Although an installation can occur by accepting all the defaults and typing a few items such as the root password, such an installation is not necessarily one that will stand up to long use. Granted, for a test environment, or to get your feet wet, this might be the best approach, but for production environments, it is best to stop and consider the options.

When upgrading to ESX version 3, the first options to consider are whether to upgrade, if there is an existing installation, or to reinstall per the initial discussion in this chapter. Many people opt to use the supported upgrade option. However, most Linux gurus perform reinstalls instead of upgrading. Upgrading the service console to use a new version is the same for ESX as it is for any other variant of or derived from Linux operating system. ESX version 2.5.2 is a derivation of Red Hat 7.2, and 2.5.3 is a derivation of RHEL 2.1 ES. ESX version 3 is a variant RHEL 3.0 ES. The difference in versions is rather extreme, and because there is no guarantee with Linux installations that all the older files and configurations will be properly removed or updated, it is generally the best choice to reinstall. This holds true for moving from ESX version 2.5.2 to ESX version 2.5.3 because this is a fairly major change to the COS version of Linux. Reinstallation makes it possible to clean up the file systems and to create a new plan for the new version of ESX. With the introduction of new features, new requirements exist, because the older options no longer apply. A case in point is the large /vmimages used to store ISO images and backups. Because ESX now can use the vmkernel NFS option to access ISO images and the local data store, this file system may no longer be needed for this purpose. In addition, having a separate large vSwap file or files is no longer necessary, so the layout of VMFS partitions is also different to make better use of resources.

However, prior to reinstallation or upgrade, ask this question:

Are you happy with your current backup?

Best Practice for Reinstallation
Always make a good backup before proceeding.

Because not much needs to be restored with a basic ESX installation, the backup is to store custom settings made after installation. These settings include Active Directory integration configuration files, user and group files, and files for other configurations not off the main installation media. In addition, any hardware agent settings will need to be saved.

If upgrading, remove any hardware agents before performing the upgrade, because different versions of ESX often require different versions of hardware agents. The VMkernel exposes different aspects of the hardware to the service console depending on the ESX version. Figures 3.15 and 3.16 illustrate this decision point.

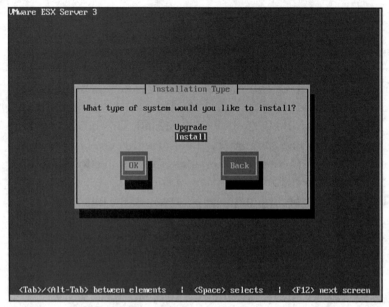

Figure 3.15 ESX upgrade or not using text install

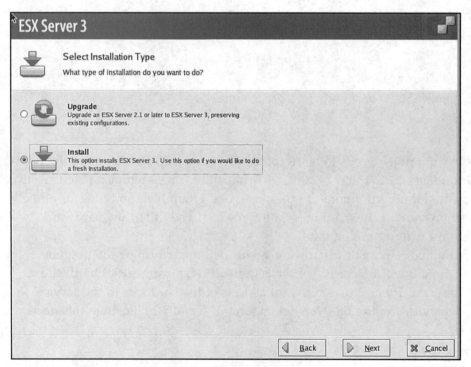

Figure 3.16 ESX upgrade or not using graphics install

The next decision point for ESX version 2.5.x is whether to enter the license keys upon installation or to wait until after installation. License keys are entered afterward in ESX version 3, so this is an ESX version 2.5.x and earlier question. If they are handy, entering the license keys during installation of ESX version 2.5.x or earlier will save a later reboot.

Next there is another series of taking the defaults, and then you are at the screens used to define the file systems for ESX and the service console. We previously defined the best practice file system layouts for ESX in Table 3.3; this is the point at which these get applied. If there is an existing VMFS on the disks, and it is desirable to keep the VMFS intact, this is definitely the time to make that selection, too. The default disk setup will wipe out all partitions, including any VMFS that may exist. Figures 3.17 through 3.19 depict how the file system layouts are changed.

The first step of this process, shown in Figure 3.17, is to choose whether to save the VMFS or any other partition on the system LUN or to wipe them out completely. This is the section of the installation that almost always requires the LUNs not be presented from a SAN or NAS. However, read carefully and choose the proper option to preserve any VMFS on the system. In addition, for ESX version 3, ensure that the installation target media is a supported IDE, SATA, SCSI, or RAID device. Any unsupported device will result in a nonrunnable system.

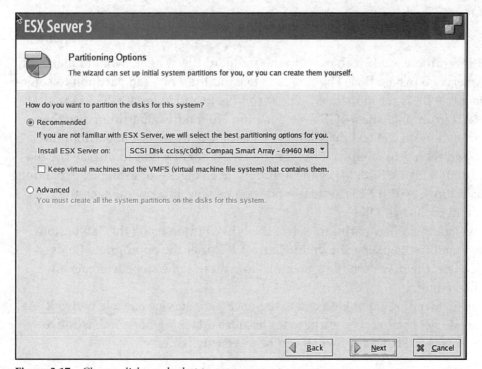

Figure 3.17   Choose disks and what to remove

It is best to choose the recommended setting and then proceed to the next step. As shown in Figure 3.18, it is possible to save existing VMFS LUNs instead of re-creating or deleting everything. When an upgrade is performed, these screens are not seen, and all the VMFS LUNs are saved. It is possible to create your own file system partitions, too, using the advanced options, but in most ESX Server installation cases, this is not required.

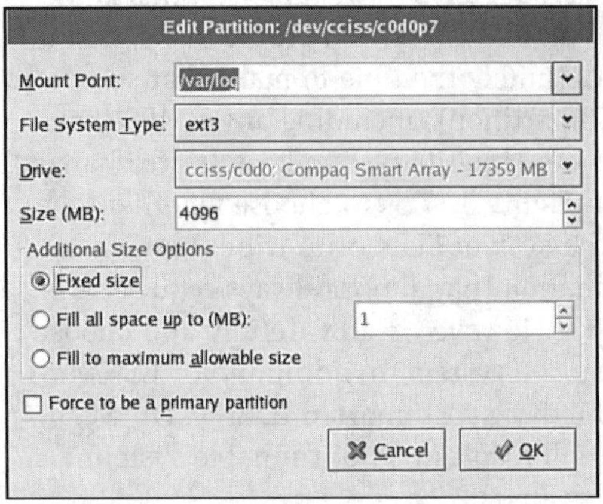

Figure 3.18   Choose the partition to change

However, there are two changes to the standard file system layout to make for an ESX Server 3 installation. The first is to expand the /var/log partition to something larger: 4GB is recommended. The second is to add at least a 2GB /tmp partition. The third is to create a 4GB /var partition. To modify a partition, use the down-arrow key on the text installation or the mouse to select the partition to modify, and then press Return for text installation or click Edit to display the dialog pictured in Figure 3.18. Make the appropriate changes—for example, expanding the maximum size of the file system—and then use the Tab key to reach the OK button, and then click OK.

When adding a new partition, select the NEW button using the Tab button, and then modify the dialog shown in Figure 3.19 to set the appropriate fields once more for the new /tmp file system. Follow these same steps to create any other file system.

The next decision point is to create the necessary service console network. At this time, do *not* create a VM port group, because attaching nonadministrative VMs to the service console vSwitch can be a security issue.

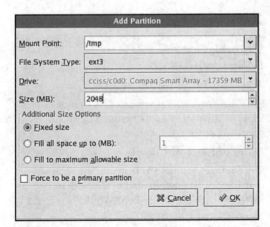

Figure 3.19 Adding a partition

After finishing the network setup, there is nothing else that is special to do, so choose the defaults until the end of the installation. After the install has completed, click Finish, and the server will reboot. Now ESX is running and ready for post-installation configuration.

Step 17: Connecting to the Management User Interface for the First Time

After the ESX Server reboots, it is time to log in to the management user interface (MUI) to complete the rest of the process. Log in to the MUI as root user and perform the post-installation configuration.

The configuration methods for ESX version 3 and earlier versions seriously differ here, but the steps are roughly the same, so they are listed here (Table 3.4) in a double column to highlight the differences. There is more about this in Chapter 8.

Table 3.4

Post-Install Configuration

ESX Version 3.0	Earlier Versions of ESX
Access MUI (webAccess)	**Access MUI**
The MUI for ESX version 3.0 will allow the download of the VIC. Access the MUI using `http://machinename/`.	The MUI for earlier versions of ESX requires a login as the root user, using the password specified during installation.
Download VIC	**Download Remote Console**
Download and install the VIC to a machine installed with a form of the Windows OS. Start the VIC and select the ESX server host, and log in using the root username and the password specified during ESX installation, or select the VC Server.	Once a login to the MUI is made, the remote console can be downloaded to a machine installed with either Linux or Windows.
Apply Appropriate Licenses	**Apply Appropriate Licenses**
License keys are distributed in a file for use either by the VMware License Server or to be loaded into the host.	If a license key was not entered during the installation phase, a license key will be required to progress. Enter the appropriate keys and the host will reboot.
Network Management	**Network Management**
The installation of ESX version 3 will result in a pre-created vSwitch for the service console. More vSwitches can be created using `esxcfg-vswitch`, and the service console vSwitch is configured using `esxcfg-vswif`. Create new vSwitches for the VMkernel NFS and VMotion networks and a VMkernel port group off the service console vSwitch for an iSCSI network. Then create a VM network as necessary. The network configurations are covered in Chapter 7, "Networking."	Create virtual switches that the VMs will use to talk to an external network. Each virtual machine can have a maximum of four virtual NICs (vNICs). Each vNIC connects to a port on the virtual switch for communicating with other VMs and servers that are on the network. Be sure to give each vSwitch a descriptive name. Most customers use either network names such as Production, Backup, or Test, or they use actual IP addresses of the networks involved.
	Create the Virtual Swap File
Not applicable, as virtual swap files are automatically created as needed per VM.	The first vSwap file for VMkernel use must be created and activated from the management tool.
	If you need to add additional swap space for VMkernel use, you must do from the service console. Each ESX server may have up to eight vSwap files, with a maximum file size of 64GB per virtual swap file.
	Here is one way of creating a secondary 1GB swap file:
	`# vmkfstools -k 1024M` `vmhba0:0:0:6:addswap.vswp`

ESX Version 3.0

Earlier Versions of ESX

To activate swap:

```
# vmkfstools -w 1024M
vmhba0:0:0:6:addswap.vswp
```

ESX Server starts using the additional swap file immediately. You can check this by using `esxtop`.

To make sure all the swap gets activated upon reboot, add the following line to `/etc/rc.local`:

```
vmkfstools -w 1024M
vmhba0:0:0:6:addswap.vswp
```

Storage Management

ESX version 3 pre-labels any VMFS created during installation. However, it is possible and recommended to change the local storage label using the VIC or from the COS command line. The symbolic link command can be used to change the local storage label, which is discussed further in Chapter 8. Without a proper label, the only way to access the VMFS is to know the UUID number assigned to the VMFS, or to know the VM HBA name. Tools such as `vmkfstools` use the VM HBA name, while the rest of ESX version 3 uses the UUID associated with the data store.

Before accessing a SAN, consider the contents of Chapter 5, "Storage with ESX."

Storage Management

Use the MUI to label the VMFS volume created by the default installation. In addition, it is now possible to create new VMFS volumes. Before accessing a SAN, consider the contents of Chapter 5.

After creating a VMFS volume or after accessing the VMFS volume automatically created upon install, give the volume a label and use that label when specifying VMFS files on that volume. For example, if you created a VMFS partition, `vmhba0:0:0:10`, to hold all test VMs, you may label this TESTVMFS. You can then refer to the `testvm1.vmdk` as `TESTVMFS:testvm1.vmdk` rather than `vmhba0:0:0:10:testvm1.vmdk` in a VM configuration file, which makes for easy reference when manipulating the VMDKs from the command line. If there is no persistent connection, it is possible that when a new LUN is presented the LUNs will be renumbered. Good labels are therefore important.

Create a Login User

It is impossible to initially log in to the ESX Server as the root user remotely. In case it is necessary to log in to manage the system by hand, it is best to create an administrative user. To further secure the system, this login is also required.

Create a Login User

This step is only necessary if the security recipe in Chapter 4, "Auditing, Monitoring, and Securing," is to be followed, because root access should be limited.

Storage Upgrade (if performing upgrade)

Using either the VIC or the command line, upgrade the appropriate VMFS-2 to VMFS-3.2:

N/A

```
vmkfstools -T /vmfs/volumes/<VMFSName>
vmkload_mod -u vmfs2; vmkload_mod vmfs2
vmkload_mod -u vmfs3; vmkload_mod vmfs3
vmkfstools -u /vmfs/volumes/<VMFSName>
```

continues...

Table 3.4   continued

Post-Install Configuration	
ESX Version 3.0	Earlier Versions of ESX
Virtual Hardware Upgrade (if performing upgrade)	N/A
Using the VIC, upgrade the virtual hardware of all VMs. This requires that the VMs first be shut down. Once rebooted, also update Vmware Tools.	

ESX Server is now installed and ready for use. However, now is the time to install optional third-party agents and other software that is necessary for the day-to-day use of ESX.

Step 18: Additional Software Packages to Install

Log in to the service console to install any additional packages. If you downloaded any of the RPM packages you plan to install on your ESX Server to your Windows workstation first, remember to FTP them over to your ESX Server in *binary* mode.

Several packages that are part of the ESX Server installation CD are not installed during installation. If you plan to send mail (not recommended) or to use the X11 graphics (never recommended) or to set up your server as an Samba server (not recommended), you may want to install the necessary packages from the install CD or from an appropriate RPM repository (see Table 3.5). For ESX version 3, the equivalent software repository is the software repository for Fedora Core 1, CentOS 3; or if there is a purchased version of RHEL, it is possible to use the RHEL installation media. Note that any addition of third-party software to a VMware ESX Server could have disastrous consequences but is sometimes necessary. Proceed with caution.

Table 3.5

Additional Software Packages and Where to Find Them		
Package Name	**Where to Find**	**Description and Use**
iptables	ESX media.	Packet-filtering firewall for the service console. This is for ESX version 2.5.2 or earlier. See Chapter 4 for more details on securing ESX.
sendmail	Choose the appropriate version based on the Linux COS version.	Necessary to send mail from various tools. Not necessary as a mail server, but as a mail client. This is sometimes required for management agents.

Package Name	Where to Find	Description and Use
Samba	ESX media.	Samba is necessary to share files between systems that use CIFS. In addition, Samba is necessary to integrate an ESX server with Active Directory. Never run as a file server.
X Windows	ESX media.	Never recommended for the COS because it is a memory hog. X Windows may be needed to run graphical tools remotely, however.
minicom	Choose the appropriate version based on the Linux COS version.	Minicom is used to access serially connected devices. A case in point is access to an MSA1xxx SAN. There is no way to configure the device using ESX and the COS except by using a serial port.
sysstat	Choose the appropriate version based on the Linux COS version.	Sysstat provides various system statistics tools for determining the COS resource utilization from an OS view. This is not from an ESX view, but is unique to the COS. This is often required by security scanners.
psacct	Choose the appropriate version based on the Linux COS version.	Psacct is a method to perform process accounting to monitor the COS for runaway processes. This is often a required by security scanners.
MTX	Choose the appropriate version based on the Linux COS version.	Software to control a local tape robot. (Not recommended.)
MT	ESX media.	Software to control a local tape drive. (Not recommended.)

Check out www.vmware.com/download/esx to see whether any new patches have been released for the server. A number of available packages might also be useful to have. You might want to install VMware ESX Server performance-monitoring tools.

This is also the right time to look into any vendor-specific diagnostic and monitoring packages that should be installed on the server. For example, on HP Proliant or blade servers, you should install the HP management packages that help you monitor the system hardware.

Automating Installation

ESX Server has a built-in mechanism to automatically set up installations or upgrades using remote servers. The Scripted Installation mechanism uses a web interface available from the MUI to create an installation. The key to the scripted installation is the creation of a kick-start file. Linux installers use the kick-start file to configure servers and to create installs that do not require human intervention.

To create a scripted installation kick-start file for ESX version 3, first enable the scripted install service within at least one ESX Server, log in to the MUI, and select the Log In to Scripted Installer link to log in and create the kick-start file.

To enable the service, run the following script from the command line; note that the line beginning with /bin/sed is very long.

```
#!/bin/bash
cd /usr/lib/vmware/webAccess/tomcat/apache-tomcat-5.5.17/webapps/ui/WEB-INF
/bin/cp struts-config.xml struts-config.xml.orig
/bin/sed 's#<action path="/scriptedInstall"
type="org.apache.struts.actions.ForwardAction" parameter="/WEB-
INF/jsp/scriptedInstall/disabled.jsp" />#<!— <action path="/scriptedInstall"
type="org.apache.struts.actions.ForwardAction" parameter="/WEB-
INF/jsp/scriptedInstall/disabled.jsp" /> —>#' struts-config.xml ¦ sed 's#<!—
$#<!— —>#' ¦ sed 's/  —>$/<!— —>/' > struts-config.xml.new
/bin/mv struts-config.xml.new struts-config.xml
/sbin/service vmware-webAccess restart
```

Figure 3.20 displays the primary screen for kick-start file creation.

The primary screen depicted has several decision points. The first is the type of scripted install choice: whether to perform a clean install or to update an existing installation. The second decision is the method of installation to use. There are three methods available:

- Using Remote is a way to specify a remote installation server. Set the Remote Server URL string to http://<hostname>/vmware. The URL specifies the location of the VMware installation files located on the given web server.

- Using CDROM it is not possible to enter a URL string. This installation method requires the CD-ROM to be available to perform the installation.

- Using NFS will tie this resultant boot floppy/kick-start file image to an NFS server to which the contents of the installation CD-ROM have been copied already. Using NFS is a way to use an NFS server and the Remote Server URL string should be <hostmachine>:<mountpoint>.

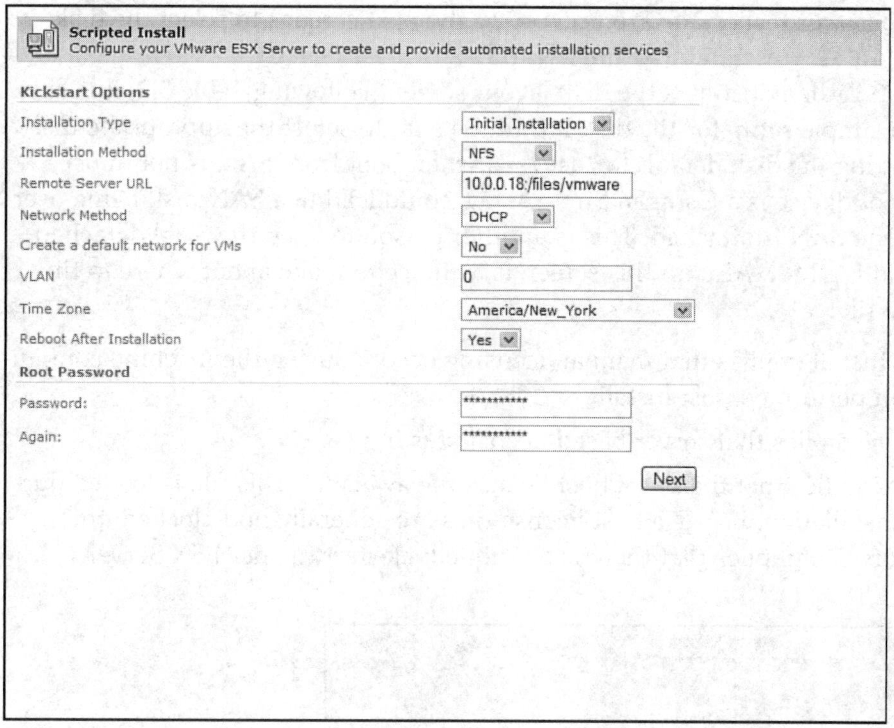

Figure 3.20 Scripted installation

The third decision point is the type of networking to use. If you choose a static network, the next screen will request the networking information for the installer to use on boot. However, there is no mechanism to set the default network port to use, so the default network port will be the first or lowest PCI device address associated with a network device, usually the on-board pNIC devices. For example, on a DL585, the pNIC labeled Port 1 that shares an IRQ with the ILO device is the primary pNIC. To force the kick start to use a different adapter for networking for ESX version 3, it is possible to change the kick-start boot to use a different device per the following boot options if the kick-start file is available remotely:

```
boot ks=http://kickStartServer/pathto/ks.cfg ksdevice=eth1
```

If the ks.cfg will live on a floppy, the ksdevice option is moot, because there are other options to place within the kick-start file as necessary.

In keeping with the disk-based installation, the recommendation prevents VMs from living on the service console network, so choose No when presented with the Create a Default Network for the VMs question. The last decision, for this screen, is to set the time zone for the installation. After you have selected the time zone and password, click Next to proceed to the next screens to select the disk layout.

Figure 3.21 demonstrates the disk layout screen. Following Table 3.2, it is easy to create a simple setup for the disk layout. Be sure to select the appropriate disk device. Letting the disk default to /dev/sda when boot from SAN is not in use, and the boot device is a Compaq SmartArray, could lead to a SAN disk being overwritten if the SAN is attached. This is another reason to keep the SAN detached when installing ESX. Also on this screen is a choice to make about where to find the license file:

- Post Install implies that manual licensing occurs during the machine configuration performed post install.

- Server implies that server-based licensing is in use.

- Host implies that there is a host license file available. This file is loaded during installation. Because host license files are generally node locked, this option also implies that there is a unique kick-start file per ESX Server.

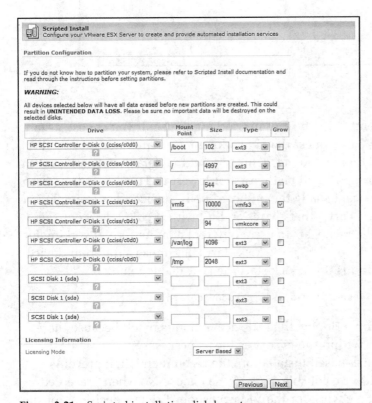

Figure 3.21   Scripted installation disk layout

Place the resultant kick-start on a floppy disk or disk image, a web server, or on a newly built CD-ROM or ISO image. Unlike version 2.5.3, ESX version 3 no longer produces a boot disk image, only a kick-start file. VMware has added some functionality to the kick-start file that should be explained. The functionality outside the normal expected for a kick-start file is in Table 3.6. You can find information about a normal kick-start file at www.redhat.com/docs/manuals/enterprise/RHEL-3-Manual/sysadmin-guide/ch-kickstart2.html.

Table 3.6

VMware Kick-Start Options	
VMware Kick-Start Option	**Definition**
vmaccepteula	Accepts the VMware license agreement.
vmlicense	Sets up licensing in the form of:
	`vmlicense –mode=server –server=<server> — features=<features> —edition=<edition>`
	Or
	`vmlicense –mode=file –features=<features> —edition=<edition>`
	Features can be backup and edition could be one of `esxFull` or `esxStartup`.
firewall	This option is deprecated in VMware ESX Server and should not be used.
%vmlicense_text section	Contains the host-based license file contents.
%post	Discussed below.

Of special note is the `%post` section of a kick-start file. This section contains a script of commands to run after the installation to configure the host, but before the first reboot of the server. The specialized configuration commands are covered in Chapters 8 through 10, and so are not covered here. However, to hook them in so that the configuration is automated, it is first required that the VMkernel be running. All the ESX-specific commands require the VMkernel to be running, and during the installation phase this is not the case. The following %post section creates a first boot script that will then configure the machine after the installation tool has rebooted the server:

```
%post
/bin/cat >> /etc/rc.d/rc.firstboot << EOF
#!/bin/bash
if [ -e /.firstboot ]
```

```
then

    # Place Configuration commands here

    /bin/rm -f /.firstboot
fi
EOF
/bin/touch /.firstboot
/bin/chmod 500 /etc/rc.d/rc.firstboot /.firstboot
/bin/echo ". /etc/rc.d/rc.firstboot" >> /etc/rc.d/rc.local
```

The code can be used anytime just by creating the file /.firstboot on the system, too. If the file does not exist, the firstboot script will not run. Also note that the firstboot script has restricted permissions, so other users cannot see the configuration changes made during boot.

Another sticky point with kick-start-based installations is that many people want to install from a VLAN. This is possible, but the ability to use virtual switch tagging is not yet available, because the VMkernel is not loaded, so any ESX Server using a VLAN needs to be plugged directly into the VLAN in question. Installations only support external switch-tagging networks. Chapter 7 goes into networking in detail and covers these concepts.

Conclusion

Before installing, be sure to have all the pertinent data at hand and all the decisions made. Although redoing one installation is simple, if there are 300 to perform, a change to the plan could take many more hours to fix. Now that the installation is complete and customized, we should make sure this server is secured and properly monitored. The next chapter discusses in detail various ways of auditing, monitoring, and securing the newly built ESX Server.

Chapter 4

Auditing, Monitoring, and Securing

Is ESX secure? That is the number one question to be answered by this chapter, and the question petrifies security specialists every time ESX is brought into the mix of equipment and software. This is because ESX is a large unknown with regard to security as ESX was designed to be placed behind a firewall. Specifically, access to any ESX Server Ethernet port is intended to be made through a firewall, as shown in Figure 4.1. Figure 4.1 depicts the basic ESX networks and the need for multiple firewalls for each exposed network.

However, here we are about to discuss how to secure ESX and how to protect your investment from the wily hacker or cracker, not to mention malicious colleagues. The key to such protection is defense in depth, where there are multiple levels of protection that aid in the overall security of the system. But before we can begin our discussion of a security recipe, we need to first understand the existing security inherent inside ESX. We need to understand what we are mixing our extra ingredients into before we do so.

The current placement of an ESX Server in the enterprise is also worth considering at this time, as the recipe is developed. Currently, there are customers that place ESX inside the network between the common dual bastions of protection referred to as the demilitarized zone (DMZ). Some ESX Servers are outside the enterprise firewall, and others are placed firmly behind the firewall. Consider these placement options when reading the rest of this chapter.

First, we look at existing ESX and VM security, and then go into detail about how to improve upon it.

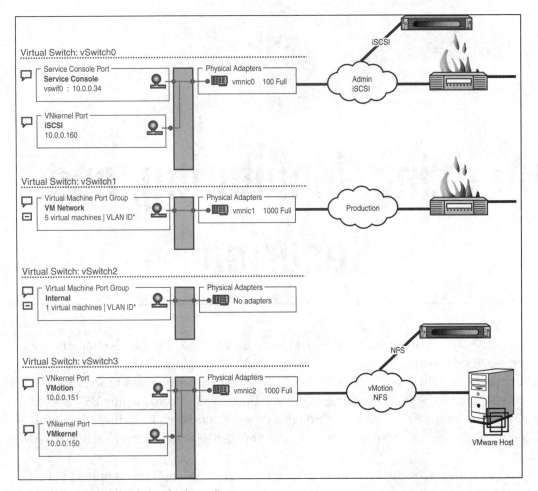

Figure 4.1 ESX Server behind a firewall

Best Practice for Security

Consider an ESX Server to be a datacenter. Datacenters house multiple servers, as do ESX Servers, so an ESX Server is a form of a datacenter.

VM Security

ESX provides some extremely advanced forms of security between VMs, and in this case we consider the service console (SC) or COS to be a very special VM, which is the way things are in ESX version 3. The same analogy holds true for ESX version 2.5.x. The COS on both ESX version 3 and ESX version 2.5.x has indirect access to those devices allowed by the VMkernel; this indirect access can be quite limited. It can be as limited as just being able to read a few status bits so hardware agents still work. As you can see, all the security necessary to protect VMs from each other is inherent in the VMkernel, which is the heart and soul of ESX. There is often a misconception that the COS is what is running ESX and not the VMkernel. Given how things used to start up this is a completely understandable, but incorrect, assumption.

The VMkernel claims all those devices and subsystems not specifically assigned to the service console, and with ESX version 3 this implies *all* the devices and memory. The VMkernel, and not the service console, assigns all the memory used by the VMs, and as such, the service console does not have access to the memory footprint of any other VM. On top of that, any memory assigned by the VMkernel is set to *null* before it is handed off to a VM, which in turn implies that a VM running in its memory segment cannot access the memory segment of another VM or the service console or vice versa. Because the COS provides administrative access to the VMkernel with no access to anything not previously assigned to it, there is no way for the COS to gain low-level access to the VMkernel. It is not possible to start any random process in the VMkernel as you can in the COS. It is just not possible, because there are *no* public interfaces to the VMkernel. This in turn makes the VMkernel extremely secure and pretty much hack proof. To aid in administration, the VMkernel exports to the COS access to the Virtual Machine File System (VMFS) upon which reside the VM runtime and disk files and some status bits and data regarding the physical hardware. With all the separation inherent in the VMkernel, the network access and VM security is dependent on the particular OS running in the VM in question and not upon the security of the COS.

In addition to the COS's access to the aspects of the physical hardware, there are other aspects of ESX to be aware of from a security perspective. The first is deployment of VM from templates and other sources, and the other is how VMotion via the VMkernel network works.

In other words, securing the COS will *not* secure your VM's runtime but can secure your VM data. Security of the VM is dependent upon the OS in use and should follow the same recipes already developed by corporate security for these operating systems as if each VM were a physical host; from a security perspective, a VM and a physical server do not differ. Outside the service console's access to the VMFS, the only way to access another VM is via its network connections, so securing the network is of the utmost importance. Because the COS can access the VM disk files, securing your service console is even more important.

The following is a list of items that need securing, over what networks data can travel, and the risk associated with not securing the component.

- **VM OS:** Secure the VM OS using the same recipes that corporate Security dictates for the OS in question. Not securing these servers can lead to a high risk to a network.

- **VM networks:** These network connections should reside behind a firewall. If the OS in the VM is properly secured, this is a low-risk item; otherwise, it is a high risk.

- **Securing the VMkernel:** The VMkernel is by its very nature extremely secure. With no public APIs, there is no known way to hack or crack this crucial software. Currently, this is a low- or no-risk component.

- **Securing VMotion or the VMkernel network:** VMotion passes memory data from ESX Server to ESX Server to help balance and manage each ESX host. Because it passes memory data in an unencrypted form for a VM over a wire, it is crucial to apply some form of security; this is a high-risk item. The VMkernel network is also used to perform NFS mounts and iSCSI access for ESX version 3.0 and VMotion. Access to the VMkernel network should be guarded at all times.

- **Console operating system:** The COS has access to everything that the VMkernel will expose. Because the VMkernel exposes hardware and the data stores for the VM disk files, this is another crucial and high-risk component. In addition, nonadministrative VMs should not have access to the COS network so as to limit attack points.

- **VM deployment:** There are a many different tools for deploying VMs that use the COS network connection. Such deployment sometimes sends an unencrypted disk image to the target ESX Server. Because this is the case, securing the deployment network is necessary and is considered a high-risk component.

- **VM backup:** There are two major ways to back up a VM; one is to back up from within the VM, which uses the network connections of the VM; and the other is to back up from outside the VM via the COS or VMware Consolidated Backup (VCB). In either case, the security associated with this could be considered a high risk, so either the VM backup network or the

COS backup network should be secured. There are other backup methods covered in Chapter 12, "Disaster Recovery and Backup," that do not use IP-based networking, and therefore are not a concern.

Now that we understand the current security of an ESX Server, it is important to realize that solving the majority of the security concerns uses physical means. That it is essential to creating a defense in depth for the individual VMs and the COS. The recipe that follows provides a defense in depth for COS for ESX because it has the access to critical data that individual VMs do not have, while also providing a list of necessary physical security measures for each exposed network.

What follows is not a replacement for your corporate security policy but a recipe to enhance, augment, or implement your existing policy. An example security policy follows.

Example Security Policy

Each host must reside behind a firewall, and no machine can host more than one network (except specific hardware routers). In addition, all machines will run Norton Antivirus daily, and spyware scanners will be employed. Internally application-based firewalls will be in use to ensure only approved applications are running on the network.

Assuming your security policy is as simple as shown here, we can immediately note some glaring problems, and an exception or restatement of the security policy is necessary to accommodate ESX. Before writing a security policy, write a security philosophy for ESX.

Example Security Philosophy

Our goal is to provide the highest security possible for a given operating system while allowing for the auditing and monitoring of the OS with minimal impact on the operation of the system applications. In addition, the goal of any security effort is to understand that eventually something will happen, and there is a need to make the necessary adjustments and provide the necessary tools before this eventually. Security is a daily learning process.

While packing a punch, the philosophy does not contradict our policy, which is what we want. Decide on a philosophy before choosing to write or implement a policy. If your philosophy is contradictory to your policy, one or the other has to change; otherwise, disaster and confusion will reign.

Best Practice for Security
Have a written security policy and a written security philosophy.

Security Recipe

Would you allow anyone to walk into your datacenter and remove disk drives from any machine therein? Of course you wouldn't, and this is what an unsecured service console can allow to happen without you even knowing it is happening. Hence, it is extremely important to keep the service console out of a DMZ or outside a firewall. The rest of this chapter presents a recipe to add auditing, monitoring, and security to the ESX Server service console with the goal of protecting your data the same way you would protect a datacenter. We are only concerned with the service console because each VM is separate and distinct, yet the service COS is a part of ESX and it has access to critical data.

From this example policy and our list of different ESX components mentioned previously, we can formulate a checklist for securing ESX (see Table 4.1), and we can use that checklist to make the necessary changes to, or to start writing, an inclusive security policy.

Table 4.1

Security Checklist		
Policy Element	**ESX Element**	**Element Type**
Firewall	iptables	Securing
Shadow passwords	pwconv/grpconv	Securing
Multiple networks	NA	Securing
Antivirus	clamav/sophos/etc.	Securing
Spyware scanner	NA	Securing
Application firewall	sudo/logcheck	Auditing/monitoring
Card key access	sudo/passwords	Security/auditing
Protection from DoS	Bastille/CISscan	Security

Policy Element	ESX Element	Element Type
Preparing for forensics	Coroner's toolkit	Auditing
Checksums	Tripwire	Auditing
Remote logging	Service console logging	Monitoring
Process accounting	sar	Monitoring
Rootkit checking	chkrootkit	Monitoring
Periodic scans	Bastille/nmap/nessus	Monitoring
Patches	By hand from VMware	Security

From the checklist, there is quite a bit that may need to change in our security policy. First off, ESX should have multiple networks; at least a network for VMs and one for management. Because access to the service console implies access to your VM disks, your management network should be limited to just those who need access and should be protected as you protect your datacenter. In addition, many of the tools listed most likely look foreign to you, because they are Linux-based tools, and that implies that a Windows-centric security policy no longer applies as the management interface to ESX is a variant of Linux but is not Linux. However, do not confuse ESX with Linux; it is *not* Linux. Just the management or service console uses a variant of Linux, not the virtualization layer, which is the VMkernel. Knowing which version of Linux is associated with a specific version of ESX will aid us in developing a security recipe and a recipe for ESX because each version of Linux has different vulnerabilities. This implies that specific mention of Windows tools such as Norton Antivirus must include the Linux equivalents for the version of Linux involved. In most cases, the version of the base Linux for the variant is the same across the board except for either a different build or version.

The version of the service COS has changed radically through the versions of ESX (see Table 4.2), but this does not imply that the following recipe will change very much. On the contrary, it will not. Note that although we are discussing versions of Red Hat Linux, the ESX kernel is quite different from that of the Red Hat kernel, and there are packages lacking from the full release of Red Hat, because ESX installs using a single CD-ROM. Therefore, and we will reiterate this throughout the rest of the book, *all patches* must *come from VMware and* not *from Red Hat.*

Table 4.2

Service Console OS Versions	
ESX Version	COS Version
ESX earlier than 2.5.3	Red Hat Linux release 7.2
ESX 2.5.3	Red Hat Enterprise Linux ES release 2.1
ESX 3.0	Red Hat Enterprise Linux ES release 3

Best Practice for Patching ESX

Apply patches *only* from VMware for ESX.

The difference between ESX version 2.5.x and ESX version 3 is in the differences between Figure 4.1 and Figure 4.2. Figure 4.1 has an extra network named VMkernel connected to a NAS device that serves up iSCSI or NAS, whereas Figure 4.2 is missing this extra connection, so the NAS serving up NFS is connected via the service console connection. iSCSI targets are not supported on ESX version 2.5. From a security perspective, it is not much of a difference and does not change our recipe any. We just need to be careful of software versions per Table 4.2. There are several goals with adding more auditing, monitoring, and security to ESX:

- To secure the service console such that it is as safe as the doors to your datacenter.

- To increase the auditing capabilities of ESX so that we can tell when something happened and by whom.

- Add some level of monitoring to ESX so that you can tell when a problem occurs that needs attention.

- Disallow malicious network activity by the hosted VMs.

- In keeping with our security philosophy, we are going to prepare the system for forensic analysis. This is because we know that eventually all secure systems can be hacked, and good security specialists prepare for this eventuality ahead of time.

Best Practice for Security

Prepare for the eventuality that your security will be breached.

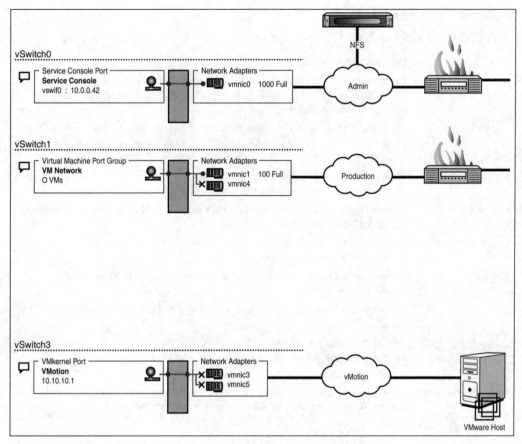

Figure 4.2 ESX version 2.5

Table 4.3 provides definitions of tools to use in our recipe and where to find them on the ESX distribution or the web.

Table 4.3

Tool Definition and Location	
Tool	**Definition and Location**
iptables	iptables is a packet-filtering firewall that is intrinsic in the Linux kernel and is part of the ESX distribution.
shadow-utils	shadow-utils is the Shadow Password package for Linux that comes stock on all versions of ESX.
clamav	clamav is a free antivirus agent for Linux available at www.clamav.org.
Sophos	Sophos is a for fee antivirus agent for Linux from www.sophos.com.

continues...

Table 4.3   continued

Tool Definition and Location	
Tool	**Definition and Location**
sudo	sudo is a tool that provides root like access to individuals using their own passwords, yet it logs all activity and can be configured to limit which commands individual users can use.
logcheck	logcheck is a tool to hourly monitor various log files and to mail the possible security and high-risk issues to the administrators. logcheck is found at http://rpmfind.net.
Bastille	Bastille is a scanning and security implementation tool that will secure a Linux box from the inside. www.bastille-linux.org.
CISscan	CISscan is a Linux security scanner that will check the security of Linux from the inside (www.cisecurity.org).
Coroner's toolkit	Coroner's toolkit will take a snapshot of a system and provide the tools to do forensics using the snapshot.
Tripwire	Tripwire provides the capability to notice if files have changed inadvertently (www.tripwire.org).
sar	sar records process data that can be used to determine how much a process is using.
chkrootkit	chkrootkit looks for root kits on a system. Rootkits are left by a hacker to facilitate logging back in later and are designed to hide themselves (www.chkrootkit.org).
NMAP and Nessus	NMAP and Nessus are tools that can periodically scan a server from outside to determine whether there is any vulnerability (www.nessus.org).

The basis for our recipe is the concept that reduced access will reduce our risk. So, the first step is to limit access to the COS through reducing the number of users who can log in directly to the COS or via the MUI, because that requires a COS login to access. We will have operators access the ESX Servers via other less-dangerous management interfaces. We will also limit access to the servers by IP address so that we always know from where access is allowed. You do not give everyone access to your datacenter, so do not give them access to your ESX Servers. Nor will we allow those administrators with the necessary privileges direct access to the super-user account, but will have a separate account for each user to aid in auditing. Note that the recipe presented herein is more for the advanced administrator with quite a bit of Linux knowledge. Another basis for our recipe is the placement of the service console on your network. Specifically, the service console shall never live external to your corporate firewall and never live within the DMZ of your network. The DMZ is a location that will trap many hackers and is a dangerous place to leave the keys to your datacenter, because the service console is the entry to your virtual datacenter. Although other VMs can live in the DMZ or outside your corporate firewall, the service console should never live inside a DMZ, because there is a higher chance of loss than with a single machine. Consider the analogy of the datacenter; most companies leave the datacenter door open off the lobby to the building? Granted, getting into the lobby may require authentication. Is it then sensible for lobby authentication to imply datacenter authentication? The lobby in this analogy is the DMZ, and the datacenter lives further in.

Although the recipe presented in the following sections will harden ESX such that it is at a much lower risk for hacking, we will still subscribe to the philosophy that eventually we will be at risk, and therefore we need to minimize all aspects of access, including access to the service console. In addition, before implementing this recipe, review and critique the recipe. Be sure it covers all the necessary requirements and meets the goals for your implementation.

Step 1

Ensure that the root (super-user) password is known by only a few people, and the fewer the better. Create an account on the system for each person you have given the root password and for any other administrator. It is best to create local accounts, but you can tie into a domain server. If you choose to go that route, you should limit access to the host through domain and firewall controls. For ESX version 3, and once the recipe is followed for ESX versions earlier than 3, logging in directly via the root user is not necessary.

Step 2

Implement shadow groups and passwords. Shadow passwords avoid the possibility of any nonroot user directly accessing user passwords and being able to crack those passwords. Enabling shadow passwords is a must, because the passwords are no longer accessible by any user. Although shadow passwords are on by default, if a scan suddenly shows them not enabled it is important to make the necessary change. To enable shadow group and user passwords, issue the following commands:

```
esxcfg-auth —enableshadow
```

Step 3

Implement a defense in depth using built-in packet-filtering firewalls and other tools such as TCP Wrappers so that all avenues of approach are covered.

ESX version 3

ESX version 3 comes with its own firewall software that can be controlled using the supplied `esxcfg-firewall` command. This is a powerful tool to allow or disallow access to your COS. In addition, the full set of rules can be set from the security profile in the Virtual Infrastructure Client (VIC). However, be careful, because the regular iptables service is disabled and use of the iptables service to reconfigure the firewall will result in no rules at all. Use the firewall service instead to restart the ESX-based firewall.

In addition to providing a firewall script, the crafters of the script thought about some of the possible agents available. There is no longer a need to look up the ports and protocols because the tool has them within for easy usage.

To see a full set of rules available, issue the following command:

```
esxcfg-firewall -s
```

Or to query the existing set of rule, there are two methods:

```
esxcfg-firewall -q
```

Or

```
iptables -L
```

However, most people will find the output of either command to be extremely cryptic or often confusing. Yet, there is some hope, because there are references available to aid in deciphering the results. The `esxcfg-firewall` query command does give a nice list of enabled services at the end of the output that takes away some of the confusion.

ESX Version 2.5.2 and Earlier Than Version 3

Using the ESX distribution CD-ROM, install the iptables package and create a rule set for use with the package. I find that making an ISO image of the ESX distribution media and placing it on the ESX Server makes it easier to install extra software and other bits; otherwise, I need to search for the media. Although iptables is extra yet available software, most people turn to the MUI to set security settings. The MUI disables or enables various servers on the system, but it does not set up a firewall.

```
- place ESX CD into CDROM drive
# dd if=/dev/cdrom of=esx.iso
# eject
# mount -o loop esx.iso /mnt/cdrom
# cd /mnt/cdrom/VMware/RPMs
# rpm -ivh iptables*.rpm
```

To create the rule set for use with iptables, we can get extremely complex or simplify our lives. Either way we need to start with the basics that Red Hat has developed and expand from there. Rules for iptables are read from top to bottom with ACCEPT or accepted connections before REJECT or rejected connections. iptables can be extremely complex and it is expected that you will use one of the iptables references in conjunction with these first steps. Refer to the References for iptables references. To allow items such as the HPSIM management tools, the ports need to be specified in the `/etc/sysconfig/iptables` file per the following. There is no script available as there is in ESX version 3.

```
edit /etc/sysconfig/iptables and enter the following lines.
*filter
:INPUT ACCEPT [0:0]
:FORWARD ACCEPT [0:0]
:OUTPUT ACCEPT [0:0]
:INPUT-RULE-1 - [0:0]
-A INPUT -j INPUT-RULE-1
-A FORWARD -j INPUT-RULE-1
-A INPUT-RULE-1 -i lo -j ACCEPT
-A INPUT-RULE-1 -p icmp -j REJECT
-A INPUT-RULE-1 -p 50 -j ACCEPT
-A INPUT-RULE-1 -p 51 -j ACCEPT
-A INPUT-RULE-1 -m state --state ESTABLISHED,RELATED -j ACCEPT
-A INPUT-RULE-1 -m state --state NEW -m tcp -p tcp --dport 8222 -j ACCEPT
-A INPUT-RULE-1 -m state --state NEW -m tcp -p tcp --dport 8333 -j ACCEPT
-A INPUT-RULE-1 -m state --state NEW -m tcp -p tcp --dport 2301 -j ACCEPT
-A INPUT-RULE-1 -m state --state NEW -m tcp -p tcp --dport 2381 -j ACCEPT
-A INPUT-RULE-1 -m state --state NEW -m tcp -p tcp --dport 443 -j ACCEPT
-A INPUT-RULE-1 -m state --state NEW -m tcp -p tcp --dport 905 -j ACCEPT
-A INPUT-RULE-1 -m state --state NEW -m tcp -p tcp --dport 902 -j ACCEPT
```

```
-A INPUT-RULE-1 -m state --state NEW -m tcp -p tcp --dport 199 -j ACCEPT
-A INPUT-RULE-1 -m state --state NEW -m tcp -p tcp --dport 22 -j ACCEPT
-A INPUT-RULE-1 -m state --state NEW -m tcp -p tcp --dport 80 -j ACCEPT
-A INPUT-RULE-1 -m state --state NEW -m tcp -p tcp --dport 21 -j ACCEPT
-A INPUT-RULE-1 -j REJECT --reject-with icmp-host-prohibited
COMMIT
```

Adding iptables will create a defense in depth for your ESX Server and allow the monitoring of the types of network attacks on your host and their origin. Although iptables can replace a hardware firewall, that is not our recommendation. The preceding rules will look familiar to administrators of a standard Red Hat system because they are pretty much direct from there, but with some modifications to account for ESX-specific issues. These are the ports and protocols necessary for VC (port 902), VMware remote console (port 905) which is no longer used in ESX version 3, ESX scripted installation (ports 8222 and 8333) which are no longer use din ESX version 3, SNMP (ports 199), the HP management agents (ports 2301 and 2381) if using HP hardware, or the appropriate management ports for your hardware. Other installed agents may require different ports and protocols to be made available. Note that protocols 50 and 51 refer to the IPv6 crypt and auth protocols.

ESX Versions Earlier Than 2.5.2

A big concern of implementing this type of firewall and any firewall, whether it be software or hardware based, is the installation of VC agents, which must occur prior to the implementation of a firewall. For ESX versions earlier than ESX 2.5.2 the agents are installed via a new protocol and set of ports that are very similar to the way the File Transfer Protocol (FTP) works. However, this protocol has yet to be documented, and it does not use TCP or UDP packets but some other transmission protocol. So to register an ESX Server into VC, a firewall cannot exist between the two, specifically not between the VC host and the service console of the ESX Server. After the agents have been installed, there is no need for ESX to *not* be behind a firewall. It is suggested then that the service consoles and VC Server live on a management network that is completely separate from the network for your VMs. Although this is not always possible, it is by far the best practice for ESX.

Step 4

Given the aforementioned ports and protocols, we can further secure them by either locking the system to specific IP addresses or limiting the number of ports further:

1. Remove all non-SSL-based web servers. Specifically, remove the 80, 2301 (or any non-SSL port dictated by your vendor-supplied system management agents), and 8222 port lines from the rules.

2. Lock down access to the SNMP port 199 to just the IP addresses of the servers who need to access SNMP. Specifically, you would allow access to the VC, HPSIM, OpenView, or other SNMP monitoring servers. [ManageIP]

3. Lock down access to the VC and remote console ports to only those hosts that need to access these capabilities. Specifically, port 902 is only accessible by the VC Server and port 905, used by the remote console, is accessible to only those hosts that need to access the remote console. Granted, disallowing access to the remote console may inadvertently reduce necessary functionality. [VCServerIP, AdminIP]

4. Allow access to the ESX scripted installation website accessed via port 8333 to be accessible from other ESX Servers. [ESXServerIP] (ESX version 2.5.x only!)

5. Allow access to port 2381 (or the port dictated by your vendor-supplied system management agents), the System Management home page, which is used to monitor the ESX Server hardware through just the HPSIM or OpenView management tools. [ManageIP] (HP Proliant hardware only!)

6. Lock down access to the MUI via ports 443 to just those administrative hosts in use. Specifically, allow access to at least those hosts that need to edit host configuration within VC. There is actually no need to allow the VC Server access to these ports. [AdminIP]

7. Lock down SSH access via port 22 to just those hosts previously assigned as administrative hosts. [AdminIP]

8. Allow access from VIC via port 902, 5989, and 5988 for all those hosts that require it via the administrative network. [AdminIP] (ESX version 3 only!)

There are three approaches to locking down servers to certain IP addresses. The first is to use entries in /etc/hosts.allow and /etc/hosts.deny to further protect your services just in case the packet-filtering firewall is not accessible. These files are used by TCP Wrappers to control who can access a server and from what IP. Unfortunately there is a limited subset of tools that use TCP Wrappers, which implies this cannot be the only defense. The simplest entries are usually the best and the following would work well to limit access to those tools such as SSH and other xinetd-based tools to only be accessible from the AdminIP while denying access for all other hosts.

```
#cat /etc/hosts.allow
ALL: AdminIP


#cat /etc/hosts.deny
ALL: ALL
```

However, this is only a small part of the big picture, because further configuration of the packet-filtering firewall is the first priority. The packet filtering firewall is the second approach. The third approach is to configure the pam_access module which is described in chapter 8. Like TCP Wrappers, pam_access provides only a limited subset of controls. Below we break out how to configure the packet filtering firewall to block via IP.

ESX Version 3

The preceding specification not only changes the rules, but it changes the manner in which the tools are used to create the firewall. Although the default firewall does limit the ports to use, it does not have a mechanism to lock down access by IP. There are two approaches to implementing the lock down by IP. The first approach is to modify the esxcfg-firewall script to accept arguments specifying source hosts to allow. The second approach is to create a secondary firewall script to accept connections only from one of the allowed servers.

Because changing the esxcfg-firewall script would create more problems in the long run, the second option is a better way to go. The problems would include the need to modify the script every time the system is updated, while a secondary script can be used to augment the security available by the firewall script. Be sure to include all open ports. For ESX version 3, the default open ports are for SSH (22), HTTP (80), HTTPS (443), BOOTPS (UDP ports 67 and 68), VMware heartbeats (UDP port 902), CIMHttpServer (5988), CIMHttpsServer (5989), and others. However, more ports can be opened using the esxcfg-firewall scripts, so it is important to realize which these are and secure them accordingly. For example, HPSIM requires port 2381 to be opened for use by the SIM Server, and by any machine that needs to access the System home page. For example, the following partial script will look for the specific rules for the listed ports and first replace the existing wide-open rule with one that disallows all other IP addresses not in the $AdminIP variable. Then set the packet-filtering firewall to add new rules above the replace closed rule that the esxcfg-firewall tool enables for each administrative IP listed in the $AdminIP variable of the script. For the complete script, see Appendix A, "Security Script."

```
…
for x in 902 80 443 2050:5000 8042:8045 427 22 5989 5988
do
        rulenum=`$IPTABLES —line-numbers -L INPUT -n ¦ grep "tcp" ¦
➡grep "$x state NEW" ¦ awk '{print $1}'`
        # Replace original rule to DROP everything from all other hosts
        $IPTABLES -R INPUT $rulenum -m state --state NEW -m tcp -p tcp
➡—dport $x -j DROP
        for y in $AdminIP
        do
              $IPTABLES -I INPUT $rulenum -m state --state NEW -s $y
➡-m tcp -p tcp --dport $x -j ACCEPT
        done
done
…
```

ESX Version 2.5.2 and Earlier

The preceding specification changes the rules quite a bit, and they now look similar to the following. However, there will need to be several substitutions made for the real IP addresses for the hosts that are allowed access to the networking available via the service console.

```
edit /etc/sysconfig/iptables and enter the following lines.
*filter
:INPUT ACCEPT [0:0]
:FORWARD ACCEPT [0:0]
:OUTPUT ACCEPT [0:0]
:INPUT-RULE-1 - [0:0]
-A INPUT -j INPUT-RULE-1
-A FORWARD -j INPUT-RULE-1
-A INPUT-RULE-1 -i lo -j ACCEPT
-A INPUT-RULE-1 -p icmp -j REJECT
-A INPUT-RULE-1 -m state --state ESTABLISHED,RELATED -j ACCEPT
-A INPUT-RULE-1 -m state --state NEW —s ESXSeverIP -m tcp -p tcp --dport 8333 -j ACCEPT
-A INPUT-RULE-1 -m state --state NEW —s AdminIP -m tcp -p tcp --dport 2381 -j ACCEPT
-A INPUT-RULE-1 -m state --state NEW —s ManageIP -m tcp -p tcp --dport 2381 -j ACCEPT
```

```
-A INPUT-RULE-1 -m state --state NEW -s AdminIP -m tcp -p tcp --dport 443 -j ACCEPT
-A INPUT-RULE-1 -m state --state NEW -s AdminIP -m tcp -p tcp --dport 905 -j ACCEPT
-A INPUT-RULE-1 -m state --state NEW -s VCServerIP -m tcp -p tcp --dport 902 -j ACCEPT
-A INPUT-RULE-1 -m state --state NEW -s ManageIP -m tcp -p tcp --dport 199 -j ACCEPT
-A INPUT-RULE-1 -m state --state NEW -s AdminIP -m tcp -p tcp --dport 22 -j ACCEPT
-A INPUT-RULE-1 -m state --state NEW -s AdminIP -m tcp -p tcp --dport 21 -j ACCEPT
-A INPUT-RULE-1 -j REJECT --reject-with icmp-host-prohibited
COMMIT
```

Step 5

We are almost done working with our secondary firewall. Note that any of these modifications can also be done at the primary firewall depending on how it is used and configured. Working with the secondary firewall for a defense in depth increases security. However, what is security without auditing, so this step is to add some advanced logging to the iptables rules so that we can catch anything extra that may be trying to reach our hosts.

ESX Version 3

ESX version 3's built-in firewall includes a fair amount of logging and provides adequate auditing of the firewall.

ESX Version 2.5.2 and Earlier

By adding the following lines before the final REJECT line in the rules shown for ESX version 2.5.2 or earlier in "Step 4," we can enable logging via the syslog facility:

```
edit /etc/sysconfig/iptables and enter the following line before the line reading:
-A INPUT-RULE-1 -j REJECT --reject-with icmp-host-prohibited
-A INPUT-RULE-1 --log-level info --log-prefix iptables -j LOG
```

The change to the iptables rules listed above will *log* to syslog all accesses of the network that are *not* picked up by the previous rules, so in essence we can track from where an attack or disallowed access was even attempted. Using the info or informational log level will allow us to redirect to which log file these reports go. And finally, if the logging takes up quite a bit of disk space, you can use the -limit 10/s iptables option to limit the amount of throughput you get to just 10 per second. Any rate of logging above that will be dropped automatically. The limit option goes just before the -j option in the previous rule.

Using limits may be required, because enabling logging in iptables could saturate a log file very quickly! This is one line that, if you do not need it at the time, you might want to disable it until it is needed. Generally, this will be either at the beginning or when you suspect a denial-of-service attack. If you suspect that type of attack on your service console, you will definitely need to implement the limit option to this rule.

VM Use of iptables

iptables rules can also be used within a VM that in turn acts as a firewall to other VMs. This type of configuration is discussed further in Chapter 7, "Networking." iptables is extremely powerful and is a stock feature of all modern Linux operating systems, and its use within ESX does not require any extra software, just a different level of knowledge.

Step 6

The next step in our recipe is to use several alternative tools to audit the current security of the system and then modify the system to increase the security to the highest possible level. We will use two tools going forward that are Linux-specific as there is nothing yet for ESX as a whole, although there is overlap between the tools, the focus is quite a bit different, because are the results. We will be using CISscan (www.cisecurity.org) for Linux, with a slight modification; otherwise, the tool does not know what it is scanning. The second tool is Bastille (www.bastille-linux.org), which CISscan has as a dependency yet is not required. To get a better score for CISscan, the sysstat RPM should be installed, which can be found at http://rpmfind.net, and download the version for Red Hat 7.2 for ESX earlier than 2.5.3. Bastille has two modes, whereas CISscan has only one. The common mode is to run assessments that you can then use to judge the security of your system, while Bastille's second mode is to actually implement the security profile you desire. The goal of both these assessment tools is to get a score that is as close to 10 as possible. Appendix A lists a security script that can be run to achieve a very high score, and so far I have not noticed any issues with the use of ESX in this mode.

CISscan and Bastille overlap in functionality for their assessments, but CISscan reviews the system network configuration at the protocol level a bit more, whereas Bastille concentrates on making sure the appropriate permissions are set on system resources and files. The overlap between the two tools is mostly on the softer aspects of security, which are just as important. The softer aspects of security are the warnings and other texts necessary to tell users that they are possibly accessing a secure system and, if they are not authorized to, dire consequences will result. Because of the legal need for such notices, it is important that your corporate security policy document these dire consequences in excruciating detail.

Step 6A

CISscan requires that the /etc/redhat-release file contain a properly formatted Red Hat string for it to identify what system is being scanned. Because we know what version of Red Hat is involved, we can formulate the contents of this file appropriately according to the Table 4.4. Note that there is no adjustment necessary for ESX version 3.

Table 4.4

/etc/redhat-release Contents for CISscan Processing	
ESX Release	Contents of /etc/redhat-release File
ESX 2.5.2 and earlier	Red Hat Linux release 7.2
ESX 2.5.3	Red Hat Enterprise Linux ES release 2.1
ESX 3.0	Red Hat Enterprise Linux ES release 3.0

After we have formulated the /etc/redhat-release, file we can install and run the assessment tool to determine what we have to modify to increase security on the system. Note that this tool requires registration to download, and the specifics of how to fix the problems this tool discovers are available in detail in the one-week security course put on by SANS.

Downloading the tool is simple. Install and run as follows:

```
mkdir /opt/cis
cd /opt/cis
tar -xzf cisscan.tgz
create the file /etc/redhat-release per table 4.3 if using ESX v2.5.x


**************************************************************************
****************** CIS Security Benchmark Checker v1.6.7 ******************
*                                                             *
* Original Developer                       : Jay Beale        *
* Lead Developer                           : Ralf Durkee      *
* Benchmark Coordinator                    : George Toft      *
*                                                             *
* Copyright 2001 - 2005 The Center for Internet Security  www.cisecurity.org *
*                                                             *
```

* Please send feedback to linux-scan@cisecurity.org.   *
****

        Investigating system...this will take a few minutes...

                                ******

Now a final check for non-standard world-writable files, Set-UID and Set-GID
programs — this can take a whole lot of time if you have a large filesystem.
Your score if there are no extra world-writable files or SUID/SGID programs
found will be 6.53 / 10.00 . If there are extra SUID/SGID programs or
world-writable files, your score could be as low as 6.25 / 10.00 .

        You can hit CTRL-C at any time to stop at this remaining step.

The preliminary log can be found at: ./cis-most-recent-log

                                ******

            Rating = 6.44 / 10.00

****
To learn more about the results, do the following:

    All results/diagnostics:
        more ./cis-ruler-log.20060417-16.52.47.7460
    Positive Results Only:
        egrep "^Positive" ./cis-ruler-log.20060417-16.52.47.7460
    Negative Results Only:
        egrep "^Negative" ./cis-ruler-log.20060417-16.52.47.7460

For each item that you score or fail to score on, please reference the
corresponding item in the CIS Benchmark Document.

    For additional instructions/support, please reference the CIS web page:

                    http://www.cisecurity.org

```
# egrep "^Negative" cis-most-recent-log
Negative: 1.3 sshd_config parameter Banner is not set.
Negative: 1.3 ssh_config must have 'Protocol 2' underneath Host *.
Negative: 1.4 sysstat system accounting package is NOT installed.
Negative: 3.1 umask not found in first /etc/rcX.d script /etc/rc3.d/S00microcode_ctl.
Negative: 3.2 xinetd is still active.
Negative: 3.6 Misc. Boot Services — gpm not deactivated.
Negative: 3.15 Web server not deactivated.
Negative: 4.1 sysctl net.ipv4.conf.default.secure_redirects=1 and should be '0'.
Negative: 4.1 sysctl net.ipv4.conf.all.secure_redirects=1 and should be '0'.
Negative: 4.1 sysctl net.ipv4.conf.all.rp_filter=0 and should be '1'.
Negative: 4.1 sysctl net.ipv4.icmp_echo_ignore_broadcasts=0 and should be '1'.
Negative: 4.1 sysctl net.ipv4.conf.all.accept_redirects=1 and should be '0'.
Negative: 4.1 sysctl net.ipv4.conf.default.accept_source_route=1 and should be '0'.
Negative: 4.1 sysctl net.ipv4.tcp_syncookies=0 and should be '1'.
Negative: 4.1 sysctl net.ipv4.conf.default.accept_redirects=1 and should be '0'.
Negative: 4.1 sysctl net.ipv4.tcp_max_syn_backlog=1024 and should be >= 4096.
Negative: 4.2 sysctl net.ipv4.conf.all.send_redirects=1 and should be '0'.
Negative: 4.2 sysctl net.ipv4.conf.default.send_redirects=1 and should be '0'.
Negative: 4.2 /etc/sysctl.conf should not be world or group readable.
Negative: 6.1 /tmp is not mounted nodev.
Negative: 6.1 /boot is not mounted nodev.
Negative: 6.1 /var/log is not mounted nodev.
Negative: 6.2 Removable filesystem /mnt/cdrom is not mounted nosuid.
Negative: 6.2 Removable filesystem /mnt/cdrom is not mounted nodev.
Negative: 6.2 Removable filesystem /mnt/floppy is not mounted nosuid.
Negative: 6.2 Removable filesystem /mnt/floppy is not mounted nodev.
Negative: 6.3 PAM allows users to mount removable media: <floppy>.
(/etc/security/console.perms)
Negative: 6.3 PAM allows users to mount removable media: <cdrom>.
(/etc/security/console.perms)
Negative: 6.3 PAM allows users to mount removable media: <pilot>.
(/etc/security/console.perms)
Negative: 6.3 PAM allows users to mount removable media: <jaz>.
(/etc/security/console.perms)
```

Negative: 6.3 PAM allows users to mount removable media: <zip>.
(/etc/security/console.perms)

Negative: 6.3 PAM allows users to mount removable media: <ls120>.
(/etc/security/console.perms)

Negative: 6.3 PAM allows users to mount removable media: <camera>.
(/etc/security/console.perms)

Negative: 6.3 PAM allows users to mount removable media: <memstick>.
(/etc/security/console.perms)

Negative: 6.3 PAM allows users to mount removable media: <flash>.
(/etc/security/console.perms)

Negative: 6.3 PAM allows users to mount removable media: <diskonkey>.
(/etc/security/console.perms)

Negative: 6.3 PAM allows users to mount removable media: <rem_ide>.
(/etc/security/console.perms)

Negative: 6.3 PAM allows users to mount removable media: <rio500>.
(/etc/security/console.perms)

Negative: 6.9 The hotplug package is installed.

Negative: 7.4 Couldn't open cron.allow

Negative: 7.4 Couldn't open at.allow

Negative: 7.5 The permissions on /etc/crontab are not sufficiently restrictive.

Negative: 7.6 xinetd either requires global 'only-from' statement or one for each service.

Negative: 7.7 /etc/securetty has a non console or tty 1-6 line: tty7.

Negative: 7.7 /etc/securetty has a non console or tty 1-6 line: tty8.

Negative: 7.7 /etc/securetty has a non console or tty 1-6 line: tty9.

Negative: 7.7 /etc/securetty has a non console or tty 1-6 line: tty10.

Negative: 7.7 /etc/securetty has a non console or tty 1-6 line: tty11.

Negative: 7.8 GRUB isn't password-protected.

Negative: 7.9 /etc/inittab needs a /sbin/sulogin line for single user mode.

Negative: 8.1 bin has a valid shell of /sbin/nologin. Remember, the /sbin/nologin shell,
when found in /etc/shells, leaves a user potentially able to use FTP.

Negative: 8.1 daemon has a valid shell of /sbin/nologin. Remember, the /sbin/nologin
shell, when found in /etc/shells, leaves a user potentially able to use FTP.

Negative: 8.1 adm has a valid shell of /sbin/nologin. Remember, the /sbin/nologin shell,
when found in /etc/shells, leaves a user potentially able to use FTP.

Negative: 8.1 lp has a valid shell of /sbin/nologin. Remember, the /sbin/nologin shell,
when found in /etc/shells, leaves a user potentially able to use FTP.

Negative: 8.1 mail has a valid shell of /sbin/nologin. Remember, the /sbin/nologin shell, when found in /etc/shells, leaves a user potentially able to use FTP.
Negative: 8.1 news has a valid shell of /bin/sh. Remember, an empty shell field in /etc/passwd signifies /bin/sh.
Negative: 8.1 uucp has a valid shell of /sbin/nologin. Remember, the /sbin/nologin shell, when found in /etc/shells, leaves a user potentially able to use FTP.
Negative: 8.1 operator has a valid shell of /sbin/nologin. Remember, the /sbin/nologin shell, when found in /etc/shells, leaves a user potentially able to use FTP.
Negative: 8.1 games has a valid shell of /sbin/nologin. Remember, the /sbin/nologin shell, when found in /etc/shells, leaves a user potentially able to use FTP.
Negative: 8.1 gopher has a valid shell of /sbin/nologin. Remember, the /sbin/nologin shell, when found in /etc/shells, leaves a user potentially able to use FTP.
Negative: 8.1 ftp has a valid shell of /sbin/nologin. Remember, the /sbin/nologin shell, when found in /etc/shells, leaves a user potentially able to use FTP.
Negative: 8.1 nobody has a valid shell of /sbin/nologin. Remember, the /sbin/nologin shell, when found in /etc/shells, leaves a user potentially able to use FTP.
Negative: 8.1 nscd has a valid shell of /sbin/nologin. Remember, the /sbin/nologin shell, when found in /etc/shells, leaves a user potentially able to use FTP.
Negative: 8.1 vcsa has a valid shell of /sbin/nologin. Remember, the /sbin/nologin shell, when found in /etc/shells, leaves a user potentially able to use FTP.
Negative: 8.1 ntp has a valid shell of /sbin/nologin. Remember, the /sbin/nologin shell, when found in /etc/shells, leaves a user potentially able to use FTP.
Negative: 8.1 sshd has a valid shell of /sbin/nologin. Remember, the /sbin/nologin shell, when found in /etc/shells, leaves a user potentially able to use FTP.
Negative: 8.1 rpc has a valid shell of /sbin/nologin. Remember, the /sbin/nologin shell, when found in /etc/shells, leaves a user potentially able to use FTP.
Negative: 8.1 rpm has a valid shell of /sbin/nologin. Remember, the /sbin/nologin shell, when found in /etc/shells, leaves a user potentially able to use FTP.
Negative: 8.3 User elh should have a minimum password life of at least 7 days.
Negative: 8.3 /etc/login.defs value PASS_MIN_DAYS = 0, but should not be less than 7.
Negative: 8.10 Current umask setting in file /etc/bashrc is 022 — it should be stronger to block world-read/write/execute.
Negative: 8.10 Current umask setting in file /etc/bashrc is 022 — it should be stronger to block group-read/write/execute.
Negative: 8.10 Current umask setting in file /etc/csh.cshrc is 002 — it should be stronger to block world-read/write/execute.

```
Negative: 8.10 Current umask setting in file /etc/csh.cshrc is 002 — it should be
stronger to block group-read/write/execute.
Negative: 8.11 Coredumps aren't deactivated.
Negative: 8.12 Compilers not removed; The gcc package is installed.
Negative: 8.13 Pam /etc/pam.d/su does not require wheel group for su access.
Negative: 9.1 /etc/motd doesn't contain an authorized usage only banner.
Negative: 9.1 /etc/issue doesn't contain an authorized usage only banner.
Negative: 6.7 Non-standard SUID program /usr/lib/vmware/bin/vmkload_app
Negative: 6.7 Non-standard SUID program /usr/lib/vmware/bin-debug/vmware-vmx
Negative: 6.7 Non-standard SUID program /usr/lib/vmware/bin/vmware-vmx
Negative: 6.7 Non-standard SUID program /usr/lib/vmware/bin-debug/vmkload_app
Negative: 6.7 Non-standard SUID program /usr/sbin/vmware-authd
```

Once run, the first assessment will show some errors that can be ignored. The score reported in the example run is for ESX version 3. For ESX version 2.5.x, the score is a low 5.62 out of 10.0, and CISscan identifies many issues that can be broken down into the following categories:

- Services that are running that should not be or which are incorrectly configured. However, we need to consider keeping those options required by ESX.

- Kernel networking options that are set incorrectly or not set.

- Soft security settings not implemented.

- User options incorrectly configured.

- Nonstandard SUID programs for ESX version 3. There are no reports of nonstandard SUID programs for ESX versions earlier than 3.

CISscan is going to investigate access to various system services to the extent of only allowing access to them from unique IP addresses. Linux provides multiple methods to implement access restrictions. iptables is just one of those methods and is discussed earlier, but others exist, and the assessment tools expect these to be implemented. iptables is the catchall to deny access to those systems not listed that are not caught by the other access restriction methods. We could, for example, use the first set of iptables rules and set up host restrictions using the other system tools. In essence, we will *not* count on any one tool always working, so we build our defense in depth further.

Many of the base system tools respond to restrictions set in TCP Wrappers, which is a library of functionality used to control access to network services via IP address, network, and domains that uses the /etc/host.allow and /etc/host.deny files. In addition, the super daemon xinetd has its own method of restricting access to its daemons, which works in conjunction with TCP Wrappers in some cases, adding yet another level of depth and for those daemons that do not speak TCP Wrappers, providing one level of access restrictions. In either case, configuring these controls in addition to iptables increases our defense in depth.

Let's review the output of the CISscan software to point out the items in ESX that require additional protections and setting changes. We will only look at the negative output per the preceding example because positive output implies that aspect of the assessment is just fine. As you can see from the output, CISscan has found many issues, but they are not impossible to fix and will secure your system extremely well. Even so, there are some choices to be made in many cases and consequences if you do not make an appropriate choice. Let's go through this output in a little detail.

First, we have the issues with SSH. The Secure Shell is the default method to access the COS over the network, but it has a nasty problem when protocol level 1 is in use. It is recommended then that only protocol level 2 be used. To ensure this, we could modify the putty or SSH clients in use to only use protocol level 2, but it is much easier to change the SSH daemon configuration files to alleviate the problem. There is also a need to add a bit of soft security changes to let users know that authorized only access is required when using SSH. Adding the following lines to the end of the file /etc/ssh/sshd_config will solve both these problems:

```
Protocol 2
Banner /etc/motd
```

Because there is a better-than-average chance that you will be using SSH from the COS to access yet another ESX Server, we should ensure that the SSH client in use from this host also only uses protocol level 2 by adding the following to the end of /etc/ssh/ssh_config, too:

```
Protocol 2
```

Second, CISscan is going to report that there are quite a few services running that should be disabled, and although some of these can be disabled and enabled from the MUI for ESX versions earlier than 3 (Options > Security), it is not an exhaustive list. Although the first two in the list are controlled by the MUI, the rest are not, and it is strongly recommended that they be disabled. Note that this list includes many protocols (NFS, SMB, sendmail, and XFS) not installed by default, but which can easily be installed from the ESX media and elsewhere, as is the case for sendmail. Judicious use of the chkconfig command can disable the offending daemons. Note that we are not disabling the SNMP agent, because hardware-monitoring tools generally need this functionality. Instead, we use iptables to protect SNMP.

```
/sbin/chkconfig telnet off
/sbin/chkconfig ftp off
/sbin/chkconfig xfs off
/sbin/chkconfig —level 0123456 gpm off
/sbin/chkconfig nfslock off
/sbin/chkconfig —level 0123456 sendmail off
/sbin/chkconfig nfs off
/sbin/chkconfig autofs off
/sbin/chkconfig smb off
/sbin/chkconfig portmap off
```

Third, CISscan will request that you add some settings to configure your kernel to prevent malicious or out-of-control network activity from affecting your COS. Mostly, this takes the form of accepting or denying redirects, broadcasts, and SYN cookies. Redirects are packets redirected from other hosts without proper handling. Broadcasts are packets sent to more than one host at a time and are generally used to determine whether something is running. SYN cookies are used by many DoS attacks and by limiting the number of SYNs we mitigate these types of attacks. Adding the following to the /etc/sysctl.conf file will remove these possibly malicious activities at the kernel level before the packets go far down the networking path:

```
net.ipv4.conf.default.secure_redirects=0
net.ipv4.conf.all.secure_redirects=0
net.ipv4.conf.all.rp_filter=1
net.ipv4.icmp_echo_ignore_broadcasts=1
net.ipv4.conf.all.accept_redirects=0
net.ipv4.conf.default.accept_source_route=0
net.ipv4.tcp_syncookies=1
net.ipv4.conf.default.accept_redirects=0
```

```
net.ipv4.tcp_max_syn_backlog=4096
net.ipv4.conf.all.send_redirects=0
net.ipv4.conf.default.send_redirects=0
```

In addition to the preceding changes, reducing the default permissions of the /etc/sysctl.conf file to read-writable *only* by the root user will secure this important file. The use of /usr/sbin/sysctl -p will read the new file and update the kernel, or a reboot will do the same.

The fourth issue that CISscan catches is the unsafe presentation of various devices. It would be best to protect your system from users mounting devices that would give them root privileges and device-level access to your system. To do that, we edit a few files, with the first being /etc/fstab. In /etc/fstab, change the files system options as shown in Table 4.5 for ESX version 3.

Table 4.5

New Options for FSTAB entries		
File System	Existing Options	New Options
/boot	Defaults	defaults,nodev
/tmp	Defaults	defaults,nodev
/var/log	Defaults	defaults,nodev
/mnt/cdrom	Kudzu	kudzu,nosuid,nodev
/mnt/floppy	Kudzu	kudzu,nosuid,nodev

The next changes are to the security settings for various plug-in devices for a system. By commenting out these lines in /etc/security/console.perms, the system protects itself from users trying to gain root access by adding other devices to the system through USB and other mechanisms. In essence, only the administrator will now be able to mount or initially access these devices, because by default any user can normally access files on these devices that can be used to subvert administrative access.

```
0660 <floppy>
0600 <cdrom>
0600 <pilot>
0600 <jaz>
0600 <zip>
0600 <ls120>
0600 <camera>
```

```
0600 <memstick>
0600 <flash>
0600 <diskonkey>
0600 <rem_ide>
0600 <rio500>
```

The fifth issue relates to how some services are started up by default. Adding various options will further secure the service (see Table 4.6).

Table 4.6

New Startup Options for Services		
Service	**Old Options**	**New Options**
wu-ftpd	-l -a	-l -a -d

The sixth issue that CISscan raises is about the users on the system. There are more users on a standard ESX box than you might be initially aware of, and these other user accounts need to be correctly set up so that other users do not subvert the root account. Specifically, it will complain about the vpxuser, news, and rpm users and perhaps others. There are three steps to take to secure these accounts.

1. Remove /sbin/nologin from the /etc/shells file, preventing various tools from listing this as a valid shell, even though it still is.

2. Use the usermod command to change the news and rpm users to have a shell of /sbin/nologin, which will deny access to these wide-open accounts.

3. For ESX version 2.5.x and earlier, move and secure the vpxuser's home directory from /tmp to a non-world-writable location. We recommend the following sequence of commands, which creates a directory under /home, setting the permissions so that the vpxuser has read-writable access and changes the vpxuser's home directory location:

   ```
   /bin/mkdir -p /home/vpxuser
   /bin/chmod 750 /home/vpxuser
   /bin/chown vpxuser /home/vpxuser
   /usr/sbin/usermod -d /home/vpxuser vpxuser
   ```

4. Eventually, you might want to age passwords, and although it is not necessary right away, it is an extremely useful way to enforce password changes as often as the corporate security policy requires. To do this modify the PASS_MAX_DAYS (maximum number of days the password will be valid) to the

number required by the corporate security policy, as well as the PASS_MIN_DAYS (minimum number of days the password will be valid), and PASS_MIN_LENGTH (minimum password length) in /etc/login.defs.

5. For ESX version 2.5.x, update the vpxuser's password-aging parameters per the values entered previously. Use the change command with the –m PASS_MIN_DAYS –M PASS_MAX_DAYS options, where PASS_MIN_DAYS and PASS_MAX_DAYS come from step 6. You might have to repeat this step for any other users reported by CISscan.

The sixth problem CISscan reports is the appearance of packages, various file permissions, and entries in various data files as being incorrect, or missing. CISscan requests you remove the hotplug package, change the permissions of /etc/crontab to be read-writable by root, and create /etc/cron.allow and /etc/at.allow so that the only entry is root, thereby not allowing any other users to use the at or crontab commands to set up jobs in batch mode. CISscan also complains about the entries in /etc/securetty being too liberal, which implies that it wants you to remove the tty7-11 entries. The last issue is the fact that the xinetd super daemon is not allowing only hosts from well known networks to access the services it controls. For example, if we want only those hosts on the 10.0.0.0 network to access the super daemon's services, we would add to /etc/xinetd.conf the following line before the end of the file:

```
only_from = 10.0.0.0
```

The seventh item CISscan uncovers is the default permissions used to create new files. By default, the permissions on new files are set up to be readable and, in some cases, executable by all users. The security specialist would rather make the opening up of permissions on various files be a conscious action and not one that is happenstance. To that end, change the umask settings in the following list of files to a more restrictive setting. umask is used by the system to mask off certain permission bits so that when files are created they are created with the desired set of permissions. CISscan requires that you mask off the group and other permissions bits so only the owner of the file can access the file. To do this, set the umask settings to the value 077. Although an in-depth discussion of permissions is beyond the scope of this book, I delve into them briefly. The permissions are in three octets (well, four, but we will ignore the fourth for now). Take the output of ls –al and you will see something similar to this for a normal file:

```
-rwxr—r— root root June 10 filename
```

This shows that the first octet is read (r), writable (w), and executable (x), and these translate to the numbers 4(r), 2(w), and 1(x). The second and third octets are set to read-only. If you add these up, they come to seven. A umask with a value of 077 would allow the first octet to retain its value, while the second and third octets would completely mask off permissions, making the permissions such that you have only the owner or first-octet permissions. Unfortunately, there is not just one place to set this value, so we need to make changes in the files /etc/bashrc and /etc/csh.cshrc. Each file requires two changes. In addition, CISscan requires that the first service script to run also share this reduced permission for file create and on ESX that implies we need to add the line umask 077 to the /etc/rc.d/init.d/ vmkhalt file for ESX version 2.5.x and /etc/rc.d/init.d/microcode_ctl for ESX version 3.

CISscan further requires an eighth change, which is to secure the system from users rebooting the machine and thereby gaining access to the administrator account. For that to occur, the user could sit at the console and press Ctrl+Alt+Del. Although normally ESX prevents this from happening, it is best to just remove the functionality entirely from /etc/inittab. In addition, if during reboot the user can edit the boot line (which is possible), the user can enter single-user mode without a password, so it's also wise to add the following to the /etc/inittab file to require a password to enter single-user mode from bootup:

```
~:S:wait:/sbin/sulogin/
```

The ninth change is to enter in some soft security text to the files /etc/motd and /etc/issue. Because /etc/issue prints before login to the system, keep it short and simple and enter AUTHORIZED USE ONLY into the file. Display of /etc/motd occurs after login and can contain the full text required by the corporate security policy. To pass this rule in CISscan successfully, AUTHORIZED USE ONLY should be somewhere in the text.

The tenth change required by CISscan is to reduce who can use the su command. Allow access to root only by those users in the wheel group, so make sure at least one user is in the wheel group. All the preceding changes (specifically to the /etc/securetty file) will force a login to a normal user account before accessing the root account from the console, and this can also be enforced for SSH, but unfortunately not the MUI. In the /etc/pam.d/su file, uncomment the line containing the pam_wheel.so string.

The last file-level issue is the report of nonstandard SUID programs. These files have the proper permissions for ESX and should not be modified. CISscan was written for Linux and not ESX, so some adjustments will need to be made when reading the output. It is also possible to modify the appropriate `cis_ruler_suid_programs_redhat_*` file to include the reported list of nonstandard SUID programs. SUID refers to a program that when executed executes as another user no matter whom starts the program. By default, programs are started as the user under which they run. So if I log in as user foo, a non-SUID program will run with an owner of foo, but with SUID, the program runs as the user who owns the program (in this case, root).

Finally, the last change is to reduce the size of core files produced to a size of zero. Because ESX abhors a full disk, we should avoid the possibility of filling a disk by a core file that is created when a program crashes, which can happen when DoS attacks occur. Add the following line to the end of the `/etc/security/limits.conf` file.

```
*          soft    core    0
```

After all these changes, you would think everything is as secure as it could possibly get, but unfortunately it is not quite there. That is why we combine the CISscan and Bastille assessments when we look at system vulnerabilities, because in the next step I will have Bastille look at file-level issues.

Step 6B

Bastille is a tool that provides the capability to assess your system for risk and to walk you through securing your system. Like CISscan, Bastille's assessment phase returns a value from 1 to 10, with 10 being the most secure. But unlike CISscan, Bastille can run in another mode that will walk you through securing your system with written explanations to why these changes are necessary. In this way, I find Bastille more user friendly and much more beneficial as a learning tool. Bastille has one of two installation requirements based on how you would like to use the program: either via CLI or graphical. For CLI, you need the perl-Curses package, and for graphics you will need the perl-Tk package, both available via CPAN (the online repository of Perl modules: www.cpan.org). If you *just* want to run the assessment, neither additional packages is required. The install is straightforward and does not require any modifications to the system. Download the RPM and install as normal:

```
rpm -ivh Bastille-3.0.8-1.0.noarch.rpm
```

However, there is a slight change necessary to Bastille to make the assessment portion more accurate for ESX, and that is to change the file `/usr/lib/Bastille/test_AccountSecurity.pm` and remove some data; otherwise, this test will constantly fail. The normal value is `rexec`, `rlogin`, `rsh`, `login`, `shell`, but the actual value should be `rexec`, `rlogin`, `rsh`. This change should make it into Bastille eventually. After these changes have been made, you can safely run an assessment on your system. The output of a standard assessment without fixing any of the issues CISscan exposes will be quite a lot larger, but we have covered many overlap areas. Run the assessment and review the results per the following example. It gives a score of 6.79 out of 10.0 on a stock ESX 2.5.x Server, whereas ESX version 3 gives a higher and better score of 8.11 out of 10. With a few minor changes, this score will increase further for all versions of the operating system.

```
# bastille -n —assessnobrowser
NOTE:      Using audit user interface module.


NOTE:      Bastille is scanning the system configuration...


===============================================================================
¦ Bastille Hardening Assessment Completed                                     ¦
¦                                                                             ¦
¦ You can find a report in HTML format at:                                    ¦
¦    file:///var/log/Bastille/Assessment/assessment-report.html               ¦
¦                                                                             ¦
¦ You can find a report in text format at:                                    ¦
¦                                                                             ¦
¦    /var/log/Bastille/Assessment/assessment-report.txt                       ¦
¦                                                                             ¦
¦ You can find a more machine-parseable report at:                            ¦
¦                                                                             ¦
¦    /var/log/Bastille/Assessment/assessment-log.txt                          ¦
===============================================================================


# cat /var/log/Bastille/Assessment/assessment-report.txt
Bastille Hardening Assessment Report
+—————————————.+————————————————+——.+———+——.
¦ Item               ¦ Question                             ¦ Yes
¦Weight¦Score
¦
¦
+—————————————.+————————————————+——.+———+——.
```

¦ generalperms_1_1	¦ Are more restrictive permissions on the	¦ No	¦ 0.00	¦ 0.00
¦ suidmount	¦ Is SUID status for mount/umount disabled	¦ Yes	¦ 1.00	¦ 1.00
¦ suidping	¦ Is SUID status for ping disabled?	¦ No	¦ 1.00	¦ 0.00
¦ suiddump	¦ Is SUID status for dump and restore disa	¦ Yes	¦ 1.00	¦ 1.00
¦ suidcard	¦ Is SUID status for cardctl disabled?	¦ Yes	¦ 1.00	¦ 1.00
¦ suidat	¦ Is SUID status for at disabled?	¦ Yes	¦ 1.00	¦ 1.00
¦ suiddos	¦ Is SUID status for DOSEMU disabled?	¦ Yes	¦ 1.00	¦ 1.00
¦ suidnews	¦ Is SUID status for news server tools dis	¦ Yes	¦ 1.00	¦ 1.00
¦ suidprint	¦ Is SUID status for printing utilities di	¦ Yes	¦ 1.00	¦ 1.00
¦ suidrtool	¦ Are the r-tools disabled?	¦ Yes	¦ 1.00	¦ 1.00
¦ suidusernetctl	¦ Is SUID status for usernetctl disabled?	¦ Yes	¦ 1.00	¦ 1.00
¦ suidtrace	¦ Is SUID status for traceroute disabled?	¦ No	¦ 1.00	¦ 0.00
¦ suidXwrapper	¦ Is SUID status for Xwrapper disabled?	¦ Yes	¦ 1.00	¦ 1.00
¦ suidXFree86	¦ Is SUID status for XFree86 disabled?	¦ Yes	¦ 1.00	¦ 1.00
¦ protectrhost	¦ Are clear-text r-protocols that use IP-b	¦ No	¦ 0.00	¦ 0.00
¦ passwdage	¦ Is password aging enforced?	¦ Yes	¦ 1.00	¦ 1.00
¦ cronuser	¦ Is the use of cron restricted to adminis	¦ Yes	¦ 1.00	¦ 1.00
¦ umaskyn	¦ Is the default umask set to a minimal va	¦ No	¦ 1.00	¦ 0.00

roottylogins	Are root logins on tty's 1-6 prohibited?	No	1.00	0.00
removeaccounts	Have extraneous accounts been deleted?	No	0.00	0.00
removegroups	Have extraneous groups been deleted?	Yes	0.00	0.00
protectgrub	Is the GRUB prompt password-protected?	No	1.00	0.00
protectlilo	Is the LILO prompt password-protected?	Yes	1.00	1.00
lilodelay	Is the LILO delay time zero?	Yes	0.00	0.00
secureinittab	Is CTRL-ALT-DELETE rebooting disabled?	Yes	0.00	0.00
passsum	Is single-user mode password-protected?	No	1.00	0.00
tcpd_default_deny	Is a default-deny on TCP Wrappers and xi	No	1.00	0.00
deactivate_telnet	Is the telnet service disabled on this s	Yes	1.00	1.00
deactivate_ftp	Is inetd's FTP service disabled on this	Yes	1.00	1.00
banners	Are "Authorized Use" messages displayed	No	1.00	0.00
compiler	Are the gcc and/or g++ compiler disabled	Yes	1.00	1.00
morelogging	Has additional logging been added?	Yes	1.00	1.00
pacct	Is process accounting set up?	No	1.00	0.00
laus	Is LAuS active?	Yes	1.00	1.00
apmd	Are acpid and apmd disabled?	Yes	1.00	1.00
remotefs	Are NFS and Samba deactivated?	Yes	1.00	1.00

pcmcia	Are PCMCIA services disabled?	Yes	1.00	1.00
dhcpd	Is the DHCP daemon disabled?	Yes	1.00	1.00
gpm	Is GPM disabled?	No	1.00	0.00
innd	Is the news server daemon disabled?	Yes	1.00	1.00
disable_routed	Is routed deactivated?	Yes	1.00	1.00
disable_gated	Is gated deactivated?	Yes	1.00	1.00
nis_server	Are NIS server programs deactivated?	Yes	1.00	1.00
nis_client	Are NIS client programs deactivated?	Yes	1.00	1.00
snmpd	Is SNMPD disabled?	Yes	1.00	1.00
disable_kudzu	Is kudzu's run at boot deactivated?	Yes	1.00	1.00
sendmaildaemon	Is sendmail's daemon mode disabled?	Yes	1.00	1.00
sendmailcron	Does sendmail process the queue via cron	Yes	0.00	0.00
vrfyexpn	Are the VRFY and EXPN sendmail commands	Yes	1.00	1.00
chrootbind	Is named in a chroot jail and is it set	Yes	0.00	0.00
namedoff	Is named deactivated?	Yes	1.00	1.00
apacheoff	Is the Apache Web server deactivated?	Yes	1.00	1.00
bindapachelocal	Is the Web server bound to listen only t	Yes	0.00	0.00
bindapachenic	Is the Web server bound to a particular	Yes	0.00	0.00

```
¦ symlink                    ¦ Is the following of symbolic links deact ¦ Yes ¦ 1.00 ¦ 1.00
¦
¦ ssi                        ¦ Are server-side includes deactivated?    ¦ Yes ¦ 1.00 ¦ 1.00
¦
¦ cgi                        ¦ Are CGI scripts disabled?                ¦ Yes ¦ 1.00 ¦ 1.00
¦
¦ apacheindex                ¦ Are indexes disabled?                    ¦ Yes ¦ 1.00 ¦ 1.00
¦
¦ printing                   ¦ Is printing disabled?                    ¦ Yes ¦ 1.00 ¦ 1.00
¦
¦ printing_cups              ¦ Is printing disabled?                    ¦ Yes ¦ 1.00 ¦ 1.00
¦
¦ printing_cups_lpd_legacy   ¦ Is CUPS' legacy LPD support disabled?    ¦ Yes ¦ 1.00 ¦ 1.00
¦
¦ userftp                    ¦ Are user privileges on the FTP daemon di ¦ Yes ¦ 1.00 ¦ 1.00
¦
¦ anonftp                    ¦ Is anonymous download disabled?          ¦ Yes ¦ 1.00 ¦ 1.00
¦
+ — — — — — — — — — — — —+— — — — — — — — — — — — — — — — — — —+— —·+— — —+— —·
Score: 8.11 / 10.00
```

First we want to clean up various overlapping items that CISscan did not pick up on. The seventh step earlier under CISscan is to make sure the permissions for new file creations are secure enough. We need to add to our list of files the following that need umask 077 entries added.

```
/etc/profile
/etc/zprofile
/etc/csh.login
/root/.bash_profile
```

Second, we need to configure the TCP Wrapper configuration files to allow only those hosts that should be allowed and deny all others. For example, if we want to allow all hosts on the 10.0.0. network, we need to add the following line to /etc/hosts.allow:

```
ALL: 10.0.0.
```

while adding the text 'ALL:ALL' to the /etc/hosts.deny file to then deny access to every other host.

Our third change is to disable FollowSymLinks in the /etc/httpd/conf/ httpd.conf Apache web server file because symlinks can allow access to your file system through the web browser. This is ESX version 2.5.x specific.

Our fourth change is to the permissions on a host of files. We will be reducing the permissions on many files and disabling some tools for use outside the administrator or root account. For a full list of these files, see Appendix A, where we host a script that will secure an ESX system. Following the script completely will result in a CISscan score of 9.45/10.00 and a Bastille score of 10.00/10.00 on ESX version 3 systems. This includes the installation of sysstat, psacct, and setting a boot-change password.

Step 7

The last step of our security recipe is to set up some form of antivirus software. Several vendors provide packages that will work on ESX (for example, Sophos, Norton Antivirus, F-Secure, and many other for-fee products). However, an open source version named clamav has a pretty wide following. Setup of antivirus for ESX is beyond the scope of this book because the number of options is staggering. Even so, it is important to note that you will never want to scan the virtual disk (VMDK) files of running VMs without first placing the VMs into REDO mode. However, doing so is really overkill because each VM will most likely be running some form of antivirus at the same time. In addition, running a virus scanner against any VMDK will result in false positives in addition to major performance issues with ESX (because this can lead to SCSI Reservation issues). To avoid this, ensure the /vmfs directory is ignored by any virus scanner.

Auditing Recipe

At this stage in the overall process, we turn to adding more auditing capabilities into ESX. Specifically, we will want to determine who is doing what and when. This stage is a little more advanced than the last and adds some new tools to the toolbox to avoid items such as root kits. It is best, however, to install most of these tools onto read-only media such as a CD-ROM, floppy, or some other file system that can only be mounted read-only. In most cases, I recommend a CD-ROM. Most of these tools, when run in a cluster of ESX Servers, should have staggered start times so that ESX itself does not get overloaded or cause unnecessary LUN locking. (See Chapter 6, "Effects on Operations," for more details on this.) The recipe for adding the additional auditing capabilities involves the following steps:

1. Force all users to use the sudo command instead of directly accessing root when doing administration via the COS. For every administrator, create a local account and do not allow a direct login as root by restricting its password; and if someone needs root access to the system, require use of sudo. sudo will log in as root using the user's password and run a set of predefined commands. This set of commands can be wide open or restricted by group and user. One thing you absolutely do not want to allow is access to the shells, because once the shells are accessed, sudo's capability to log actions disappears completely. sudo has its own log file, and it records *when* a command was run, *what* the command was that was run, and by *whom* the command was run. The most simplistic /etc/sudoers file is to allow access to everything but the shells by adding the following line to the file. In addition, we do not want nonadministrative users to edit the /etc/sudoers file directly.

```
%wheel ALL=  /*bin/*,/usr/*bin/*,!/bin/*sh,!/usr/bin/ksh,!/bin/vi
➥ /etc/sudoers,!/usr/sbin/nano /etc/sudoers
```

2. Run a periodic check for root kits. Root kits are malicious code that will be placed on a system when a system is hacked, to make logging in once more as root easier. That enables someone to launch further attacks on the internal systems, whether VM or a physical machine. It is a good idea to keep this tool on read-only media and to keep it up-to-date from time to time by checking (www.chkrootkit.org). chkrootkit will spit out a large amount of detail about the checks it has made. The key is to check this output for *any* positives. Any positive requires investigation and could imply, at the very least, that something has failed on the system on which it occurred. Earlier versions of chkrootkit did have some false positives, so run it and investigate often.

3. Periodically run the CISscan and Bastille assessments so that you know whether your security stance has changed. At the very least, run the tools after applying any patches. Run the assessments and make the necessary adjustments per the scripts in Appendix A. The idea here is to ensure that your score is either at least what it was or higher.

4. Install and configure Tripwire or a similar tool. Tripwire and its primary database should be on read-only media so that modification is impossible.

Tripwire creates a database of checksums for critical files and will enable you to check whether these files have changed. This auditing tool will catch changes to critical files nightly when the audit normally runs. However, like most tools, it needs adjustments for ESX, so we should make some changes to the configuration files to include ESX configuration directories, VM configuration files, and any nonpersistent VMDK files. For ESX version 2.5.x, the following is a list of changes suggested for Tripwire to work best on ESX. To get the best out of Tripwire, the sendmail RPM should also be installed, which has dependencies on `openldap`, `cyrus-sasl`, and `cyrus-sasl-md5` RPMs. The default configuration file is extremely useful without modification. Adding the following lines will add ESX-specific items for ESX version 2.5.x. The ESX version 3 file is very similar.

```
##############
#           ##
############# #
#          # #
# VMware dirs # #
#           ##
#############
(
   rulename = "VMware dir",
   severity = $(SIG_MED)
)
{
   /usr/lib/vmware                  -> $(SEC_BIN) ;
   /var/lib/vmware                  -> $(SEC_BIN) ;
   # Following is only if scripted install in use
   /var/vmware                      -> $(SEC_BIN) ;
}


   ###############################
   #                           ##
   ############################ #
   #                          # #
   # VMware Administration Programs # #
   #                           ##
```

```
###################################

(
  rulename = "VMware Administration Programs",
  severity = $(SIG_HI)
)
{
  /usr/sbin/vmAddRedo.pl          -> $(SEC_CRIT) ;
  /usr/sbin/vmkuptime.pl          -> $(SEC_CRIT) ;
  /usr/sbin/vmware-ccagent        -> $(SEC_CRIT) ;
  /usr/sbin/vmCommit.pl           -> $(SEC_CRIT) ;
  /usr/bin/vmkusage               -> $(SEC_CRIT) ;
  /usr/bin/vmware-cmd             -> $(SEC_CRIT) ;
  /usr/sbin/vmdbsh                -> $(SEC_CRIT) ;
  /usr/bin/vmkusagectl            -> $(SEC_CRIT) ;
  /usr/bin/vmware-config-mui.pl   -> $(SEC_CRIT) ;
  /usr/bin/vmfs_ftp               -> $(SEC_CRIT) ;
  /usr/bin/vmnet-bridge           -> $(SEC_CRIT) ;
  /usr/bin/vmware-config.pl       -> $(SEC_CRIT) ;
  /usr/sbin/vmfs_ftpd             -> $(SEC_CRIT) ;
  /usr/bin/vmnet-dhcpd            -> $(SEC_CRIT) ;
  /usr/bin/vmware-loop            -> $(SEC_CRIT) ;
  /usr/sbin/vmkblkopen.pl         -> $(SEC_CRIT) ;
  /usr/bin/vmnet-natd             -> $(SEC_CRIT) ;
  /usr/bin/vmware-mount.pl        -> $(SEC_CRIT) ;
  /usr/sbin/vmkchdev              -> $(SEC_CRIT) ;
  /usr/bin/vmnet-netifup          -> $(SEC_CRIT) ;
  /usr/bin/vmware-nmbd            -> $(SEC_CRIT) ;
  /usr/sbin/vmkdump               -> $(SEC_CRIT) ;
  /usr/bin/vmnet-sniffer          -> $(SEC_CRIT) ;
  /usr/bin/vmware-ping            -> $(SEC_CRIT) ;
  /usr/sbin/vmkfstools            -> $(SEC_CRIT) ;
  /usr/sbin/vmres.pl              -> $(SEC_CRIT) ;
  /usr/sbin/vmware-serverd        -> $(SEC_CRIT) ;
  /usr/sbin/vmkloader             -> $(SEC_CRIT) ;
  /usr/sbin/vmsnap_all            -> $(SEC_CRIT) ;
```

```
/sbin/vmware-sfdisk              -> $(SEC_CRIT) ;
/usr/sbin/vmkload_mod            -> $(SEC_CRIT) ;
/usr/sbin/vmsnap.pl              -> $(SEC_CRIT) ;
/usr/bin/vmware-smbd             -> $(SEC_CRIT) ;
/usr/sbin/vmklogger              -> $(SEC_CRIT) ;
/usr/bin/vmstat                  -> $(SEC_CRIT) ;
/usr/bin/vmware-smbpasswd        -> $(SEC_CRIT) ;
/usr/sbin/vmkmultipath           -> $(SEC_CRIT) ;
/usr/bin/vm-support              -> $(SEC_CRIT) ;
/usr/bin/vmware-smbpasswd.bin    -> $(SEC_CRIT) ;
/usr/sbin/vmkpcicheck            -> $(SEC_CRIT) ;
/usr/bin/vmware                  -> $(SEC_CRIT) ;
/usr/sbin/vmware-snmpd           -> $(SEC_CRIT) ;
/usr/sbin/vmkpcidivy             -> $(SEC_CRIT) ;
/usr/sbin/vmware-authd           -> $(SEC_CRIT) ;
/usr/sbin/vmware-snmptrap        -> $(SEC_CRIT) ;
/usr/sbin/vmkstatus              -> $(SEC_CRIT) ;
/usr/bin/vmware-authtrusted      -> $(SEC_CRIT) ;
}
```

There are two configuration files for Tripwire: `twcfg.txt` and `twpol.txt`. The suggested changes are for `twpol.txt` and can be added to the end of the file. To make use of these changes, run the following commands, which will initialize and sign the files and databases, and run a baseline scan of the system for the sake of comparison. Quite a few errors will be reported, and they can either be ignored or the `twpol.txt` file can be edited to comment out the offending lines. If you do comment out the offending lines, rerun the following commands to resign and recompile the database. To sign and encrypt the files against change, several pass phrases will be required and will need to be repeated to re-create the policy and database files.

```
twinstall.sh
tripwire —init
```

Any time you patch the system, the database for Tripwire should be re-created. Use the second of the preceding commands to do this. It is not recommended that VMX files be included in the Tripwire database explicitly because they move from system to system with a VMotion with ESX 2.5.3 and earlier. However, for ESX 3.0, adding the VMX files is a great addition. The contents would look similar to the following. If a VMDK is in nonpersistent mode, including that in a Tripwire database would ensure notification in case it changes. This last one implies that only one host that accesses the SAN should have the VMDK in its Tripwire database. Having it on more than one host would be a duplication of effort

```
###########################
#                              ##
############################### #
#                              # #
# VMware VMX/VMDK              # #
#                              ##
###############################

(
    rulename = "VMware VMX/VMDK",
    severity = $(SIG_HI)
)
{
    /vmfs/VMFS-SAN-1/vMachine/vMachine.vmx        -> $(SEC_CRIT) ;
}
```

5. Enable process accounting on ESX so that you can tell when a process is started or stopped, or to gather other information. Although not incredibly important, an increase in processing time could imply someone is running something that should *not* be running, the server is experiencing a DoS-style attack, or the system is generally not behaving well. Because we already installed sysstat as a dependency to CISscan, we have enabled process accounting using the sar tool to perform reporting. The results of the automatic report generation are in the /var/log/sa/ directory and are sardd, where dd is the day of the month. The use of sar itself is beyond the scope of this chapter because we are only concerned with using this data to see whether you have a process running, taking up resources, that you

do not normally have, which is a possible sign of a break in. The sa1 and sa2 tools should be on read-only media and sar itself. The added benefit to the use of sysstat and psacct is tracking of valuable performance data to determine whether there are any performance issues or to use in conjunction with other tools to determine whether there is a need for more ESX hosts.

6. From a remote system, or a special VM you only run when this test is to be performed, periodically run tools such as Nessus (www.nessus.org) and NMAP to scan your service console's network connectivity for vulnerabilities. The output of Nessus can be extremely verbose. Investigate any negative result. See below for a detailed look at Nessus output. At least run this tool to get a baseline, and if there is a difference between the baseline and your new run, you should investigate, because some part of the defense in depth we are trying to establish has failed.

7. The last auditing tool to install is not really a part of ESX or anything else; log the console to a file using a script that can talk to the ILO or similar remote console access card if available. This script may be available from your hardware vendor; otherwise, it is something that will have to be written, usually involving the expect tool. This script has a two-fold effect. The first is to gather any console text that appears for later forensic analysis or for support analysis, because it will capture any crash or "purple screens of death" data that is necessary for the support specialist. The drawback to this is that many times a text-based access to the console for logging will *not* allow access by any other means, including sitting at the console when necessary. Writing this type of script is beyond the scope of this book, and although I have written one, there needs to be a control mechanism to interrupt the script to allow other users to log in remotely.

8. Although the previous item was the last general tool, two other tools could be used. The first is the Coroner's toolkit, which will take a checksum of *all* files on the system, which will produce gigabytes of data. Do this once just after the machine is fully configured to get baseline data. Without this baseline data, forensic analysis can fail quickly, so gathering a baseline initially and any time the system is patched will be a great benefit for when forensic analysis is required. Because it is gigabytes of data *and* it is important for forensics, this data should be stored on some form of removable media (tape, DVD-ROM, USB disk [mounted remotely], and so on). The other tool, named Tara, is yet another assessment tool that can add some

value and reams of data just like the Coroner's toolkit. Tara is another means of getting a baseline of the system that is slightly different. Having both of these baselines will be useful for future analysis. These two tools should be run *only* after the system is initially configured and then when it is patched. Do not overwrite old data; keep it around and safe, preferably in a vault. Forensic analysis will piece together what should be there from this data and compare it to what is there now. It could be that the root cause is back several revisions, which makes each baseline valuable data.

Monitoring Recipe

Now that the recipes for setting up security and auditing are complete, it is time to turn our hand to the issues of monitoring your ESX Server in a more automated fashion and for security and support issues. All the changes to date have been specifically for the purposes of security, but now we can add monitoring for security reasons and for better handling of the data available, which is quite a bit. ESX has quite a few methods to monitor the system, including, but not limited to, the MUI (and by hand looking at log files), VC and its various reports and alarms, HPSIM and VMM for determination of whether VMs are running and for host monitoring of hardware, ESXCharter for monitoring VMs, and open source tools such as Nagios that can monitor various subsystems for VMs or hosts. Because there are many tools available, we really only cover items that improve security monitoring more than system monitoring. We concentrate on the host, not the VMs, in this discussion.

ESX comes with one extremely useful tool already, which is the logrotate command. logrotate will rotate the log files on a set basis for us. However, we need to improve this rotation because it does not account for VMs and the VMkernel log files. By rotating on a regular basis all the log files, we will gain the capability to better control and monitor disk space and get a better handle on support issues. The second issue to address is a way to deal with the quantity of data that does get logged so that only the most crucial items are sent on to the administrators in some automated fashion. If it is not automated and the data is not reduced, it implies that someone needs to check log files regularly, and we all know this only happens when a problem occurs. From a security point of view, we have to address issues *when* they happen and proactively, not after the fact. The sooner we address things after the occurrence of the problem, the easier it will be to prevent them from becoming a real issue.

It is important to understand log rotation before we modify the scripts. ESX Server has built-in log rotation monthly for 36 months, as well as rotation when the system boots. VM logs rotate only when they boot. Because logs can get too large and fill a disk (which can be a sign of a support or security issue), changing this rotation is important. But because log rotations happen frequently, you could suddenly have 50 or more VMkernel log files. Which given some possible sizes is a bit much.

Tied in with log rotation is the need for a way to peruse the possible gigabytes of data inside the log files to bring problems to your attention without the need to sift through the data. To your rescue is the logcheck tool, which will by default run hourly and will report security violations and other important information. All of these reports can be customized to ignore unnecessary log file lines. Because e-mail is sent hourly, or whenever desired, the monitoring provided is pretty good, and it is independent of other tools to monitor the health of your hardware (hardware agents), the uptime of your host (various management tools), and other aspects of your host (utilization). This type of monitoring is designed to show you when problems occur and provide a tool to read the pesky log files so that you can determine *when* a problem occurred and possibly what or even who caused it. In addition, this could help with support issues. As an example of this, an ESX Server with an attached tape library had a VM that used the tape drive constantly and crashed sometime during the night. Because it was difficult to determine when the crash occurred or what possibly caused the failure, the use of the logcheck allowed us to determine the hour in which the problem occurred. The actual nature of the problem was available, because there were SCSI errors and VM failures that provided notifications via e-mail, which narrowed our search for the root cause. It ended up being one of the tape drives in the library. Without this helpful tool, it would have taken days longer to determine this because there were gigabytes of possible log files.

Following is the recipe for improving logging by first improving log rotation and second adding in a method to read the log files for security and other issues:

1. Implementing different log rotation schemes can save disk space and create smaller logs for easier perusal. However, do not trim too many logs. You will need at least four and they should not all be from the same day; a little history is useful. Note that later versions of ESX do provide rotation periods for everything but VMkernel. By changing the /etc/logrotate.d/ vmkwarning file to look like the following, you will put it in sync with both the VMkernel and vmksummary files in the same directory:

```
/var/log/vmkwarning{
      missingok
      sharedscripts
      rotate 36
      postrotate
             /bin/kill -HUP \`cat /var/run/syslog.pid 2> /dev/null\` 2>
➥/dev/null ¦¦ true
      endscript
}
```

These changes add the three-year backup of files that both VMkernel and vmksummary have in common other than the hundreds of log files that are created. If it is desired only to keep a year of log files, the rotate line would have a 12 rather than 36.

In addition to the preceding, we need to rotate the log files produced by the VMs if they exist. We can add the following file to /etc/logrotate.d to do this. The file can be called vmware.log and will rotate any .log file in the /home/vmware/* or VM configuration directories for ESX version 3 VMs, which is represented by storage1 below, which is the default name for a local VMFS.

```
/vmfs/volumes/storage1/*/vmware.log {
      monthly
      rotate 8
      missingok
      copytruncate
      compress
      postrotate

      endscript
}
```

The use of copytruncate could lose a very small amount of data because it is not possible to update a VM with a newly created log file. A copy is the best we can do. In most cases, the loss of one line of data may not be important. If the VM has need of debugging for some reason, it is important to disable this rotation.

2. Implementing `logcheck` will allow the automated perusal of log files for critical information. However, there are multiple versions of `logcheck` available; the one that works best and requires less modification is the earliest one (version 1.1.1) from before Cisco bought the company and before it was re-created for the Debian Linux distribution. The `logcheck` RPM is on http://rpmfind.net. To use `logcheck`, the main script file needs to have some additions made to it to make it more useful; otherwise, all it peruses is the messages, secure, and maillog files in /var/log. This short list of log files is insufficient, so it needs to be changed. Because a mail daemon should *never* be run on the ESX host, the maillog file can be dumped, and we should add in the VMkernel file. Granted most of the VMkernel information that is important is also in the vmkwarning and vmksummary files, but not everything is in these files, so grabbing all the information we can is a pretty good idea. Change the lines in /usr/sbin/logcheck as such to grab the most useful data:

```
# Linux Red Hat Version 3.x, 4.x, 5.x
$LOGTAIL /var/log/messages > $TMPDIR/check.$$
$LOGTAIL /var/log/secure >> $TMPDIR/check.$$
#$LOGTAIL /var/log/maillog >> $TMPDIR/check.$$
$LOGTAIL /var/log/vmkernel >> $TMPDIR/check.$$
#$LOGTAIL /var/log/vmkwarning >> $TMPDIR/check.$$
#$LOGTAIL /var/log/vmksummary >> $TMPDIR/check.$$
$LOGTAIL /var/log/vmware/vmware-ccagent.log >> $TMPDIR/check.$$
$LOGTAIL /var/log/vmware-mui/error_log >> $TMPDIR/check.$$
```

After the preceding lines are added and changed once an hour by default, the logs will be reviewed and important data sent to the root user. Because reading mail on an ESX Server host is not a great idea, and perhaps you will want to send this information to a mailing list, modify the `logcheck` script once more to change the SYSADMIN setting to be the corporate e-mail address of your mailing list or administrator.

However, we are not yet done because the default rules for `logcheck` are geared toward security violations on standard Linux distributions, and we have it checking more files than it did before. So, we need to add some rules of our own; otherwise, we will just get the complete log file sent to us once an hour, which does not save us from much pain. We want to modify two files depending on what we are trying to ignore. Both these files are in /etc/logcheck and end in .ignore. These will be regular expressions containing the lines to not report.

The following are the default lines for ESX version 2.5.x added to logcheck.ignore:

```
hb: vmk loaded
loaded vmkernel
starting system...
vmkernel:.*^I
syslogd 1.4.1: restart
sshd.*: session opened for user root
sshd.*: session closed for user root
ucd-snmp.*: Connection from 127.0.0.1
sshd.*: Accepted password for
sshd.*: Did not receive identification
vmkernel: .*Init:
vmkernel: .*nfshaper: init_module
vmkernel: .*MTRR:
vmkernel: .*Timer:
vmkernel: .*IDT:
vmkernel: .*ISA:
vmkernel: .*PCI:
vmkernel: .*Log:
vmkernel: .*Mod:
vmkernel: .*LinPCI:
vmkernel: .*LinStubs:
vmkernel: .*LinSCSI:
vmkernel: .*LinNet:
vmkernel: .*Host: 3254
vmkernel: .*Host: 3448
vmkernel: .*Host: 3693
vmkernel: .*Host: 3753
vmkernel: .*Host: 3235
vmkernel: .*Host: 5246
vmkernel: .*Host: 3703
vmkernel: .*XMap:
```

```
vmkernel: .*Chipset:

vmkernel: .*APIC:

vmkernel: .*SMP:

vmkernel: .*CpuSched:

vmkernel: .*scheduling reap

vmkernel: .*cleanup via module table

vmkernel: .*cleanup done

vmkernel: .*Successfully created new world

vmkernel: .*status = 0/1 0x0 0x0 0x0

vmkernel: .*status = 0/7 0x0 0x0 0x0

vmkernel: .*destroying world from host

vmkernel: .*cpuidFeatures

vmkernel: .*Creating slave world

vmkernel: .*is emulated by vmkernel

vmkernel: .*vmware ham_hot_add module

vmkernel: .*transfers

vmkernel: .*VMNIX: 1531

vmkernel: .*SCSI Id: Supported VPD

vmkernel: .*SCSI Id: Id for vmhb

vmkernel: .*SCSI Id: Device id info for vmhb

vmkernel: .*SCSI: 1466:

vmkernel: .*SCSI: 2059:

vmkernel: .*SCSI: 771:

vmkernel: .*SCSI: 1457

vmkernel: .*SCSI: 1214

vmkernel: .*SCSI: 2868

vmkernel: .*SCSI: 8979

vmkernel: .*SCSI: 8946

vmkernel: .*SCSI: 2761

vmkernel: .*SCSI: 2953

vmkernel: .*SCSI: 2582

vmkernel: .*SCSI: 2810

vmkernel: .*versionNumber

vmkernel: .* =

vmkernel: .*e1000: vmnic1 NIC Link

vmkernel: .*Network connection
```

```
vmkernel: .*watchdog timer
vmkernel: .*VMNIX: ShrDev:
vmkernel: .*VMNIX: VmkDev:
vmkernel: .*cpqarray
vmkernel: .*SMART2 Driver
vmkernel: .*Vendor:
vmkernel: .*Type:
vmkernel: .*Intel
vmkernel: .*Swap: 1639
vmkernel: .*\*\*\*
vmkernel: .*File descriptr
vmkernel: .*\^I
vmkernel: .*Total allocated pe
vmkernel: .*DUMPING PE
vmkernel: .*END PE
vmkernel: .*File descriptor
last message repeated
ipt_REJECT
app.*module
app.*<[a-z]
app\¦.*Op
app\¦.*SP:
app\¦.*VMServerd
app\¦.*VM suddenly changed state
app\¦.*cleanup
app\¦.*Lost connection to vmx
hpvmmcntsvc: hpvmmcnt shutdown succeeded
START: vmware-authd
vmware-authd.*: login from
app\¦.*accessVM
app\¦.*IPC
app\¦.*Accepted new connection
app\¦.*Set my connection
app\¦.*VM already present
app\¦.*\[DATASTORE\]
app\¦.*\[VMCOPYSERVER\]
```

```
app\¦.*\[VMCopierServer\]
app\¦.*SNMPConfig:
app\¦.*NFC
app\¦.*Debug level
app\¦.*DB Handle
app\¦.*Serverd hostname
app\¦.*Setting up serverd
app\¦.*Successfully set up
app\¦.*Waiting for tools
app\¦.*Performed:
app\¦.*OVL_STATUS_EOF
app\¦.*Accepted connection
app\¦.*Trimming
app\¦.*Program:
app\¦.*CWD:
app\¦.*LimitResources:
app\¦.*vmsd_register:
app\¦.*Files included
app\¦.*New connection on socket
```

Add the following to the `logcheck.violations.ignore` file:

```
ipt_REJECT
hpvmmcntsvc: hpvmmcnt shutdown succeeded
app\¦.*Failed to start LRO
```

Even after these changes, modifications may still be needed to remove even more lines from the output. The goal should be to remove anything that is not informative. For example, if the line states a VM powered on but did not mention the VM, why keep the line in the output? Use this tool to read your log files and strip out unnecessary debris. After making the changes to test, the changes remove the `/var/log/*.offset` files and run the command `logcheck`. It is also possible to use `logcheck` to scan the `/home/vmware/*/vmware.log` files for issues and any other location for VM configuration and logging data. This last change is left as an exercise for the reader.

3. Run Bastille or CISscan in scan mode periodically, perhaps once a week, to determine whether there has been a change to the security of the system. Have these results mailed to the system administrator, and investigate any change.

4. Run Nessus and NMAP against your system to produce an external security report to determine what external vulnerabilities exist. Nessus should be run from a machine on the administrative network. Nessus will output the following when ESX is not secured. This is a look at ESX version 3 when the VMkernel for NAS access and the COS share the same virtual switch, which is similar to ESX version 2.5, except for the multiple networks in ESX version 3.

```
Nessus Scan Report
— — — — — — — —

SUMMARY

 - Number of hosts which were alive during the test : 2
 - Number of security holes found : 0
 - Number of security warnings found : 0
 - Number of security notes found : 26


TESTED HOSTS

  10.0.0.42 (COS, Security notes found)
  10.0.0.150 (VM Kernel, Security notes found)


DETAILS

+ 10.0.0.42 :

 . List of open ports :

   o ssh (22/tcp) (Security notes found)

   o http (80/tcp) (Security notes found)

   o https (443/tcp) (Security notes found)

   o ideafarm-chat (902/tcp) (Security notes found)

   o ideafarm-catch (903/tcp) (Security notes found)

   o wbem-http (5988/tcp) (Security notes found)

   o wbem-https (5989/tcp)

   o general/udp (Security notes found)

   o general/tcp (Security notes found)
```

. Information found on port ssh (22/tcp)

    An ssh server is running on this port

. Information found on port ssh (22/tcp)

    Remote SSH version : SSH-2.0-OpenSSH_3.6.1p2

. Information found on port ssh (22/tcp)

    The remote SSH daemon supports the following versions of the

    SSH protocol :

     . 1.99

     . 2.0

    SSHv2 host key fingerprint : ...

. Information found on port http (80/tcp)

    A web server is running on this port

. Information found on port http (80/tcp)

    The following directories were discovered:

    /downloads, /client

    While this is not, in and of itself, a bug, you should manually inspect

    these directories to ensure that they are in compliance with company

    security standards

    Other references : OWASP:OWASP-CM-006

. Information found on port https (443/tcp)

    A SSLv2 server answered on this port

. Information found on port https (443/tcp)

    A web server is running on this port through SSL

. Information found on port https (443/tcp)

    Synopsis :

    The remote service encrypts traffic using a protocol with known

    weaknesses.

Description :

The remote service accepts connections encrypted using SSL 2.0, which

reportedly suffers from several cryptographic flaws and has been

deprecated for several years. An attacker may be able to exploit these

issues to conduct man-in-the-middle attacks or decrypt communications

between the affected service and clients.

...

. Information found on port https (443/tcp)

Here is the SSLv2 server certificate:

Certificate:

Data:

...

Solution: disable those ciphers and upgrade your client

software if necessary.

...

. Information found on port https (443/tcp)

The following directories were discovered:

/downloads, /client

...

. Information found on port https (443/tcp)

The following CGI have been discovered :

...

. Information found on port ideafarm-chat (902/tcp)

A VMWare authentication daemon is running on this port:

...

. Information found on port ideafarm-chat (902/tcp)

Synopsis :

The remote host appears to be running VMware ESX or GSX Server.

Description :

According to its banner, the remote host appears to be running a VMWare

server authentication daemon, which likely indicates the remote host is

    running VMware ESX or GSX Server.

...

 . Information found on port ideafarm-catch (903/tcp)

    A VMWare authentication daemon is running on this port:

...

 . Information found on port wbem-http (5988/tcp)

    A web server is running on this port

 . Information found on port wbem-http (5988/tcp)

    The remote web server is very slow - it took 95 seconds to

    execute the plugin no404.nasl (it usually only takes a few seconds).

...

 . Information found on port general/udp

...

 . Information found on port general/tcp

    Synopsis :

    The remote host seems to be a VMWare virtual machine.

    Description :

    The remote host seems to be a VMWare virtual machine running

    the Microsoft Windows Operating system. Because it is

physically

    accessible through the network, you should ensure that its

    configuration matches the one of your corporate security policy.

...

 . Information found on port general/tcp

...

 . Information found on port general/tcp

    Nessus was not able to reliably identify the remote operating

system. It

        might be:

...

 + 10.0.0.150 :

 . List of open ports :

    o irdmi (8000/tcp)

```
o general/icmp (Security notes found)

o general/udp (Security notes found)

o general/tcp (Security notes found)


. Information found on port general/icmp
   Synopsis :
   It is possible to determine the exact time set on the remote host.
   Description :
   The remote host answers to an ICMP timestamp request. This allows an
    attacker
   to know the date which is set on your machine.
...
. Information found on port general/udp
...
. Information found on port general/tcp
   Synopsis :
   The remote host seems to be a VMWare virtual machine.
   Description :
...
. Information found on port general/tcp
   Nessus was not able to reliably identify the remote operating
system. It
   might be:
...
  — — — — — — — — — — — — — — — — — — — — — — — — — — —
This file was generated by the Nessus Security Scanner
```

Although the output is mostly notes about your server, this information
can be used to craft an attack utilizing any one of the weaknesses mentioned about the server and in some cases actually break into the system
using various methods available. However, a secured ESX Server using all
the tools mentioned in this chapter will have the following resulting
Nessus scan, which does not give off any additional information about the
server that could be used to craft an attack. However, the information
about the VMkernel stays the same because the VMkernel interface does
not contain any form of firewall functionality.

```
Nessus Scan Report
_ _ _ _ _ _ _ _ _
SUMMARY
 - Number of hosts which were alive during the test : 1
 - Number of security holes found : 0
 - Number of security warnings found : 0
 - Number of security notes found : 1


TESTED HOSTS
 10.0.0.42 (COS, Security notes found)
 10.0.0.150 (VM Kernel, Security notes found)


DETAILS
+ 10.0.0.42 :
 . List of open ports :
 . Information found on port general/udp

...


+ 10.0.0.150 :
 . List of open ports :
   o irdmi (8000/tcp)
   o general/icmp (Security notes found)
   o general/udp (Security notes found)
   o general/tcp (Security notes found)


 . Information found on port general/icmp
   Synopsis :
   It is possible to determine the exact time set on the remote host.
   Description :
   The remote host answers to an ICMP timestamp request. This allows an
    attacker
   to know the date which is set on your machine.
 ...
 . Information found on port general/udp
 ...
 . Information found on port general/tcp
```

```
Synopsis :
The remote host seems to be a VMWare virtual machine.
Description :
...

 . Information found on port general/tcp
    Nessus was not able to reliably identify the remote operating
system. It
    might be:

...

 _ _ _ _ _ _ _ _ _ _ _ _ _ _ _ _ _ _ _ _ _ _ _ _ _ _ _ _ _ _
This file was generated by the Nessus Security Scanner
```

5. Now that the log files and security are being monitored better we should turn our thoughts to what services to monitor, too. Monitoring services will let you know whether for some reason they are not available and various monitoring programs go about this in different ways. For example VC monitors port 902 with its alarm system. If suddenly the ESX Server were no longer available, first alarms will go off, and then eventually the ESX Server would automatically disconnect telling you that there was an issue. However, there is a bit more to monitor than just port 902.

If you are using HPSIM, for example, it will let you know whether SNMP, and whether the machine itself, is reachable via the network. Both VC and VMM will track disk, load, memory, and swap usage on the VMs, but neither tool will tell you by default if the MUI or other management interfaces such as the System Management home page are available. To check these, we need to check to see whether the web servers running on their ports are also available. Although VC does not provide this functionality, HPSIM and other vendor tools do, as well as the open source Nagios program (www.nagios.org). Not specifically designed for ESX, Nagios will monitor everything at a service level.

The basic steps to setting up remote monitoring of systems and services follow.

    a. For VC, create new alarms for each VM and ESX Server to send e-mail when there is a disconnect or when a failure state is reached for each VM.

    b. For HPSIM, set up an alarm to send e-mail or a page when the ESX Server or VM is no longer running or reachable by HPSIM.

c. Using Nagios, set up a service-level alarm to send e-mail when the MUI, System Management home page, or a service within a VM is no longer available.

From a security perspective, a failure to access a service could imply that a DoS attack has been launched against that service and perhaps the host. However, from a support perspective, knowing when a system or service is unreachable proves extremely useful to debug problems. For monitoring, security and support concerns go hand in hand.

ESX-Specific Security concerns

The previous sections of this chapter deal with ways to secure the service COS, which is a variant of Linux. The recipe presented is a pretty standard recipe for generic Linux that accounts for the ESX peculiarities. Now it is time to delve into the ESX-specific issues related to the virtualization of machines into ESX guests and the various modes of networking available: specifically, the split between the networks for the service console, VMs, and VMotion. Ideally, neither network should overlap. From a security point of view, if a break in occurs on the COS, the COS should *not* be able to sniff the packets coming from the VMs and absolutely should *not* be able to sniff the packets for the VMotion network. This network transmits a memory footprint, and access to this will allow a hacker to see what is currently in memory, which should be prevented at all costs. Allowing someone to not only grab your data, but to see what is currently in running memory is a recipe for security disaster, so be sure that the service console network is not shared with the VMs or the VMotion networks. There is only one way for this to even be possible in ESX earlier than version 3.0, and that is to employ the vmxnet_console driver used in low port density network environments. If this feature is in use or ESX version 3.0 is in use, the service console should be attached to its own virtual switch (vSwitch) that has no other attachments except the service console. There should be other vSwitches for the VMs and VMotion. Let the service console have a vSwitch just for itself, thereby not allowing the service console to gain access to the VM or VMotion networks.

VMkernel Security Considerations

VMkernel security should be addressed differently from VMotion security because with ESX version 3 it is possible to have multiple VMkernel connections. Given the output of the Nessus scan, the VMkernel connections require physical security as there is no packet-filtering firewall for the VMkernel yet and because it is possible to use this connection for iSCSI or NAS, which contain information about VMDKs and possibly the VMs in use. It is important to realize that access to this network could imply access to the VMDKs, so access to the VMkernel NAS and iSCSI directories should be on their own private network

VMotion Security Considerations

VMotion security should be addressed separately. As stated earlier, the VMotion network transmits a current running clear-text memory image from one ESX host to another. The only way to prevent this is to not use VMotion, which is not desirable. Not even the administrative network should be able to access the VMotion network, because a break in on the admin network could allow the sniffing of the clear-text memory image. A little simple decoding makes it possible to see all your data for the running VM, which could include credit card and other personal identification information. The only way to prevent packet sniffing is to place the VMotion network on its own physical switch or VLAN segmented and detached from any other network. This physical security will keep any other computer from being able to sniff VMotion packets as they happen. This includes making sure no VM is attached to the VMotion vSwitch.

Other ESX Security Considerations

In addition to the vSwitch layout, we need to consider the VMs themselves. Because many VMs will share the same physical NIC, it is best to lay some ground rules for both the VMs and the service console:

1. VM deployments happen over the administrative network or locally within the service console, so the administrative network needs to have some form of physical security.

2. Do not configure any network card in promiscuous mode, and disallow the VMs from doing so.

   There is no way to prevent the service console from running its network interfaces in promiscuous mode prior to ESX version 3, but by not having any VM or VMotion networks on the same network as the service console promiscuous settings will not grab private data not already belonging to the service console. However, it is possible to prevent the VMs from running promiscuous network drivers by using the following option in the VM configuration file for ESX version 2.5.x and earlier versions:

```
Ethernet<n>.noPromisc = TRUE
```

For ESX version 3, these settings are attached to vSwitches and port groups rather than to the individual VM. To make these changes, use the Virtual Switch Security Properties displayed in Figure 4.3, where promiscuous mode changes can be rejected at the virtual switch. It is possible to also make these changes for each network, instead of directly on the virtual network, by selecting the appropriate network configuration and not the virtual switch.

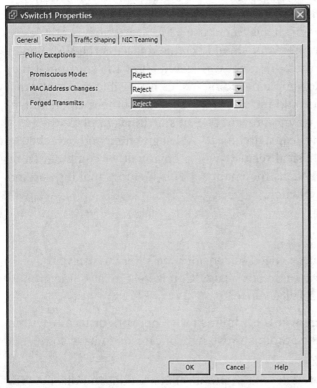

Figure 4.3   vSwitch security properties

3. Do not allow the VMs to spoof MAC addresses. It is very easy and extremely common for hackers to spoof MAC addresses to attack another host or gain access to protected networks. To prevent your VMs from being able to do this and prevent crackers from using the VMs as a base to hack other computers using this method, it is possible to disable the capability by using the following options in the VM configuration file for ESX version 2.5.x and earlier versions:

```
Ethernet<n>.downWhenAddrMisMatch = TRUE
```

For ESX version 3, this setting is part of the vSwitches and port groups rather than the individual VM. To make these changes, use the vSwitch security properties displayed in Figure 4.3, where MAC address changes can be rejected at the vSwitch. Because it is possible to have multiple networks on each vSwitch, these changes apply to the vNetwork, the vSwitch, or both.

4. Do not allow forged retransmits. Forged transmits are a cracker's way of trying to get around IP-based security settings by modifying a packet to have a different source address. It is possible to disable the capability by using the following options in the VM configuration file for ESX version 2.5.x and earlier versions:

```
Ethernet<n>.noForgedSrcAddr = TRUE
```

For ESX version 3, this setting is part of the vSwitches and port groups rather than the individual VM. To make these changes, use the vSwitch security properties displayed in Figure 4.3, where forged source address changes can be rejected at the vSwitch. Because it is possible to have multiple networks on each vSwitch, these changes apply to the vNetwork, the vSwitch, or both.

5. Disable copy and paste into and out of a VM when using the remote console, thereby requiring users of a VM to use existing secure mechanisms to transfer data. On ESX versions earlier than version 3, adding the following options to the VM configuration file will force users to use normal and secured data transfer methods to move data from machine to machine whether virtual or otherwise:

```
isolation.tools.copy = FALSE
isolation.tools.paste = FALSE
```

For ESX version 3, these are set using VM advanced options, which allows the addition of new VM configuration settings via a graphical interface, using the same options as earlier versions.

Roles and Permissions

The Virtual Infrastructure Client (VIC) and VC Server 2.0 have roles and permissions built in. Should these be part of a security recipe? Yes, the VIC can modify ESX settings, it too should be protected. Roles and permissions do this. The communication from the VIC to the ESX Server is over an SSL-encrypted transport, which is secure and runs only over your protected administrative network. Just like picking good administrative passwords, all those users who have access to the VIC need to pick strong passwords. The VIC can be used to communicate with the server, which allows any users who have privileges on the ESX Server to log in. This type of user is a direct user. An indirect user is one who can log in to the VC Server and from there see all the ESX Servers at once, enabling the movement of VMs between hosts and many other configuration possibilities. This is where roles and permissions come in handy. The VIC is a .NET application that has security credentials on all objects. The permissions are for all these objects. A role is a user with a set of VIC permissions listing the actions a user can take based on their role within the organization. Direct or indirect users must have strong passwords, and all these users have the possibility to impact ESX or VM security. Roles and permissions are available to reduce users permissions and limit impact to ESX or VM security.

Roles and permissions offer a granular approach to security within the VIC and applies when using the VIC whether the user is a direct or indirect user. This allows the administrator to set limits on what a user can actually do within the environment when work is performed through the VIC. A bad example is that it is possible to give everyone administrator access via the VIC, whether the users are domain or system administrators or not. A good example is to grant the NOC the ability to VMotion VMs from one host to another if they detect a failed component, yet the NOC is not allowed to do anything else within the system except use the monitor functionality inherent within the VIC.

Roles and permissions are inherited. In Figure 4.4, we can see that the Administrator group has Full Administrator rights within the VIC starting at the very top of the inventory, rights that are therefore inherited all the way through the list of VMs, resources, and hosts. Figure 4.4 shows the use of permissions for Virtual Machines & Templates inventory items within the VIC. There are similar permissions for the Hosts & Clusters inventory pane and for datacenters, which can use either pane to set. The permissions show the inherited roles of the VIC permissions; for example, the C1I1 account can see and manipulate every VM under the Students folder. However, the C1S1 user can only see those VMs within its folder and nowhere else.

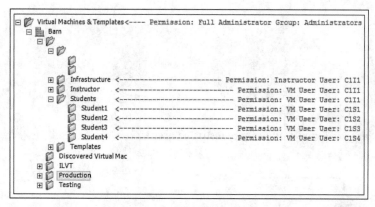

Figure 4.4   VIC Virtual Machines & Templates inventory pane w/roles added

When dealing with roles and permissions inheritance, which can be disabled when setting up a permission on a folder (permission only applies to that folder or entity and is not inherited), the most restrictive permission wins. So if there were a general "No Access" for all users but those in the Administrators group set on the datacenter, the C1I1 user could not see anything because the more restrictive "No Access" is higher in the inheritance than "VM User." This implies that to set permissions you need to start at the bottom of your inventory tree and work backward to get it correct. Judicious use of groups is very useful.

In Figure 4.4, there are Virtual Machine User permissions for user C1I1 on the Instructor and Students folder and Instructor permissions on the Infrastructure folder, which implies that when the C1I1 user log ins to the VIC, that user can see only the VMs in those folders and no other VMs or folders on the system (see Figure 4.5).

We added and used the Instructor role to the roles and permissions by following these simple steps.

1. Click the Admin button within the VIC.

2. Right-click in the Roles pane and select the Add menu item.

3. Give the new role a name and select the options that apply to the role. In Figure 4.6, we have chosen to only allow this role to access the remote console and disconnect or connect devices.

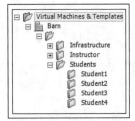

Figure 4.5 VIC Virtual Machines & Templates inventory restricted user view

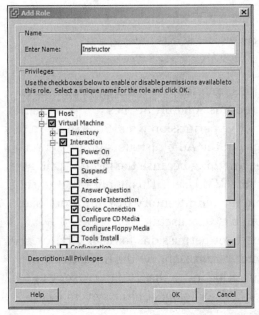

Figure 4.6 VIC add role

4. Click the OK button to save.

5. Click the Virtual Machines and Templates Inventory button.

6. Right-click the folder on which to add the roles and permission, and select Add Permission from the menu.

7. Add the user; in this case, we are using the domain INTERNAL and the user m2-c1i1. Then select the role to apply to the user for this folder. If you desire the role to propagate to all children, check the box (the default) or uncheck to keep the role and permission from applying to any existing children (see Figure 4.7).

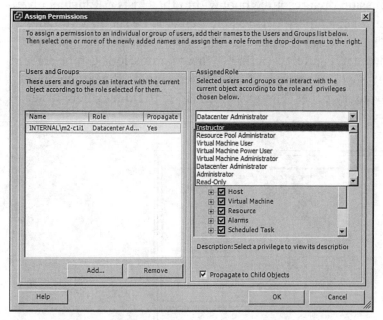

Figure 4.7 VIC adding permission

8. Click OK to apply the desired role.

Because the use of these is like the use of groups, there are no hard-and-fast rules except as defined in the following list:

- Use strong passwords for users.
- Have at least one full administrator role defined.
- To synchronize between VC VIC access and ESX Server VIC access roles and permissions, be sure the same users and groups as exist on the ESX Server.
- Read-only access is a very good role for those who need to review ESX and VC reporting.

- Apply roles to the proper inventory pane; otherwise, they will not be effective.

- Test all proposed changes with a secure user, to be sure you do not give away too much access.

- Specifically add roles based on groups of users or specific users. Be careful of just using a No Access role without understanding its restrictions. Unless a role is explicitly defined, there is no way to do anything in the VIC.

Setting a VM permission on a resource pool within the Hosts & Clusters inventory pane will not take effect as those permissions can only be set on VM folders and individual VMs. The same holds true for setting a resource permission on a VM; it will not go into effect. Figure 4.8 outlines where permissions can be set and what the role affects. It is extremely easy to set a permission on the wrong object within the multiple inventory panes. Figure 4.8 will aid in deciding where to set your permissions.

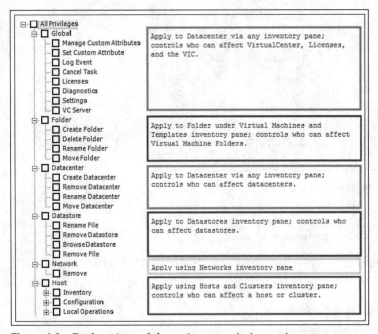

Figure 4.8   Explanations of the various permission options

Figure 4.8 Explanations of the various permission options

What to Do If There Is a Break-In

In the beginning of this chapter, we mentioned that one of our goals was to be prepared for forensic analysis, because we will assume that even our most rigid security recipe can eventually be cracked. To reach this goal, we have implemented additional auditing that will result in more logs to keep so we can determine *who* did *what, when,* from *where,* and *how.* Although it looks good in words, the *where* and the *how* are often times the hardest things for forensic analysis to determine, and with the advent of antiforensic cracking tools, forensic analysis for computing systems is a difficult task. We need to make this easier for the experts. Here is a list of tasks to perform once a break-in has been determined to have occurred. Note that these steps are suggestions, and the corporate security policy should be consulted. If such a policy does not exist, the following list makes a good starting point for any digital forensics:

1. Notify corporate security of a break-in or any attempt at a break-in.
2. Because we mirrored the OS drive, break the mirror and place the tainted disk into an antistatic bag and seal it. Tag the bag with the date, time, and

from where it was removed, and lock it away in a safe until needed.

3. In another bag, place a copy of your original baseline data for the system in question, plus any additional baseline data created. Ensure this bag is sealed and tagged with the appropriate date, time, and hostname.

4. VMotion all live VMs off the system in question and cold migrate any VMs powered down.

5. Reinstall the host from original media, patch, and secure using an appropriate script. At this time, we start to wonder whether the backup was also tainted so original media is best.

6. Get a fresh baseline! This is extremely important.

7. Bring the host back into service by using VMotion to move VMs to the host in question.

As you can see from the previous discussion, a break-in does not have to be catastrophic with ESX, but it should be taken seriously and dealt with. Step 5 says to reinstall from original media, and this advice is offered mostly from experience: In an analysis of a break-in, it was determined that the break-in was only noticed recently, because the cracker covered his tracks exceedingly well, and that the original break-in happened sometime ago. This meant all recent backups were tainted. In this case, a restore from backup would have had to have been done from a backup made three or so years earlier. So, reinstallation from original media is strongly suggested.

Conclusion

Securing any machine is generally a task for those who understand the OS in question in great detail, but the judicious use of preformed scripts from trusted sources, additional logging, and quite a bit of common sense will lead to a secure system, one that can monitor itself for possible security, performance, and support issues. In addition, if you follow the advice in this chapter, you will be prepared for the eventuality of a break-in, and you will audit and monitor your system so that you do not rest on our laurels. Keeping a secure system is an active task, and the system should be audited and monitored closely.

In Chapter 5, "Storage with ESX," we delve into the SAN and NAS fabric as it relates to ESX, and we can be thankful that this fabric currently just needs physical security.

Chapter 5

Storage with ESX

The need for fast, dependable, highly available, and easily managed storage is certainly a design component vital to ensuring a virtual infrastructure implementation is successful in all aspects. Successful in the situation means the implementation meets the organization's expectations moving into this new virtualization world of computing. Up to this point, we have discussed planning your server hardware and implementing the best server configuration requirements. Now let's consider doing the same decisive planning for our virtual data stores.

When implementing and planning new or using existing storage in an ESX virtual datacenter, it is essential to have a thorough understanding of the VM requirements in the present, and far into the future, to get the most out of storage. After selecting the optimal storage hardware based on a design (see Chapter 1, "System Considerations"), it is essential to understand the best practices when managing the storage environment from the ESX perspective. As the virtual datacenter grows, it will deal with growing volumes of data that will increase at an unexpected pace. With the high cost of storage products, an organization may consider cutting corners, which might come back later to hit you where it hurts, which ends up being in the wallet. Take the time to purchase the correct storage hardware components and verify that your existing or new SAN, NAS, iSCSI, or locally attached storage configuration is acceptable to use with the virtual infrastructure and the anticipated capacity. This preliminary step will save you time, money, and anguish. After selecting the storage hardware best for meeting the design goal, it is essential to understand how to connect this storage to your ESX Server, and then understand how to manage this storage using the provided tools. Because many organizations have separate groups that manage servers, and for data stores companywide, it is best to provide a view from how the remote storage sees the ESX Server, and also how ESX sees the remote storage. Such a view will assist both groups in communicating productively.

Best Practice for Getting Started with Storage for ESX
Review the storage compatibility guide at www.vmware.com/support/pubs/vi_pubs.html.

Overview of Storage Technology with ESX

To construct a storage infrastructure for your virtual datacenter that will operate easily, dependably, and optimally, it is extremely important to have a basic understanding of the storage technologies available for ESX in today's market. With today's computing datacenter dealing with volumes of data in the gigabyte, terabyte, and possibly the petabyte range, organizations will be faced with dealing with larger, faster, more reliable storage products to get the job done. As mentioned in Chapter 1, the storage technologies include local attached storage (either SCSI or SATA), SAN (either SCSI or SATA), iSCSI, and NAS-based NFS storage. Storage within ESX refers to where a VM disk file (VMDK) can live.

From an ESX perspective on storage, the hosted VMs may access the storage components whether accessing them physically or by protocol, just like SCSI devices or volumes within the VMs themselves. When a VM issues a read or write command to what the VM thinks is a local SCSI controller with locally connected drives, the guest OS accesses this storage just like it does on a physical server. When an OS receives a request from an application for a file read/write operation, this request is handled by the OS as a file to block translation, and the request is then passed to the driver serving the OS. Because the VM driver does not directly access the hardware, the driver subsequently passes the block read/write request on to the VMkernel, where another translation takes place, and then it is passed on to the physical hardware device driver and sent to the storage controller. This storage controller could be a local on-board SCSI controller serving SCSI devices local to a server, external SCSI RAID devices, a FC HBA accessing a SAN array via multiple paths, or network cards serving access to an iSCSI target. No matter what the physical storage devices are, the VM knows nothing about their attributes or access methods, and ESX does a great job of making the guest operating systems believe the storage is the same as a physical server. On the ESX Server, all storage bus traffic from all the hosted VMs appears to be coming from a single source from the storage controller's perspective. The two ways of making storage volumes available to VMs are using a VMDK and using a raw disk map, which is a LUN formatted with the one of the VM operating system's native file systems.

In production, most ESX installations use local storage for the COS, all swap files, and local backups for disaster recovery, incorporating an external data store to access VM disk files. The choices of storage now available with ESX version 3 for formatting as a VMFS volume are SANs, iSCSI, and local SCSI storage. VMDKs can also be placed on an NFS-based NAS. These are essential components of a virtual datacenter due to the sheer volume of disk space required to meet the demands of virtual computing, as well as providing the flexibility to manage VMs with ease. By implementing shared storage into the computing environment, administrators now have the capability for multiple hosts to access a common storage repository and uncoupling storage from single physical servers. The need for megabytes, terabytes, or petabytes of data space to store and run your VMs in an enterprise environment is simply not satisfactory when using local system storage, especially when you would like to use clustered servers, dynamic resource load balancing (DRLB), and disaster recovery (DR) technology. Equally important is having a common storage platform for all ESX Servers for ease of movement between and access to VMs from any host. Designing enough capacity and an easily accessible storage implementation complements any DR plan, which is always critical in today's computing environment.

With the early versions of ESX earlier than version 3, storage was limited to local attached storage and SANs with which to implement a virtual infrastructure. ESX version 3 supports NAS-based NFS storage for VM configuration and disk files and other sundry data files, including ISO images, iSCSI, and SAN using either SCSI, SAS, or SATA drives from which to run and store VM disk files. Administrators now have more choices to assist in implementing ESX. As storage options become available with new releases of ESX, the potential for unanticipated problems and roadblocks increases, which makes understanding and planning storage imperative.

SCSI Versus SAS Versus ATA Versus SATA

What disk technology to use is of the utmost importance to a high-performance ESX Server. The use of SCSI has always been the best choice in the past, but newer technologies have now come into their own. ESX supports VMs on two different storage technologies: VMFS or NFS. VMFS is the highest performance option and requires that disks be presented to the ESX Server as some form of SCSI device (iSCSI, SAN, local storage), whereas NFS can be of any disk technology and is presented by some form of NAS. Because VMFS requires SCSI, this rules out locally attached ATA or SATA drives, but does include SCSI and SAS drives for local VMFS storage. Any other supported local storage can run ESX but cannot launch any VMs. ESX has few disk drivers, and if the appropriate driver exists for the ATA and SATA drives, use of these devices is supported. However, it is best to have all local disks be some form of SCSI or SAS drive. Set up the ATA and SATA drives in a NAS or SAN and present them as SCSI to the ESX Server. SATA will be supported with ESX v3.5.

Best Practice for ATA or SATA
Present these disk types via iSCSI or use within a SAN or NAS (NFS) server.

SATA drives, although they can hold a larger amount of data than SCSI, tend to run slower than SCSI devices, and this speed difference will affect an ESX Server farm. Using SATA drives as the backup media for a LUN-to-LUN mirror is wise because fewer disks will be necessary. However, using them directly for VMFS storage is not recommended except in a DR mode. SATA and ATA are more failure prone than their SCSI counterparts.

Best Practice for Use of SATA
Use SATA-based devices as the target for LUN to LUN backups.

iSCSI (SCSI over IP)

iSCSI appliances are low cost, very simple to use, and utilize SCSI protocols over TCP/IP. iSCSI disk arrays or servers are accessible from IP network-attached processors that allow direct access to a networked LUN that hosts a VMFS from which to run VMs. In effect, iSCSI uses Ethernet rather than Fibre to form a storage fabric. iSCSI, as compared to SAN, is generally less expensive and integrates with existing networks. However, for best performance, iSCSI usually has its own network. Another key attribute of having your VMs on iSCSI is now VMs can run from an ESX Server that is on a LAN (local area network) or WAN (wide area network) to enable data access across long distances, which is beneficial for utilizing remote resources and disaster recovery. iSCSI is comparable to Fibre Channel when using bonded network devices until 10G is cost-effective on the server. However, single networks currently run at 1Gb speeds, compared to 4Gb for Fibre Channel. iSCSI is gaining a lot of attention, with HP, EMC, Cisco, NetApp, along with many other smaller companies producing iSCSI components in hopes of competing with the SAN market at a lower cost. The low-cost benefit of iSCSI is due to the capability to use existing hardware and topologies to now act as data stores, and in addition, current network administration organizations do not need to add new skills or hardware to manage iSCSI. iSCSI uses authentication and encryption available through IP and can also utilize VPN connections. Because iSCSI uses IP, any standard firewall can control access to the iSCSI servers or network.

iSCSI is a client/server technology where the initiator, or client (a server), initiates requests to a server, or storage device, which is the target. There are two types of initiators: software and hardware. The software initiator is a driver that manages all requests and matches them with the network interface drivers and SCSI drivers. The downside to the software initiator is that the OS implements the whole stack, which is processor intensive. A hardware initiator is an iSCSI HBA that is essentially an Ethernet card containing a SCSI ASIC (application-specific integrated circuit) board designed to manage the SCSI requests rather than the server's CPU assuming this job. VMware uses a software initiator, which is a port of the SourceForge-based Cisco initiator. The initiator lives inside the service console with some in the VMkernel, and therefore it is important to have the service console network participate in the iSCSI network. There is an experimental iSCSI HBA for ESX, the Qlogic 4010. This device appears just like any other SCSI HBA and acts as a TCP Offload Engine (TOE) with its own network stack to offload iSCSI protocol from the system processor. ESX provides the VIC20 to manage the ESX Server and its SCSI cards such as the Qlogic 4010, as well as other iSCSI connections.

NAS (Network-Attached Storage)

NAS devices can share many different protocols, with the most prevalent being NFS (Network File System), CIFS (Common Information File System), and iSCSI. ESX can make use of NFS and iSCSI, but not CIFS. iSCSI can be fully used by ESX, but it has some slight security and networking considerations, as covered in Chapter 4, "Auditing, Monitoring, and Securing," and Chapter 8, "Configuring ESX from a Host Connection." NFS, on the other hand, has its own limitations, including the NFS protocol to use. ESX supports NFS over TCP only. NFS can store ISO images used to build VMs, and 2Gb sparse VMDKs, or the format of virtual disk files exported out of ESX versions earlier than version 3 or usable by VMware Workstation. In future discussions, iSCSI and SAN are synonymous.

SANs (Storage Area Networks)

SANs can meet the extreme requirements of data storage for ESX. SANs make use of dedicated network connections to one or many variable-sized disk arrays, which provide ESX Servers and many other systems in a datacenter with a common, shared data access container. SANs provide an optimum storage area that ensures high availability, desired performance, and ease of disaster recovery for data accessed from the applications running on VMs. SANs provide an ideal complementary technology to run, manage, and store VMs with the capability to grow far into the future. SANs are similar in concept to Ethernet networking connecting hosts, but the difference is we are not connecting servers together. We are connecting servers to a data space that is larger than is achievable with locally attached storage with SANs, often providing data access that is as fast or faster than that of locally attached storage. In addition to directly presenting storage to a physical host, many SANs can present iSCSI to hosts via a dedicated Ethernet connection to connect hosts to the data space. SANs connecting directly to hosts use a Fibre Channel card utilizing 2Gb or 4Gb connections. On average, iSCSI connects using 1Gb via network cards. However, this is changing as faster network cards become available.

Although this might be a review for some readers, I believe that a review of what makes up a SAN would be useful. So, in short, here we go.

Gigabit Interface Converters (GBICs)

GBICs enable Fibre Channel devices such as HBAs, switches, and routers to interconnect with the Fibre Channel cable. The reason for the GBIC is to translate a Fibre Channel signal from the Fibre Channel cable into a format that is interpretable by the HBA or Fibre Channel switches. What GBICs provide is the capability to interconnect physical media such as optical and copper in the SAN. Because of the lack of standardization for SAN connectivity, the GBIC allows switch manufacturers to focus their products on solutions and not on a specific medium type. This can be handy when changing the Fibre Channel type; just upgrade the GBIC instead of upgrading a switch. This is a great advantage considering the price of Fibre Channel switches.

Fibre Channel Switch

Fibre Channel switches are the intelligent devices that create what is called the "SAN fabric" by interconnecting all the Fibre Channel devices making up the SAN: the servers, storage arrays, hubs, and routers to tape libraries. Fibre Channel switches provide the capability to create arbitrated-loop and switched-fabric SAN designs. Ports on some switches use GBICS, whereas others permit a direct Fibre Channel cable connection. The type of ports available on switches dictate what type of Fibre Channel network may be connected.

The types of Fibre Channel switch ports are as follows:

- **FL_PORT:** For Fibre Channel arbitrated loop (FC-AL) designs
- **F_PORT:** For switched-fabric designs
- **U_PORT:** For universal port (FC-AL or fabric) designs
- **E_PORT:** For connecting Fibre Channel switches together

Newer Fibre Channel switches now provide additional switch ports that allow connectivity for IP networks to support protocols such as iSCSI.

Bridge

The bridge, or what is referred to as a router, is used to connect a Fibre Channel SAN to a SCSI device like a tape library, jukeboxes, or disk arrays. The purpose of this device is to bridge or route Fibre Channel protocol communication to a SCSI bus, which allows interconnection between the SAN and backup or secondary storage. This device is beneficial when you have existing investment in secondary storage and you want to integrate these devices for use in your SAN.

Topologies

Now that we have a "brief" description of SAN components, let's take a moment to review the manner in which these components interconnect in the SAN fabric.

Point-to-Point Topology

Point-to-point topology, as depicted in Figure 5.1, is the simplest method for connecting a SAN array to a server by connecting a Fibre Channel cable from the storage array's storage processor (SP) port directly to the server's FC HBA. This is the lowest-cost solution, but this topology has a high risk of failure simply because there is no redundancy available. You may connect an MSA1000 to a server in this topology, but many other SAN storage arrays do not support this connection (for example, the EVA and HP series). This topology, although supported by VMware, is highly discouraged, and only suggested for testing and proof of concept. Another problem with this topology is that to expand you must do a total shutdown.

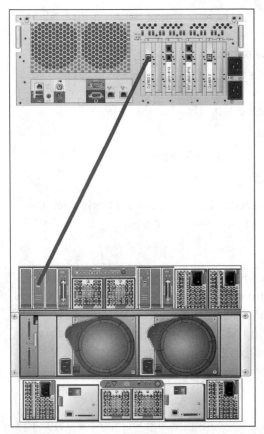

Figure 5.1 Point-to-point topology
Visio templates for image courtesy of Hewlett-Packard.

Switched Fabric

The switched fabric or trivial fabric topology, as shown in Figure 5.2, shows an addition to the direct connect topology by adding a Fibre Channel switch, which allows several point-to-point connections for more storage and servers. The problem with this topology is that is still presents many points of failure, making this topology a non-fault-tolerant solution. Although not a best practice for an ESX environment, it is supported.

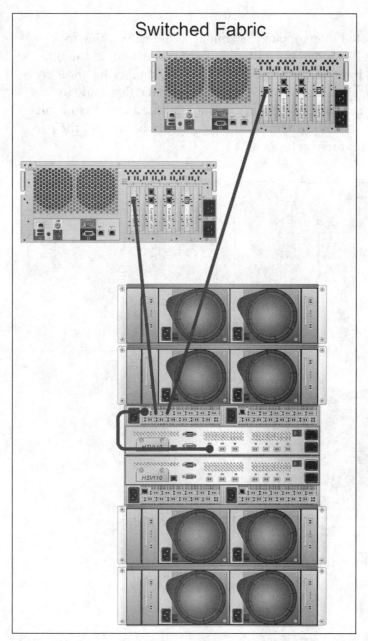

Figure 5.2 Switched fabric topology
Visio templates for image courtesy of Hewlett-Packard.

Arbitrated Loop

The Fibre Channel arbitrated loop topology is similar to the networking topology known as Token Ring, as illustrated in Figure 5.3. Each component in the ring transmits data during an interval. This topology is popular due to the lower costs of Fiber Channel hubs compared to switches, even though the downside to this topology is the lack of scalability and efficiency. The arbitrated loop has no support within ESX and will have no support in the near future because of the performance limitations of this architecture.

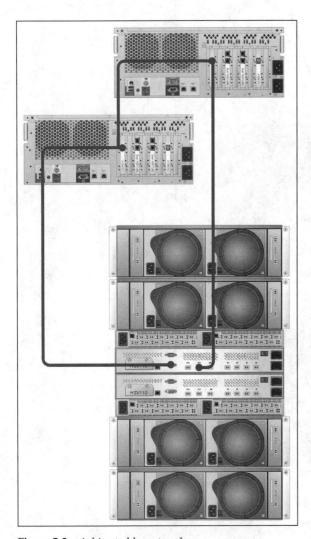

Figure 5.3   Arbitrated loop topology
Visio templates for image courtesy of Hewlett-Packard.

Multipath Fabric

Multipath fabric, or multipath switched-fabric topology, introduces a highly fault-tolerant design with redundant storage processors on the storage array and FC HBAs on the servers, as shown in Figure 5.4. With multipath fabric topology, if an FC HBA or a storage processor fails, the ESX Server has a backup path to fail over to continue to access virtual disk files on the VMFS. ESX Server supports failover aspects of multipath but not automated load balancing and port aggregation.

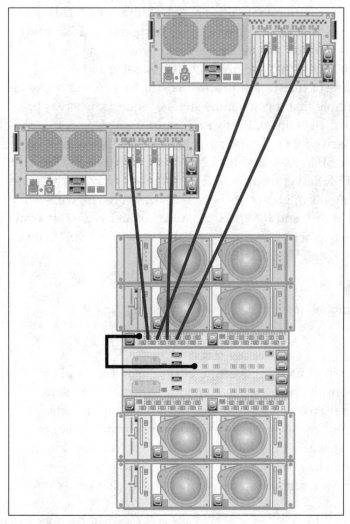

Figure 5.4 Multipath fabric topology
Visio templates for image courtesy of Hewlett-Packard.

Redundant Fabric

The redundant fabric is the most popular topology and the preferred SAN topology for the ESX Server environment. It is illustrated in Figure 5.5. When a second Fibre Channel switch is included into the topology, the fabric becomes completely redundant. Fault-tolerant fabric eliminates all single points of failure. However, when using a single active/passive SAN, where only one storage processor (SP) is active at a time, ensure that all primary FC HBAs on every ESX Server in the same farm point at the same SP, while the secondary FC HBAs point to another SP. This is extremely important to pay attention to, to prevent "LUN thrashing." This is a situation where the storage ports ping-pong connections back and forth, creating storage access degradation. However, this is not necessary when using an active/active SAN or multiple active/passive SANs. Active/passive and active/active describe the state of the storage processors. The SP is either active or passive. Active processors imply that it can handle storage requests, whereas passive processors cannot immediately do so. Passive SPs must first become active to handle requests. When a passive SP becomes active, it moves all the connections in use on the previous active SP to itself and then handles the request. So, be sure to present all LUNs for an ESX Server on an active/passive SAN through the same SP to alleviate LUN thrashing. Examples of active/active arrays are Hitachi 9900, EMC Symmetrix, HP XP (Hitachi), and IBM ESS. Examples of active/passive arrays are HP MSA1x00 (HP has active/active firmware available now for all MSA1x00 devices), HP EVA, IBM FAStT, and EMC Clariion.

Other SAN Options and Components

Other SAN options and components include replication, zoning, and multipath.

Replication

If a company has an interest in disaster recovery, to ensure high data availability for their VMs, they might consider using replication for their SAN array data. It may be stored at one or more separate locations that are strategically selected to provide data availability when any one or more locations are compromised, rendering them inoperable. As discussed in Chapter 12, "Disaster Recovery and Backup," disaster recovery can be achieved with the use of clustering, snapshots, backups, and, when using SANs, replication to a remote site or sites using WAN technologies.

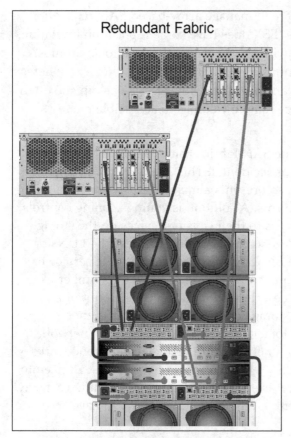

Figure 5.5   Redundant fabric topology
Visio templates for image courtesy of Hewlett-Packard.

Fibre Channel over IP (FCIP) is the lowest-cost solution, which allows the use of the IP over the Internet to interconnect SAN arrays for replication. Some Fibre Channel switches provide the transfer link to allow Fibre Channel data to pass to FCIP across the Internet to a remote SAN to mirror the disk array data. In essence, SANs are connected to each other using an IP network protocol similar to the way servers are connected using Ethernet. applications such as EMC's Symmetrix Remote Data Facility (SDRF), Peer-to-Peer Remote Copy (PPRC), and HP's

Continuous Access provide the software to manage array-based SAN replication by synchronizing data at a remote site. ESX does have some replication limitations because there is no direct integration with third-party replication tools. In most cases, array vendors support synchronous replication up to 10 kilometers, whereas asynchronous replication can be over any distance. Failover to a backup site often requires manual intervention to change remote volumes to accessible mode.

Zoning

It is not desirable that any server on the SAN fabric arbitrarily access any data on a VMFS volume, whether intentional or accidental. This presents a data-integrity issue for the whole data store, but it also presents a major security concern, and it promotes the spread of viruses and worms. A solution is zoning. Zoning controls the specific allocation of data path access to the LUNs or devices on the storage array. Zoning ensures that certain servers or users can only access the LUNs or devices they should be accessing on a SAN. Zoning also provides the service of device load balancing. Another attribute is that zoning reduces the number of LUNs or targets that the ESX Server sees, thereby reducing the amount of boot time for ESX or any servers scanning storage on the array. Think of a zone as essentially equivalent to a file system folder, or directory, or similar to network VLANs, or the concept of segmenting a network into many logical subnetworks that cannot cross data paths. When a SAN has many ESX Servers that all need to have data access to a common VMFS, it is essential to implement zoning correctly. To use VMotion in an ESX environment, all the ESX Servers have to have access to the same zone.

There are two types of SAN zoning: hard and soft zoning. With hard zoning, assign each device to a specific zone at the switch level. A method of hard zoning is to allow selected switch ports to communicate with other switch ports. Soft zoning allocates each device based on different server needs in the SAN topology. Soft zoning is at the storage processor level; for example, soft zoning uses World Wide Names (WWNs) to identify the storage processor on the fabric. A WWN is a unique 64-bit address represented in hexadecimal format that identifies an individual storage processor on the fabric. In some cases, storage arrays have multiple ports, each identified with an individual WWNN (World Wide Name Number). Similar to PCI networks cards that use MAC (Media Access Control) addresses to identify the ports on a LAN, WWNs are similar in concept to a SAN fabric. The advantage of zoning using a WWN is that all device or device ports have the flexibility of moving to another location on the fabric, while changing the device switch port but not changing the current zoning configuration. With ESX, it is essential that all servers in a farm be located in the same zone, so it is best to use soft-zoning policy if possible.

ESX Server provides a third zoning mechanism: LUN masking. LUN masking reduces the number of LUNs seen by the ESX Server, which may take a long time to boot if there are many LUNs to scan. All servers in a farm must see all LUNs for VMotion, and it is best to perform LUN masking at the storage processor level.

Multipath

Multipath failover allows a LUN on the SAN to be available, through multiple fabric paths, to an OS or application in the event of a failure somewhere in the fabric. If there is an event such as an FC HBA, switch, storage controller, or a Fibre Channel cable failure that causes the current path accessing a LUN to be severed, a failover happens automatically, with a configurable delay. With multipath failover, only one path to any particular LUN is active at any time. There are two other aspects of multipath: port aggregation and load balancing. Port aggregation enables, in the case of an active/active SAN, multiple HBAs, and hence multiple paths to the SPs, to be used, thereby gaining at least roughly a 2x performance improvement with storage queries and replies. Load balancing also makes use of multiple paths to the SPs and balances the traffic over all the paths to alleviate fabric bottlenecks.

ESX does support multipath failover, but it does not support port aggregation or load balancing, to maintain a consistent connection between the LUNs the VMkernel or the server manages. Path management is an important topic when it comes to multipath functionality within ESX. ESX has made two policies available: MRU (most recently used), which is the default; and fixed (preferred path). Because the default policy is MRU, there could be problems with path management if using the default setting with an active/active array. When using the ESX MRU setting, which is used with active/passive arrays such as the MSA1x00, once a failover occurs to the backup path, that path will continue to remain in use until an administrator changes it back to the original preferred path. When you are using active/active arrays or multiple arrays, the "fixed" failover policy is best. In the event of a path failure with the selected preferred path, ESX attempts the alternate path to maintain access to the storage, but as soon as the preferred path regains connectivity, ESX reverts to the preferred path.

Best Practice Path Management

Use an MRU policy only for instances where there are single active/passive arrays or where multiple active/passive arrays are in use and zoned through to the same FC HBA.

Use a fixed policy for instances where there are active/active arrays or when multiple active/passive arrays are in use and zoned through multiple FC HBAs.

When adding in multiple FC HBAs to an ESX Server, be sure to use the same type of adapter, because there is limited support for multiple types of adapters. As an example, it is not possible to set up multipath failover when using an Emulex and a Qlogic FC HBA. The limitation is inherent in the drivers used. The FC HBAs must share the same driver to allow multipath failover functionality.

For ESX version 3, there are several ways to investigate the state of multipath failover. The first is to log in to the COS and use the `esxcfg-mpath` command. The other method is to use the VIC20 client (see Figure 5.6).

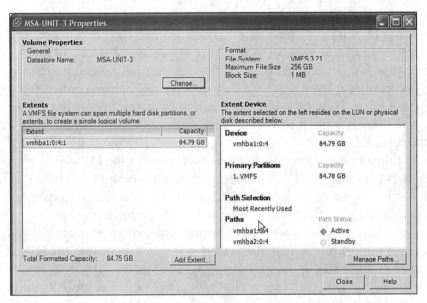

Figure 5.6 VIC20, reviewing multipath settings

For ESX versions earlier than version 3, several tools are available to review the state of multipath failover. The first is from the MUI under the Options tab, where there is a storage management link that leads to another tab. If desired ,the `vmk-multipath -q` command can be issued when logged in to the COS shell.

Support for third-party multipath software products is *not* available for ESX, including HP's SecurePath and EMC's PowerPath.

Overview of Storage Technology with ESX

Storage technology can be divided into SAN and iSCSI/NFS

SAN Best Practices

SANs are extremely flexible and provide a common large data store for use by the datacenter.

There are also some limitations and best practices:

- Do not share the FC HBA between the VMs and COS when using ESX versions earlier than version 3 because this can cause contention for the SAN resources. This is no longer an issue for ESX version 3.

- If implementing boot from SAN (BFS) on ESX, do not include on the boot LUN, presented by the SAN, any form of VMFS. VMFS SCSI Reservations lock the whole LUN and not just the assigned partition, which will contribute to contention for SAN resources.

- For ESX versions earlier than ESX version 3, sharing the FC HBA between the VMs and the COS (as required for BFS) is mutually exclusive with shared disk clusters such as Microsoft Cluster Suite (MSCS).

- ESX does not contain true multipath capability, just failover modes. Multipath can include some form of load balancing among all FC HBAs. Therefore, more than two ports add more failover paths and not more bandwidth.

- The "sort of" exception to the preceding practice is this: When there is an active/active SAN or multiple active/passive SANs, it is possible to zone LUNs presented through each available FC HBA. However, this is *not* multipath, but a zoning and presentation possibility, which then requires some form of failover.

- When placing FC HBAs in a server, be sure to place each card in its own PCI bus. Most servers have more than one PCI slot. Review Chapter 1 for more details on this.

- It is important to use the SAN array BIOS recommended by the vendor. If you use the wrong BIOS, ESX will fail to work properly with a SAN.

- When using multipath failover, always match FC HBA cards make and model.

- It is important to keep your FC HBA BIOS at the latest approved and supplied by the vendor for ESX, which is available from the vendor's website. Because there is no current method available to update firmware from the COS, reboot the server and use the maintenance mode kernel.

iSCSI/NFS Best Practices

iSCSI and NFS additions to ESX version 3 increase flexibility and provide more options for a common large data store for use by the datacenter.

There are also some limitations and best practices:

- iSCSI and NFS are not available as a data store for VMs until ESX version 3. However, NFS can be used prior to ESX version 3, just not as a data store location.

- The iSCSI VMkernel device *must* be part of at least one service console vSwitch, which implies that the service console must be on the same network as the iSCSI servers. This is required whether using CHAP authentication, or not, to pass credentials to the iSCSI server.

- The NFS VMkernel device can be separate from the service console vSwitch.

- The VMkernel default route and netmask must include both the iSCSI and NFS servers, which implies the service console default route and netmask should include at least the iSCSI server.

- Adding more NICs to the iSCSI vSwitch does not necessarily increase bandwidth. See Chapter 7, "Networks," for complete details on vSwitches.

- So far, I have not been able to attach more than one iSCSI server to an ESX Server; but according to the ESX 3.x SAN guide, ESX 3.x supports eight iSCSI targets.

Virtual Machine File System

VMFS is a simple, efficient, distributed file system that is used by the VMkernel to enable high-performance access to large files such as virtual disks for VMs with very low overhead. VMFS is the native file system in ESX, which enables the VMkernel to perform read/writes as efficiently as performing operations on a raw disk, with fast data structures used exclusively by the VMkernel, whether the VMFS is located on a local server or remote storage. VMFS is the only file system that can host VMDKs for ESX versions earlier than version 3. ESX version 3 can host monolithic VMDKs on a VMFS and multiple file VMDKs on NFS.

Versions of ESX earlier than version 3 used either VMFS-1 or VMFS-2 depending on the build level. VMFS-1 and VMFS-2 are flat block file systems that did not permit a directory structure hierarchy for the reason of maintaining fast access to virtual disk files from the VMkernel. ESX version 3 introduces VMFS-3, which adds a directory structure allowing for the storage of VM configuration, disk, and swap files in one place. A single LUN may only house exactly one VMFS, which in turn will provide a container for many VM disk files from many ESX Servers if the VMFS is located on shared or local storage. The VMkernel organizes access to the VMFS by using SCSI-2 Reservation on the entire volume or LUN. SCSI-2 Reservations are covered later is this chapter.

A VMFS volume contains a metadata area to manage all the files that live in the VMFS, as well as the attributes of the VMFS volume. The metadata file includes the VMFS label, number of files in the VMFS, attributes about the files, and file locks. Creating, deleting, and modifying the size of a file or its attributes updates the metadata. Because the VMFS is a cluster (distributed) file system, any update to the metadata requires locking the LUN on which the VMFS resides using a SCSI-2 Reservation. ESX uses the lock to synchronize data across all the ESX nodes accessing the VMFS.

The primary reason for a VMFS is the storage of VMDK files and VM swap files. These files are often out on shared storage, and therefore require not only the intrinsic features of the VMFS, but the clustering features, too. Other files also exist on a VMFS. Table 5.1 lists important file extensions, their use, and the version of ESX that uses them. A full list is available in Chapter 9, "Configuring ESX from a Virtual Center or Host."

Table 5.1

VMFS Files by Extension		
Extension	Usage	Notes
.dsk	VM disk file	Early versions of ESX
.vmdk	VM disk file	
.hlog	Log file formed by VMotion	Often left hanging around, safe to remove
.vswp	Virtual swap file	Per VM in ESX version 3, monolithic before version 3
.vmss	VM suspend file	
.vmtd	VM template disk files	Exported form of a VMDK (prior to version 3)
.vmtx	VM template configuration files	Prior to version 3 only
.REDO	Files produced when VM is in REDO mode	Should disappear on a commit
.vmx	VM configuration files	
.log	VM log files	
.nvram	Nonvolatile RAM file	

VMDK and VMFS Manipulation

VMFS volumes are managed by the VMkernel, but are also available from the service console. They are available from the /vmfs mount point, which is automatically created when VMFS volumes are added or created by ESX. The mount point is handy when working in the service console. However, normal Linux commands do no report anything about the mounted VMFS LUNs, so be sure to use the vdf command to see disk usage information, and the vmkfstools command to manage the VMFS volume(s). In addition, manipulating VMDKs using normal Linux could result in corrupt virtual disks. The safest way to move VMDKs from machine to machine is to either use secure copy or scp for transferring disk images from VMFS to VMFS or first export the VMDK or convert it to the 2Gb sparse disk type. The 2Gb sparse VMDK type is safe to move using any Linux-based tool. 2Gb sparse VMDK files can be executed within the VMkernel from an NFS volume on ESX version 3. The following is the way to convert to 2Gb sparse files:

```
ESX 2.5.x: vmkfstools -e /vmfs/vmhbaX:Y:Z/file.vmdk /tmp/file.vmdk

ESX 3: vmkfstools -i /vmfs/volumes/VOLUMENAME/file.vmdk -d 2gbsparse
➥/tmp/file.vmdk
```

In addition, it's simple to create a VMFS from the command line. First, it is important to remember that there is a basic rule of one VMFS per LUN due to the way ESX invokes SCSI-2 Reservations. See Chapter 8, "Configuring ESX from a Host Connection," for information about creating VMFS volumes from the command line, but for performance reasons it is best to use the VIC to create a VMFS because it provides 64KB track-boundary alignment.

Best Practice for VMDK Movement

Use scp to move VMDKs from VMFS on one host to VMFS on another host.

To move VMDKs to a non-VMFS location, convert the VMDK to a 2Gb sparse file first. Then use any tool to move the resultant VMDK files.

VMFS Types

The VM file system has gone through three forms (see Table 5.2) and has been designed to optimize VM runtime. The VMFS is a clustered file system shared among ESX Servers.

Table 5.2

Virtual Machine File System Differences	
VMFS Type	**Notes**
VMFS-1	No directory structure, limited files per VMFS, public access mode
VMFS-2	No directory structure, configuration files stored on boot storage device, BFS supported, public and shared access modes, raw disk map support, enhanced to support multiple ESX servers
VMFS-3	Directory structure, configuration, and vSwap files stored with VM disk file, public access mode only enhanced to support multiple ESX servers

Structure of VMFS

VMFS contains a header of the VMware file system metadata that includes all the attributes for the VMFS volume and holds the files within the volume. When a metadata update is required, the VMkernel of the ESX Server places a nonpersistent SCSI-2 Reservation on the complete VMFS volume, which creates a lock until the operation is completed. This is essential to keep other ESX Servers accessing the same VMFS volume from updating the metadata while another update is happening, which prevents metadata corruption, which is necessary for any clustered file system. The VMFS metadata attributes include the size, type, and extents of the VMFS, and information about each file. The file attributes within the metadata are a files types, permissions, ownerships, access and modification times, sizes, names, locations within the VMFS, or if a raw disk map (RDM), a direct pointer to the LUN location. After the metadata are the actual files and directories within the VMFS. The overall VMFS layout is shown in Figure 5.7.

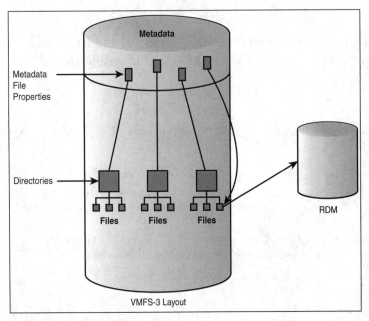

Figure 5.7   VMFS layout

VMFS Accessibility Modes

For ESX versions earlier than version 3, there are two types of VMFS access modes, which define how the ESX Servers may access the VMFS and files in the volume. The two types of access modes in are public and shared, and it is important to understand the difference between these modes. VMFS-1 used public mode exclusively because only a single ESX Server would be accessing the VMFS volume, and so the file read/writes locked the whole volume. With VMFS-2, public mode has enhanced the locking algorithm that allows multiple ESX Servers to access the VMFS volume in an atomic mode by only locking at the file level during reads/writes. In shared access mode, the VMFS is in read-only mode, where the VMkernel controls file accesses. Public mode locks the entire VMFS only during a metadata update. With ESX version 3, shared access mode goes away, leaving only public access mode. Because the shared access mode was exclusively available for VMDKs used as shared disks of clustered VMs, a new shared-disk mechanism is available with ESX version 3. That is the use of RDMs.

Raw Disk Maps

RDMs provide VMs direct access to the underlying LUN presented by remote storage, either iSCSI or SAN. RDMs either use a physical mode, where the VM controls all access and ESX places the virtual SCSI adapters in pass through mode, or the ESX Server can manage the RDM, providing all the normal disk-level functionality, including snapshots and other virtual disk modes. The latter occurs only if the RDM is a virtual RDM.

SCSI Pass Thru

Similar to RDMs in physical mode, SCSI pass thru mode allows a VM direct access to any SCSI device attached to the ESX Server. The main use is to gain access to a tape device. For this to happen, the SCSI host adapter is assigned to the VM for ESX versions earlier than version 3. Tape devices are only supported using Adaptec SCSI host adapters. Fibre Channel tape devices are accessible through Fibre Channel switches and are presented like any LUN.

VMFS Error Conditions

ESX VMFSs can have several error conditions that are important to understand. Understanding the causes of these errors will help to govern how to implement ESX with remote storage. Some of the error conditions do not actually point to a problem on the ESX Server, but they will nonetheless cause problems on ESX and need to be addressed at the SAN and ESX Server levels. All these errors will show up in the /var/log/vmkwarning file, or via the MUI under the Options tab and its System Logs link (for ESX versions earlier than version 3). For ESX versions earlier than version 3, when using the MUI, this is the first of the system logs shown. What follows in the rest of this section is a breakdown of the common errors, their implications, and steps to alleviate them. With ESX version 3, the VMFS non-VM I/O is throttled in an attempt to alleviate any of these conditions.

SCSI: 24/0

This is just a warning and usually ignorable. It implies that there was a delay in the SCSI Reservation request and the request was reissued. As the advanced option scsiconflictretries increases from the default to the maximum suggested of 20, the number of these messages will increase. Only increase this value if you see SCSI Reservation conflicts and there are no other ways to alleviate them. A full discussion of SCSI Reservation conflicts follows. The default value for ESX versions earlier than version 3 is four; the default value for ESX version 3 is eight.

SCSI: 24/7

This is a SCSI Reservation conflict. See the section "0xbad0023" for more details.

SCSI: 2/0

This message implies that the SCSI subsystem is experiencing a BUSY WAIT condition. The common case is by exhausting the FC HBA Q Depth for the LUN. Either that or the SAN/iSCSI server is very busy and so there are pending SCSI requests that are delayed. Increasing the Q Depth for the FC HBA can alleviate pending requests. If the problem persists, there could be an issue with an overload of the cache on the storage device.

SCSI: 0/1

This message implies that the SCSI subsystem could not connect to the previously specified LUN.

SCSI: 0/4

This message implies that the SCSI subsystem is trying to reach a previously defined LUN but now considers the target LUN to be a bad target. This error could be caused by the array suddenly going offline or the LUN no longer being available.

SCSI: 0/7

This message implies that the SCSI subsystem is experiencing an internal error, which could be related to any of the other 0xbadXXXX conditions. This message often appeared for SCSI Reservation conflicts, but has been replaced with 24/7 error discussed earlier.

0xbad0010

This message implies that the SCSI subsystem has I/O errors and usually points to hardware issues and not ESX Server issues. In some cases, these errors will appear if the Fibre fabric is overloaded and needs rebalancing between paths. The action that received this message will abort and would need a reissue.

0xbad0023

This message implies that there were SCSI Reservation conflicts. Reception of this message implies cancellation of the operation on the LUN. The conflict message happens when the `scsiconflictretries` setting is exhausted, but before the 0xbad0023 error appears and the operation is cancelled, many `SCSI: 24/0` messages will appear. SCSI Reservation is the name for the SCSI-2 locking that occurs within ESX whenever modification of the VMFS metadata occurs. The metadata of the VMFS holds the properties of all the files on the file system, including that for each file the name, size, access, and modification times, permissions, owner, and group names.

A SCSI Reservation occurs whenever there is a request to update the metadata of a VMFS with new information or modification of old information. These reservations will lock the entire LUN, and although the standard states that a SCSI-2 Reservation can lock an extent or partition, it is important to realize that in ESX it requests a lock of the entire LUN. Because multiple machines can update the metadata per LUN at any time, these reservation requests can occur quite often and at the same time (and thus the possibility of SCSI Reservation conflicts occurs). Each reservation request that occurs will, once accepted, take anywhere from 1 millisecond to 12 milliseconds to complete, with an average of 7 milliseconds. Some operations take only 1 to 2 milliseconds from SCSI Reservation request, acceptance, and release. These fast operations are generally ones that change permissions, access and modification times, owner, and group names. All other operations generally lock the LUN for 7 milliseconds.

Operation changes are often the only ways to alleviate a SCSI Reservation conflict. To do so, it is best to understand what can cause them. Because SCSI Reservations are issued only for those items that modify the metadata of the VMFS, there is a definitive list of operations that can cause these. REDO mode refers to the creation of snapshots (-delta.vmdk files) and the traditional REDO mode.

That list is as follows:

- When a file is first created.
- When a file is deleted.
- When a VMDK is placed into REDO mode, specifically a SCSI Reservation is required for the REDO file when it is first created and every time the REDO log size is increased. This size increase happens in 15MB chunks.
- When a 2Gb sparse or thin-formatted VMDK changes size on a VMFS, the size increase happens in 15MB chunks. If a 2Gb sparse or thin-formatted VMDK resides on an NFS partition, no SCSI-2 Reservation is made, only an NFS lock.
- When the VMDK is migrated, two reservations are actually required: one on the source system, and one on the target to make sure the files do not change in the middle of an operation, whether via a hot migration (VMotion) or a cold migration. Conflicts can cause the VMotion to fail outright.
- When the VMDK is suspended because there is a suspend file written.

- When the VMDK is in nonpersistent mode because there is a REDO log created that will be removed when the VM is shutdown, and then for every 16MB added to the REDO log.

- When the VMDK is created via a template. If the template also resides on a VMFS, there is a SCSI Reservation for the source and also one for the target so that the template does not get destroyed in the middle of a deployment.

- When a template is created from a VMDK. If the template target is also on a VMFS, there is a SCSI Reservation every 16MB for the target and a single lock for the source. The source SCSI Reservation is to ensure that the VMDK is not modified as it is made into a template.

- When the VMDK is exported.

- When the file system is modified via `fdisk` or similar disk-manipulation tools run from the service console.

- When `vm-support` is run from the service console.

- When running `vdf` from the service console after a modification to the file system is made. This is a nonexclusive reservation.

- When a file on the VMFS has its ownership, permissions, access times, or modification times changed.

- When a file on the VMFS changes its size, a reservation is requested every 15MB.

- When a LUN is first attached to ESX.

The problem is not only an issue of a SCSI Reservation conflict, but the time it takes to return a status that the reservation request is good. SCSI Reservation requests are immediately handled by all arrays, but it could take up to 200ms for the status to be reported back to ESX. Running a Fibre analyzer against an array leads to the results shown in the rest of this section.

Here the reservation request was issued, and 70ms later there was a response to the ESX Server. The time for this type of situation ranges from 1ms to 120ms. There is no way currently available to predict the exact time a lock request will report back to ESX.

```
00:30.243_596_192,SCSI Cmd = Reserve(6); LUN = 0000; FCP_DL = 00000000; ,00,4AD8
00:30.313_070_422,SCSI Status = Good; ,,4AD8
70ms response on lock.
```

Here the reservation release request was issued, and .340ms later the array responded to the ESX Server:

```
00:30.313_652_818,SCSI Cmd = Release(6); LUN = 0000; FCP_DL = 00000000; ,00,4B20
00:30.313_922_280,SCSI Status = Good; ,,4B20
.340 ms response on lock release.
```

Here is a case in which two locks were requested at the same time from differ-ent machines. There is a 107ms lock response delay, which results in a SCSI Reservation conflict. This will exhaust the scsiconflictretries setting of 20 and result in a SCSI Reservation conflict within ESX, and the operation on the LUN metadata will fail outright.

```
00:31.955_514_678,FC_i7 1,SCSI Cmd = Reserve(6); LUN = 0000; FCP_DL = 00000000; ,00,2630
00:32.015_103_122,FC_i6 3,SCSI Cmd = Reserve(6); LUN = 0000; FCP_DL = 00000000; ,00,30F8
00:32.015_391_568,FC_i6 4,SCSI Status = Resv Cnft; ,,30F8
00:32.062_289_994,FC_i7 2,SCSI Status = Good; ,,2630
107ms for Lock response.
```

0xbad0004

Although not the last, this error implies that the LUN is busy and cannot handle the request submitted. In general, this could occur if the Fibre Channel queue depth is too small or there is an issue with the fabric or array.

Storage Checklist

Now that you understand storage hardware and concerns, it is possible to formu-late a checklist for the use of storage with ESX. SANs, iSCSI, and NAS are truly complementary technologies to virtualization, providing increased flexibility in addition to what VMs already offer. After presentation of storage to the server by the storage administrator (SAN, iSCSI, or NFS), ESX does not need any other changes to manage the LUNs. A benefit of remote storage is that it provides the capability to create any amount of storage for all ESX Servers to share and dis-perse workloads evenly and effectively. The benefits include provisioning VMs from template, convenient backup and disaster recovery, boot from SAN or iSCSI for various environments, providing storage for diskless environments, and pro-viding a common storage interface needed for clustering using SCSI reservations.

Having NAS, iSCSI, or SANs being able to traverse long distances means that ESX Servers from many locations can access the same data store. There is also an advantage to spreading storage and backup server to many different facilities because doing so can also reduce the risk of disasters. When VM disks and config-uration files are stored on a remote data store, any VM can run on any host and have the capability to migrate to another host at will. Discussion of these possibilities occurs in later chapters. However, one of the main drawbacks of remote storage is the lack of standardization with SAN and NAS technologies. Granted, SCSI and iSCSI are standards, but the implementation by vendors is by no means standard. Just look at SCSI-2 Reservation request response times. No standard governs how fast these need to be. Each array has different mechanisms to control the storage, so VMware is continuously working to validate as much storage vendor equipment as possible. Table 5.3 presents a checklist to follow when using remote storage with ESX.

Table 5.3

Storage Checklist	
Element	**Comments**
Storage arrays	Determine supportability of the array by finding the make and model on the SAN compatibility guide. This includes iSCSI devices. If the SAN is not in the ESX storage compatibility matrix, do not use it.
Firmware	Verify the minimum firmware levels recommended by the storage vendor. This includes any switch and FC HBA or iSCSI TOE HBA firmware.
Multipathing (SAN)	There is no specialized multipath software for ESX. When there is more than one active SP for ESX, there is the capability to zone through multiple HBAs by the array. ESX cannot perform this zoning. Be sure not to zone through multiple HBAs on the same ESX server because there is only an active/passive array. Be aware of the limited number of targets ESX can "see," and know that multipathing counts against the target limit.
LUN masking	Mask all LUNs at the storage level. Use the ESX LUN masking only if necessary. Never mask off LUN 0.
Switches	Outside of ensuring the proper level of firmware for a switch concerning an array, there is nothing to consider from an ESX perspective.
Cabling	Ensure cabling is performed to avoid LUN thrashing, which occurs when an active HBA is connected to a passive storage processor when there are only two paths to an array (multipath fabric). In four-path configurations, this is not a big issue (redundant fabric).
HBA (FC/iSCSI)	Verify the supportability of the HBA by reviewing the I/O compatibility guide. If an HBA is not in the compatibility matrix, do *not* use it.
Clustering	ESX version 3 requires remote storage for an RDM for *all* shared disk clusters. Ensure there is enough LUN to support this. Also confirm that the array supports clustering by looking at the HCL. In addition, shared disk clusters require the boot volume of the VM to be on local storage.
Storage processors	Understand which storage processors are active and passive and how they are zoned and presented to ESX.
RAID level	Ensure a LUN is at the proper RAID level. RAID 5 or ADG are generally best.

Element	Comments
Connection type	When presenting to ESX, a SAN will need the proper connection type, which is a value used during LUN presentation. This information is available from the SAN vendor.
Limitations	Review and understand all limitations from the storage compatibility matrix and from the storage vendor.
Shared HBA	For ESX versions earlier than version 3, will the FC HBA be shared between the SC and the VMs? Remember that shared FC HBA is mutually exclusive with cluster support for ESX versions earlier than version 3.
Access	Record the WWPN or network IP and netmask for the ESX server for use by the storage device.
ESX	Verify the patch level and configuration of ESX against the storage compatibility matrix for the remote storage device in use.
Storage topology	When formulating a storage topology design, consider all forms of available storage and LUN sizes for ESX: SAN, iSCSI, local storage, direct attach storage, NAS, SATA usage, and so on.
VMotion	Which LUNs are visible to which servers.
LUN 0	Is there a LUN 0 or controlling LUN associated with the storage device? This can affect BFS. In addition, this LUN is always presented to every host.
Control	Who controls the storage device? Ensure there are clear lines of communication.
Documentation	Is there supporting documentation for re-creating the ESX environment as needed? Include diagrams highlighting any possible single points of failure.
Space	Are there enough LUNs and LUN space for business continuity and disaster recovery? See Chapter 12 for full details.

Assessing Storage and Space Requirements

When considering what ESX storage needs may be, many people look past the assessment of their VM requirements and concentrate only on the storage product suite. The question is, from where are the VMs going to run and therefore be stored? When designing an ESX storage infrastructure from the ground up, or utilizing an existing storage implementation, it is vital to categorize and validate the storage on which to run VMs. Even though the perception of how important an organization's VMs are depends upon criticality, performance, availability, or DR requirements, this same information will assist in determining what storage design will be appropriate.

It is best to perform an unbiased poll for each VM's requirements as to the criticality of the applications that are running. How fast does this VM need to perform? Will this VM need point-in-time recovery? How does this VM need to be backed up? Would this VM ever need to be replicated? By collecting this data about the VM that will be running today, tomorrow, and down the road, the data will aid in answering these important questions:

- Is the current storage configuration acceptable, and if so what limitations may be expected, or is all new storage required to accomplish your goal?
- What level of storage will meet all virtualization goals, and which storage solution is most cost-effective?

One problem is over time the level of storage may change due to technology advances; in addition, your VM requirements may change as applications become less or more important, and therefore storage will also change. In addition, peak storage needs could be different depending on what is running, specifically back-ups. This can be a difficult task because many VMs accessing a VMFS have varied peak characterization attributes to optimize your storage access. The more VMs accessing a VMFS, the greater the possibility of high I/O contention leading to performance degradation. A suggestion to manage possible I/O contention is to create LUNs or volumes that separate test, development, template storage, and production.

A topic that is certain to appear when configuring storage for ESX Servers is the size of the LUN. Should the VMs use many small LUNs or a few large LUNs?

The claims made in support of many smaller LUNs or volumes center around the idea that with more LUNs per ESX Server, there is an increase in the number of simultaneous actions (thus possibly reducing the number of SCSI Reservations). Small LUNs equate to less wasted space when managing the SAN. Different types of application may require different levels of RAID, so you may need specific LUNs for these scenarios. If you need to use clusters across ESX Servers, these will need their own LUNs for quorum and data access.

The claims made for support of fewer, larger LUNs for VMFS are based on the idea that a SAN administrator can create large LUNs to provision disk space ahead of time, which allows the ESX Server administrator to use the space as desired. An advantage of fewer LUNs is the reduction of the amount of heap used by the server to manage many LUNs. If there are fewer LUNs to view, you have less to worry about concerning tne visibility of LUNs due to zoning or LUN masking policies. Also, with a large VMFSs, there is the freedom to resize virtual disks to larger sizes and use delta/REDO files.

It is common to have a difficult time choosing whether to use big or small LUNs. It is important to characterize the VMs to choose to go with many small

LUNs or just a few large LUNs. Consider testing the VMs in both scenarios, and collect some data that will assist in deciding which size LUN to use for production. First, choose a sample set of applications from the production environment.

For one testing data store, create a large LUN with RAID 5 or RAID 1+0 and make sure it is write-cache enabled. Format the VMFS-2 or -3, as appropriate, on this LUN, and deploy three virtual disks, and monitor the disk performance on the data store. If all is running well, increase the number of virtual disk files by three more, and continue to monitor disk performance while running the appropriate applications within the VM. Continue to add virtual disk files until there is an unacceptable level of application performance. This will flesh out a threshold as to how many virtual disks with the chosen applications running in them. It is possible to have up to 32 lightweight VMs, meaning very low resource-consuming VMs, or 10 heavyweight VMs with high-resource usage.

On the other test data store with many small LUNs or volumes, create many small LUNs with various storage characteristics and format a VMFS-2 or -3 in each LUN, and be sure to label each LUN with its respective characteristic. Place each virtual disk file in the VMFS appropriately configured for the application the VM is running, and again monitor disk usage. Add VM disk files once more to find the threshold.

A third test is whether VMFS extents can be used to gather a bunch of smaller LUNs into one large LUN. Although extents allow multiple LUNs to be part of a single VMFS, there are issues when trying to remove an extent. However, this is also a valid test for comparison with the other two mechanisms. Yet, the extent size should be at least the common size of a VMDK.

How big a LUN is, is a fundamental question of storage, and unfortunately not easily answered because the answer is a moving target based on VM resource utilization. The method outline previously is one method to try. The next big question is how many VMs to place on each LUN, and this can also define LUN size. If each VM is 200GB, for example, the size of the LUN could be rather large and still accommodate only a few VMs. Five VMs implies at least 1TB of storage for a given LUN. This number is a minimum, because the following should also be part of any consideration: the size of REDO logs, snapshots (ESX version 3 only), VMotion logs, vSwap (ESX version 3 only), VM log files (ESX version 3 only), suspend files, and so on. Table 5.1 shows all the possible files. Consider the sizes of all these files when sizing a LUN. Although five 200GB VMs may be possible on a 1TB LUN, it might be better to only place 3VMs on this LUN to accommodate all the other files. Use the checklist presented in Table 5.4 to size LUNs.

Table 5.4

LUN Size Checklist		
Element	Common Size/ Value	Notes
Performance threshold	None	This is the results of the tests defined previously.
Default size of individual VMDKs	None	Calculate based on the real values. Many implementations standardize on a single VMDK size and always use increments of that size.
RDM size	None	An RDM will use a slot in the VMFS table of contents but take up no other VMFS space. Many implementations choose a default lower limit with which to decide whether a VMDK should actually be an RDM. Anything over 200GB is common.
REDO log size	15MB increments	The longer a VM is in REDO mode, the larger this file becomes. Undoable VMs are always in REDO mode for the life of the VM. Monitor the size of REDO files created for each VMDK backup.
Snapshot file size	15MB increments	A snapshot is an improved form of a REDO file that creates a point-in-time copy of memory, disk, and settings. In addition, it is now possible to choose from which snapshot to start processing. The longer the runtime of a snapshot dictates the size of the file.
VM configuration file	2K	There are two per VM for ESX version 3 if the VM configuration file is stored with the VMDK.
VMDK configuration file	.5K	There is one VMDK configuration file per VMDK for ESX version 3 stored with the VMDK.
vSwap file	Size of VM Memory	There is always one per VM, the size of the VM memory, for ESX version 3, and it is usually stored with the VMDK.
NVRAM file	8K	There is one NVRAM file per VM for ESX version 3 usually stored with the VMDK.
VM log file	20K Minimum	The VM log file can be any size from 20K to the largest file allowed on the file system. This file can remain less than 100K, and there are up to seven of them. If there is a problem, this log file can grow to gigabytes very quickly.
Snapshot configuration file	.5K	There is usually one file per VM.
VMotion log file	.5K	There is one file per VMotion.

It is important to realize that most of the values used are based entirely on the environment being modeled. There is only one hard-and-fast rule: The more VMFS there are, the more actions that can happen simultaneously, as described in

Chapter 6, "Effects on Operations."

Example of LUN Sizing

As an example, let's review the following possible configuration. In the nonvirtualized world, each of 12 servers has 2GB of memory and 200GB of hard disk space allocated per machine. However, when the usage statistics for the hosts were uncovered, it was discovered that only 512MB of memory and 20GB of disk space were actually used. From Table 5.4, the static size of a VM's disk usage is around 31.5KB of disk space. Because the limit on the memory was only 512MB, we may want to only allocate that much memory for the VM so that a vSwap file would be created of that size. Then, because the disk usage is 20GB, it might be wise to start off with 25GB VMs. The math leads to 25GB + 512MB + 31.5KB of necessary disk space, or roughly 25.6GB. However, it has been decided that snapshots will be used and that two snapshots will be necessary for recovery purposes. This implies that now at most 25.6GB * 3 or 76.8GB of space will now be required per VM. If a snapshot memory image will be required, an addition 1GB of space is required. With 12 VMs, the total required disk space is now 933.6GB.

The next decision point is whether to keep all 12 VMs on the same LUN. The suggested answer is *no*, which implies using less disk space per LUN. Assuming it was decided to split the 12 VMs between 2 LUNs, each LUN could be .5TB or some value greater than or equal to 466.8GB. Increasing this value to 512GB gives some leeway for increasing memory and increasing a VMDK file or adding another VMDK as necessary to a VM.

In this example, it is important to realize what the minimums are and increase that value to allow for future growth of the VM. For ESX versions earlier than version 3, it is important to realize that there is a set limit on the number of files per LUN; that limit is 192 plus 32 files per additional extent. Assuming there are at least 6 files per VM (1 VMotion log file, 1 suspend file, 2 VMDKs, 2 REDO), there is a maximum of 32 VMs allowed per VMFS.

Storage-Specific Issues

Some of the most common storage issues encountered while using ESX are discussed in this section, as are several solutions. There are usually three ways to address each storage problem; however, the most useful happens to be the use of the service console or command line. Although not a definitive list of issues, they are common. Most storage solutions will use the `vmkfstools` command-line tool.

`vmkfstools` is the VMDK and VMFS management tool for the command line to create, modify, or delete VMDKs, RDMs, VMFS, and vSwap files (for those ESX versions that need them created).

Increasing the Size of a VMDK

There are mixed feelings about the need to increase VMDK sizes when it is easily possible to add a new virtual disk to a VM, and with ESX version 3 it is possible to add a VMDK on-the-fly while the VM is running from the Virtual Infrastructure Client. Earlier versions of ESX required the VM to be shut down prior to VMDK addition. To change the size of a VMDK, you must shut down the VM. Note that changing the size of the VMDK does *not* change the size of the file system or systems held within the VMDK. Resizing a VMDK is extremely dangerous, and in most cases should never happen. Add a new VMDK instead, or create a new VMDK and copy the contents from the old to the larger using the standard VM OS tools.

As an example, let's look at a VMDK holding an NTFS for the Windows 2003 OS used by the VM. Because this VM has one file system and it is the C: partition, the OS does not necessarily allow the resizing of this partition directly. A third-party tool will be required to do so, such as DiskPart, which must be used from other boot media. That aside, the command to use to resize the VMDK follows. Note that it is also possible to shrink a VMDK, which *will* destroy data. Any use of the following commands is risky and should only be performed if you can safely answer this question:

Are you satisfied with your backup?

If you can answer yes to the preceding question, proceed. Otherwise, do not, because these commands are destructive.

```
vmkfstools -X xxG /vmfs/vmhbaC:T:L:P/yyyyy.vmdk
```

Note that xx is the number of gigabytes to which to set the size of the VMDK, and yyyyy is the name of the VMDK to manipulate. If xx is less than the original size of the VMDK, it is possible to shrink the VMDK, and that would result in data loss. ESX version 3 prevents the shrinking of files. The next step is to boot from a virtual floppy or CD-ROM that contains DiskPart or equivalent utility and manipulate the VMDK partitions by either increasing the size of the original partition or by creating secondary partitions. However, if creation of secondary partitions is to be performed, it is much safer and recommended that a new VMDK be created instead. If the OS within the VM supports some form of logical volume or dynamic disk technology, however, it is possible to add the new partition to the existing file system. Linux has this capability for its partitions, whereas Windows has this functionality only for nonboot partitions or C: drives.

Increasing the Size of a VMFS

Like increasing the size of a VMDK, increasing the size of a VMFS should be approached with care. It general, the recommendation is *not* to resize a VMFS, but instead to create a new VMFS and copy over all the files from one to another, or even better, use multiple VMFSs to increase the number of simultaneous operations. To increase a VMFS, first the LUN size must be increased, but this does not automatically increase the size of the VMFS; however, it does allow multiple partitions on the LUN to be created. But, because there is a rule of one VMFS per LUN, doing this will cause contention and therefore performance issues. ESX does have the means to logically increase the size of the VMFS by extending a VMFS across multiple LUNs, referred to as extents. However, using extents also has some drawbacks; for ESX versions earlier than version 3, the use of extents adds only 32 more files to the VMDK, no matter the size of the extent added. Deleting an extent often results in massive data loss.

Adding Extents

To add an extent, use the MUI for ESX versions earlier than version 3 by selecting the extent to add while reviewing the properties of the VMFS to which to add the extent or by using the VIC for ESX versions 3. With ESX version 3 and the VIC, review the VMFS properties in question, and then use the Add Extent Wizard.

Deleting Extents

Do not delete an extent unless you can first answer the following question:

Are you satisfied with your backup?

If you can answer yes to the preceding question, proceed. Deleting an extent is destructive. There are two ways to delete an extent. The first is to remove presentation of the underlying LUN of the extent, and the second is to perform a complex chain of actions using the DiskMaskLUN advanced setting for ESX versions earlier than version 3 (which does *not* work for ESX version 3). These actions are as follows:

1. Determine the LUN to delete from the extent.
2. Record the current values of the DiskMaskLUN advanced option.

3. Set the DiskMaskLUN advanced option to include the LUN or LUNs to delete from the extent. Apply the advanced option.

4. Rescan the Fibre Channel and revisit the VMFS in question using the MUI.

5. Set the DiskMaskLUN back to what was recorded.

6. Rescan the Fibre Channel.

7. Now it is safe to delete or manipulate the LUN in question because it is now an independent VMFS and LUN.

Searching for New LUNs

To search for new LUNs presented to the ESX Server, just use the Rescan buttons in the MUI or the VIC. However, sometimes this does not work for ESX versions earlier than version 3, and then it is the work of a command line command to do so. The command is explained for version 3 and earlier versions in the following sections.

ESX Version 3

The C in the following command implies the controller to rescan listed when running the command esxcfg-vmhbadevs. If the controller was not used prior to the rescan, finding the controller is based on extrapolating the results of the esxcfg-vmhbadevs command results:

```
esxcfg-rescan vmhbaC
```

ESX Versions Earlier Than Version 3

The C in the following command implies the controller. The controller number can be found using the vmkmultipath -q command:

```
cos-rescan vmhbaC
```

VMFS Created on One ESX Server Not Appearing on Another

In some cases, a VMFS does not appear on all ESX Servers when a rescan is issued. This common storage problem is not really an ESX issue but could be related to the advanced options DiskMaskLUN or DiskMaxLUN settings. If the LUN to be presented is greater than eight, it is related to DiskMaxLUN. If DiskMaxLUN and DiskMaskLUN are set properly, it is related to how the LUN is zoned or presented, and that points directly to the storage array and the WWID

(World Wide ID) and WWPN (World Wide Port Number) used in zoning and presentation. It is possible to find the WWPN of all the ESX Servers by visiting the Storage Controllers buttons and tabs in the VIC (see Figure 5.8) or MUI (see Figure 5.9) to relay this information to the storage array administrators.

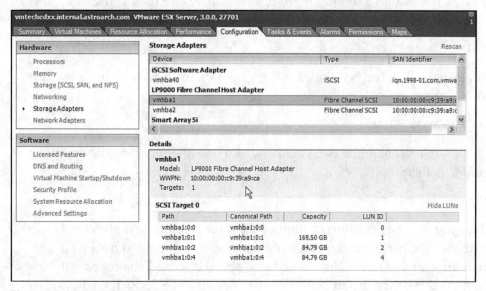

Figure 5.8   WWPN via VIC

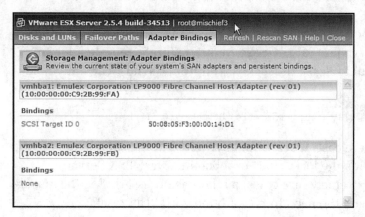

Figure 5.9   WWPN via MUI

How to Unlock a LUN

In some cases, when attempting to manipulate a VMDK the result is that there is a lock imposed by another host and the action cannot occur. Remember from our initial discussion on SCSI Reservation conflicts that a lock is imposed on the entire LUN, not just on a single file. To reset the LUN and release the lock, run the following command:

```
vmkfstools -L lunreset vmhbaC:T:L:0
```

To verify the lock has been released, get the lock info on the volume by running this:

```
vmkfstools -D vmhbaC:T:L:P
```

It is possible to chain the two commands on one line separating them with a semicolon, as follows:

```
vmkfstools -L lunreset vmhbaC:T:L:0; vmkfstools -D vmhbaC:T:L:P
```

The C implies the controller, T implies the track or path, L implies the LUN, and P implies the partition number. Note that the first command uses 0 for the partition number to address the whole LUN, and the second command will have a partition to address the extent or VMFS only. Because ESX locks the whole LUN when it performs SCSI Reservations, it is never suggested to have more than one partition per LUN for a VMFS, so the P should always be 1 in this case. The only exception to this is a VMFS on a local SCSI controller that does not have the same locking issues, because they can never be shared. Assuming that when trying to manipulate the file /vmfs/vmhba1:0:1:1/test.vmdk a failure is reported due to locking, the following would release the locks if run from the host currently holding the lock:

```
vmkfstools -L lunreset vmhba1\:0\:1\:0; vmkfstools -D vmhba1\:0\:1\:1
```

There is no method to release a lock from anywhere but the command line of the host that currently holds the lock, short of rebooting every ESX Server attached to the LUN. In extremely rare cases, a reboot is necessary. See the discussion in Chapter 6 to alleviate the need to play around with LUN resets.

Boot from SAN or iSCSI

Although boot from iSCSI is not currently supported but available using an iSCSI-HBA, there is a chance that it will be supported shortly after this book arrives.

However, boot from SAN and boot from iSCSI share similar issues. As previously mentioned, ESX locks the entire LUN when operating upon the metadata of a VMFS, and because at least one VMFS will be available when BFS is enabled, it is vitally important that the disk layout for the boot device *not* include a VMFS. If this happens, an operation on the VMFS will also lock the file systems for the console operating system and ESX generally becomes unstable. To alleviate this problem, always make sure there are at least two LUNs available for BFS. The first is private to the host in question and is the boot LUN; the second is the LUN to use for VMFS.

The BFS configuration is not recommended for ESX versions earlier than version 3 because of the need to share the Fibre Channel between the service console and the VMs, which results in unstable results. One way to alleviate this is to make sure there are two active SAN controllers and to zone each LUN through different active controllers. The result is separate control, with each controller responsible for either the service console or the VMs but never both.

In odd cases with those arrays that have a controlling LUN 0 that must be presented to every host attached to the SAN, it might be necessary to have three LUNs mapped to the host (LUN 0 and two others) to even install ESX versions earlier than version 3.

Conclusion

With careful planning and diligence, it is possible to have a very strong SAN-, iSCSI-, or NFS-based storage network for ESX Server. The key to all this is understanding how storage works within ESX to help plan around any issues that could occur. This chapter complements the storage whitepapers provided by VMware on their documentation website. The next chapter reviews some operational concerns to assist in better planning of the virtualized storage network.

Chapter 6

Effects on Operations

ESX creates a myriad of problems for administrators, specifically problems having to do with the scheduling of various operations around the use of normal tools and other everyday activities such as deployments, VMotion to balance nodes, and backups. Most, if not all, the limitations revolve around issues related to performance gathering and the data stores upon which VMs are placed, whether SCSI, including iSCSI, or non-VMDK files accessed from NFS shared off a NAS or some other system.

The performance-gathering issues dictate which tools to use to gather performance data and how to use the tools that gather this data. A certain level of understanding is required to interpret the results, and this knowledge will assist in balancing the VMs across multiple ESX Servers.

The data store limitations consist of bandwidth issues; each has a limited pipe between the ESX Server and the remote storage and reservation or locking issues. These two issues dictate quite a bit how ESX should be managed. As discussed in Chapter 5, "Storage with ESX," SCSI reservations will occur whenever the metadata of the VMFS is changed and the reservation happens for the whole LUN and not an extent of the LUN. This also dictates the layout of VMFS on each LUN; specifically, a VMFS should take up a whole LUN and not a part of the LUN.

This chapter covers data store performance or bandwidth issues, SCSI-2 reservation issues, and performance-gathering agents, and then finishes with some other issues and a discussion of the impact of Sarbanes-Oxley. Note that some of the solutions discussed within this chapter are utopian and not easy to implement within large-scale ESX environments. These are documented for completeness and to give information that will aid in debugging these common problems.

Data Store Performance or Bandwidth Issues

Because bandwidth is an issue, it is important to make sure that all your data stores have as much bandwidth as possible and to use this bandwidth sparingly for each data store. Normal operational behavior of a VM often includes such things as full disk virus scans, backups, spyware scans, and other items that are extremely disk-intensive activities. Although none of these activities will require any form of locking of the data store on which the VMDK resides, they all take a serious amount of bandwidth to accomplish. The bandwidth requirements for a single VM are not very large compared to an ESX Server with more VMs. Staggering the activities in time will greatly reduce the strain on the storage environment, but remember that staggering across ESX Servers is a good idea as long as different data stores are in use on each ESX Server. For example, it would cause locking issues for VMs that reside on the same LUN but different ESX Servers to be backed up at the same time. This should be avoided. However, virus scans will not cause many issues when done from multiple VMs on the same LUN from multiple ESX Servers, because operations on the VMDK do not cause locks at the LUN level. It is possible that running of disk-intensive tools within a VM could cause results similar to those that occur with SCSI Reservations, but are not reservations. Instead, they are load issues that cause the SAN or NAS to be overworked and therefore present failures similar to SCSI-2 Reservations.

Best Practice for Internal VM Operations
Stagger all disk-intensive operations internal to the VM over time and ESX hosts to reduce strain on the storage network.

SCSI–2 Reservation Issues

With the possibility of drastic failures during crucial operations, we need to understand how we can alleviate the possibility of SCSI Reservation conflicts. We can eliminate these issues by changing our operational behaviors to cover the possibility of failure. Although these practices are generally simple, they are nonetheless fairly difficult to implement unless all the operators and administrators know how to tell whether an operation is occurring, and whether the new operation would cause a SCSI Reservation conflict if it were implemented. This is where monitoring tools make the biggest impact. SCSI Reservation conflicts will be avoided if a simple rule is followed: Verify that any other operation has first completed on a given file, LUN, or set of LUNs before proceeding with the next operation.

> **Best Practice**
> Verify that any other operation has first completed on a given file, LUN, or set of LUNs before proceeding with the next operation.

To verify that any operation is in use, we need to perform all these operations using a similar management interface so that there is only one place to check. The use of Virtual Center or HPSIM with VMM will assist because it gives you one place to check for any operation that could cause a conflict. Verify in your management tool that all operations upon a given LUN or set of LUNs have been completed before proceeding with the next operation. In other words, serialize your actions per LUN or set of LUNs. In addition to checking your management tools, check the state of your backups and whether any current open service console operations have also completed. If a VMDK backup is running, let that take precedence and proceed with the next operation after the backup has completed. To check whether a backup is running, you can quickly look at the VMFS via the MUI or VIC to determine whether there are any REDO files out on the LUNs in question. If there are, either a backup is running or a backup has left a REDO file on the file system, which means the backup most likely failed for some reason. To check to see whether service console operations that could affect a LUN or set of LUNS have completed, judicious use of sudo is recommended. Sudo can log all your operations to a file that you can peruse and then you, as the administrator, can check the process lists for all servers. No user interface combines backups, VMotion, and service console actions.

As an example, let's look at a system of three ESX Servers with five identical LUNs presented to the servers via XP12000 storage. Because each of the three servers shares each LUN we need, we should limit our LUN activity to one operation per LUN at any given time. In this case, we could perform five operations simultaneously as long as those operations were LUN specific. Once LUN boundaries are crossed, the number of simultaneous operations drops. To illustrate the second case, consider a VM with two disk files, one for the C: drive and one for the D: drive. Normally in ESX, we would place the C: and D: drives on separate LUNs to improve performance, among other things. In this case, because the

C: and D: drives live on separate LUNs, manipulation of this VM, say with VMotion, counts as four simultaneous VM operations. This count is due to one operation affecting two LUNs. Therefore, five LUN operations could equate to fewer VM operations. This is the most careful of methods. However, instead of LUN, we can use FILE in many of these suggestions that follow, except where we are changing the metadata.

Using the preceding example as a basis, the suggested operational behaviors are as follows:

- Simplify deployments so that a VM does not span more than one LUN. In this way, operations on a VM are operations on a single LUN.

- Determine whether any operation is happening on the LUN you want to operate on. If your VM spans multiple LUNs, check the full set of LUNs by visiting the management tools in use and making sure that no other operation is happening on the LUN in question.

- Verify that there is no current backup operation happening and that the VM is not in REDO mode.

- Choose one ESX Server as your deployment server. In this way, it is easy to limit deployment operations, imports, or template creations to only one host and therefore one LUN at a time.

- Use a naming convention for VMs that also tells what LUN or LUNs are in use for the VM. This way it is easy to tell what LUN could be affected by VM operation. This is an idealistic solution to a problem, but at least label VMs as spanning LUNs.

- Inside VC or any other management tool, limit access to the administrative operations so that only those who know the process can actually enact an operation. In the case of VC only the administrative users should have any form of administrative privileges. All others should only have VM user or read-only privileges.

- Administrators should only be allowed to power on or off a VM. For reboots required by patch application, schedule each reboot so that there is only one reboot per LUN at any given time. A power-off and power-on are considered separate operations. However, there are more than just SCSI Reservation concerns with this case. For example, if you have 80 VMs across 4 hosts, rebooting all 80 at the same time would create a performance issue, and some of the VMs could fail to boot. The standard boot process for an ESX Server is to boot only the next VM after the VMware Tools are started, guaranteeing that there is no initial performance issue. The necessary time of the lock for a power-on or -off operation is less than 7 microseconds, so many can be done in the span of a minute. However, this is not recommended because the increase in load on ESX could adversely affect your other VMs. Limiting this is a wise move from a performance viewpoint.

- Use care when scheduling VMDK-level backups. It is best to have one host schedule all backups and to have one script to start backups on all other hosts. In this way, backups can be serialized per LUN. For ESX version 3, this problem is solved by using the VMware Consolidated Backup tool. However, for ESX versions 2.5.x and earlier, use the built-in ESX tool, vmsnap_all, to start a backup, or use the vmsnap_all tool to serialize all activities per VM and LUN. This is discussed further in Chapter 12, "Disaster Recovery and Backup." Using the following pseudo-code may assist with backups where ssh-keygen was employed to make SSH not require a password be entered. By having one host and only one ESX Server run the following, you are guaranteed a serialized action for each backup regardless of the number of LUNs in use. In addition, third-party tools such as ESXRanger can serialize backups:

```
for x in $hosts
   do
      for y in $vms
      do
        ssh $x vmsnap.pl $y &
      done
   done
```

This pseudo-code demonstrates for ESX version 2.5.x and earlier releases that we can also change the behavior so more than one backup can occur simultaneously as long each VM in the list of VMs in $vms has all its disks on a single separate LUN. If you go with this approach, it is better for performance reasons to have each ESX Server doing backups on a different LUN at any given time. For example, our three machines can each do a backup using a separate LUN. Even so, the activity is still controlled by only *one* host so that there is no mix up or issue with timing. Let the backup process limit and tell you what it is doing. Find tools that will:

- Never start another backup on a LUN while another is still running.
- Signal the administrators that backups have finished either via e-mail, message board, or pager(s). This way there is less to check per operation.

- Limit VMotion (hot migrations), fast migrates, and cold migrations to one per LUN. If you must do a huge number of VMotion migrations at the same time, limit this to one per LUN. With our example there are five LUNs, so there would be the possibility of five simultaneous VMotions, each on its own LUN, at any time. This assumes the VMs do not cross LUN boundaries. VMotion needs to be fast, and the more you attempt to do VMotions at the same time, the slower all will become. There is a chance that the OS inside the VM will start to complain if this time lag is too great. Using VMotion on ten VMs at the same time could be a serious issue for the performance and health of the VM regardless of SCSI Reservations. Make sure the VM has no REDO logs before invoking VMotion.

- Only use the persistent VM disk modes. The other modes create lots of files on the LUNs that will require locking. In ESX version 3, persistent disk modes lead to not being able to perform snapshots and use the consolidated backup tools. These limitations make this item a lower priority from an operational point of view.

- Do not suspend VMs as this also creates a file and therefore requires a SCSI Reservation.

- Do not run vm-support requests unless all other operations have completed.

- Do not use the vdf tool when any other modification operation is being performed.

- Do not rescan storage subsystems unless all other operations have completed.

- Limit use of `vmkmultipath`, `vmkfstools`, and other VMware-specific COS commands until all other operations have completed.

- Create, modify, or delete a VMFS only when all other operations have completed.

- Be sure no third-party agents are accessing your storage subsystem via vdf, or direct access to the `/vmfs` directory. Although vdf does not normally force a reservation, it could experience one if another host, due to a metadata modification, locked the LUN.

- Do not run scripts that modify VMFS ownership, permissions, access times, or modification times from more than one host. Localize such scripts to a single host. It is suggested that you use the deployment server as the host for such scripts.

- Stagger any scripts or agents that affect a LUN so that they run from a management node that can control when actions can occur.

- Stagger the running of disk-intensive tools within a VM such as virus scan. The extra load on your SAN could cause results similar to those that occur with SCSI Reservations but which are not reservations errors but are instead queue-full or unavailable-target errors.

- Use only one file system per LUN.

- Do not mix file systems on the same LUN.

- Do not store a VM's VMX configuration files on shared ext3 partitions on a SAN LUN. In ESX 3.0, you can place a VMX configuration of virtual machines on VMFS volumes (locally or on the SAN).

What this all boils down to is ensuring that any possible operation that could somehow affect a LUN is limited to only one operation per LUN at any given time. The biggest hitters of this are automated power operations, backups, VMotion, and deployments. A little careful monitoring and changes to operational procedures can limit the possibility of SCSI Reservation conflicts and failures to various operations. A case in point follows. One company under review due to constant, debilitating SCSI Reservation conflicts reviewed the list of 23 items and fixed one or two possible items but missed the most critical item. This customer had an automated tool that ran simultaneously on all hosts at the same time to modify the owner and group of every file on every VMFS attached to the host. The resultant metadata updates caused hundreds of SCSI-2 reservations to occur. The solution was to run this script from a single ESX Server for all LUNs. By limiting the run of the script to a single host, all the reservations disappeared, because no two hosts were attempting to manipulate the file systems at the same time, and the single host, in effect, serialized the actions.

Hot and cold migrations of VMs can change the behavior of automatic boot methodologies. Setting a dependency on one VM or a time for a boot to occur deals with a single ESX Server where you can start VMs at boot of ESX, after VMware Tools start in the previous VM, after a certain amount of time, or not at all. This gets much more difficult with more than one ESX Server, so a new method has to be used. Although starting a VM after a certain amount of time is extremely useful, what happens when three VMs start almost simultaneously on the same LUN? Remember we want to limit operations to just one per LUN at any time. We have a few options:

- Stagger the boot or reboot of your ESX Server and ensure that your VMs only start after the previous VMs' VMware Tools start, to ensure that all the disk activity associated with the boot sequence finishes before the next VM boots, thereby helping with boot performance and eliminating conflicts. VM boots are naturally staggered by ESX when it reboots anyway.

■ Similar to doing backups, have one ESX Server that controls the boot of all VMs, guaranteeing that you can boot multiple VMs but only one VM per LUN at any time. So, if you have multiple ESX Servers, more than one VM can start at any time on each LUN. In essence, we use the VMware PERL API to gather information about each VM from each ESX Server and correlate the VMs to a LUN and create a list of VMs that can start simultaneously; that is, each VM is to start on a separate LUN. Then we wait a bit of time before starting the next batch of VMs.

All the listed operational changes will limit the amount of SCSI subsystem errors that will be experienced. Although it is possible to implement more than one operation per LUN at any given time, we cannot guarantee success with more than one operation. This depends on the type of operation, the SAN, settings, and most of all, timings for operations.

There are several other considerations, too. Most people want to perform multiple operations simultaneously, and this is possible as long as the operations are on separate LUNs. To increase the number of simultaneous operations, increase the number of LUNs available. Table 6.1 shows the maximum number of operations allowed per number of hosts connected to the LUN for various arrays. The table is broken into categories of risk based on the number of operations per LUN and the SCSI conflict retry count. In this table, gaps exist between the number of hosts per LUN and the number of operations per LUN; assume that if you are above the listed number, you are in the next-highest category.

Table 6.1

Risk Associated with Number of Operations per LUN					
Array Type	# of Host(s)	Low Risk (0% to 10% failure)	Medium Risk (30% to 60% failure)	High Risk (> 60% failure)	SCSI Conflict Retry Count
Entry level - MSA	1	4	8	10	20
	2	2	4	5	20
	4	2	3	4	20
	8	1	2	3	20
Enterprise – EVA, Symmetrics	1	8	12	16	8
	2	2	4	6	8
	4	2	3	4	8
	8	1	2	3	8

Array Type	# of Host(s)	Low Risk (0% to 10% failure)	Medium Risk (30% to 60% failure)	High Risk (> 60% failure)	SCSI Conflict Retry Count
Hitachi/HDS	1	6	10	12	20
	2	2	4	6	20
	4	2	3	4	20
	8	1	2	3	20

Note that no more than eight hosts should be attached to any one given LUN at a time. Also note that as firmware is modified, these values can change to be higher or lower.

Performance–Gathering Agents

Performance and other monitoring is an important issue from an operational point of view. Many customers monitor the health of their hardware and servers by monitoring hardware and performance agents. Although hardware agents monitor the health of the ESX Server, they should not monitor the health of a VM, because the virtual hardware is truly dependent on the physical hardware. In addition, most agents are talking to specific chips, and these do not exist inside a VM. So using hardware agents will often slow down your VM.

Best Practice for Hardware Agents
Do *not* install hardware agents into a VM; they will cause noticeable performance issues.

Because these agents will adversely affect performance, measuring performance now is a very important tool for the Virtual Infrastructure and will tell you when to invest in a new ESX Server and to how to balance load among the ESX Servers. Although there are automated ways to balance the load among ESX Servers (they are covered in Chapter 11, "Dynamic Resource Load Balancing"), most if not all balancing of VM load across hosts is performed by hand, because there are more than just a few markers to review when moving VMs from host to host.

The first item to understand is that the addition of a VM to a host will impact the performance of the ESX Server; sometimes in small ways, and sometimes in other ways that are more noticeable. The second item to understand is that the performance tools that run within a VM depend on real clock cycles to determine the performance of the VM and that a VM is not always given full clock cycles. Because there are often more VMs than CPUs or cores, a VM will share a CPU with others, and as more VMs are added the slice of time the VM gets to run on a CPU is reduced even further. Therefore, there is a greater time lag between each usage of the CPU and thus a longer CPU cycle. Because performance tools use the CPU cycle to measure performance and to keep time, the data received is relatively inaccurate. However, the experimental descheduler VMware tool can be used to counteract this effect. When the system is loaded to the desired level, a set of baseline data should be discovered.

Once a set of baseline data is available, the internal to the VM performance tools can determine whether a change in performance has occurred, but it cannot give you raw numbers, just a ratio of change from the baseline. For example, if the baseline for CPU utilization is roughly 20% measured from within the VM and suddenly shows 40%, we know that there was a 2x change from the original value. The original value is not really 20%, but some other number. However, even though this shows 2x more CPU utilization for the VM, it does not imply a 2x change to the actual server utilization. Therefore, other tools need to be used to gain performance data for a VM that do not run from within the VM. Although useful for baselines, they are not useful overall. In this case, VC, a third-party VM manager, ESXCharter, and the use of esxtop from the command line are the tools to use. These all measure the VM and ESX Server performance from outside the VM, to gain a clearer picture of the entire server. The key item to realize is that when there is a sustained over 80% utilization of an ESX Server as measured by VC or one of the tools, a new ESX Server is warranted and the load on the ESX Server needs to be rebalanced.

Balancing of ESX Servers can happen daily or even periodically during the day by using the VMotion technology to migrate running VMs from host to host with zero downtime. Although this can be dynamic (covered in Chapter 11, "Dynamic Resource Load Balancing"), using VMotion by hand can give a better view of the system and the ability to rebalance as necessary. For example, if an ESX Server's CPU utilization goes to 95%, the VM that is the culprit needs to be found using one of the tools; once found, the VM can be moved to an unused or lightly used ESX Server using VMotion. If this movement becomes a normal behavior, it might be best to place the VM on a lesser-used machine permanently. This is often the major reason an N+1 host configuration is recommended.

Another item that can increase CPU utilization is the deployment of VMs. Deployment is discussed in detail in a later chapter, but the recommendation is to create a deployment server that can see all LUNs. This server would be responsible for deploying any new VM, which allows the VM to be tested on the deployment server until it is ready to be migrated to a true production server using VMotion.

For example, a customer desired to measure the performance of all VMs to determine how loaded the ESX Server could become with their current networking configuration. To do so, we explained the CPU cycle issues and developed a plan of action. We employed three tools in this example, VC, vmkusage (now rolled into VC 2.0), and esxtop running from the service console. We found that the granularity of VC was less than vmkusage, which was less than esxtop. For performance-problem resolution, esxtop is the best tool to use, but it spits out reams of data for later graphing. VC averages things over 30-minute or larger increments unless the graph is exported then the raw data can be manipulated in Excel. vmkusage averages all data over 5-minute distributions. esxtop uses real and not averaged data. The plan was to measure performance using each tool as each VM was running its application. Performance of ESX truly depends on the application within each VM. It is extremely important to realize this, and when discussing performance issues to not localize to just a single VM, but to look at the host as a whole. This is why VMware generally does not allow performance numbers to be published, because without a common set of applications running within each VM, there is no way to compare all the apples to oranges. It is best to do your own analysis using your applications, because one company's virtualized application suite has nothing to do with another companies, and therefore will have major implications on performance.

Other Operational Issues

Because ESX makes extensive use of memory, there are operational concerns regarding the use of memory, too. The main issue with memory is to prevent the overcommitment of memory during runtime of the VMs. The runtime covers the memory actually used, and not always what is allocated. A VM may have 16GB of memory allocated to it. If this much memory is allocated to all the VMs, on a 32GB ESX Server, only one VM could be created unless the memory is overcommitted as the OS takes some memory. If the goal is to run ten VMs, there is a memory requirement of 160GB, which is quite a bit over the 64GB server memory limit inherent in ESX. Which means that if all the 16GB of memory is actually used by a VM, the ESX Server will need to start swapping (or paging) memory out in large chunks to accommodate the running of another VM. However, if in reality only 1GB of each VM is used, there is only 10GB of the available 32GB of memory in use at any time, allowing more VMs to be created and used without swapping memory, even though there is potential for up to 160GB of memory to be used. In this case, it is best to assign memory sparingly and to only give a VM what it needs to run. This way memory management will allow a denser population of VMs to run. Note it is not possible to create a VM that will exceed the physical memory of the machine.

Consider the following thought: with ESX we are now back in time to the realm of limited resources. There are no longer gobs of memory and disk available for any particular machine, but a realm where memory and disk can be vast; but as more VMs are added, more resources are used. The goal is now to preserve memory. As an example, consider programming the old Commodore 64, where no more than 360K would fit on a single floppy; to go past this, more than one floppy had to be used. Everyone programmed to the 360K limit of the floppy so that code would fit on a single disk. Once another floppy was in use, the applications usage went downhill, performance suffered, and wait time increased. With ESX, we are back in this realm where we need to be cognizant of the limitations of the host, which is trying to do much, much more with less than ever before.

Best Practice for ESX
The mindset for ESX is to only give out the necessary resources to each VM rather than give out all the resources.

All VMs affect the resource limits of the host and therefore resource management becomes a huge issue (as covered in another chapter). Note, however, that changes to the way resources are used, assigned, and managed can inadvertently affect all VMs on a host or in a farm.

Limiting memory assignment to VMs can allow more VMs to run in a single ESX host without impacting memory or performance limits.

Sarbanes–Oxley

Sarbanes-Oxley can also impact performance of an ESX Server, because the gathering up of log files at incorrect times will inadvertently cause a load on the system. With the advent of ESX version 3, it is now possible to store VM log files with the VMDK, and access to the file system holding these logs has been throttled so that copies to and from do not adversely impact performance. What logs are necessary? Those logs that tell who did what and when are ultimately required, but many system administrators are streaming *all* logs to tape for later retrieval. For ESX, this will be all the logs from each VM running on the host and all the VM log files and service console log files in /var/log. Once more, a single host is best to use to gather all this information so that no one LUN or server is overloaded. Because the ESX service console is Linux, the network features of syslog can be used to create a logging server so that all data is logged to one host from where it can be conveniently archived. The key is to make use of syslog to send the logs to the remote host and the local host. To do that, modify the /etc/syslog file as follows: Duplicate each uncommented line and add to the end instead of the local filename the @ipaddress option to force log files to not only be stored locally but remotely to the IP address of the syslog server.

Conclusion

By paying careful attention to operational issues, it is possible to successfully manage ESX and remove some of the most common issues related to poor operational use of ESX. ESX is designed to be centrally managed and care should be taken to do so. It is also important to realize that each implementation of ESX has different operational concerns.

Chapter 7

Networking

As mentioned in Chapter 1, "System Considerations," there are certain best practices in relation to networking, particularly the physical network interface card (pNIC) count associated with ESX. We look at networking in more detail to explain the capabilities of ESX in this arena. In this chapter, I begin with some of the basic building blocks that make up a network. Then I turn to network definitions. Discussion of a network requirements checklist follows. Next, some brief examples of networks are presented. Finally, I spend a little time on the subject of configuration.

Basic Building Blocks

In the physical world, there are basic building blocks to a network, and this does not change in the virtual world. The most basic of building blocks exist within the virtual world: NICs and switches. Table 7.1 shows a mapping of the physical to virtual building blocks of a network.

Table 7.1

Basic Network Building Blocks		
Physical	**Virtual**	**Comments**
Physical network interface card (pNIC)	Virtual network interface card (vNIC)	VMs are limited to PCNET32 or vmxnet devices and in some cases the Intel e1000 device
Physical network switch (pSwitch)	Virtual switch (vSwitch)	vSwitch has less functionality than pSwitch
Network router	N/A	Performed via software in a VM
Firewall	N/A	Performed via software in a VM
Gateway	N/A	Performed via software in a VM

Reviewing Table 7.1, there is no doubt that the virtual environment appears to have less functionality than the physical equivalent. But that is to be expected because ESX virtualizes everything into software and cannot compete, nor does it want to do so, with the varied network components and diversity of products. It has simplified everything to the most basic of necessary networking components while leaving some critical (but not necessary for basic networking) devices to be implemented in software by the administrators. These devices are: the router, gateway, and firewall components. There are extremely good software versions available that can be implemented within a VM. VMware has a number of these VM appliances on their website at www.vmware.com/appliances/. The appliances contain many different firewall, gateway, and router entries for VMs preinstalled with software and easy-to-use configurations.

There are very few limits and caveats associated with the virtual hardware. The most interesting and handicapping limitation is the fact that the vSwitches cannot be layered; however, this is only a minor hiccup. Similar to blocks played with by children, the virtual network (vNetwork) components can be placed together to create complex networks.

Consider the following example presented by a customer: The customer usually took infected physical boxes to a lab bench on a stand-alone network for testing, cleaning, rebuilding, and staging before placing them back into the wild. The customer wants to be able to do similar things in a virtual environment, but the machines on the lab bench must have access to the administrative VMs and other installation server VMs that the whole enterprise uses. However, everything must be secure, and viruses cannot infect other parts of the network.

Figure 7.1 lays out a possible network to meet our customer requirements. As shown in Figure 7.1, we used our basic building blocks to interconnect our networking bits. We have used pNICs, vNICs, pSwitches, and vSwitches, and a VM that acts as a firewall (vFW) between the lab bench and the real world. Several operating systems provide this type of firewall capability, including Linux and Windows. The customer used Linux as the packet-filtering firewall, allowing access only to what was absolutely necessary. In addition, the firewall was designed to block all outgoing traffic to prevent further spread of infections. In this way, if a VM became infected for some reason, it could quickly be moved to a quarantined network. Figure 7.1 does depend on an external firewall for those VMs not in the internal quarantined network. The use of two independent pNICs each connected to their own vSwitch allows the lab bench to connect independently of the enterprise. The vFW between the two vSwitches allows traffic from the installation servers to reach the lab bench but does not allow infections to reach the enterprise.

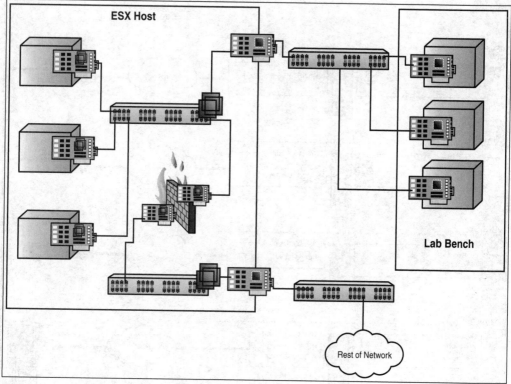

Figure 7.1   Customer example using basic network building blocks

Details of the Building Blocks

Given the example just discussed and Figure 7.1, we should define our basic build-ing blocks more and list out any limitations or characteristics. Let's look at Figure 7.2 when defining the basic roles of the building blocks. Figure 7.2 is a simplified network that displays some practices for configuring networking for ESX. In the following sections, I define the basic network building blocks for both the physical network and for ESX.

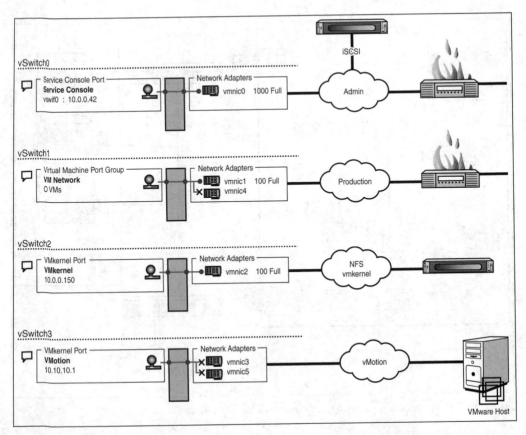

Figure 7.2 ESX physical and virtual network layout

Physical Switch (pSwitch)

The pSwitch can be any network switch from any vendor. The best practice is to have at least two pSwitches attached for VMs so that if one goes down the other can handle the load and provide a level of load balancing and redundancy represented by the production cloud. The best practice for all pSwitches is to have gigabit ports. There should be an administrative network for the service console as outlined in Chapter 4, "Auditing, Monitoring, and Security." There should be a separate pSwitch or VLAN for VMotion, so that when VMotion is used, the memory footprint to be transferred is not sniffable and so as to provide unimpeded connectivity. Other systems besides ESX Servers on the VMotion network put at risk the necessary high-speed migration of a running VM. For ESX version 3, new VMkernel networks are available to handle iSCSI and NAS connections; these networks should have their own pSwitch, too.

Physical NIC (pNIC)

The pNIC is the most basic of building blocks and comes in a myriad of forms from twisted-pair to Fibre with speeds from 10Mbps to 10Gbps, and there are thousands of different types of these available from almost the same number of vendors. As listed in Chapter 1, there is support only for a few vendors and flavors with ESX. ESX uses the pNIC to communicate to the outside world from the service console, to use VMotion to move running VMs from host to host, and for the host and VMs to communicate with the rest of the world. With the exception of the service console for ESX versions earlier than 3.0, all pNICs are attached to one or more vSwitches. As shown in Figure 7.2, there are at least two pNICs attached to the VM network. Each of these pNICs is attached to a separate pSwitch, yet both are teamed together to the vSwitch. Usually the service console has its own pNIC, as does the VMotion network; however, these also can have two pNICs associated with them.

When looking at Figure 7.2, note that each vSwitch could have associated with it any number of pNICs. For ESX version 3, this is true, but for ESX version 2.5.x and earlier, there are only two necessary vSwitches, and having redundancy for everything else is somewhat troublesome. Later in this chapter, we discuss how to make everything redundant for ESX version 2.5.x.

Virtual Switch (vSwitch)

In Figure 7.2, there are four distinct vSwitches, each connected to at least one pNIC associated with the service console, VMkernel, VMotion, and VM network. The service console and VM network vSwitches are connected to pNICs on one side and VMs on the other. The VMkernel and VMotion vSwitches are not connected to any VM on the inside, because the ESX Server VMkernel uses these vSwitches. On ESX versions earlier than version 3, the VMkernel and service console vSwitches do not exist. Although on ESX versions earlier than ESX version 3 there can be a service console vSwitch if necessary, this is not recommended. A vSwitch supports NIC teaming, port groups, 802.3ad, 802.1q, and various flavors of load balancing. However, it is not a full switch. Nor is there a way to manage the individual ports on the switch like you can with a pSwitch. Consider it a very smart but extremely thin bit of software and not equivalent to a physical switch. The vSwitch NIC teaming is not equivalent to 802.3ad, yet the vSwitch can support 802.3ad, too. NIC teaming is a way to bond or team pNICs together to gain failover and load balancing capabilities within the virtual environment. Support for 802.1q or VLAN tagging is at three different levels. A vSwitch without a pNIC can exist and creates a network that is internal to the ESX Server and is a valuable tool for creating stand-alone systems. An unfortunate downside is that any VM connected to an internal vSwitch cannot be VMotioned.

Table 7.2

vSwitch Functionality	
Function	**Definition in vSwitch Terms**
802.3ad	802.3ad or EtherChannel bonds two or more pNICs together with a single IP address. Each end of the connection (pSwitch and vSwitch) must agree that this bond exists.
VMware NIC teaming	This functionality is very similar to Linux bonding drivers and differs from 802.3ad in that both ends do not need to agree that the bond exists. The only side that needs to know that a bond exists is the vSwitch side of the network. VMware NIC teams can be attached to the same or multiple pSwitches.
pNIC failover	Each vSwitch can failover a network connection if there is more than one pNIC connected to it. This is a feature of VMware NIC teaming. This failover occurs at the pNIC level once a network path disappears from a failed pNIC, pNIC port, pSwitch, or cable issue.
Load Balancing	
Out-mac	Distribute load based on source MAC addresses (default for ESX versions earlier than 3)
IP address	Distribute load based on source IP protocol; all other protocols are load balanced sequentially.
Port ID	Distribute load based on the source port ID (ESX version 3 only, and the default for that version).
802.1q	Each vSwitch supports three forms of 802.1q, which is often referred to as trunking or VLAN tagging.

Function	Definition in vSwitch Terms
EST	With external switch tagging, the trunk leads to the pSwitches and from there to a pNIC pair that exists for each port group on the trunk. Each VM connects to the vSwitch, and no port groups are needed on the vSwitch. However, more pNIC will be necessary for each port group on the pSwitch.
VST	The most common use of 802.1q is the virtual switch tagging, which passes the trunk from the pSwitch through the pNICs and to the vSwitch. On the vSwitch, the VMs connect to virtual port groups. This method reduces the hardware requirements to only the pair of pNICs needed for redundancy and moves possible complex network management to the hands of the ESX administrators.
VGT	In virtual guest tagging, the trunk goes from the pSwitch to the pNIC to the vSwitch and then to the vNIC for the VM in question, and special drivers on the VM will decide how to handle the trunk. Windows by default does not support this, and there are very few drivers for any operating system to handle the trunk directly. This method is not recommended.
Traffic shaping	Shape traffic for the port group or vSwitch to control bandwidth utilization.

Virtual NIC (vNIC)

The vNIC is the last bit of the puzzle, because it is used to connect the VMs to the vSwitch and thereby possibly to a pNIC. The vNIC comes in two flavors (internal to the VM): PC-NET32 and vmxnet. The PC-NET32 vNIC is a simple 10/100Mbps network adapter that is easy to virtualize because it does not have much complexity to it. It is not a smart NIC, but nearly every operating system has a driver for this NIC; therefore it was a perfect candidate for virtualization. The other vNIC is the vmxnet NIC developed by VMware. The vmxnet vNIC has more smarts than PC-NET32 because it will take some shortcuts in the virtualization as it truly understands the virtualization layer and can hook directly into it to get better performance. However, this performance gain requires a vSwitch that is gigabit to the pSwitch. The choice of which to use, vmxnet or PCNET32, depends on the VM configuration and is discussed in Chapter 10, "Virtual Machines." External to the VM, there is no choice in an available vNIC for ESX version 3, yet internally there still exists a choice. The external choice for ESX version 3 is a type of Flexible, which implies that the driver used within the VM (PC-NET32 or vmxnet) dictates whether or not vmxnet is used.

Virtual Firewall (vFW)

ESX does not contain a vFW like a vSwitch and vNIC, but consists of any firewall software that is installable into a VM. There are firewalls that are part of a single floppy, installed on top of an OS, or already part of full-blown operating systems; all can be used. When it comes to a vFW, you will be relying on software to perform your firewall capabilities, and the Linux-based systems tend to work out very well in this environment.

Virtual Router (vRouter)

The vRouter, like the vFW, is a not built into ESX, but would be a VM with an OS that would support routing. Once more, Linux systems often fill this software role, and there exist VM appliances available based on a form of Linux.

Virtual Gateway (vGateway)

The vGateway is like the vRouter, and once more would be a form of a VM. Linux systems often fill this software role, and VM appliances based on a form of Linux do exist and are available.

Network Definitions

Because we have looked at the basic hardware components, we should look at the other basic components of an ESX Server network. Although some of this is a bit repetitive, it is nonetheless important to understand how ESX connects to the outside. Although the material presented in the previous section goes into the virtual and physical hardware in use, this section is a deep dive into each network shown in Figure 7.2.

Administration Network

The administration network (see Figure 7.3) is a secure network that in general only administrators can access directly. The VC Server, remote access cards (ILO), and ESX Server service consoles should be on this network. Chapter 4, "Auditing, Monitoring, and Securing," covers the security reasons for this. However, there is a more pragmatic reason. Those people who need to access these Virtual Infrastructure elements are administrators only. No others have the need to do so, so they should not be granted the right to do so. The utility of the administrative network is to create, deploy, and manage VMs and can be unencrypted depending on the tools used. All cold migrations, which are also unencrypted, travel over this network, as do the initial instructions for a VMotion. On ESX versions earlier than version 3.0, there was no best practice for having redundant networking for the admin network. For ESX version 3.0, it is as simple as it is for the VMs; just create a NIC team on the service console vSwitch. Internally, the service console uses the vmxnet_console driver to communicate with the vSwitch, but there is a new device created named vswifX. The vswifX device is the device associated with the service console vSwitch. This is a very different driver configuration than that used in ESX version 2.5.x and earlier releases, and it does not suffer the issues that the old vmxnet_console driver suffered. Since the service console must participate in any use of an iSCSI network, they are combined here for convenience. It is possible to have multiple vSwif devices with one for Administration and one for iSCSI.

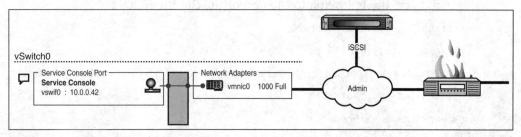

Figure 7.3   Administration and iSCSI network

For ESX versions between 2.0 and 2.5.3, there is the vmxnet_console driver that will attach the service console to its own vNIC, which allows it to be connected to a vSwitch and thereby a pNIC. In this way, failover is at least achieved; however, there is no load balancing. The following list is the recipe that will allow this behavior. It is not recommended, but it is sometimes necessary. To alleviate any impact when using vmxnet_console, it is recommended that you use matched hardware and that this hardware be different from your VMs to limit the amount of possible impact. For example, if your computer has a pair of on-board Broadcom adapters, and you add two dual-port Intel adapters into your ESX host, this creates an ideal situation where you can use the Broadcom adapters for the service console using the vmxnet_console driver, and the Intel adapters for the VMs and VMotion. VMware states that vmxnet_console should not be used except in the case where there is low port density, perhaps a blade or 1U device. The following recipe for enabling vmxnet_console work only on ESX version 2.5.x, assuming that there are no currently defined NIC teams or bonds, and that there are only two pNICs in the server. In addition, it assumes that the name of the NIC team will be Network0. It can be extrapolated to more than one pNIC as desired.

1. Log in to the service console.

2. Enter # `vmkpcidivy -i`.

3. When you come to the pNIC that is assigned to the [c]onsole, change the setting to [s]hared.

4. Leave all other items as the default.

5. Save and reboot the server.

6. Assume the ports are now labeled as `vmnic0` and `vmnic1` (two-port 1U server).

7. To add the vmxnet_console device to a NIC team, edit `/etc/vmware/hwconfig` and add the following to the end of the file the following:

```
nicteam.vmnic0.team = "bond0"

nicteam.vmnic1.team = "bond0"
```

8. Edit `/etc/vmware/netmap.conf` and add the following to the end of the file:

```
network1.name = "Network0"

network1.name = "bond0"
```

Because using vmxnet_console is not recommended for ESX versions earlier than version 3, there is another option for creating a redundant admin network. This alternative method is to have two pNICs for the service console, but to only have one operational at any time and to write a script to do IP-based failover from within the service console. Both pNICs would be configured with the same IP address and with only one active at the same time. Failover would consist of bringing down the primary network and then once down, bring up the secondary network. This option provides IP-based failover only and does not support 802.1q VLAN tagging, the various forms of load balancing, or 802.3ad, because there are no drivers for any of this functionality within the service console per the following script. ESX 3.0 does change this, however, and all the vSwitch functionality is supported.

```
#!/bin/sh
running=eth0
second=eth1
GatewayIP=10.0.0.141
while [ 1 ]
do
        data=`ping -c 1 $GatewayIP | grep -i unreachable`
        if [ X$date != "" ]
        then
                # reset
                ifdown $running
```

```
        ifup $second
        # reset running device
        foo=$running
        running=$second
        second=$foo
    fi
    sleep 300
end
```

The preceding code above assumes that devices eth0 and eth1 of the service console are defined with exactly the same information but eth1 is not configured to start on boot. The script will attempt to ping the gateway, and if it cannot be reached it will bring down the network device and start the secondary device.

Best Practice for Admin Network

Use IP-based failover for ESX versions earlier than 3.0 and NIC teams for ESX version 3.0 or later. Secure this network with some form of firewall.

For ESX versions earlier than version 3, use of vmxnet_console for redundancy purposes is strongly discouraged. It is, however, necessary for low network port density configurations because of the conflicting notions about who controls the pNIC: the service console or the VMkernel.

For ESX version 3, the iSCSI VMkernel device must share the same subnet as the service console, which generally implies sharing the same vSwitch, because half the iSCSI code lives in the service console. The use of iSCSI throws a huge monkey wrench into the security of the COS and the need to have the administrative network handle nonadministrative traffic. At this time, there is only one way to alleviate the possible conflicts between administration and iSCSI: Use port ID-based load balancing so that each port has its own pNIC. Even so, there is no guarantee that the iSCSI server will end up coming in over a different pNIC than the standard COS traffic. Another option is to perhaps use two service console vSwitches on two distinct networks, thereby having one vSwitch for the admin network and a second for the iSCSI network.

VMotion Network

The VMotion network (see Figure 7.4) is used to transfer the memory image and VM configuration of a running VM from ESX Server to ESX Server, and therefore requires its own private network. Placing this network unprotected within your public network would allow someone to grab the memory footprint of the VM, which in security circles would be considered catastrophic. It is recommended that this network be on a private pSwitch or pSwitch VLAN as this memory footprint is sent over the wire unencrypted. The VMotion network requires a pNIC connected to a vSwitch. This vSwitch would not be connected to any VMs, but instead is connected to the ESX VMkernel for VMotion only. The VMotion network can be a redundant network where two pNICs are connected to the VMotion vSwitch. However, in this mode, there is only failover support and not load balancing.

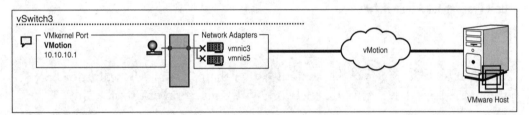

Figure 7.4   VMotion network

Best Practice for VMotion Network
Connect pNICs of the VMotion network to their own private pSwitch or VLAN for performance and security reasons.

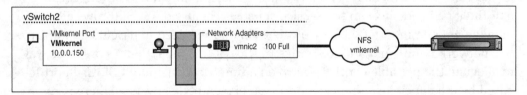

Figure 7.5   VMkernel network

VMkernel Network

The VMkernel network (see Figure 7.5) does not exist in versions of ESX earlier than version 3, and its use is to mount or access network-based data stores. Note that SAN fabric is accessed through other means, not via this network. iSCSI-based storage is part of the admin network, so only NFS-based NAS servers can be accessed over this network. Because this is a data store network, it is important to configure this network with at least two pNICs and to connect the pNICs to multiple pSwitches. In addition, for security reasons outlined in Chapter 4, the networks should be private to the data stores. The VMkernel network would not have any VMs on it. To make this network look like ESX versions earlier than version 3, attach this network to the vSwitch associated with the service console, which is the most common configuration, yet can be a private VMkernel network depending on port density. iSCSI will still require a vmkernel network device, the one caveat about the use of iSCSI is that a port on the service console must participate in the iSCSI network.

Best Practice for the VMkernel Network
Use multiple pNICs and pSwitches for redundancy and bandwidth. The VMkernel network is not usable for VMs.

VM Network

The VM network (see Figure 7.6) by default consists of at least two pNICs connected to a single vSwitch. For redundancy reasons, each of these pNICs should be connected to different pSwitches, but it is not required. The VM network should always consist of a pair of pNICs, because the vSwitch will provide load balancing and failover functionality to increase throughput and redundancy for each VM. Each vSwitch for the VMs can handle all the various flavors of load balancing, VLAN tagging, and redundancy. In general, there is no need for more than two pNICs for the VM network even with a host full of machines because with load balancing there is a 2Gb pipe going out to the world. When talking to network people, most, if not all, of our customers firmly believe that no ESX host needs more than 2Gb of bandwidth. However, if there is a need for more bandwidth, it is strongly suggested that another pair of pNICs be added and another vSwitch added, and that the NIC team limit this to two pNICs per vSwitch. The round-robin approach used for assigning network paths, when there is a path failure, causes what amounts to a fair amount of thrashing on the pSwitches until the system once more balances out, with an elapsed time in minutes and not seconds. Limiting the network paths to two alleviates this issue.

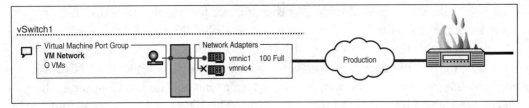

Figure 7.6 VM network

Best Practice for VM Network

Always connect two pNICs to each VM vSwitch that needs outside access for redundancy and load balancing. In addition, use multiple pSwitches.

Do not use more than two pNICs per vSwitch.

Checklist

Now that we understand the components that make up networks within and outside of an ESX Server, we can expand on this and break down our network requirements to a checklist. This checklist will display what is required for networking the ESX Server and the VM guests. Without this information the implementation of ESX could be seriously delayed. As an example, we went to a customer site that did not have all this information. The initial deployment of the server was delayed by two days, and then the final deployment by at least two weeks as new cables needed to be pulled, pNICs added, and IP addresses allocated. It is best to take care of this before you need them to speed up the deployment of an ESX Server.

As shown in Table 7.3, quite a bit of information is needed before ESX installation, and although any change to the networking setup can occur after installation with judicious use of the appropriate commands and configuration files, it is always better to have this information prior to installation. In addition, the VMs side of the network must be known prior to implementation so that the appropriate vSwitches can be created. As you can see, some dissections need to be made to properly configure the network for the VMs and for the host. Outside of the standard IP addresses for VMs and the host, there are some important items to consider and review.

Table 7.3

ESX Server Networking Checklist		
Element	**Host or Guest**	**Comments**
pSwitch (2)	Host	The recommendation is for two pSwitches for redundancy.
pNIC (4) or (6)	Host	The recommendation is for four pNICs. One for the service console, two for the VMs, and the fourth for VMotion. If ultimate redundancy is required, use two for the service console, two for the VMs, and two for vMotion.
SC IP address	Host	The IP address of the service console
SC netmask	Host	The netmask of the service console
SC gateway	Host	The Gateway of the service console
SC DNS	Host	DNS servers for the service console
SC redundancy method	Host	Will we be using vmxnet_console, IP-based failover, or nothing?
vMotion IP address	Host	IP address for the vMotion network. This should be nonroutable.
802.1q state	Host	Are the networks heading to the ESX Server trunked to the pSwitch or through to the vSwitch? If 802.1q is not in use, this is important to note.
vSwitch load-balancing method	Host	Are the vSwitches going to use port ID-, MAC address-, or IP address-based load balancing?
IP address for all the VMs	VMs	A list of IP addresses for the VMs. If DHCP is in use, this is not necessary.
Netmask for all the VMs	VMs	The netmask for the VM networks in use if DHCP is not in use.
Gateway for all the VMs	VMs	The gateway to use for the VM networks in use if DHCP is not in use.
DNS servers for all the VMs	VMs	The DNS server for use within the VM network if DHCP is not in use.
vSwitch names	VMs	Naming your vSwitches appropriately will aid in finding which vSwitch to connect a vNIC to.
vSwitch port group names	VMs	If VST is in use, the port group names will be helpful before beginning.
pSwitch configuration	pSwitch	Is spanning tree disabled or PortFast enabled?

Starting with the IP addresses required, we need an IP address for the service console, *not* for each vSwitch, but instead for the VMs attached to the vSwitch. But we have pNICs, so IP addresses are required? The pNICs assigned to vSwitches are placed into a bridge mode that bridges the pSwitches to the vSwitches and thus do not require their own IP address. In this mode, the VMs require IP addresses as does the service console, but not the pNICs themselves. Nor do the vSwitches require IP addresses, because they are not IP-based managed switches and do not have all the functionality of pSwitches.

vSwitch Settings

Each vSwitch has various capabilities, as defined in this section. These capabilities dictate how the vSwitch will work in the ESX environment. Note that because a vSwitch is an extremely thin layer of code, it looks like a pSwitch, but does not behave the same. What follows is a description of the vSwitch capabilities.

802.1q

802.1q is the same as trunking or VLAN tagging and is an important consideration for the design of an ESX Server network because it could change the physical and virtual networking within or outside of ESX. 802.1q routes multiple networks or subnetworks over the same set of cables, thereby limiting the number of cables used, VLANs, pSwitches, and hopefully the number of pNICs in use on the network. For low-port-density devices such as blades, 802.1q can be very important. ESX supports three mechanisms for 802.1q, and each contains different constraints and requirements. EST has a higher hardware investment, VST has a higher configuration investment, and VGT has a high driver investment.

EST (external switch tagging) is configured such that the trunk comes to the pSwitches, and then each network in the trunk needed by ESX is sent over a pair of network cards. Figure 7.7 displays a trunked network with four VLANs with only two going to ESX via a pair of network cards for each VLAN. Even with quad-port pNICs, ESX can only handle up to a certain number of networks or subnetworks, and this could lead to requiring more hardware than can be used with the server chosen.

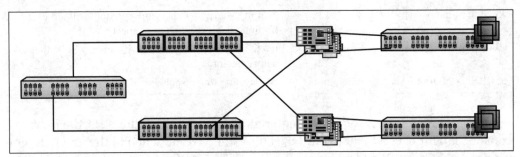

Figure 7.7 External switch tagging with two VLANS

VGT (virtual guest tagging) requires the VM to host specialized software drivers to interpret the 802.1q packets (see Figure 7.8). In this case, the trunk goes from the pSwitch direct to the VM without interpretation by any other device. Although this is possible with some operating systems, it is not a commonly available driver available for Windows. VGT is almost never recommended.

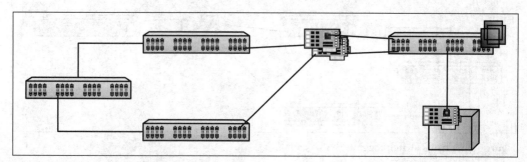

Figure 7.8   Virtual guest tagging

VST (virtual switch tagging) is the commonly recommended method of implementing 802.1q because there is no need to purchase more hardware, yet it moves some network configuration out of the hands of networking teams and into the hands of the ESX Server administrators. In Figure 7.9, all networks are trunked until they reach the vSwitch, which has four port groups representing the four VLANs/networks trunked together. In many cases, VST is recommended by networking teams who are only concerned about the hardware connectivity and not the virtual environment. VST reduces the number of physical cable pulls, pNICs, and pSwitches required and moves these items into the simplified virtual environment, where vNICs connect to port groups on the vSwitches. Although adding complexity to an ESX Server administrator's job, the network administrator's job just got quite a bit simpler when VST is in use. The ESX Server administrator only needs to define port groups on the vSwitch and assign VMs to the required port groups for VST to be configured.

Unfortunately, it is not possible to layer vSwitches and to trunk between them. Unlike pSwitches, the vSwitch is not a true switch and does not have the same capabilities. At best they are just connection points on a network and cannot be layered without first going through a VM. It is important to consider your virtual networking (vNetwork) layout before you begin creating VMs. The network needs to be thought out before VMs are created, because the vNIC selections within the VM must exist before the VM can have any network connections. If networking is not required for the VMs, nothing needs to be done. However, we have yet to see this as an implementation used by customers. Even though most, if not all, of the vNetwork can be changed throughout the life of an ESX Server, reattaching vNICs to vSwitches requires that the VM be shut down to make any changes.

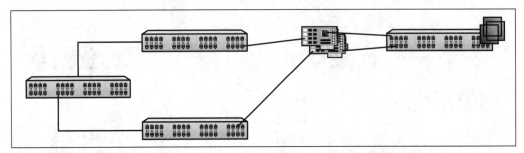

Figure 7.9   Virtual switch tagging

There are other features of the vSwitch to set up that pertain to load balancing, redundancy, and beacon monitoring.

Load–Balancing pNICs

vSwitches can load balance the network packets between multiple pNICs and pSwitches as a feature of VMware NIC teaming. The type of load balancing employed can be chosen by the creator of the vNetwork, but by default ESX version 2.5.x vSwitches use source MAC address-based load balancing and is named out-mac load balancing; whereas ESX version 3 vSwitches default to a new form of load balancing based on the source port ID. The other option is out-ip load balancing or IP-based load balancing. In either case, load balancing in the vSwitch affects only the outbound traffic, because the inbound traffic is controlled by the pSwitch, not by the VMkernel. With out-mac and port-ID load balancing, all traffic is load balanced. However, with out-ip, only the IP protocol is load balanced, and all other protocols use a sequential approach on a fixed volume of packets. Unless there is an absolute need to use out-ip, port ID or out-mac are preferred. To set up load balancing, use the following instructions.

ESX Version 3

Once a vSwitch exists, it is possible to select the Edit option for each vSwitch off the Networking Configuration screen in the VIC. When the dialog appears, click the Edit button again to bring up the vSwitch properties window, where you can set the load-balancing mode, as displayed in Figure 7.10. Just pick the appropriate form of load balancing and click OK.

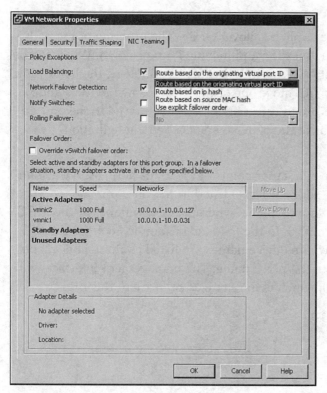

Figure 7.10 Load-balancing and failover modes

ESX Version 2.5.x or Earlier

To disable or set a NIC team to out-mac mode, substitute the term out-mac for out-ip in the following example:

```
Log into the Service Console as root
# vi /etc/vmware/hwconfig
Set the load balancing mode to out-ip for bond1
nicteam.bond1.load_balance_mode = "out-ip"
```

Redundant pNICs

Instead of load balancing, the vSwitch can be set to redundant mode, which implies only one network path is available at any given time. Setting redundancy on a NIC team overrides load balancing. Setting this option is similar to setting the load-balance mode previously.

ESX Version 3

As shown Figure 7.10, select Use Explicit Failover Order. The ordering of the pNICs can be set by selecting a pNIC in question and moving it up or down. Whichever is on the top is selected as the first pNIC, or in ESX 2.5.x terminology, the home_link. To finish making a redundant pNIC, move one of the pNICs down to the standby section. If more than two pNICs are in use, a pNIC could be moved to the unused portion of the pNIC listing. Arrange the pNIC to any desired configuration.

ESX Version 2.5.x and Earlier

That is also fairly easy. There is an adapter name and PCI bus address in the management interface. The PCI bus address is also listed in the file /etc/vmware/hwconfig and will translate to a vmnicX name, where *X* is the number of the pNIC. In our case, we are looking at vmnic0. In the following example, look for the PCI bus address in the file section where device names are listed as these lines map the devicename.PCI:BUS.Address to the pNIC name. The management interface will list the PCI bus address as 7.3.0, which is the same as 007:03.0 in this file.

```
Log into the Service Console as root
# vi /etc/vmware/hwconfig
Find the name of the pNIC
    devicenames.007:03.0.nic = "vmnic0"
    devicenames.007:03.1.nic = "vmnic1"
Set redundancy mode for bond1
nicteam.bond1.home_link = "vmnic0"
```

Beacon Monitoring

ESX uses beacon monitoring as a secondary method to determine whether network paths are dead in addition to the link state it automatically detects. Link state could imply the pNIC, pSwitch, or cable is bad. Using beacon monitoring could determine whether the pSwitch is down for some reason. A beacon is sent out on all network paths addressed to the other network paths. ESX then waits for the beacons to return. If there is a failure to return, it determines that the network path in question is dead. If a pSwitch traps beacon packets and does not forward them, beacon monitoring within ESX can detect this as a dead network path and resend data down one of the other network paths, which could mean duplicate data is received by the target. This could cause the target to get fairly confused quickly. This will cause false positives, and it might be necessary to change the type of beacon to send to another value to bypass. In most cases, beacon monitoring should not be used.

ESX Version 3

Setting up beacon monitoring on ESX version 3 is extremely simple. Go to the vSwitch Properties window shown in Figure 7.11 and select Beacon Probing for the network failover detection mode. The default is Link Status Detection.

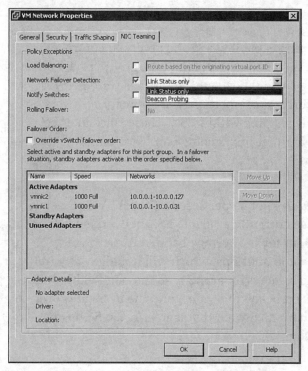

Figure 7.11 Change Link Status to Beacon Probing

ESX Version 2.5.x

Beacon monitoring has two values that define the beacon failure interval used to determine whether a network path is dead. The first element is set by advanced options is the SwitchFailoverBeaconInterval, and the other is the SwitchFailoverThreshold, which can be set via advanced options for all vSwitches or individually for every vSwitch. By default, the threshold is set to 0, effectively disabling beacon monitoring.

```
Log into the Service Console as root
# vi /etc/vmware/hwconfig
Find the name of the pNIC
```

```
devicenames.007:03.0.nic = "vmnic0"
devicenames.007:03.1.nic = "vmnic1"
Set beacon monitoring threshold for bond1
nicteam.bond1.switch_failover_threshold = "2"
```

Traffic Shaping

Each vSwitch has basic traffic-shaping capabilities or the ability to control or shape what runs over the network on a per-vSwitch and port group level. Earlier versions of ESX had traffic shaping capabilities, but the settings were per VM rather than per vSwitch and per portgroup, where they are now for ESX version 3. There are three basic rules to traffic shaping within ESX. These rules in effect implement a subset of traffic shaping that implements bandwidth limiting and not any form of service differentiation.

Average Bandwidth

The average bandwidth is specified in kilobits per second (Kbps). A GbE network has 102,400Kbps or 1Gbps. Because currently available ESX network speeds are no more than 1Gbps, the higher limit for the average bandwidth setting is 102,400Kbps. The lower limit is a value of 0Kbps, which will not allow any traffic through the vSwitch. Note that this value is an average, so the bandwidth utilization can go above this value and even below this value, and the average is over time. For example, if you want to have a vSwitch that is in effect a .5Gbps network, the value for this is 51,200Kbps.

Peak Bandwidth

The peak bandwidth is the maximum amount bandwidth available at any time. The amount of bandwidth can never go above this value. The maximum and minimum limits are the same as for average bandwidth. If we follow the example for average bandwidth, we may only want the vSwitch to peak at three-fourths of gigabits per second, so the value would be set to 76,800Kbps.

Burst Size

If a value is given in kilobytes and represents the maximum size of the data to be transmitted at any given time or the size of a burst of data over the network targeted for the vSwitch, it is possible to set any limit on this value, but remember this is not just the payload of the data packet sent over the network but the envelope, too. This limits the size of the maximum size of the packets that can be sent through the vSwitch, too.

pSwitch Settings

One of the most important, but often overlooked, items on the checklist is the settings on the pSwitch. It is important to realize that ESX vSwitches do not understand the Spanning Tree Protocol and so cannot be made the root of your spanning-tree network, which might happen if the root fails for some reason. The ESX vSwitches need to be protected from this within the physical network. In addition, ESX requires either spanning tree be disabled or PortFast to be enabled on all ports connecting pSwitches to the pNICs associated with an ESX Server. In cases of failover, PortFast will speed up the process by which paths become available to ESX as some of the spanning tree checks are bypassed. And finally, if out-ip is the load-balance mode of choice, set the switch ports for each pNIC in the NIC team to 802.3ad mode or EtherChannel; otherwise, it is possible that each switch port in use will see the same MAC address, which confuses most switches.

Best Practices for the pNIC/pSwitch Configuration

This best practice is made up of three aspects:

- Disable the Spanning Tree Protocol or enable PortFast on the pSwitch ports associated with ESX pNICS.
- IP load balancing requires the setting up of EtherChannel or 802.3ad on the pSwitch for the pNICs in the NIC team.
- Use beacon monitoring with care, and, if necessary, use beacon monitoring with multiple pSwitches, and make sure that all pSwitches are in the same broadcast network.

Example vNetworks

The following example vNetworks can be created within ESX using the basic building blocks discussed earlier.

- The use of a virtual staging network firewalled from the rest of the vNetwork so that new software can be installed in an extremely safe environment. This is shown in Figure 7.12. The pNICs for the VMs are attached to a vSwitch labeled Network0. Connected to this vSwitch are many VMs; one of these is a vFW, which also connects to the vSwitch labeled Staging. Any new VM created is first attached to the Staging vSwitch, and because the vFW uses NAT and provides DHCP services, the VM can initiate network-based application installation techniques. This protects the VM and any other VM connected to the Staging vSwitch. The external network is also protected from the VMs attached to the Staging network.

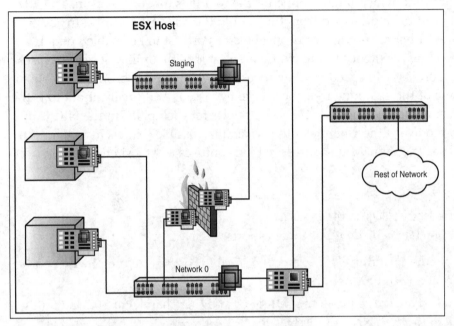

Figure 7.12 Use of a vFW to form an internal staging vNetwork

- The use of a vNetwork to formulate a lab environment can provide the capability to test network functionality for implementation in the real world. Figure 7.13 shows a version of this type of vNetwork in which there is a vSwitch labeled as VirtualLab to which many VMs attach. In addition, there is a second vSwitch labeled VirtualLab1 that is connected to VirtualLab via a vFW to test how various daemons react with a firewall between them and the target machine. Many customers use the virtual lab environment to test Active Directory, Samba, DHCP, and other network tools currently in use by the physical network. A vNetwork of this nature alleviates the need to purchase pSwitches and machines to test network daemons. The virtual lab network can be as complex as the real world and can test the deployment and proposed networking changes.

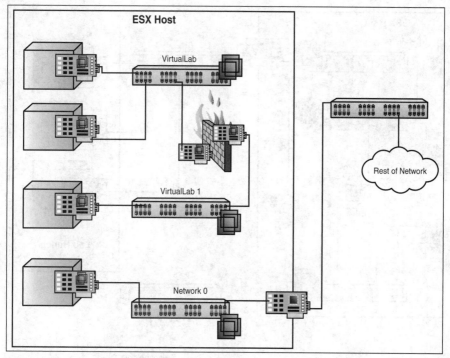

Figure 7.13 vNetwork containing a stand-alone virtual lab

- Figure 7.14 shows the use of a vNetwork to attach a physical lab bench to a vNetwork using all the basic building blocks to protect the rest of the network from the infected computers on the lab bench. It is also possible to improve on this to create a DMZ where installation servers can exist, as well as another vFW, to create the virtual lab bench for infected VMs per Figure 7.14. This provides a vNetwork that segregates infected machines from the rest of the network, whether virtual or physical.

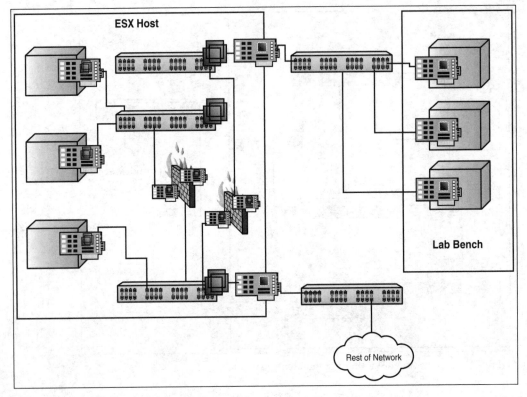

Figure 7.14 vNetwork containing a physical and virtual lab bench

As you can see, the creation of the vNetwork is extremely simple and requires only the creation of vSwitches, and the creation of VMs that act as vFWs, vGateways, and other appliances. We are only limited by our imaginations. Having the vNetwork plan in writing before beginning will give a semblance of order to the implementation of ESX. The design phase of the VI network does not start with logging into the VIC. It should all be mapped out well ahead of time using Visio network diagrams or some other tool. Implement and configure the design through the VIC or command line, and then test the design before rolling out the system to production.

Best Practice for vNetwork
Create a vNetwork diagram/design prior to implementation so that the number of vSwitches and other virtual network building blocks are known.

Configuration

We have been discussing vSwitches and vNICs as if they already existed, and we just need to grab one and hook it up. However, these devices need to be created first, and there are a few ways to do this. For ESX version 3, the Virtual Infrastructure Client 2.0 (VIC20) or the command line can be used. For ESX version 2.5.x and earlier, there are also multiple methods: using the MUI is the most common approach. However, it is also possible to use the command line. Creating or modifying networks through the COS will *not* automatically commit changes and make them active. If a vSwitch is not created using the MUI, the vmware-serverd (or vmware-ccagent if you are using VC) process must be restarted. The majority of vNetwork is covered in Chapter 10, "Virtual Machines," but the rest of this section is a review of steps necessary before any vNetwork element is created.

The first thing to do is determine which pNIC is represented by the physical adapter list within ESX. Because there is no easy way to determine this by just looking at the hardware, it will require someone moving Ethernet cables and someone watching and refreshing the physical adapter list within the management console. In many cases, it is only necessary to do this to the edge cards to determine which way the PCI bus is numbered. For example, at a recent customer site, there were six pNICs involved on a Proliant DL580 G2, which did not have any on-board pNIC ports. To understand the bus ordering, someone pulled all the cables and working together built up a map of all pNIC ports and ESX adapter numbers by first determining which PCI addresses were associated with which adapter number on the left side of the PCI slots, and then the right side, which automatically gave us the ordering of the middle card, and incidentally told us which pNIC port was associated with the service console. Figure 7.15 shows a map and also lays out what connectivity is required for each vSwitch. In this case, there are three: VMotion, Network0, and Network1. Additional notes can be added to the map to depict which PCI slots have which cards, disks, and RAID types, as well as ILO and other necessary labels.

Best Practice for pNIC Determination
When trying to map pNIC port to ESX adapter numbers, work from the outside in. In addition, make a drawing of the back of the chassis and label placement of cables (and label the cables). Documenting the hardware device mapping and cabling can prove helpful later for troubleshooting.

After the adapter number to the pNIC map has been determined, it is time to continue and create all the vSwitches needed by the vNetwork. There are multiple ways to do this in ESX, but there is only one supported method, and that is to use one of the management interfaces. Although there is a command-line method, use of it could require a reboot and can be extremely dangerous. For all ESX versions earlier than version 3.0, vSwitch creation methods edit the file /etc/vmware/netmap.conf so that vSwitches survive a reboot of the ESX Server. There is nothing tricky about using a management interface to create a vSwitch; however, that is covered in the next chapter.

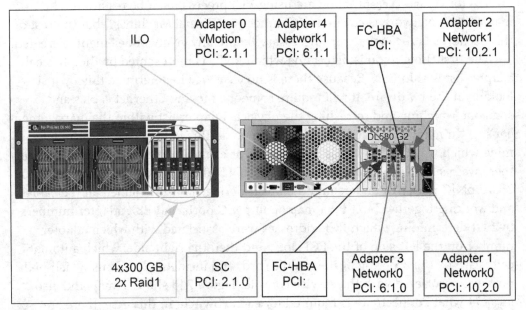

Figure 7.15 pNIC to vSwitch example map
Visio templates for image courtesy of Hewlett-Packard.

Conclusion

Creating a vNetwork is just like playing with so many tinker toys that connect everything together. Now that we have created the vNetwork, it is now possible to create VMs and install them with an appropriate OS. Like networking in ESX, it is important to understand the underlying layers before creating any VMs. The next chapter delves into the management of ESX, where vNetworks will be created, modified, and destroyed.

Chapter 8

Configuring ESX from a Host Connection

There are many aspects of managing ESX. The key, however, is to first understand how to configure a single ESX Server and from there branch out to multiple machines. However, where do you start with ESX management? Should we dive directly into everyday management tasks? All our elders state to start at the beginning, so that is what we will do. In the previous chapters, the ESX Server has been chosen, installed, secured, and storage usage has been decided, so now it is time to perform an initial configuration of ESX. The steps to configure ESX version 3 differ slightly from the steps to configure earlier versions, yet the actual interface you use differs quite a bit.

The goal of this chapter is to somehow logically lay out the configuration tasks that might be needed at the beginning of ESX usage and the everyday tasks necessary to continue the usage of ESX. To do this, the organization of this chapter approaches configuration from the tasks necessary to configure ESX after installation. Remember, however, that all the previous chapters, once read, will make management easier.

In addition, the Virtual Infrastructure Client 2.0 (VIC20) can attach to an ESX Server, running version 3, just as easily as it can attach to Virtual Center (VC) 2.0. However, the VIC cannot attach to earlier versions of ESX, so the web-based management user interface (MUI) will be necessary.

This chapter is more of a collection of how-to's with general discussion on why these work. There are plenty of references available to discuss the details of the configurations either in previous chapters or in other books. Refer to the References element at the end of this book for more details. The tasks include a Rosetta stone of sorts where they are broken down by command line, VIC20, and the MUI of older versions of ESX.

Configuration Tasks

The set of tasks to configure ESX are finite, but they have no specific order. Some things are necessary prior to VM creation, and the order is independent of ESX. Most if not all the tasks can also be completed from the COS, but the graphical and web-based interfaces seem to be easier. With large numbers of machines, however, scripting the configuration is necessary. Table 8.1 outlines the tasks necessary to configure ESX, whether they can be accomplished from the MUI, VIC, or the command line. In addition, any dependency on order will be highlighted.

Table 8.1

Configuration Tasks				
Task	VIC	MUI	COS	Dependency/Notes
Administrative user	ESX Server only	Yes	useradd	Chapter 4, "Auditing, Monitoring, and Securing"
Security configuration	ESX Server only	Limited	esxcfg-firewall	Chapter 4
Network Time Protocol	N/A	N/A	By hand	VIC v2.5 will contain this capability for ESX 3i at the very least.
Service console resources	Yes	Yes	N/A	Requires reboot

Server-Specific Tasks

A few of the listed tasks can take place only when logged into the ESX Server in question either via the VIC20, MUI, or command line. These tasks are not available via the VC or any other management tools. Actually, access to the MUI for ESX versions earlier than version 3 is always direct access to the ESX Server. However, for ESX version 3, the MUI has disappeared, and now only the VIC20 is available for configuring ESX.

The tools chosen to configure an ESX Server via the command line can be used to create a configuration script that can be run over multiple hosts as needed.

Administrative User

For all versions of ESX, it is imperative that you create administrative users. Whether or not the users use local or network-based passwords depends on the network security in place. See Chapter 4 for more information on security. There are various ways to create an administrative user via all mechanisms. For ESX versions earlier than version 3, the administrative user can be created during installation.

Command Line

The command-line methods encompass more than just one way to create users. A user can be added with a local or remote password. If using a remote password, the user can be a member of an Active Directory (AD) domain or part of NIS.

Local User

To create an administrative user via the command line with a local password, use the following commands. Note that `adminuser` is the name of the administrative user to create. In addition to creating or adding the user, it is important to set the local password for the administrative user.

```
useradd adminuser
passwd adminuser
```

In order for this user to be usable via the VIC, you will need to add the appropriate lines to the `/etc/vmware/hostd/authorization.xml` file as well. Assuming no other users are added you can simple add the following lines after the first `</ACEdata>` tag. Note the id number will need to be increased as new users are added. this includes changing the ACEDataID field.

```
<ACEData id="12">
    <ACEDataEntity>ha-folder-root</ACEDataEntity>
    <ACEDataID>12</ACEDataID>
    <ACEDataIsGroup>false</ACEDataIsGroup>
    <ACEDataPropagate>true</ACEDataProagate>
    <ACEDataRoleID>-1</ACEDataRoleID>
    <ACEDataUser>adminuser</ACEDataUser>
</ACEData>
```

Non-Active Directory Network User

All versions of ESX support various forms of non-AD network users from Kerberos, NIS (Yellow Pages), and LDAP. Because most users of ESX use AD rather than the others, these are briefly outlined for ESX version 3. ESX versions earlier than version 3 do not provide the necessary system tools, but all the changes can be made by hand. However, that is beyond the scope of this book.

It is suggested that a level of Linux experience is necessary to configure these sub-systems for ESX earlier than version 3. For every `enable` command that follows, there is a `disable` command, too, that does not take any of the extra arguments.

NIS

For NIS, all that is needed is the following command, because the service console knows to get the user information from the NIS server:

```
esxcfg-auth --enablenis --nisdomain=domain --nisserver=server
```

Kerberos

For Kerberos, the user information is added using `useradd`, because the remote Kerberos server does not provide user information for the service console:

```
esxcfg-auth --enablekrb5 --krb5realm=domain --krb5kdc=server --krb5adminserver=adminServer
useradd adminUser
```

LDAP

LDAP can provide authentication, and if it is being used, enable the LDAP TLS option, because it provides a secure path to the LDAP server. Otherwise, credential information is passed to the server using clear text, which would invalidate LDAP as a tool for authentication. LDAP authentication is enabled as follows and requires a local user to complete it, because only the authentication details are available via LDAP:

```
esxcfg-auth --enableldapauth --enableldaptls --ldapserver=server --ldapbasedn=basedn
useradd adminUser
```

LDAP User Information

Because the goal of many systems is to *not* store user information locally, another option is available for Kerberos and LDAP authentication, and that is to use LDAP to store the user information. User information is the username, groups, and anything unrelated to authentication credentials. To enable LDAP user information, use the following command:

```
esxcfg-auth --enableldap --ldapserver=server --ldapbasedn=basedn
```

Active Directory Domain User

For ESX version 3, there is a very simple method to allow AD authentication. For ESX versions earlier than version 3, the standard Linux tools are available to enable AD authentication. It is important to realize that unless Winbind (Samba) or LDAP is involved, a local user is also required for AD authentication to be in use. Winbind provides an encrypted mechanism to gain user and group information from the AD server. LDAP can provide the same but uses a clear-text transfer.

ESX Version 3

To set up AD authentication for ESX version 3, first configure your AD server if necessary; this depends on the version of Winbind being used. The latest versions of the Samba package does not require these changes. You can find the latest versions of Samba and pam_krb5 that will work with ESX to authenticate ESX using AD at www.astroarch.com/virtual/samba.html.

```
Start->Administrative Tools->Domain Controller Security Policy
     Security Settings->Local Policies->Security Options
Disable both:
     Domain member: Digitally encrypt or sign secure channel data (always)
     Microsoft network server: Digitally sign communications (always)
```

To set up AD authentication for ESX version 3, use the following commands:

```
Download krb5-workstation from http://www.gtlib.gatech.edu/pub/startcom/AS-
3.0.6/updates/repodata/repoview/krb5-workstation-0-1.2.7-61.html
# rpm -ivh krb5-workstation-1.2.7-61.i386.rpm


Upgrade pam_krb5-1.77-1 to pam_krb5-2.2.11-1
Upgrade samba-client-3.0.9-1.3E.10vmw to samba-client-3.0.25-2
Upgrade samba-common-3.0.9-1.3E.10vmw to samba-common-3.0.25-2


# esxcfg-firewall -e activeDirectorKerberos
# esxcfg-firewall -o 445,tcp,out,MicrosoftDS
# esxcfg-firewall -o 445,udp,out,MicrosoftDS
# esxcfg-firewall -o 389,tcp,out,LDAP
# esxcfg-firewall -o 464,udp,out,kpasswd
# esxcfg-auth —enablead —addomain=VMWARELAB.INTERNAL.COM
➥ —addc=w2k3-ad.vmwarelab.internal.com
```

Now test the Kerberos connection:

```
# /usr/kerberos/bin/kinit Administrator
Password for Administrator@VMWARELAB.INTERNAL.COM:
kinit(v5): Clock skew too great while getting initial credentials
```

Fix any issues that appear from this command. Without `krb5-workstation` installed, the `kinit` command does not exist. In this case, the AD server's time and the ESX Server's time are too different, and one of them needs to be fixed. It is best for both servers to use the same time source. After the Kerberos problems have been solved, it's time to set up the configuration files to talk to AD.

In some cases, it is necessary to specify the proper encryption types used by the AD server. The error that leads up to this is a report on incorrect `enctypes`. Update the `/etc/krb5.conf` file to be similar to the following:

```
# Autogenerated by esxcfg-auth


[domain_realm]
vmwarelab.internal.com = VMWARELAB.INTERNAL.COM
.vmwarelab.internal.com = VMWARELAB.INTERNAL.COM


[libdefaults]
default_realm = VMWARELAB.INTERNAL.COM
default_tkt_enctypes = des3-hmac-sha1 des-cbc-crc des-cbc-md5 rc4-hmac
default_tgs_enctypes = des3-hmac-sha1 des-cbc-crc des-cbc-md5 rc4-hmac


[realms]
VMWARELAB.INTERNAL.COM = {
      admin_server = w2k3-ad.vmwarelab.internal.com:464
      default_domain = vmwarelab.internal.com
      kdc = w2k3-ad.vmwarelab.internal.com:88
}
```

Note that there are not many changes needed to this file, and that other changes usually used for Linux can be made after you have a working AD authentication. Another key file to AD authentication within ESX is the `/etc/pam.d/system-auth` file. You also need to tweak it:

```
#%PAM-1.0
# Autogenerated by esxcfg-auth

account      required    /lib/security/$ISA/pam_unix.so      broken_shadow
account      [default=bad success=ok user_unknown=ignore]
/lib/security/$ISA/pam_krb5.so
account [default=bad success=ok user_unknown=ignore]  /lib/security/$ISA/pam_access.so

auth         required    /lib/security/$ISA/pam_env.so
auth         sufficient  /lib/security/$ISA/pam_unix.so      likeauth nullok
auth         sufficient  /lib/security/$ISA/pam_krb5.so      use_first_pass
auth         required    /lib/security/$ISA/pam_deny.so

password     required    /lib/security/$ISA/pam_cracklib.so retry=3
password     sufficient  /lib/security/$ISA/pam_unix.so      nullok use_authtok md5
shadow
password     sufficient  /lib/security/$ISA/pam_krb5.so      use_authtok
password     required    /lib/security/$ISA/pam_deny.so

session      required    /lib/security/$ISA/pam_limits.so
session      required    /lib/security/$ISA/pam_unix.so
session      optional    /lib/security/$ISA/pam_krb5.so
session      required    /lib/security/$ISA/pam_mkhomedir.so skel=/etc/skel umask=0077
```

Note the first pam_krb5.so line will allow account authentication if there is a local account without errors. Also note the last line will create a home directory for the AD user automatically. A home directory is required when logging into Linux-based systems such as ESX. Also, use this file as is, because the use_first_pass and use_authtok options are required; otherwise, you will be asked for passwords many, many times.

The last line of the account section of the system-auth file references pam_access.so which allows the administrator to control who can login from which systems. An example of the /etc/security/access.conf file follows. This file allows root access from crond, console, ttys 1-6, IP Address 127.0.0.1 and not from anywhere else. It also allows those users in the vmadmins group (whether from a local group or AD) to gain access to the system from any IP except for the user badadmin who can gain access ONLY from the IP address of 192.168.1.100. All other access is denied. The manual page on access.conf (man access.conf) will give many more details on how to set this up. This is an important step to take or it may be possible for others to gain access to information they should not have, like the configuration of the virtual machines.

```
# Access.conf
+ : root : crond console tty1 tty2 tty3 tty3 tty5 tty6
+ : root : 127.0.0.1
+ : @vmadmins EXCEPT badadmin : ALL
+ : badadmin : 192.168.1.100
- : root : ALL
- : ALL : ALL
```

Another critical file is the Samba configuration file that will be used by Winbind to communicate with the AD server for user information in an encrypted form. LDAP, on the other hand, is not encrypted. The /etc/samba/smb.conf should look like the following:

```
[global]
        workgroup = VMWARELAB
        server string = Samba Server
        printcap name = /etc/printcap
        load printers = yes
        cups options = raw
        log file = /var/log/samba/%m.log
        max log size = 50
        security = ads
        socket options = TCP_NODELAY SO_RCVBUF=8192 SO_SNDBUF=8192
        dns proxy = no
        idmap uid = 16777216-33554431
        idmap gid = 16777216-33554431
        template shell = /bin/bash
        template homedir = /home/%D/%U
        winbind use default domain = yes
        password server = w2k3-ad.vmwarelab.internal.com
        realm = VMWARELAB.INTERNAL.COM
```

Of special importance is the workgroup and realm fields; these define the domain and Kerberos realm, respectively. The template lines also provide the location in which to create home directories. Because home directories are owned by the users themselves, they are created by the user so, special attention needs to be paid to permission on the `template_homedir` directory. Note the %D in the line, which refers to the domain to be used (in our case, VMWARELAB). The final requirements for Winbind and `pam_mkhomedir` follow:

```
# mkdir /home/VMWARELAB
# chmod 1777 /home/VMWARELAB
# mkdir /var/log/samba
```

Before you can use AD authentication, you need to tell the system where to find the user information. Therefore, the `/etc/nsswitch.conf` file needs to be told to use Winbind, as in the following example, which appends Winbind to the group, passwd, and shadow lines. By appending, we are stating that the local files should be consulted first, thereby allowing local users to authenticate through normal means:

```
# Autogenerated by esxcfg-auth

aliases:        files nisplus
automount:      files nisplus
bootparams:     nisplus [NOTFOUND=return] files
ethers:         files
group:          files winbind
hosts:          files dns
netgroup:       nisplus
netmasks:       files
networks:       files
passwd:         files winbind
protocols:      files
publickey:      nisplus
rpc:            files
services:       files
shadow:         files winbind
```

Now that every file is configured properly, we are ready to join the ESX Server to the AD domain using the following commands. These will join the machine to the domain and enable Winbind and ensure that Winbind runs on reboot:

```
# net ads join -UAdministrator
Administrator's password:
Using short domain name — VMWARELAB
Joined 'AURORA01' to realm 'VMWARELAB.INTERNAL.COM'
# service winbind start
# chkconfg winbind on
```

And last, we test everything to make sure it works. The following commands and outputs are examples; your AD server will have more users and groups. Testauser is just an example user. The last command verifies that the groups are resolved for an individual user:

```
#wbinfo -g
domain computers
domain controllers
schema admins
enterprise admins
domain admins
domain users
domain guests
group policy creator owners
# wbinfo -u
administrator
guest
support_388945a0
krbtgt
testauser
smbservice
# wbinfo -t
checking the trust secret via RPC calls succeeded
# getent group
root:x:0:root
...
domain computers:*:16777220:
```

```
domain controllers:*:16777218:
schema admins:*:16777222:administrator
enterprise admins:*:16777223:administrator
domain admins:*:16777219:administrator
domain users:*:16777216:
domain guests:*:16777217:
group policy creator owners:*:16777224:administrator
# getent passwd
root:x:0:0:root:/root:/bin/bash
...
administrator:*:16777216:16777216:Administrator:/home/VMWARELAB/administrator:/bin/bash
guest:*:16777217:16777217:Guest:/home/VMWARELAB/guest:/bin/bash
...
krbtgt:*:16777220:16777216:krbtgt:/home/VMWARELAB/krbtgt:/bin/bash
# id testauser
uid=16777221(testauser) gid=16777216(domain users) groups=16777216(domain users)
```

ESX is now integrated in with Active Directory.

ESX Versions Earlier Than Version 3

The setup is similar to ESX version 3, except that there is no `esxcfg-auth` command, so the files mentioned must be edited and created by hand. Also, there is no pam_access.so capabilities so other tools are necessary to limit access to the system.

Virtual Infrastructure Client

The use of the VIC20 to create an administrative user only works if the user in question is going to be a local user. Remote users have their own methods for creating the user. However, the configuration for a remote user is available only from the command line. The first step is to launch the VIC20 and specify as the server the hostname of the ESX version 3 server to configure, providing the root user and password credentials. The root user and password credentials must be provided in step 26 of the ESX version 3 server installation, as shown in Appendix B and Appendix C. These same credentials are a requirement to initially log in via the VIC20.

1. Once logged in, select the Users & Groups tab, and right-click within the list to produce the add user menu per Figure 8.1. Note that this tab does not exist if the VIC20 connects to the VC Server.

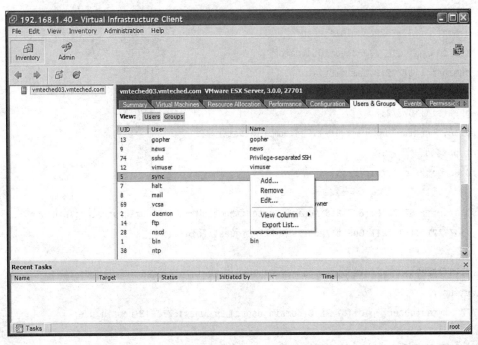

Figure 8.1   Accessing the Add User menu

2. Within the Add User dialog, enter the administrative user login.

3. Within the Add User dialog, enter the administrative username and password twice. The second entry is to confirm the first is correct.

4. Enter the group of wheel, and click the Add button next to the Group entry field.

5. Click OK and add the administrative user with a group of wheel (see Figure 8.2). Note the Group Membership box now contains wheel.

6. And finally, verify that the user has actually been entered by reviewing the users displayed in the Users & Groups tab (see Figure 8.3).

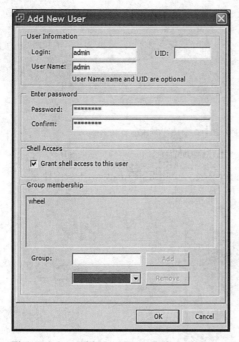

Figure 8.2   Add New User dialog

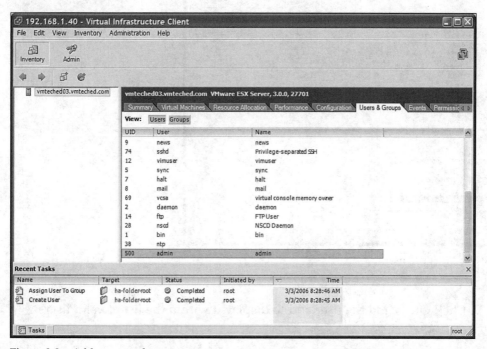

Figure 8.3   Add user results

Management User Interface (MUI)

You can add a user via the MUI as follows:

1. Log in to the MUI.

2. Select the Options tab.

3. Select the Users and Groups link.

4. Enter the appropriate credentials for the administrative user.

5. Click the Add link to add this new user to a group.

6. Select the wheel group name from the drop-down list. The results of the last three steps are shown in Figure 8.4.

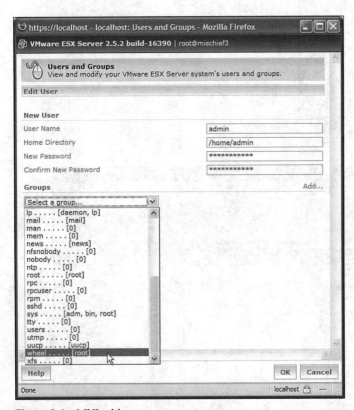

Figure 8.4 MUI add user

7. Click OK to add the user and to display it within the list of valid users.

Security Configuration

Similar to adding an administrative user, the security configuration of ESX can occur only with a direct connection to the ESX Server in question. Refer to Chapter 4, "Auditing, Monitoring, and Securing," and Appendix A, "Security Script," for details on hardening ESX. The security configuration of ESX covered herein is how to access the tools, not how to harden the server.

Command Line

ESX versions earlier than version 3 do not contain a direct command-line mechanism to control the security of ESX. Multiple tools achieve the same level of changes via the MUI; but for these versions of ESX, there is really no sense of security. ESX version 3, however, changes all that with the implementation of a real firewall and security protocol.

ESX Version 3

ESX version 3 has a single tool that controls security via the command line. The use of the `esxcfg-firewall` is the same as using the VIC20, because it modifies the same local ESX Server databases. By default, ESX version 3 has most services and ports disabled, but some services and ports should be enabled to allow for outbound SSH, Network Time Protocol, and the use of HP Insight Manager agents. The HP Insight Manager agents modify the security settings on their own, and similar tools from other vendors should do the same. We are therefore only concerned with allowing the Network Time Protocol and outbound SSH. The following commands will do this:

```
/usr/sbin/esxcfg-firewall -e ntpClient
/usr/sbin/esxcfg-firewall -e sshClient
```

To determine all the possible `esxcfg-firewall` settings, run `esxcfg-firewall -h` and use the `-l` option to list the current firewall rules and the `-s` option to find a full list of protocols and ports to open or close.

ESX Versions Earlier Than Version 3

The command-line commands that provide functionality equivalent to the MUI are the `service` and `chkconfig` commands. All the security options in the MUI do is turn on and off various services (specifically, SSH, unencrypted MUI, unencrypted remote console, FTP, Telnet, and NFS). For example, *high* security disables SSH to the server. To do the same from the command line, issue the following commands:

```
service ssh stop
chkconfig ssh off
```

The `service` command stops the server, and the `chkconfig` command makes the change permanent past a reboot. Other than the listed services, the MUI cannot affect any others or any other security functionality. See Chapter 4 for more information about ESX security.

VIC20

The VIC20, when connected directly to the ESX Server, can modify the ESX Server firewall. Although many changes can be made, the equivalents to the command-line changes are outlined in the following steps.

1. Once logged in to the VIC20, select the Configuration tab, and then the Security Profile software configuration element (see Figure 8.5). Click the Properties link.

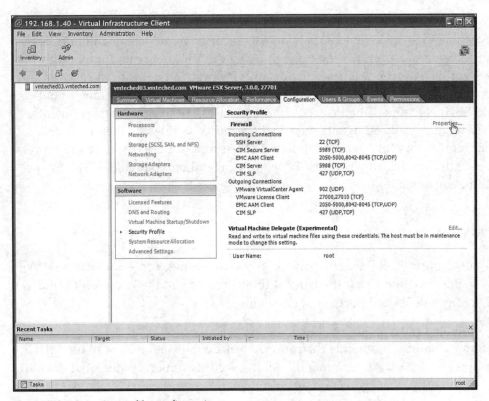

Figure 8.5 Security profile configuration

2. When the Security Profile dialog appears, check the SSH Client and NTP Client boxes (see Figure 8.6), and then select OK.

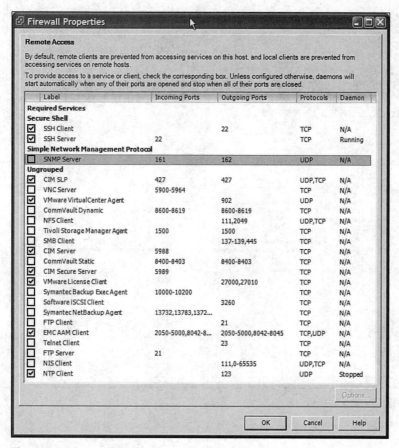

Figure 8.6 Security Profile Properties dialog

3. Review the changes to the security profile in the resulting configuration screen (see Figure 8.7).

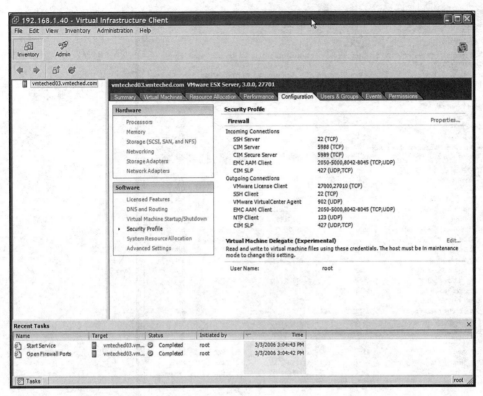

Figure 8.7 Security profile properties review

MUI

The MUI has a simple security settings web page that controls which services are running by either selecting High (SSH service), Medium (SSH and FTP services), or Low (all services). As outlined in Chapter 4, this is not an adequate tool for setting security on an ESX Server, but it does provide some rudimentary service-level security. Figure 8.8 shows the full capabilities of the settings.

Figure 8.8 MUI security profile properties

Network Time Protocol (NTP)

Configuring the Network Time Protocol is the same for all versions of ESX, and there is no way to do this except from the command line until VIC 2.5 is available. Although there are plenty of references on NTP, what is provided is more a how-to than a discussion of why this configuration works. Timekeeping is extremely important in ESX, and VMware has many knowledge briefs and white papers on the subject. These steps, however, work for all ESX OS versions. If the ESX Server time is not in sync with VC, performance information will suffer; or with other ESX Servers, VMware tools will not properly track time.

1. Add the IP addresses of each time source to the `/etc/ntp/step-tickers` file:

```
timesources="a.b.c.d e.f.g.h"
for x in $timesources
do
        echo $x >> /etc/ntp/step-tickers
done
```

2. Modify the NTP service configuration file, `/etc/ntp.conf`, to comment out any restrictions.

```
/bin/sed '/^restrict/s/^/\#/' /etc/ntp.conf > /tmp/ntp.conf
/bin/mv -f /tmp/ntp.conf /etc/ntp.conf
```

3. Modify the NTP service configuration file, `/etc/ntp.conf`,, to add in the IP address of each time source as a server:

```
timesources="a.b.c.d e.f.g.h"
for x in $timesources
do
        echo "server $x" >> /etc/ntp.conf
done
```

4. Ensure the firewall allows the NTP client to work (see the section "Security Configuration," earlier in this chapter).

5. Start the NTP service and configure it to autostart:

```
/sbin/service ntpd start
/sbin/chkconfig ntpd on
```

Service Console Memory

There is no simple command-line mechanism to change the amount of memory allocated to the service console. In general, for ESX versions earlier than version 3, most times the setting of the service console memory resources are set during installation. Any change to the memory resources of the service console requires a reboot. If you are running software or hardware agents within the ESX service console it is important to properly allocate the memory. The default settings of 272MB (or thereabout) is in most cases not enough for everything.

Command Line

For ESX version 3, there is no easy way to change the amount of memory allocated to the service console. However, earlier versions of ESX do have a command-line tool to change the amount of service console memory.

ESX Version 3

To change the amount of memory from the command line in ESX version 3, there are several steps. Be forewarned, however, that these steps are dangerous, and unless there is sufficient Linux experience available, they should be avoided.

1. Edit the file /etc/grub.conf,.
2. Copy the first stanza in the file. The first line of the stanza will start with title and end the line before the next title. This copy provides a way to get back to where the system was prior to these changes.
3. Rename the new stanza by changing the title line appropriately.
4. Edit the uppermem line to reflect the total amount of allocated memory in kilobytes assigned to the service console.
5. Edit the kernel line to change the mem=XXXM parameter. XXX reflects the total amount of memory in megabytes assigned to the service console.
6. Save and exit the file.
7. Reboot the server and select the new title from the boot screen. Once this works, change the default setting in /etc/grub.conf to reflect the new stanza number.
8. It now will be necessary to modify the /etc/esx.conf file to reflect the proper setting for /boot/memSize.
9. Or use the following script to change the value. Note we are changing the memory size of the service console from 272 to 512MB:

```
sed -e 's/boot\/memSize = \"272\"/boot\/memSize = \"512\"/g'
/etc/vmware/esx.conf > /tmp/esx.conf
sed -e 's/uppermem 277504/uppermem 523264/g' -e 's/mem=272M/mem=512M/g'
/boot/grub/grub.conf > /tmp/grub.conf
/bin/mv /tmp/esx.conf /etc/vmware/esx.conf
/bin/mv /tmp/grub.conf /boot/grub/grub.conf
```

Remember that the preceding steps are extremely dangerous and should be avoided unless absolutely necessary.

Earlier Versions of ESX

To change the service console memory for ESX versions earlier than ESX version 3 involves some of the steps listed previously or the use of the commands shown in the following listing. The recommendation is to use the command shown in the listing. The commands will raise many questions, but it is important not to make any changes to the configuration except to change the amount of memory for the service console. The final command reboots the server for the changes to take place:

```
vmkpcidivy -i
reboot
```

VIC20

The VIC20, when connected directly or indirectly to the ESX Server, can modify the ESX service console resources.

1. Once logged in to the VIC20, select the Configuration tab, and then Memory Configuration (see Figure 8.9).

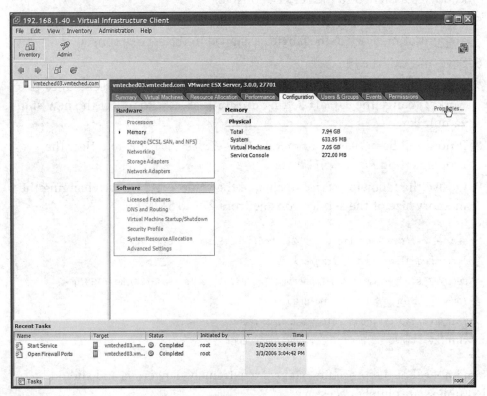

Figure 8.9   Service console memory configuration

2. Click the Properties link to display the dialog in which to change the service console memory allocation (see Figure 8.10).

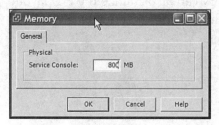

Figure 8.10 Service Console Memory dialog

3. Change the value of the allocated memory to the appropriate number, and then click OK and review the changes to the memory in the resulting configuration screen. Remember this change requires a reboot (see Figure 8.11).

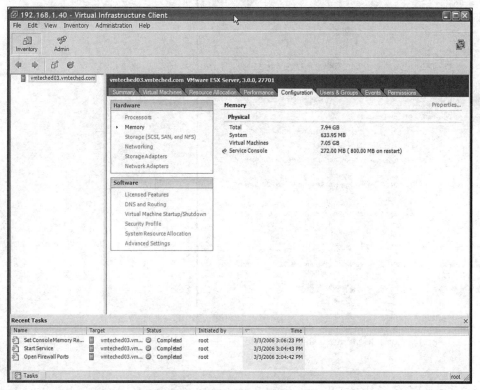

Figure 8.11 Service Console Memory dialog review

MUI

Changing the service console memory via the MUI is quite simple, but also dangerous, because the location to change the memory can also change the PCI layout of the system. Extreme caution is desirable. In addition, this step forces a reboot; so do this when you are ready to reboot the server.

1. Log in to the MUI.

2. Select the Options tab.

3. Click the Startup Profile link.

4. Select the appropriate reserved memory setting from the drop-down list, or enter a value by hand in megabytes (see Figure 8.12).

Figure 8.12   Service Console Memory startup profile

5. Click OK, and then OK again, to force a server reboot.

Conclusion

In this chapter, we have gone through the configuration of an ESX Server when connected directly to the host. Many of these items need to be done prior to creating VMs, specifically anything related to networking and the service console, because these items can require reboots. The next chapter covers those tasks that can be completed either while connected to the host or via VC and do not require reboots to complete.

Chapter 9

Configuring ESX from a Virtual Center or Host

This chapter is really a continuation of Chapter 8, "Configuring ESX from a Host Connection." However, this chapter makes use of the VIC connected to either the host or through the VC, whereas Chapter 8 does not make use of VC. This chapter continues the Rosetta stone approach to configuring the ESX Server following the steps that I find most useful. Although these steps are by no means a complete list of configuration tasks, most common and some uncommon ones are discussed.

Configuration Tasks

The following list of configuration tasks (Table 9.1) starts where the list in Chapter 8 left off. These tasks cover the intricacies of configuring the system for future virtual machines hosting.

Table 9.1

Configuration Tasks				
Task	**VIC**	**MUI**	**COS**	**Dependency/Notes**
Join host to VC	Yes	N/A	N/A	Before using the VC, configure servers
Licensing	Yes	Yes	Special script	Prior to HA/DRS
vSwap	N/A	Yes	vmkfstools	ESX v2.x only
Local VMFS	Yes	Yes	vmkfstools	Usually part of install

continues...

Table 9.1 continued

Configuration Tasks

Task	VIC	MUI	COS	Dependency/Notes
FC HBA VMFS	Yes	Yes	cos-rescan (ESX version 2)	Chapters 5, "Storage with ESX, and 6, "Effects on ESX"
			vmkmultipath	
			esxcfg-vmhbadevs	
			esxcfg-rescan	
Virtual networking	Yes	Yes	esxcfg-vmnic	
			esxcfg-vswitch	
			esxcfg-route	Chapter 7, "Networking"
iSCSI VMFS	Yes	N/A	esxcfg-swiscis	Chapters 5, 6, and 7
NFS	Yes	N/A	esxcfg-nas	Chapter 7

Add Host to VC

If VC is available, now is the time to add it into the system. The process is the same for VC versions 1 and 2. However, if VC is not available, all the VIC items that follow apply strictly to a host connection. VC is the main tool for managing multiple ESX Servers, and VC 2.0 can manage ESX 3 and earlier versions of ESX. It is a common interface and the only way to get access to the advanced features of ESX version 3 such as VMware HA, and VMware DRS, which are covered in Chapter 12, "Disaster Recovery and Backup." The steps for adding into VC follow:

1. Log in to VC.
2. Create a datacenter (*File > New > Datacenter*) and give the new datacenter a name. All hosts within a datacenter can share templates and so on.
3. Select the datacenter, and then add a host to the datacenter (*File > Add Host*).
4. Make the hostname resolvable by DNS. It is strongly urged that the FQDN be used; otherwise, VMware HA will have issues. It is also important that the ESX Server can ping itself and other hosts by hostname; otherwise, there can be VMware HA issues.
5. Enter the username and password for the root account for the host.
6. VC will now contact the host in question and present some information about the host, including the machine type and VMs it has. For ESX versions earlier than version 3, the next step is to configure VMotion. That is handled by other means in ESX version 3.

7. Next pick a location or VM folder in which to place the VMs within that host. A VM folder can be created at any time, and they are independent of hosts and are covered in Chapter 10, "Virtual Machines." This step is new for ESX version 3.

8. Click Finish to add the host to VC.

Now VC can be used to manage the host in question. Although VC 2 can manage ESX versions earlier than version 3, it will still direct the user to the MUI to manipulate ESX. However, for ESX version 3, the VIC will offer all but the preceding configuration options.

Licensing

There is no simple command-line mechanism to modify the ESX Server licensing, and for ESX versions earlier than version 3, license strings were either entered in during installation or directly after installation. ESX Server version 3, however, uses a new type of license from MacroVision called FlexLM. FlexLM licenses are either host based or server based. However, a FlexLM server is required for any advanced ESX features such as VMotion, VMware HA, or DR. The best practice for a License Server is to make it the same as the VC Server and to have both of them running as a separate physical machine and not as a VM. The reason for this may not be obvious, but it is important. If a license expires, the ESX Server will cache the license key for 14 days. If the License Server is not accessible, after those 14 days VMs will fail to boot. Therefore, if there is a slip, it is possible that all the VMs will fail to boot on an ESX system reboot. FlexLM is beyond the scope of this book, but you can find FlexLM documentation at www.macrovision.com/pdfs/flexnet_licensing_end_user_guide.pdf.

If the License Server or the VC Server is also running as a VM, then on an ESX Server failure where these VMs are running, no form of VMware-based redundancy will take effect. The best practice, therefore, is for the VC and License Servers to reside on a pair of clustered physical machines.

In addition, when you purchase a license from VMware or a reseller, you receive an activation code. This code is *not* your license. You need to log in to your VMware account and register the activation code to retrieve your license file.

Command Line

There is no easy command-line mechanism available to enter ESX license keys.

ESX Version 3

If the license is for a server and not a host license, it is possible to configure the server to see the License Server. To do this, modify the file /etc/vmware/ license.cfg and set the MODE option to be server and the SERVER option to be 27000@licenseServerIPAddress. The hostname of the License Server can also be used. If the License Server is unreachable due to a DNS issue for more than 14 days, all licenses are revoked and no new VMs can be booted on the ESX Server until such time as the problem is fixed.

Earlier Versions of ESX

There are two license files possible to use in /etc/vmware on ESX Servers earlier than version 3; unfortunately, creation of these files is not available. However, if they are configured and backed up to tape, restoration of the files will restore the appropriate host licenses. Note that the file names start with the word *license.*

VIC

The VIC, when connected directly or indirectly to the ESX Server, can modify the ESX Server licenses.

1. Once logged in to the VIC, select the Configuration tab and then the *Licensed Feature* software configuration element (see Figure 9.1). When this is displayed, click the first blue Edit link.

2. Elect whether to use a host-based license or to use a License Server. When choosing a License Server, enter the FQDN or the IP address of the License Server per Figure 9.2, and select OK.

3. On the Licensed Features configuration screen, click the next highlighted Edit link opposite ESX Server License Type. The license type served by the License Server is selectable. If only Unlicensed is available, this indicates that the License Server has no more licenses. Select the server license, in this case ESX Server Standard (see Figure 9.3), and press OK.

4. On the Licensed Features configuration screen, click the next highlighted Edit link opposite Add-Ons. Enable those add-ons available to the license granted. The add-ons include VMware DR and HA and consolidated backups.

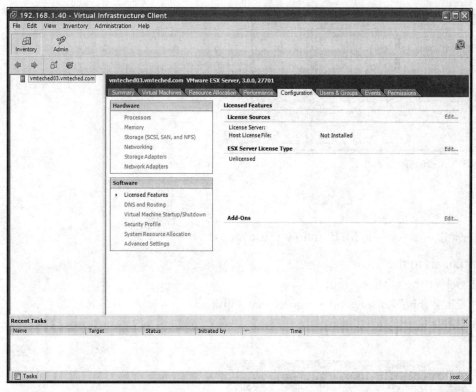

Figure 9.1   Licensed Features configuration

Figure 9.2   License Sources dialog

Figure 9.3   License Type dialog

MUI

To enter a license via the MUI, follow these steps:

1. Log in to the MUI.
2. Select the Options tab.
3. Click the *Licensing and Serial Numbers* link.
4. Enter in the serial numbers for this server per Figure 9.4 and press OK.

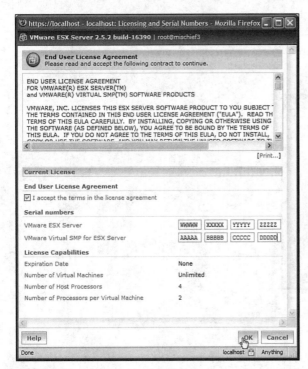

Figure 9.4   Serial Number dialog

Virtual Swap

The virtual swap (vSwap) file is incredibly important for ESX versions earlier than version 3 because it dictates how much memory can be overcommitted for use with the VMs. It is possible to create many VMs that have allocated a large amount of memory due to vSwap. However, with ESX version 3, vSwap is now allocated per VM as needed and no longer has a separately configurable option. For ESX versions earlier than version 3, it often was required to create multiple vSwap files as they were limited in size, scope, and possibly location.

Command Line

For ESX versions earlier than version 3, the process to create a vSwap file is straightforward, as shown in the following script segment where C implies the controller, T implies the track or path, L implies the LUN, P implies the partition number, and XX implies the size of the file to create in gigabytes:

```
vmkfstools -k XXG /vmfs/vmhbaC\:T\:L\:P/filename.vswp    # create
vmkfstools -w /vmfs/vmhbaC\:T\:L\:P/filename.vswp        # activate
```

Note that to remove an existing vSwap file, the vSwap file should first be deactivated. Each vSwap file in use has an ID. The ID is used to deactivate the vSwap file, which will then allow the file to be removed or moved and activated in a new location.

VIC

ESX version 3 no longer requires this functionality, so no VIC mechanism is available.

MUI

The MUI has one drawback to it with regard to vSwap files. It can only create and use one vSwap file at a time. However, it is possible to create, activate, and manage others from the command line. It is recommended that the vSwap file be 2x or 4x the available memory. However, each vSwap file can be a maximum of 64GB. Therefore, for large memory systems, it is necessary to use the command line to create multiple vSwap files. The steps to create or modify the vSwap file are as follows:

1. Log in to the MUI.
2. Select the Options tab.

3. Click the *Swap Configuration* link.

4. Enter in the size of the vSwap file (see Figure 9.5).

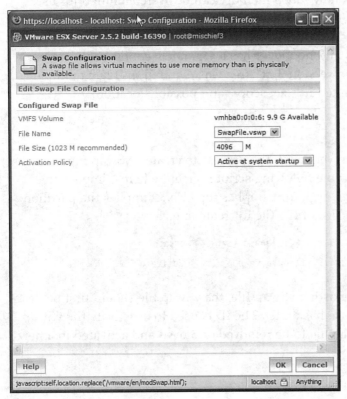

Figure 9.5 vSwap dialog

5. Click the *Activate* link to activate the swap file created.

6. Press OK to exit the dialog.

If this is the first time the server MUI has been accessed after installation, there might be a warning on the home page after logging in that provides a short-cut to the Swap Configuration dialog, because ESX versions earlier than version 3 absolutely require a vSwap file.

Local VMFS

Adding a local disk-based VMFS can be accomplished via all methods. Unlike network- or Fibre Channel-based disks, no delicate cables are involved, but the steps are pretty much the same. Generally, the local VMFS is created during installation. However, if it is not, there are various ways to add a local VMFS. It is important, especially in ESX version 3, to use unique names for each local storage device across all hosts. The reason for this is that the VIC sees all storage devices at once, and having multiple names such as storage1 can be confusing to the end users. The best practice then is to use the machine hostname as part of the local storage device name.

Command Line

Because the local VMFS is defined as a cryptic name, vmhbaC:T:L:P, it is important to rename this to be something more readable. If the file system is to be created—that is, it is not already existent—there is an option in vmkfstools to name the file system. However, this option works only on creation. So, there are two choices for an existing VMFS: either delete and re-create or label the volume somehow.

Renaming a VMFS

For ESX versions earlier than version 3, there is no way to label the VMFS outside the MUI or re-creation. For ESX version 3, the following script can be used to rename the local volume. For ESX version 3, we take advantage of the default naming convention for local storage, which is a VMFS logically named storage1:

```
cd /vmfs/volumes
uid=`/bin/ls -al storage1 ¦ /bin/awk '{print $11}'`
/bin/ln -s $uid HOSTNAME
```

Note that HOSTNAME is the first part of the fully qualified domain name (FQDN). Assuming the FQDN is vmwareyy.example.com, the HOSTNAME is vmwareyy. Note that this code only works on ESX version 3.

Creating a VMFS

The steps to create a VMFS for all forms of media are the same. Our example, however, use the local disk partition names, but remote partition names can also be used. Follow these steps to create a local VMFS. Our example uses HP hardware as its basis. A LUN (logical unit) in the following discussion is a generic term that implies either a single drive or a RAID array of drives. Note that these steps can wreak great havoc on a system and require a level of expertise with Linux. In addition, the partition should be on 64MB boundaries for best performance. For these reasons, it is best to use the VIC to create a VM. The following does not align the VMFS on any boundaries and is used as an example.

1. Determine the controller and LUN to use. Remember, that a VMFS desires to be the *only* partition on a given LUN. For example, we will be using controller 0 or the built-in RAID controller for an HP Proliant server, and the LUN to use is the second RAID array created on the controller. That implies the device we will be using is /dev/cciss/c0d1, where c0d1 refers to controller 0 and LUN 1, while c0d0 is the default boot volume.

2. Partition the new device to create one giant partition using the fdisk command. First we delete any existing partitions and then add a new one:

```
fdisk /dev/cciss/c0d1
The number of cylinders for this disk is set to 19929.
There is nothing wrong with that, but this is larger than 1024,
and could in certain setups cause problems with:
1) software that runs at boot time (e.g., old versions of LILO)
2) booting and partitioning software from other OSs
    (e.g., DOS FDISK, OS/2 FDISK)


Command (m for help): d
Selected partition 1


Command (m for help): n
Command action
   e   extended
   p   primary partition (1-4)
p
Partition number (1-4): 1
First cylinder (1-19929, default 1):
Using default value 1
Last cylinder or +size or +sizeM or +sizeK (1-19929, default 19929):
Using default value 19929


Command (m for help): t
Selected partition 1
Hex code (type L to list codes): fb
Changed system type of partition 1 to fb (Unknown)


Command (m for help): w
```

3. Once the device is created, run the following to determine the device's cryptic name. The cryptic name is crucial to know and is sometimes extremely hard to determine. If the following commands do not get the cryptic name of the device, it might be necessary to revert to tried-and-true Linux methods by reviewing the boot log of the server and extrapolating the name of the device. If there is an existing local VMFS, the cryptic name is easy to extrapolate from the existing name. The controller and target values should be the same, but the LUN value should be unique, and the partition value should always be 1 because of locking considerations discussed in previous chapters:

```
esxcfg-vmhbadevs   # available only in ESX version 3
```

Or

```
vmkpcidivy -q vmhba_devs
```

4. Now use the vmkfstools command to create the VMFS on the new device. Note that XXXX is the file system human-readable name and should include the hostname of the server. For our example, vmwareyyA is a suitable name. Also, the P or partition to use will be 1 because there is only one partition on the device. The cryptic name must be used until the volume is named:

```
vmkfstools -C vmfs3 -S XXXX /vmfs/volumes/vmhbaC\:T\:L\:P # ESX version 3
```

Or

```
vmkfstools -C vmfs2 -S XXXX /vmfs/vmhbaC\:T\:L\:P # Prior Versions of ESX
```

Extending a VMFS

Another useful feature of a VMFS is the capability to add an extent to an existing VMFS. An extent as described previously is a disk partition that is not originally part of the VMFS. Keep in mind that there is a limit of one VMFS per LUN and therefore only one LUN per VMFS. The extent capability allows more partitions from separate devices to be added to the VMFS so that the VMFS can cross device boundaries. This is similar to the Logical Volume Manager (LVM) that is common with Linux and UNIX systems, or dynamic disks in Windows, but unlike these options, there is no performance gain. First create a new partition on a new device as shown in Steps 1 through 3 earlier, and now there is a new step, Step 4.

1. See earlier.

2. See earlier.

3. See earlier.

4. Extend an existing VMFS by adding another partition to the existing pool that comprises the existing VMFS. Use the cryptic name as the name of the partition to add and use the noncryptic VMFS name as the last argument:

```
vmkfstools -Z vmhbaC\:T\:L\:P /vmfs/volumes/vmfsName # ESX Versions 3
```

Or

```
vmkfstools -Z vmhbaC\:T\:L\:P /vmfs/vmfsName # Prior versions of ESX
```

Deleting a VMFS Extent

There is no safe way to delete an extent on a local SCSI device short of repartitioning the extent, and when extents are in use, this will tend to destroy *all* data on the disk. If there is not enough space to create a new VMFS to hold the existing VMs, please do *not* follow these instructions unless the following question can be answered affirmatively:

Are you satisfied with your backup?

Follow the steps for deleting a VMFS. In ESX version 3, deleting an extent partition using `fdisk` will *not* delete the extent from the logical volume manager; however, it will delete the space from the VMFS. The original size of the VMFS will still be reported by all tools, but the space remaining will be correct. In the ESX versions earlier than version 3, deleting an extent partition effectively removes the extent because the logical volume manager was not in use.

Deleting a VMFS

Deleting a VMFS is catastrophic to all data on the VMFS. If there is not enough space to create a new VMFS to hold the existing VMs, do *not* follow these instructions unless the following question can be answered affirmatively.

Are you satisfied with your backup?

If there are no existing VMs, by all means proceed:

1. Create a new VMFS the full size of the old VMFS, plus all the extents (see 1–4 earlier under *"Creating a VMFS"*).

2. Shut down all the VMs currently residing on the old VMFS. The following script snippet takes as an argument the noncryptic name of the VMFS in question:

```
vol=`/bin/ls -al /vmfs/volumes/$1 | /usr/bin/awk '{print $11}'`
# uncomment below for ESX versions prior to version 3
#vol=`/bin/ls -al /vmfs/$1 | /usr/bin/awk '{print $11}'` for x in
`/usr/bin/vmware-cmd -l|/usr/bin/grep $vol`
do
        state=`/usr/bin/vmware-cmd $x getstate|/usr/bin/awk '{print $3}'`
        if [ $state -eq "on" ]
        then
                /usr/bin/vmware-cmd $x stop
        fi
done
```

3. Unregister all the VMs currently residing on the old VMFS. (This step could be considered optional, but because the names stay around inside VC and the MUI, it is best to unregister prior to moving.) The following script snippet takes as an argument the noncryptic name of the VMFS in question:

```
vol=`/bin/ls -al /vmfs/volumes/$1 | /usr/bin/awk '{print $11}'`
# uncomment below for ESX versions prior to version 3
#vol=`/bin/ls -al /vmfs/$1 | /usr/bin/awk '{print $11}'`
for x in `/usr/bin/vmware-cmd -l|/usr/bin/grep $vol`
do
        /usr/bin/vmware-cmd -s unregister $x
done
```

4. Move all the VMs from the old VMFS to the new:

```
cd /vmfs/volumes/oldVMFS; mv * /vmfs/volumes/newVMFS
```

5. Using `fdisk`, remove the disk partition from the old VMFS related to the extent. This is a dangerous step and requires expertise with Linux. Note that although this will remove the space allocated to the VMFS, it will *not* remove the VMFS from the LVM on ESX version 3. Re-creating the partition as a VMFS will once more show the old partition as part of an existing LVM volume or VMFS. For earlier versions of ESX, this does not hold true:

```
fdisk /dev/cciss/c0d1

The number of cylinders for this disk is set to 19929.

There is nothing wrong with that, but this is larger than 1024,

and could in certain setups cause problems with:

1) software that runs at boot time (e.g., old versions of LILO)

2) booting and partitioning software from other OSs

    (e.g., DOS FDISK, OS/2 FDISK)


Command (m for help): d
Selected partition 1


Command (m for help): w
```

6. Modify any VM configuration files left on the new VMFS so that the files all point to the proper location. Edit the files with the ending .vmdk (but not any with the word *flat* in them), .vmxf, .vmsd, and .vmx to change the location if necessary of all the VMDK (disk files) currently in use by the VM. For ESX version 3, this is not necessary, but it is for ESX versions earlier than version 3. This requires knowledge of the Linux editors nano or vi.

7. Reregister all the VMs from their current VMFS locations. The following is for ESX version 3:

```
/usr/bin/find /vmfs/volumes/newVMFS –name '*.vmx' –exec
↪/usr/bin/vmware-cmd –s register {} \;
```

Or for ESX versions earlier than version 3:

```
/usr/bin/find /vmfs/newVMFS –name '*.vmx' –exec /usr/bin/vmware-cmd
↪-s register {} \;
```

VIC

Once more, there are two tasks for a local VMFS. The first is to change the name of any local VMFS; the other is to create a new VMFS.

Renaming a VMFS
For ESX version 3, there are two ways to rename a VMFS. The two methods are presented here. Remember, it is a good practice to name the VMFS using some

form of the FQDN. The first method is to go directly to the data store for the ESX Server in question and rename the local VMFS.

1. Log in to the VIC.

2. Select the host in question.

3. Select the Configuration tab for the host in question.

4. Click the *Storage (SCSI, SAN, and NFS)* link.

5. Select the local storage device to rename.

6. Click the existing name of the local storage device to change to an entry box.

7. Change the name as appropriate (see Figure 9.6) and press Return.

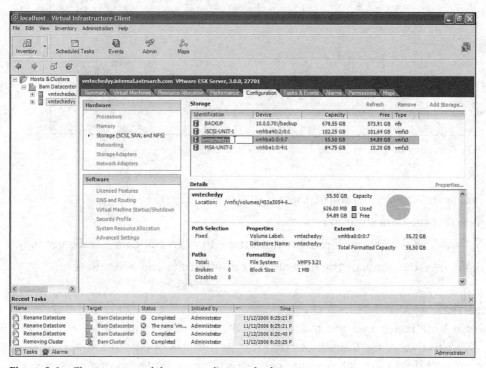

Figure 9.6 Change name of data store, first method

The second method is to look at all the data stores and rename the data store without knowing which ESX Server is involved:

1. Log in to the VIC.

2. Click on the down arrow next to the Inventory button (see Figure 9.7).

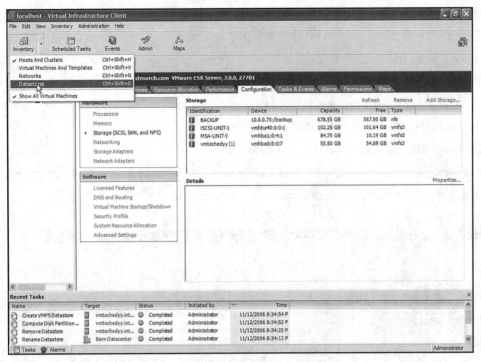

Figure 9.7   Inventory drop-down menu

3. Select *Datastores* from the menu.

4. Select the data store to rename.

5. Click the data store to rename until the entry box appears (see Figure 9.8).

6. Change the name of the data store as appropriate and press Return.

Creating a VMFS

Creating a VMFS uses a wizard to answer all the questions required for adding a local VMFS to the server. Remember that it is best to use one partition per SCSI device for a VMFS to alleviate locking concerns. Our example, however, using a default installation, does not do this due to disk space limitations:

1. Log in to the VIC.

2. Select the host in question.

3. Select the Configuration tab for the host in question.

4. Click the *Storage (SCSI, SAN, and NFS)* link.

5. Click the *Add Storage* link.

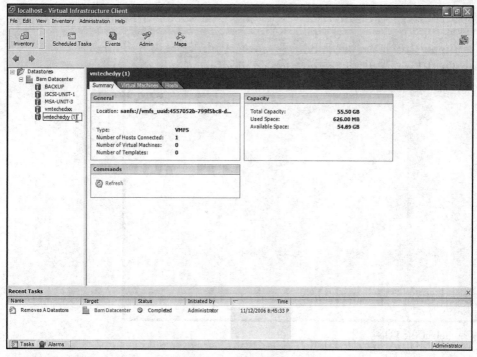

Figure 9.8 Change name of data store, second method

6. Select *Disk/LUN* from the resultant wizard and then Next.

7. Select the local device using the device cryptic name vmhbaC:T:L:P, where C implies the controller, T implies the track or path, L implies the LUN, and P implies the partition number (see Figure 9.9). Note that it is possible to determine which device is associated with each VM HBA due to the size of the LUN. Click Next to continue.

It is possible that at this juncture a screen will appear that states *unable to read partition information*. When this occurs, it implies that the disk in question has a partition table on the LUN that is somehow broken. The fix for this is to find out which device maps to the device in question. Using the cryptic name of the device do the following:

  a. Log in to the console operating system as the root user.

  b. Run the command esxcfg-vmhbadevs.

  c. Find the /dev/sdX device name associated with the cryptic name, where x refers to a letter or series of letters that represents the Linux SCSI disk device associated with the cryptic name.

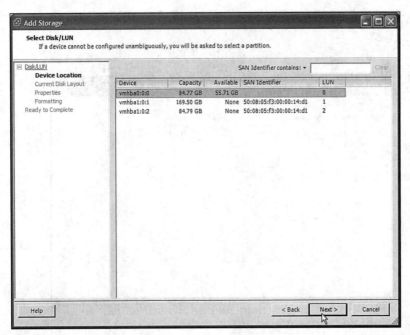

Figure 9.9   Select the LUN

   d. Use the `fdisk /dev/sdX` command per the command-line option above to remove any partitions on the device to make room for the VMFS.

The preceding steps will remove the error from the VIC Wizard when creating a VMFS, however do this carefully as removal of the partitions is a permanent action and if you select the wrong volume, it will be a catastrophic mistake.

8. Select *Use free space,* and then click Next. This wizard page also gives more information about the LUN. In this case, it is the installation LUN and shows other partitions in use. If these are valuable partitions, because they are in this case, the *Use free space* option (see Figure 9.10) is warranted. If you want to use the whole LUN, however, select *Use the Entire Device.*

9. Provide a name to the data store (see Figure 9.11) and click Next. Once more, it best to use some form of the FQDN to aid in knowing which local data store belongs to which host.

10. Click Next. It is not necessary to change the LUN formatting (see Figure 9.12). In essence, the block size to be used depends on the maximum size of a VMDK to reside on the VMFS.

11. Review all the changes (see Figure 9.13) and click Next.

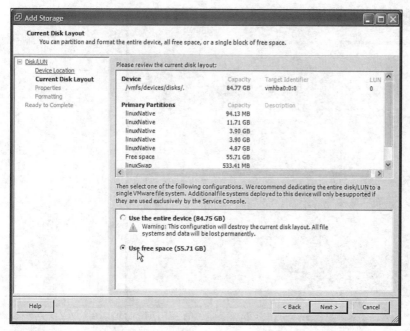

Figure 9.10 Select the LUN partition

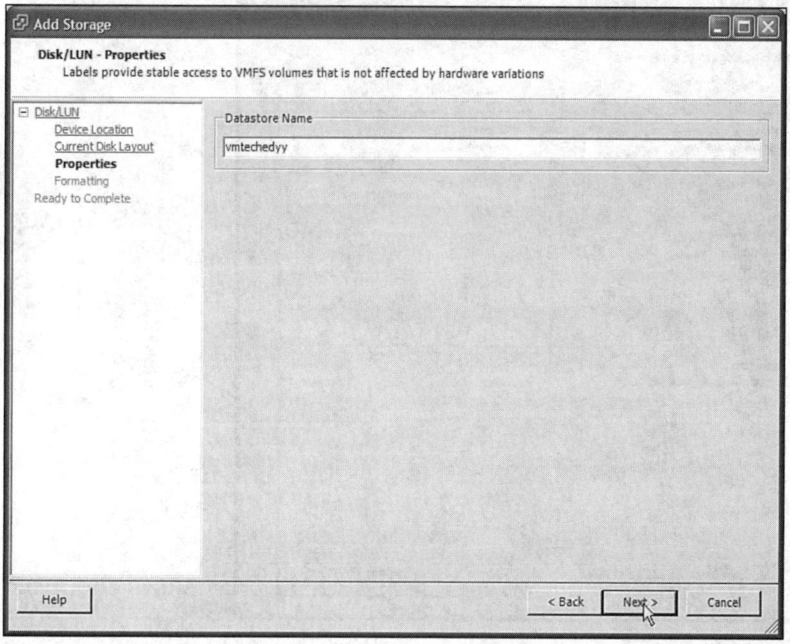

Figure 9.11 Name the new LUN

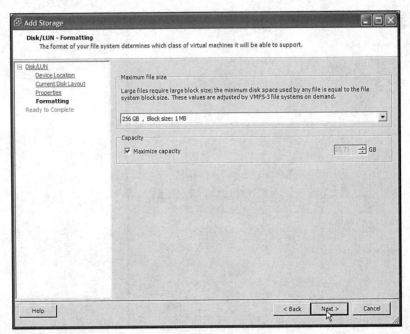

Figure 9.12   Review the LUN format

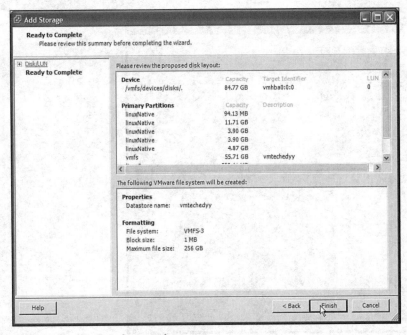

Figure 9.13   Review the new data store

12. Wait for the *Create VMFS Datastore* task to finish by monitoring the Recent Tasks window.

Extending a VMFS

Extending a VMFS in ESX version 3 is quite a bit different than in earlier versions of ESX. In earlier versions of ESX, the VMFS handled the extents, and no matter how large the extent was, only a certain number of files could be created on an extent. ESX version 3, however, uses a Logical Volume Manager (LVM) to combine LUNs before the VMFS is created. In essence, you should not use extents because the removal of an extent requires the removal of the entire VMFS. Extents are mainly for emergency use and tying together lots of small LUNs for limited use.

Best Practice for Extents

Do not use extents. To remove an extent requires the removal of the entire VMFS, not the individual extent.

VMFS is above LVM, which is above the hardware. There is a one-to-one mapping between a VMFS and a logical volume, but a one-to-many mapping of a logical volume to physical LUN. Therefore, the VMFS sees only a single large volume regardless of how many disks, RAID arrays, or SAN LUNs are involved.

To extend a VMFS, do the following:

1. Log in to the VIC.

2. Select the host in question.

3. Select the Configuration tab for the host in question.

4. Click the *Storage (SCSI, SAN, and NFS)* link.

5. Select the storage identifier to manipulate.

6. Select the *properties* for the identifier chosen.

7. Click the *Add Extent* button on the resulting dialog (see Figure 9.14).

8. Select the extent to add. Note that the devices listed in the wizard are all devices not already defined as a VMFS, which will include any and all raw disk maps defined (see Figure 9.15). Click the *Next* button.

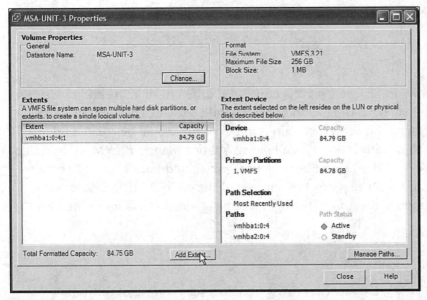

Figure 9.14 Data store properties

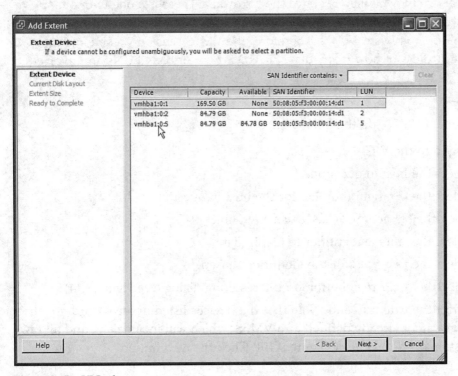

Figure 9.15 VIC, choose extent

9. Review the partition layout of the extent to add and click *Next*. If the partition layout does not include a VMFS (see Figure 9.16), clicking *Next* will be catastrophic.

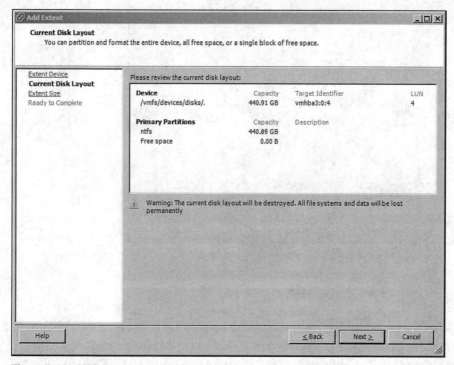

Figure 9.16 VIC extent partition layout

10. Review the VMFS information (see Figure 9.17) and click *Next*.

11. Review the new extent and click *Finish*.

Deleting a VMFS Extent

Deleting a VMFS extent is catastrophic. It is extremely important to shut down and migrate all existing VMs from the VMFS to be manipulated. Barring that, the only other concern is an affirmative answer to the following question:

Are you satisfied with your backup?

If there are no existing VMs, templates, or ISOs, and so forth on the VMFS, by all means proceed. To delete an extent, see "Deleting a VMFS" (the following section), because it's the same for local disks.

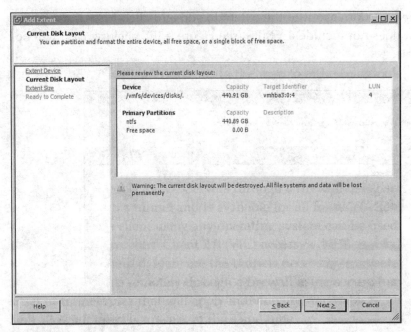

Figure 9.17 VIC extent VMFS layout

Deleting a VMFS

Deleting a VMFS within the VIC requires some functionality covered two chapters from now in more detail: that is, the movement of one VM from a data store to another. Although this is mentioned as a step, peruse Chapter 11, "Dynamic Resource Load Balancing," for further details. The steps to delete a VMFS within the VIC follow. Once more, there are two methods.

The first method is to use the storage configuration of the host in question as follows:

1. Log in to the VIC.

2. Shut down and migrate all VMs residing on this data store to a different data store.

3. Select the host in question.

4. Select the Configuration tab for the host in question.

5. Click the *Storage (SCSI, SAN, and NFS)* link.

6. Select the local storage device to remove.

7. Right-click the local storage device name and select the *Remove* menu item (see Figure 9.18).

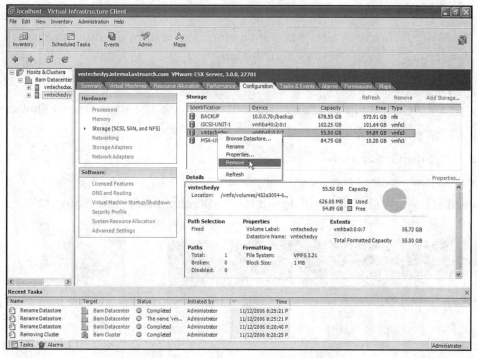

Figure 9.18   Remove Data Store menu

8. Answer Yes to the dialog about removing the VMFS.

9. Wait for the remove request to finish.

The second method is to use the data store inventory directly, as follows:

1. Log in to the VIC.

2. Migrate all VMs residing on this data store to a different data store.

3. Click the down arrow next to the Inventory button.

4. Select *Datastores* from the menu.

5. Select the data store to remove.

6. Right-click the local storage device name and select the *Remove* menu item.

7. Answer Yes to the dialog about removing the VMFS.

8. Wait for the remove request to finish.

MUI

Using the MUI to work with VMFS is quite a bit different from the other mechanisms, but it does provide the same functionality.

Renaming a VMFS

Renaming a VMFS can only take place from the MUI, and the steps are as follows:

1. Log in to the MUI.
2. Select the Options tab.
3. Click the *Storage Management* link.
4. Click the *Edit* link associated with the VMFS to rename (see Figure 9.19).

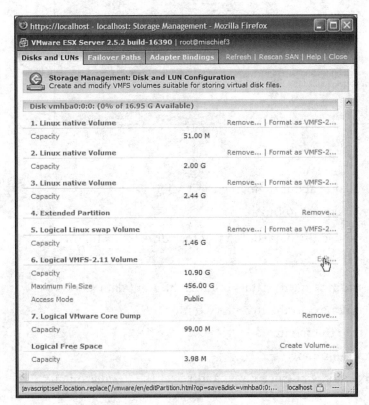

Figure 9.19 Storage Management dialog

5. Provide a new volume label for the VMFS.
6. Click OK to accept (see Figure 9.20).

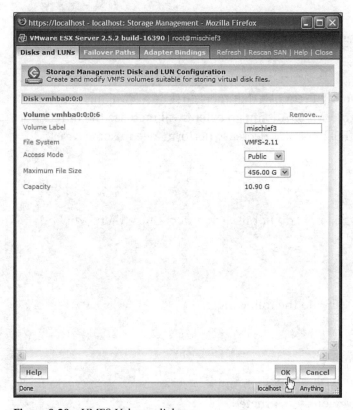

Figure 9.20 VMFS Volume dialog

Creating a VMFS

Creation of an extent from the MUI is extremely straightforward, but it does have its own issues dealing with the Storage Management dialog because all partitions available to the system are listed, including *any* boot or Linux partitions. Manipulation of anything but logical free space should be avoided, unless there is an understanding of the partition in question's purpose, which can take knowledge of Linux. To create a VMFS do the following:

1. Log in to the MUI.

2. Select the Options tab.

3. Click the *Storage Management* link.

4. Click the *Create Volume* link associated with the any logical free space or *click Format as VMFS-2* for an existing unformatted partition. However, be aware that formatting an existing partition as a VMFS-2 will be

catastrophic for the volume and requires a high level of Linux experience to determine whether this is safe.

Extending a VMFS

Extending a VMFS within the MUI requires that there first be a VMFS in which to add as an extent to an existing VMFS. Adding an extent will increase the number of files that can reside on a VMFS-2 but also decrease performance in some cases.

Best Practice for Extents

For ESX versions prior to version 3, do not use extents because there will be performance problems .

Nevertheless, to extend a VMFS, do the following:

1. Log in to the MUI.
2. Select the Options tab.
3. Click the *Storage Management* link.
4. Create a VMFS as previously instructed.
5. Click the *Edit* link associated with the VMFS to manipulate.
6. Select the extents to add to the VMFS. This list will be a series of check boxes associated with all existing VMFS partitions available to the server.
7. Click OK and proceed to add the extent to the VMFS.

Deleting a VMFS Extent

Deleting a VMFS extent is catastrophic and unfortunately cannot be completed from the MUI when dealing with a local VMFS. It is extremely important that you shut down and migrate all existing VMs from the VMFS to be manipulated. Barring that, the only other concern is an affirmative answer to the following question:

Are you satisfied with your backup?

If there are no existing VMs, by all means proceed:

1. Log in to the MUI.
2. Shut down all existing VMs on the VMFS.

3. Migrate all existing VMs on the VMFS to another VMFS.

4. Go to the service console and remove the partition using the `fdisk` command described earlier in this chapter.

Deleting a VMFS

Deleting a VMFS is catastrophic. It is extremely important that you shut down and migrate all existing VMs from the VMFS to be manipulated. Barring that, the only other concern is an affirmative answer to the following question:

Are you satisfied with your backup?

If there are no existing VMs, by all means proceed:

1. Log in to the MUI.

2. Shut down all existing VMs on the VMFS.

3. Migrate all existing VMs on the VMFS to another VMFS.

4. Select the Options tab.

5. Click the *Storage Management* link.

6. Click the *Edit* link associated with the VMFS to remove.

7. Click the *Remove* link.

8. Click OK in the Warning dialog.

FC HBA VMFS

Adding a remote Fibre Channel disk-based VMFS can be accomplished via all methods. Unlike a local VMFS disk, one other device involved needs to be configured prior to access via an ESX Server. There are two major stages to adding an FC HBA VMFS to an ESX Server. Generally, the first information has to be handed off to a SAN group, who will then configure the SAN to allow the ESX Server access. When that is completed, the rest of the ESX Server can be configured. In addition to the zoning and presentation available from the SAN side, ESX can limit the number of LUNs to use and to mask off LUNs and provide its own zoning independent of the SAN.

In this section, only the exception to the practice of manipulating local VMFS is listed. Wherever the local device has been listed in those instructions, the cryptic name of the SAN-based LUN can be exchanged.

Finding the WWPN

The first step to add a Fibre Channel VMFS to an ESX Server is to discover the WWPN for the ESX Server's FC HBA and hand these values off to the SAN group so that the SAN can be properly configured with LUNs presented and zoned appropriately. Furthermore, the WWPN in use will aid in determining the controller and LUN to use in the cryptic name of the LUN to manipulate.

Command Line

Determining the WWPN for all versions of ESX via the command line is quite simple, and the following command lines can be used only if a LUN already exists:

```
esxcfg-mpath -a # ESX version 3
```

Or

```
vmkmultipath -q # ESX versions prior to version 3
```

The output of the preceding commands, however, can be rather cryptic, and for ESX version 3 the output could be similar to the following. This output shows a total of two controllers present in the format of `cryptic name WWPN PCI device port`. For ESX versions earlier than version 3, the output of the command is a little different, but the same relative information is provided:

```
vmhba1 10000000c932a2c6 4:4.0
vmhba2 10000000c932a2c7 4:5.0
```

However, if an existing LUN does not exist, it is necessary to inspect the boot and kernel messages log files for the failure reason:

```
grep SCSI /var/log/boot.log /var/log/messages /var/log/vmkernel
```

VIC

When using the VIC, the process for finding the WWPN is simply the following:

1. Log in to the VIC either through the VC Server or directly to the host.
2. Select the ESX host in question.
3. Select the *Configuration* tab.
4. Click the *Storage Adapters* link.

5. Review the list of Fibre Channel SCSI adapters for the SAN identifier (see Figure 9.21). This will be the value or values to give to a SAN management group.

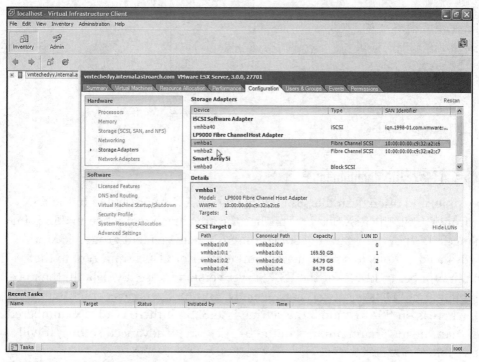

Figure 9.21 VIC SAN identifier

MUI

When using the MUI, the process for finding the WWPN is simply the following:

1. Log in to the MUI.
2. Select the *Options* tab.
3. Click the *Storage Management* link.
4. Select the *Adapter Bindings* tab and review the Fibre Channel adapters listed and the WWPN associated with each adapter. The WWPN will be the value or values to give to a SAN management group (see Figure 9.22).

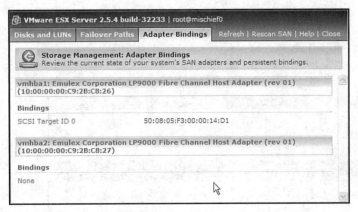

Figure 9.22   Adapter Bindings

Masking and Max LUN Manipulations

It is possible, and often desirable, to manipulate the LUNs presented to the ESX Server from within the ESX Server. This has the advantage that when making simple changes it is not necessary to contact the SAN management group. ESX provides advanced options to set the maximum number of LUNs from zero to the maximum number of LUNs for the ESX Server version in use. By default, the maximum number of LUNs is set very low, usually 8 on ESX versions earlier than version 3, whereas on ESX version 3 the setting is 128. So if there is a LUN numbered greater than the maximum number in the `Disk.MaxLUN` advanced setting, it will not be visible to the ESX Server.

In addition to this, there is an advanced setting that will mask off LUNs from view by the ESX Server. The `Disk.MaskLUN` setting will set which LUNs the ESX Server will *not* see and can be used to change the presentation LUN numbering. For example, if all ESX LUNs on the SAN were presented with LUN numbers greater than 256, it is possible to use `Disk.MaskLUN` to mask all LUNs from 1 through 256, which sets LUN 1 on the ESX Server to be the real LUN 257 as presented by the SAN.

These two options allow the ESX Server to work around some of the SAN limitations within ESX.

Command Line

There are mechanisms to manipulate LUN masks and max LUN settings from the command line, too.

ESX Version 3

For ESX version 3, there is the esxcfg-advcfg command to make advanced modifications. This command manipulates the contents of the files in /proc/vmware/config, which is *not* a direct mapping to the advanced options shown in the VIC. For the options we are discussing, Disk.MaxLUN and Disk.MaskLUNs, use the following commands to make the modifications. Note that although the files in the /proc/vmware/config file system can be manipulated directly, it is strongly recommended that this *not* happen. Use the provided command to have the changes last through a reboot.

To change the maximum LUN from the default 128 to a value of 16, use the following:

```
esxcfg-advcfg -s 16 /Disk/MaxLUN
```

To change the LUN mask to *not* allow LUN 5 to appear from either of the redundant FC HBAs in use, enter this command:

```
esxcfg-advcfg -s vmhba1:0:5\;vmhba2:0:5 /Disk/MaskLUNs
```

Now when rescanning the FC HBA for new devices and the VMFS, LUN 5 will not appear (as shown in the following). Any change to these configuration options requires performing a rescan.

```
# esxcfg-rescan vmhba1
Rescanning vmhba1...done.
On scsi0, removing: 0:0 0:1 0:2 0:4 0:5.
On scsi0, adding: 0:0 0:1 0:2 0:4.
```

ESX Versions Earlier Than Version 3

Manipulation of the ESX Server configuration files is generally the only way to change the advanced options from the command line, and this manipulation implies that the ESX Server must be rebooted to make use of the modifications for ESX versions earlier than version 3.

To change the maximum LUN count from the default of 8 to the value of 16, add the following to the /etc/vmware/vmkconfig file :

```
Disk/MaxLUN = "16"
```

To change the mask LUN settings, edit the /etc/vmware/vmkconfig file by adding or changing the following line. The following change, for example, excludes LUN 5 from appearing from either FC HBA:

```
Disk/MaskLUNs = "vmhba1:0:5;vmhba2:0:5"
```

Because these changes do not take place immediately, they can be forced by running the following commands from the command line or by rebooting the system. A reboot of the system will present the least possibility of damage.

Note that manipulation of the /proc file system can cause catastrophic damage and should only be performed by a Linux administrator, and even then extremely carefully. It is best to use the MUI to manipulate these values. Because any change to the Disk configuration options also requires a rescan of the SAN, perform one from the command line, as follows :

```
echo "16" > /proc/vmware/config/Disk/MaxLUN
echo "vmhba1:0:5;vmhba2:0:5" > /proc/vmware/config/Disk/MaskLUNs
cos-rescan.sh
```

VIC

To set LUN advanced settings using the VIC, follow these instructions:

1. Log in to the VIC either through the VC Server or directly to the host.

2. Select the ESX host in question.

3. Select the *Configuration* tab.

4. Click the *Advanced Settings* link.

5. Modify the desired entries and click OK to commit the changes and close the dialog (see Figure 9.23).

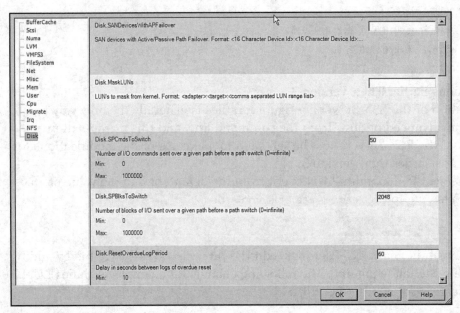

Figure 9.23 VIC advanced settings

MUI

The same settings can be manipulated from the MUI:

1. Log in to the MUI
2. Select the *Options* tab.
3. Click the *Advanced Settings* link.
4. Modify the desired entries and click OK to commit the changes and close the dialog (see Figure 9.24). Any change will pop up a dialog to edit the entry.

Figure 9.24 MUI advanced settings

Deleting a VMFS Extent

Deleting a VMFS extent is very dangerous to do because it can wipe out existing data. However, it is often necessary. Here are the mechanisms to do this.

Command Line

The command-line method is the same as for the local VMFS case and requires catastrophic destruction of the LUN that contains the extent. However, other avenues are available if the SAN group is directly involved. The LUN can be unformatted by the local ESX administrator, or can be zoned such that the LUN no longer appears to the ESX Server, or is unpresented from the ESX Server in question. If the last two are used, the SAN group is required.

ESX Versions Earlier Than Version 3

Follow these steps to delete an extent:

1. Are you satisfied with your backup?
2. Shut down all existing VMs on the VMFS.
3. Migrate all existing VMs on the VMFS to another VMFS.
4. Run the following, assuming the cryptic name of the extent is vmhba1:0:5. Substitute in the appropriate cryptic name. This also assumes that Disk.MaskLUNs was empty at the start; otherwise, use the appropriate values:

```
echo "vmhba1:0:5;vmhba2:0:5" > /proc/vmware/config/Disk/MaskLUNs
cos-rescan.sh
echo "" > /proc/vmware/config/Disk/MaskLUNs
cos-rescan.sh
```

VIC

There is no way to remove an extent short of deleting the VMFS to which it is attached completely. It is possible to exclude the LUN using the Disk.MaskLUNs advanced option, yet any time the LUN is removed from the list it will appear back as an extent. In some cases, the space will appear, but there will be *no* extent listed. Like the command-line version, removing the VMFS completely is the best way to go on ESX version 3, because anything else will seriously confuse the interface and ESX.

It is possible for the SAN administrators to remove the LUN from either the zoning or presentation to the ESX Servers in question. But any use of this LUN number in the future for ESX will once more place the LUN in question as an extent to the VMFS. This makes a LUN number impossible to use in the future until the VMFS is deleted, which will create confusion for the two teams. Therefore, the best method is to remove the VMFS completely; but first, before removing the VMFS, migrate all VMs.

MUI

There is only one complex way to delete an extent from the MUI. Although deleting an extent is considered to be destructive to a VMFS, it generally requires the removal of the LUN at the hardware in other cases. The following is a less-destructive approach, allowing the extent to be used for a future VMFS without getting the local hardware administrator involved or using the command line. It is extremely important to shut down and migrate all existing VMs from the VMFS to be manipulated. Barring that, the only other concern is an affirmative answer to the following question:

Are you satisfied with your backup?

If there are no existing VMs, by all means proceed. *Note* that this only works for ESX versions earlier than version 3; the same cannot be said for ESX version 3.

1. Log in to the MUI.
2. Shut down all existing VMs on the VMFS.
3. Migrate all existing VMs on the VMFS to another VMFS.
4. Select the *Options* tab.
5. Click the *Advanced Configuration* link.
6. Scroll until `Disk.MaskLUNs` is displayed and change its value to include the LUN to be excluded.
7. Click the *Storage Management* link.
8. Click the *Rescan SAN* link.
9. Click the *Advanced Configuration* link.
10. Scroll until `Disk.MaskLUNs` is displayed and change its value to not include the LUN previously excluded.
11. Click the *Storage Management* link.
12. Click the *Rescan SAN* link.
13. Click the *Edit* link associated with the VMFS on the extent LUN manipulated previously.
14. Click the *Remove* link.

Virtual Networking

The description of virtual network concepts is in the preceding chapter. What follows are the steps necessary to create and manage vSwitches from the command line using the VIC or the MUI for versions earlier than version 3. ESX requires a vSwitch to work correctly. Although this might not always appear to be necessary for an end environment, it is necessary from a security and functionality viewpoint. The security issue, for ESX versions earlier than version 3, flows directly into functionality and is the fact that if a VM is created with a vNIC and there is no single vSwitch, and the COS is connected to the outside, the VM will also be able to find a network connection to the outside. Because the COS is connected on an administrative network, this implies that the VM can get to that network. However, if there is even a single vSwitch, the vNIC, even if not connected to the vSwitch, cannot find a path through the service console.

> **Best Practice for Virtual Switches**
> Always have at least one vSwitch.
>
> If a VM has a vNIC, always attach it to a vSwitch.

In the following discussion, it is assumed that there are six total pNICs to be used by every form of vNetwork available for ESX, including the administrative, iSCSI, NFS, VMotion, and a private network.

Configuring the Service Console

The service console has its own networking credentials separate from the rest of the ESX Server, as Chapter 7 outlined. The service console must be configured with its own IP address and netmask. Use of DHCP could cause serious issues with ESX if the DHCP lease expires and the DHCP server is *not* available. The consequences of this action would at a minimum be the loss of management capability and the failure of the ESX Server.

Command Line

When using the command line to configure the service console, it is important to realize that the ESX Server must use static IP, unlike potential VMs.

ESX Version 3

For ESX version 3, the following commands can be used to create a new vSwitch for use by the service console. When installing ESX version 3, the VM network is also created whether that is desired or not. To ensure that vSwitch0 is assigned the service console, it is desirable to remove the VM network vSwitch and assign the appropriate pNIC to the vSwitch for use by the service console. In this example, the first Broadcom adapter of the six pNICs in the server is to be assigned to the service console. In addition, because of the use of iSCSI, which resides on its own network, the netmask for the service console includes both the admin network and the iSCSI network. And finally, the default `routerIPAddress` is set for use by all the VMkernel devices:

```
snic=`/usr/sbin/esxcfg-nics -l ¦ /bin/grep Broadcom ¦ /bin/grep Up ¦ /usr/bin/head -1 ¦
/bin/awk '{print $1}'`

/usr/sbin/esxcfg-vswitch -D "VM Network" vSwitch0

/usr/sbin/esxcfg-vswitch -U vmnic0 vSwitch0

/usr/sbin/esxcfg-vswitch -L $snic vSwitch0

/usr/sbin/esxcfg-vswif -i esxServerIPAddress -n 255.255.0.0 vswif0

/usr/sbin/esxcfg-route defaultRouterIPAddress
```

ESX Versions Earlier Than Version 3

Use the `netconfig` command to configure the service console networking information; alternatively, it is possible to create a service console vSwitch using `vmxnet_console`. The use of `vmxnet_console` is not recommended except for low-port-density situations. To configure `vmxnet_console`, follow these steps. However, note that this can be extremely dangerous to do:

1. Log in to the service console:

   ```
   # vmkpcidivy -i
   ```

   When you come to the pNIC that is assigned to the [c]onsole, change the setting to [s]hared.

   Leave all other items as the default.

2. Assume the ports are now labeled as `vmnic0` and `vmnic1` (two port 1U server).

3. To add the `vmxnet_console` device to a NIC team, edit `/etc/vmware/hwconfig` and add the following to the end of the file:

   ```
   nicteam.vmnic0.team = "bond0"

   nicteam.vmnic1.team = "bond0"
   ```

4. Edit `/etc/vmware/netmap.conf` and add the following to the end of the file:

   ```
   network1.name = "Network0"

   network1.device = "bond0"
   ```

5. Save and reboot the server.

VIC

By default, the service console vSwitch will already be created when ESX is installed, and there is no need to create another vSwitch for the service console. In the future, it might be nice to add more pNICs to the service console, but the default is already there for your use, as shown in Figure 9.25.

1. Log in to the VIC, either into the VC Server or directly to the host.

2. Select the ESX host in question.

3. Select the *Configuration* tab.

4. Click the *Networking* link to display as shown in Figure 9.25.

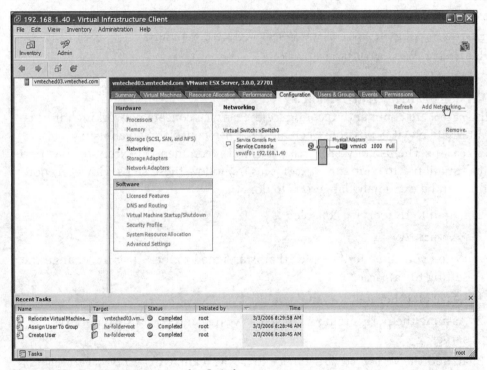

Figure 9.25 Existing service console vSwitch

MUI

There is no mechanism in the MUI to create a service console vSwitch or to configure the networking information.

Creating a VM Network vSwitch

The creation of a VM network vSwitch is required for ESX versions earlier than version 3 and highly recommended for ESX version 3. This vSwitch allows the VMs to communicate with the outside world. Of course, they could talk to the outside world using the vSwitch created for the service console but, as discussed in Chapter 4, "Auditing, Monitoring, and Securing," we know that has several risks. The following sections outline the ways to create a VM network vSwitch.

Command Line

In this code example, the system takes the first two Intel-based pNICs and uses them to form vSwitch1, which is labeled as the VM network. After the vSwitch is added, the pNICs are then added to the vSwitch1:

```
unic=`/usr/sbin/esxcfg-nics -l ¦ /bin/grep Intel ¦ /bin/grep Up ¦ head -
2 ¦ head -1 ¦ /bin/awk '{print $1}'`
vnic=`/usr/sbin/esxcfg-nics -l ¦ /bin/grep Intel ¦ /bin/grep Up ¦
➥head -2 ¦ tail -1 ¦ /bin/awk '{print $1}'`
/usr/sbin/esxcfg-vswitch -a vSwitch1
/usr/sbin/esxcfg-vswitch -A "VM Network" vSwitch1
/usr/sbin/esxcfg-vswitch -L $unic vSwitch1
/usr/sbin/esxcfg-vswitch -L $vnic vSwitch1
```

VIC

You can create a VM network vSwitch in the VIC by doing the following:

1. Log in to the VIC, either into the VC Server or directly to the host.
2. Select the ESX host in question.
3. Select the *Configuration* tab.
4. Click the *Networking* link.
5. Click the Add *Networking* link.
6. Select the *Virtual Machine* connection type, as shown in Figure 9.26.
7. Select at least one pNIC for the VM network vSwitch, as shown in Figure 9.27; however, two would be the best practice. More than two can be chosen, but this could cause performance problems if load balancing is used.

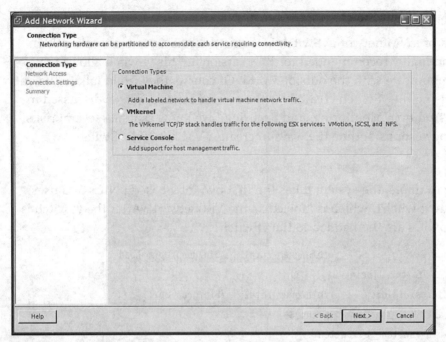

Figure 9.26 vSwitch Connection Type

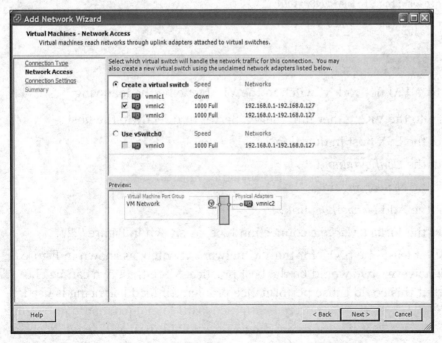

Figure 9.27 Assign pNIC to vSwitch

8. Click Next or change the vSwitch name, and then click Next, as in Figure 9.28.

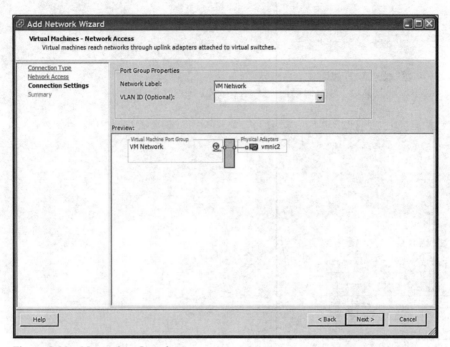

Figure 9.28 Name the vSwitch

9. Click Finish to complete the creation of the vSwitch.

MUI

To create a VM network vSwitch in the MUI, do the following:

1. Log in to the MUI.

2. Select the *Options* tab.

3. Click the *Network Connections* link.

4. Select *Click Here,* as shown at the bottom of Figure 9.29. Once the first vSwitch is created, this screen is no longer displayed.

5. Write in a network label, select an outbound adapter, as shown in Figure 9.30, and select *Create Switch.*

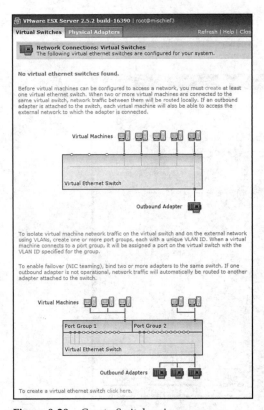

Figure 9.29 Create Switch primary screen

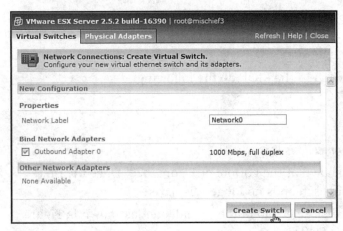

Figure 9.30 Create switch

Creating a VMotion vSwitch

A major feature of VMware ESX is the capability to move VMs from one machine to another machine while the VM is still running. The requirements for this are fairly simple yet sometimes hard to meet:

- The ESX Servers must have some form of shared storage, either NFS, iSCSI or SAN.
- The ESX Servers must have vSwitches named identically.
- The ESX Servers must have the same family of processor and in most cases share the same processor instruction set.
- The VMs must not have their CD-ROM or floppy components connected. More on this is covered in Chapter 10, "Virtual Machines."
- The VMs must be connected to a nonlocal vSwitch.
- The appropriate VMotion license must exist and be available to the ESX Server.
- It is strongly recommended that a dedicated gigabit network be used.

If all these conditions are met, it is possible to use VMotion. VMotion requires a vSwitch or a port on a vSwitch (for ESX version 3) set up just for VMotion.

Command Line

This code example uses the first of the last two Intel-based pNICs. vSwitch2 is created, relabeled as VMotion, and then the pNIC is assigned to the vSwitch. And finally, the pNIC assigned to the VMotion vSwitch is converted to a VMkernel pNIC and given a nonroutable IP and netmask:

```
wnic=`/usr/sbin/esxcfg-nics -l ¦ /bin/grep Intel ¦ /bin/grep Up ¦
➥tail -2 ¦ head -1 ¦ /bin/awk '{print $1}'`
mip="192.168.1.1" # or some other non-routable IP
/usr/sbin/esxcfg-vswitch -a vSwitch2
/usr/sbin/esxcfg-vswitch -A "vMotion" vSwitch2
/usr/sbin/esxcfg-vswitch -L $wnic vSwitch2
/usr/sbin/esxcfg-vmknic -a -i $mip -n 255.255.255.0 vMotion
vMotion=`esxcfg-vswitch -l ¦ awk '/vMotion/ {print $2}'`
cat > /etc/vmware/hostd/hostsvc.xml << EOF
<ConfigRoot>
<vmotion>
<nic>$vMotion</nic>
</vmotion>
```

```
</ConfigRoot>
EOF
esxcfg-advcfg -s 1 /Migrate/Enabled
```

VIC

Using the VIC to create a VMotion vSwitch is similar to the creation of the VM Network vSwitch:

1. Log in to the VIC, either into the VC Server or directly to the host.

2. Select the ESX host in question.

3. Select the *Configuration* tab.

4. Click the *Networking* link.

5. Click the Add *Networking* link.

6. Select the *VMkernel* connection type that is available (refer to Figure 9.26).

7. Select at least one pNIC for the VMotion vSwitch (refer to Figure 9.27). However, two would be the best practice for redundancy. Note that this does not provide any capability to load balance.

8. Change the vSwitch name to VMotion, select *Use This* Port Group for VMotion, and set the IP address and subnet mask of the VMotion *network* as shown in Figure 9.31. The best practice for the VMotion network is to use a private pSwitch or VLAN.

9. Click Finish to complete the creation of the vSwitch.

Note that now the system will ask you to specify the default gateway for all VMkernel-based port groups on all vSwitches. There are two gateways for ESX version 3, one for the service console that was set during installation time and one for all VMkernel devices. VMotion can be routed and therefore able to send VMs across networks. Remember the limitations discussed in Chapter 4.

MUI

Using the MUI to create a VMotion vSwitch is very similar to the creation of the VM network vSwitch. Because this is the second vSwitch, Step 4 is slightly different:

1. Log in to the MUI.

2. Select the *Options* tab.

3. Click the *Network Connections* link.

4. Click the *Add* link opposite the Virtual Switches label (see Figure 9.32).

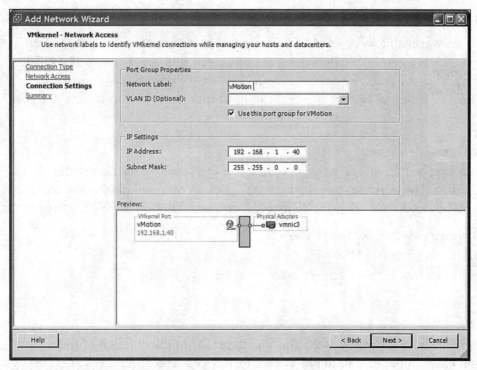

Figure 9.31   VMotion vSwitch settings

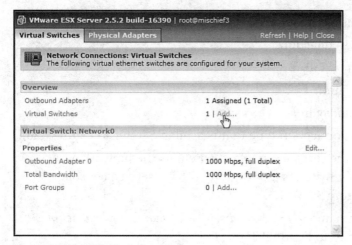

Figure 9.32   MUI vSwitch creation

5. Write in a network label, select an outbound adapter (see Figure 9.32), and select *Create Switch*.

Adding an iSCSI Network to the Service Console vSwitch

iSCSI is only available to be used by ESX directly as a data store for ESX version 3. Therefore, there is no MUI mechanism to implement this new feature. The iSCSI vSwitch port group must be part of the service console due to the nature of the iSCSI implementation. Half of the iSCSI implementation is within the service console.

Command Line

The following code creates a new port group on the service console vSwitch named iSCSI. The port group is then converted to a VMkernel device and assigned an IP and netmask. Note that the netmask is restricted to just the iSCSI network:

```
/usr/sbin/esxcfg-vswitch -A "iSCSI" vSwitch0
iip="10.0.1.34" # IP on iSCSI network
/usr/sbin/esxcfg-vmknic -a -i $iip -n 255.255.255.0 iSCSI
```

VIC

The setup of the iSCSI vSwitch via the VIC is similar to the creation of the VMotion vSwitch because both are VMkernel devices. The differences are that instead of picking a pNIC, another vSwitch is chosen, and that the device is not assigned to be used by VMotion:

1. Log in to the VIC, either into the VC Server or directly to the host.

2. Select the ESX host in question.

3. Select the *Configuration* tab.

4. Click the *Networking* link.

5. Click the Add *Networking* link.

6. Select the *VMkernel* connection type that is available (refer to Figure 9.26).

7. Select vSwitch0 (or the service console vSwitch) as the network access device, because this vSwitch is a port group off the service console vSwitch (refer to Figure 9.33).

8. Change the vSwitch name to iSCSI, *and set the IP address and subnet mask of the iSCSI network* (refer to Figure 9.31).

9. Click Finish to complete the creation of the vSwitch port group.

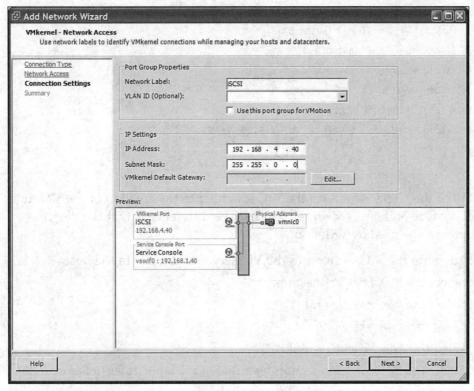

Figure 9.33 VIC iSCSI port group creation

Adding a NAS vSwitch for Use by NFS

NFS for use by ESX is handled in different ways in the various versions. For ESX version 3, NFS file systems can hold VMs but they cannot be placed there in earlier versions. However, NFS can be used to hold ISO images and other bits of information in the earlier versions of ESX. Only ESX version 3 requires the creation of a specialized vSwitch or vSwitch port group for the use of NFS as a data store. NFS file systems can be mounted directly to the service console, too, but they have a different use.

Command Line

Like the iSCSI device, NFS is its own port group on a vSwitch. In this code example, we take the last Intel-based pNIC and add it to a vSwitch labeled NFS and convert it to a VMkernel port group with the appropriate IP address and netmask:

```
znic=`/usr/sbin/esxcfg-nics -l ¦ /bin/grep Intel ¦ /bin/grep Up ¦
➥tail -2 ¦ tail -1 ¦ /bin/awk '{print $1}'`
zip="10.0.2.34" # on th NFS network
/usr/sbin/esxcfg-vswitch -a vSwitch3
/usr/sbin/esxcfg-vswitch -A "NFS" vSwitch3
/usr/sbin/esxcfg-vswitch -L $znic vSwitch3
/usr/sbin/esxcfg-vmknic -a -i $zip -n 255.255.255.0 NFS
```

VIC

The setup of the NFS vSwitch via the VIC is similar to the creation of the VMotion vSwitch because both are VMkernel devices. The difference is that the device is not assigned to be used by VMotion:

1. Log in to the VIC, either into the VC Server or directly to the host.
2. Select the ESX host in question.
3. Select the *Configuration* tab.
4. Click the *Networking* link.
5. Click the Add *Networking* link.
6. Select the *VMkernel* connection type that is available (refer to Figure 9.26).
7. Select the pNIC to assign to this vSwitch.
8. Change the vSwitch name to NFS, *and set the IP address and subnet mask of the NFS network*.
9. Click Finish to complete the creation of the vSwitch port group.

Adding a Private vSwitch

Adding a private vSwitch to an ESX Server implies that any VM attached to it is local to the ESX Server. This is extremely useful when duplicating network environments or placing VM-based firewalls between various subnets. A VM connected to a private vSwitch that is not also connected to a pNIC is a VM that cannot be hot migrated or used in conjunction with VMotion.

Command Line

From the ESX version 3 command line, create a private vSwitch by simply adding a vSwitch with the appropriate label. Our example code uses "Private Network" as the local vSwitch name:

```
/usr/sbin/esxcfg-vswitch -A "Private Network" vSwitch4
```

VIC

The setup of the local vSwitch via the VIC is similar to the creation of the VM network vSwitch. The difference is that the device is not assigned a pNIC:

1. Log in to the VIC, either into the VC Server or directly to the host.
2. Select the ESX host in question.
3. Select the *Configuration* tab.
4. Click the *Networking* link.
5. Click the Add *Networking* link.
6. Select the *VMkernel* connection type that is available (refer to Figure 9.26).
7. Unselect any pNIC previously selected, and do not select a pNIC.
8. Change the vSwitch name to `"Private Network"`, *and set the IP address and subnet mask of the NFS network*.
9. Click Finish to complete the creation of the vSwitch port group.

MUI

From the MUI, creating a local vSwitch is similar to the creation of a VM network vSwitch. The only difference is you do *not* select any pNICS to assign to the vSwitch:

1. Log in to the MUI.
2. Select the *Options* tab.
3. Click the *Network Connections* link.
4. Click the *Add* link opposite the Virtual Switches label (refer to Figure 9.32).
5. Write in a network label and select *Create Switch*.

Adding Additional pNICs to a vSwitch

It some cases, it would be very nice to add a secondary pNIC to an existing vSwitch.

Command Line

For adding a secondary pNIC to the service console vSwitch of ESX version 3, the following code finds the first Broadcom adapter and adds it to vSwitch0, which is the vSwitch for the service console:

```
mnic=`/usr/sbin/esxcfg-nics -l ¦ /bin/grep Broadcom ¦ /bin/grep Up ¦
➥head -1 ¦ /bin/awk '{print $1}'`
/usr/sbin/esxcfg-vswitch -L $mnic vSwitch0
```

VIC

Within the VIC, it is possible to add a pNIC to an existing vSwitch by editing the vSwitch in question, as follows:

1. Log in to the VIC, either into the VC Server or directly to the host.
2. Select the ESX host in question.
3. Select the *Configuration* tab.
4. Click the *Networking* link.
5. Select the "Properties" for the vSwitch to edit.
6. Select the *Network Adapters* tab
7. Select the *Add* button
8. Click on the *NIC to Add to the vSwitch* and then *Next*. Review the output and select *Next* and *Finish* to complete the addition of the NIC to a vSwitch.

MUI

Within the MUI, it is possible to add a pNIC to an existing vSwitch by editing the vSwitch in question, as follows:

1. Log in to the MUI.
2. Select the *Options* tab.
3. Click the *Network Connections* link.
4. Click the *Edit* link opposite the vSwitch to modify.
5. Select an unassigned adapter to bind to the vSwitch.
6. Click OK to save the change.

Adding vSwitch Port Groups

It is often important to add port groups to a vSwitch as VLANs are added to the physical switches and the cabling requirements when using external switch tagging (EST) is just too high. VST will work best and therefore vSwitches, need VLANs.

Command Line

Adding a port group to a vSwitch from the ESX version 3 command line is done using the following command:

```
esxcfg-vswitch –A portGroupName –v vlanID vSwitchName
```

VIC

Adding a vSwitch port group is the same as adding a vSwitch except that instead of selecting a pNIC, select the appropriate vSwitch and specify the VLAN ID. An example of this is shown earlier in the section "Adding an iSCSI Network to the Service Console vSwitch."

MUI

Adding a vSwitch port group from the MUI is done as follows:

1. Log in to the MUI.
2. Select the *Options* tab.
3. Click the *Network Connections* link.
4. Click the *Add* link under the virtual switch to modify.
5. Enter a port group label and a VLAN ID.
6. Click OK to save the change.

Removing vSwitch Port Groups
Command Line

To delete a port group from a vSwitch from the ESX version 3 command line, use the following command:

```
esxcfg-vswitch -D portGroupName vSwitchName
```

VIC

Deleting a port group from a vSwitch from the VIC goes like this:

1. Log in to the VIC, either into the VC Server or directly to the host.
2. Select the ESX host in question.
3. Select the *Configuration* tab.
4. Click the *Networking* link.
5. Click the *Properties* link opposite the vSwitch label to edit.
6. Select the port group to remove.
7. Click the *Remove* button.
8. Select *Yes* when asked *"Are you sure you want to remove this vSwitch port group?"*

MUI

Deleting a port group from a vSwitch through the MUI can be done by following these steps:

    1. Log in to the MUI.

    2. Select the *Options* tab.

    3. Click the *Network Connections* link.

    4. Click *Edit* opposite the virtual switch port group to modify.

    5. Select *Remote Port Group.*

vSwitch Removal

vSwitch removal is quite straightforward and is often necessary because of networking modifications or other issues.

Command Line

Deleting vSwitches from the ESX version 3 command line is as simple as using the following, where # is the number of the vSwitch as listed using the `esxcfg-vswitch -l` command. This one command will remove all port groups from the vSwitch, too:

```
esxcfg-vswitch -D vSwitch#
```

VIC

Deleting vSwitches using the VIC can be accomplished by following these steps:

    1. Log in to the VIC, either into the VC Server or directly to the host.

    2. Select the ESX host in question.

    3. Select the *Configuration* tab.

    4. Click the *Networking* link.

    5. Click the *Remove* link opposite the vSwitch label to remove.

    6. Select *Yes* when asked *"Are you sure you want to remove this vSwitch?"*

MUI

Within the MUI, it is sometimes necessary to remove a vSwitch. To do so, follow these steps:

    1. Log in to the MUI.

    2. Select the *Options* tab.

3. Click the *Network Connections* link.

4. Click the *Edit* link opposite the virtual switch to modify.

5. Select *Remove Switch*.

vSwitch Security

In ESX version 3, each vSwitch and each attached port group has several properties that are in the realm of security. These settings are the capability to disable VMs from forging source IP address and MAC addresses, and from entering promiscuous mode. On earlier versions of ESX, these settings are available to each VM, independent of the vSwitch or its port groups. Moving these to the vSwitch makes much more sense.

Command Line

For ESX version 3, there is no easy way to set these through the command line. However, for earlier versions of ESX, use Table 9.2 to determine what to add to the VM configuration file to achieve the same results. Note that the <n> in each configuration file entry refers to the network number used elsewhere in the configuration file. Table 9.2 will also detail the keyword to look for in the ESX version 3 /etc/vmware/esx.conf file. It is possible to change this file, but these changes may require a reboot. For ESX versions earlier than version 3, the change requires the VM to be restarted.

Table 9.2

ESX Network Security Settings		
Action	**VM Configuration file Entry (Earlier Than Version 3)**	**Key to esx.conf (Version 3)**
Disable forged source addresses	`Ethernet<n>.noForgedSrcAddr = TRUE`	`ForgedTx`
Disable MAC address spoofing	`Ethernet<n>.downWhenAddrMisMatch = TRUE`	`MacChange`
Disable promiscuous mode	`Ethernet<n>.noPromisc = TRUE`	`Promiscuous`

For ESX version 3, it is possible to edit the /etc/vmware/esx.conf settings and set the values appropriately. However, doing this will require a refresh in VC and most likely a reboot to handle the change. To modify the appropriate setting in the esx.conf file, first find the vSwitch in question and then the key specified in Table 9.2 with your favorite editor, and then modify the value to the right side of the equal sign. To allow the option, set the value to false. To disallow, set the value to true.

VIC

It is possible to set the security settings on the vSwitch or the individual port group:

1. Log in to the VIC, either into the VC Server or directly to the host.

2. Select the ESX host in question.

3. Select the *Configuration* tab.

4. Click the *Networking* link.

5. Click the *Edit Properties* link opposite the vSwitch to edit.

6. Select the vSwitch from the left-side display.

7. Click the *Edit* button.

8. Select the *Security* tab.

9. Using the drop-downs, select the *Accept* or *Reject* options as appropriate (see Figure 9.34).

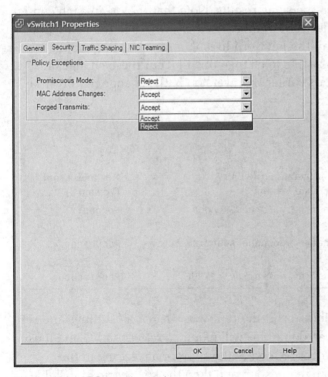

Figure 9.34 VIC security setting

To set the settings on the port group at Step 6, select the port group to modify, press Edit, and then use the check box to override the default vSwitch settings before selecting from the drop-down (see Figure 9.35).

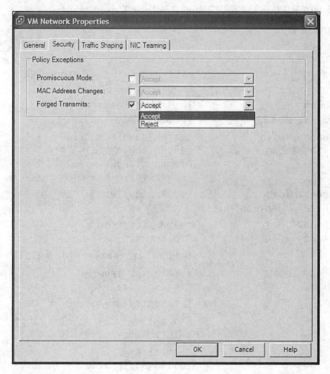

Figure 9.35 VIC security settings

MUI

No MUI method is available to change these settings. They must be added by hand to the VM configuration files.

vSwitch Properties

Each vSwitch also has several properties associated with it. Specifically, the settings are those for load balancing, failover, and pNIC state detection. For ESX version 3, there are additional properties, including the number of ports to assign to the vSwitch.

Command Line

Similar to setting security settings, it is possible to set various vSwitch properties from the command line, but it requires editing key system files. Edits of these types are very dangerous and can result in faulty systems, so be careful. See the previous section on how to edit the ESX version 3 files. Table 9.3 displays the property settings in the appropriate files.

Table 9.3

ESX vSwitch Property Settings		
Action	hwconfig entry (Earlier Than Version 3)	Key/Value to esx.conf (Version 3)
Beacon monitoring[1]	`nicteam.bondX.switch_ failover_threshold = "2"`	`beacon/enable = "true"` `beacon/threshold = "1"` `beacon/timeout = "5"` `linkCriteria/beacon = "true"`
Out-ip load balancing	`nicteam.bondX.load_ balance_mode = "out-ip"`	`teamPolicy/team = "lb_ip"`
Out-mac load balancing[2]	`nicteam.bondX.load_ balance_mode = "out-mac"`	`teamPolicy/team = "lb_srcmac"`
Port-ID load balancing[3]	N/A	`teamPolicy/team = "lb_srcid"`
EtherChannel	`nicteam.bondX.home_ link = "vmnicY"`	`teamPolicy/team = "fo_explicit"` `teamPolicy/maxActive = "1"` The active link is the first pNIC added to the NIC Team.
Rolling	N/A	`teamPolicy/ rollingRestoration = "true"`
Number of ports[4]	N/A	`numPorts = "56"`

[1] *In ESX version 3, settable on vSwitch and Port group*

[2] *Default for versions of ESX prior to version 3*

[3] *Default for ESX version 3*

[4] *Settable to 8, 24, 56, 120, 248, 504, or 1016 in ESX version 3*

To make the changes in the ESX versions earlier than version 3, open up the configuration file and append the appropriate lines to the file; if they already exist, edit the right side appropriately.

VIC

To make the changes outlined in Table 9.3 using the VIC, follow these steps:

1. Log in to the VIC, either into the VC Server or directly to the host.

2. Select the ESX host in question.

3. Select the *Configuration* tab.

4. Click the *Networking* link.

5. Click the *Edit Properties* link opposite the vSwitch to edit.

6. Select the vSwitch from the left-side display.

7. Click the *Edit* button.

8. Select the *NIC Teaming* tab.

9. Using the following actions to modify options as appropriate. Note the letters and their corresponding settings in Figure 9.36:

   a. Select the load balancing method (1 of 4).

   b. Enable or disable beacon monitoring. Only enable if requested to by support (Yes or No).

   c. Enable or disable vSwitch notifications (Yes or No).

   d. Enable or disable rolling mode (Yes or No).

   e. Change which pNIC is the default pNIC by moving a pNIC up or down or move a pNIC to standby mode.

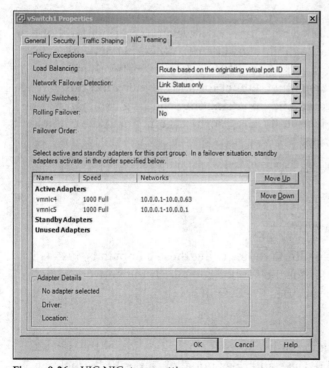

Figure 9.36   VIC NIC team settings

10. Select the *General* tab.

11. Using the drop-down, select the number of ports on the vSwitch. This is not the same as the number of ports per port group and requires a reboot.

MUI

There is no MUI method to make these changes; they must be added by hand to the end of the ESX Server configuration file `/etc/vmware/hwconfig`. In Table 9.3, there are items such as `bondX` and `vmnicY`; these represent the NIC team name and the pNIC respectively. The `X` is the bond number, and the `Y` is the pNIC number.

Changing VMkernel Gateways

The VMkernel gateway was introduced in ESX version 3 as a way to tell each VMkernel network its gateway. In earlier versions of ESX, there was only one VMkernel device, and that was the one set aside for VMotion. This is no longer the case with version 3, and because each VMkernel device can be part of its own network, it is important to set the VMkernel gateway and netmask appropriately.

Command Line

The VIC lets you set a generic VMkernel gateway. However, for a finer level of control, the command line offers the capability to set a per-VMkernel network gateway and netmask. For example, if you want to have a Class B network mask for one network and a Class C or some other subnet for another network, this can be achieved quite easily from the command line using the following commands. The dotted-decimal network format is used for each of the arguments to the command. To delete a route, use the following:

```
esxcfg-route -d network netmask gateway
```

To add a route, use this command:

```
esxcfg-route -a network netmask gateway
```

It is also possible to specify multiple routes using these commands, just as it is possible to specify multiple routes for the service console. If the network to be modified is named default, this specifies the default route.

VIC

The VIC network route modification only allows the modification of the default generic routes for all VMkernel devices and does not allow a per-VMkernel network granularity.

1. Log in to the VIC, either into the VC Server or directly to the host.
2. Select the ESX host in question.
3. Select the *Configuration* tab.
4. Click the *DNS and Routing* link.
5. Edit the VMkernel Default gateway values (see Figure 9.37).
6. Click OK.

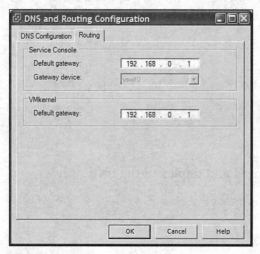

Figure 9.37   VIC setting the default route

Changing pNIC Settings

It is also desirable to disable autonegotiate on a pNIC. To do that, use the tools for each version of ESX outlined in the following sections. It is a VMware best practice to configure gigabit pNICS to gigabit pSwitches for autonegotiate.

Command Line

There is no real way to do this in ESX versions earlier than version 3 short of a reboot. However, the following will work for ESX version 3:

```
esxcfg-nics –s [10¦100¦1000¦10000] –d [full¦half] vmnic#
```

For versions earlier than version 3 of ESX, adding an entry to the bottom of /etc/vmware/hwconfig will, on a reboot, disable autonegotiate for a pNIC. The line would be similar to the following. The difference would be the speed setting of 1000, 100, or 10 and a full_duplex setting of 1 for full and 0 for half. The other major change to your environment will be to specify the x, Y, and z values per the vmnic device in question, which will be found further up in the hwconfig file:

```
device.esx.X.Y.Z.options = "line_speed=1000 auto_speed=1 full_duplex=1"
```

VIC

Within the VIC, it is sometimes necessary to disable autonegotiation:

1. Log in to the VIC, either into the VC Server or directly to the host.
2. Select the ESX host in question.
3. Select the *Configuration* tab.
4. Click the *Networking* link.
5. Click the *Edit Properties* link opposite the vSwitch to edit.
6. Select the *Network Adapters* tab.
7. Select the pNIC to modify.
8. Click the *Edit* button.
9. Using the drop-down, select the speed and duplex of the pNIC (see Figure 9.38).

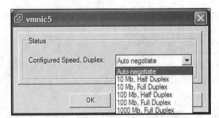

Figure 9.38 VIC Speed and Duplex settings

MUI

Within the MUI, it is sometimes required to set a pNIC to not autonegotiate:

1. Log in to the MUI.
2. Select the *Options* tab.
3. Click the *Network Connections* link.
4. Select the *Physical Adapters* tab.
5. Click the *Edit* link opposite the physical adapter to modify.
6. Choose the speed from the *Configured Speed, Duplex* drop-down (see Figure 9.39).

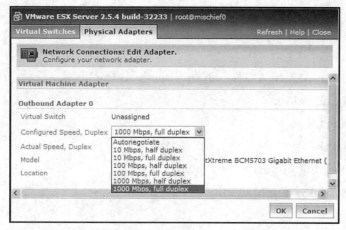

Figure 9.39   MUI setting physical adapter speed

7. Click *OK*.

Changing Traffic-Shaping Settings

It is also desirable to limit the amount of traffic a vSwitch or port group can accept. This uses the concept of traffic shaping where it is possible to limit, by the average amount of bandwidth, the peak possible bandwidth, and the burst size allowed.

Command Line

For ESX versions earlier than version 3, add a similar line to the individual VM configuration file for the VM. This will limit the bandwidth of the VM on the next reboot of the VM. Note that *xxx* is the average bandwidth limit, *YYY* is the peak bandwidth limit, and *zzz* is the burst limit. In this case, everything is in megabits (m), but could be specified using kilobits per second (k), or bits per second.

```
sched.net.filter.args = "XXXm YYYm ZZZm"
```

For ESX version 3, it is also possible to set this from the command line by looking for the following keys associated with either the vSwitch or the port group in question in the /etc/vmware/esx.conf file and modify as appropriate. Note that this requires a reboot of the server to effect the change:

```
.../shapingPolicy/avgBps = "104857600"
.../shapingPolicy/burstSize = "104857600"
.../shapingPolicy/enabled = "true"
.../shapingPolicy/peakBps = "104857600"
```

VIC

Changing traffic-shaping settings can be accomplished in the VIC by doing the following:

1. Log in to the VIC, either into the VC Server or directly to the host.

2. Select the ESX host in question.

3. Select the *Configuration* tab.

4. Click the *Networking* link.

5. Click the *Edit Properties* link opposite the vSwitch to edit.

6. Select the vSwitch or port group to modify.

7. Click the *Edit* button.

8. Select the Traffic Shaping tab.

9. Using the drop-down for Status (see Figure 9.40), select Enable Traffic Shaping, and then set the values appropriately, and finish by clicking *OK*.

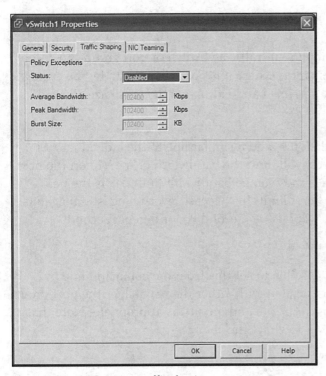

Figure 9.40   VIC setting traffic shaping

MUI

For ESX versions earlier than version 3, traffic shaping was a feature of each VM and not the vSwitch. It was then necessary to modify each VM that would need network limits:

1. Log in to the MUI.
2. Select the VM name of the VM to modify.
3. Select the *Network* tab.
4. Click the *Edit* link.
5. Enable Traffic Shaping and set the values appropriately and Click *OK* (see Figure 9.41).

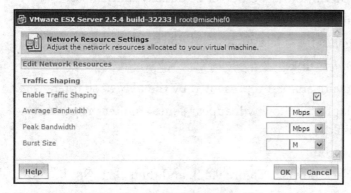

Figure 9.41   MUI Setting Traffic Shaping per VM

iSCSI VMFS

An iSCSI-based VMFS looks and acts just like a SAN-based VMFS except in the configuration of the iSCSI device. To connect to an iSCSI server, the device must be enabled first and the proper port group on the service console vSwitch created (as discussed previously). Because there is no difference between manipulating a SAN VMFS and an iSCSI VMFS, only the enabling and configuration of an iSCSI device is covered.

Command Line

It is possible to configure iSCSI from the command line by first enabling iSCSI using the following:

```
esxcfg-swiscsi -e
```

Specify an iSCSI target using the following, where staticTarget is the IP address or a hostname:

```
vmkiscsi-tool -D -a staticTarget vmhba40
```

To scan an iSCSI target for VMFS or new LUNs, use the following:

```
esxcfg-swiscsi -s
```

VIC

The alternative to the command line is to use the VIC to configure an iSCSI device. To do so, follow these steps:

1. Log in to the VIC, either into the VC Server or directly to the host.

2. Select the ESX host in question.

3. Select the *Configuration* tab.

4. Click the *Storage Adapters* link.

5. Select the iSCSI Software adapter represented by the *vhba40* adapter.

6. Below the storage adapter window will appear some adapter properties. Click the *Properties* link.

7. Click the *Configure* button.

8. Check the *Enabled* check box (see Figure 9.42), and then click *OK*. Be prepared to wait.

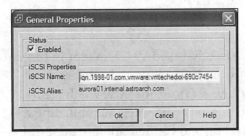

Figure 9.42 VIC Enable iSCSI

9. Select the *Dynamic Discovery* tab (see Figure 9.43).

10. Enter an IP address or system name in the Dynamic Discovery window in the form of ipAddress:3260 or systemName:3260. The :3260 represents the iSCSI port to use on the server specified. Finally, click *Add*, and be prepared to wait a while.

Figure 9.43 VIC Dynamic Discovery

11. Now it is possible to exit the properties window and inspect the iSCSI adapter details (see Figure 9.44) for the LUN or LUNs presented by the iSCSI server.

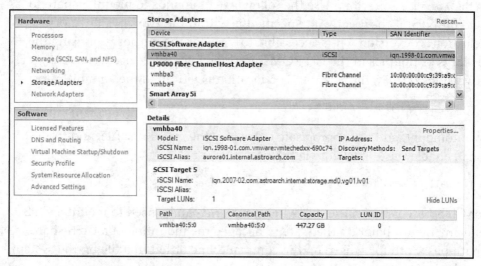

Figure 9.44 VIC iSCSI adapter details

When the iSCSI adapter can see the LUNs, all the standard SAN-based VMFS actions discussed earlier apply. A common problem is that the iSCSI VMkernel network adapter is not a port group off the service console vSwitch or that the netmask for the iSCSI gateway is not set properly.

Network–Attached Storage

In ESX version 3, it is possible to use NFS-based NAS as a VM data store in addition to storing anything else the ESX Server might require. In ESX versions earlier than version 3, NFS was used primarily to hold ISO, floppy, and other image files that the ESX Server could then use in the deployment of VMs. The major changes in ESX version 3 are that only one local directory is available to the VMs for use as a storage point for ISO or floppy images, and that is /vmimages, and NFS-based data stores are not mounted by the COS but by the VMkernel. This gives quite a bit of increased security because any COS file is no longer directly accessible by VMs, if they were misconfigured. There are three approaches for accessing NFS-based shares and only one for CIFS (Windows)-based shares. These approaches are covered either by the command line or the VIC.

Command Line

All versions of ESX can mount CIFS- or NFS-based shares directly to the COS; but in ESX version 3, these COS mounted shares can only be accessed if they are under the /vmimages directory. Use the following commands to mount a share to the COS for NFS. If the mountPoint specified is within the /vmimages directory umbrella, for ESX version 3 it is accessible to VMs for the purposes of using the files as ISOs or floppies in the CD-ROM and floppy virtual devices. However, for earlier versions of ESX, the mountPoint location is left up to the administrator:

```
mount -o nfs server:/share /mountPoint
```

To automount, add the appropriate entry into the /etc/fstab file, and for ESX version 3, enable the NFS client via the firewall:

```
esxcfg-firewall -e nfsClient
```

For CIFS-based shares, the following command can be used to mount a CIFS share to any mount point on the system. Because the mounting of a CIFS share requires a password to be used on the command line or left in a file on the system, it is not the most secure mechanism and is not recommended.

```
mount -t smbfs -o username=username,password=password
//server/share mountPoint
```

To automount, add the appropriate entry into the `/etc/fstab` file. If you want to hide the username and password, you can use a `credentials=/etc/.credentials` and place in `.credentials` two lines similar to the following. The credentials file can be named anything you want:

```
username=user
password=pass
```

To allow SMB-style mounts to the service console, enable the firewall for ESX version 3 using the following:

```
esxcfg-firewall -e smbClient
```

It is also possible to use the `smbmount` or `smbclient` commands to access remote shares. The `smbclient` command is used to transfer data or test connectivity. There are many ways to mount shares with the Samba tools, and they are covered in detail in other books.

ESX version 3 can, however, use the VMkernel to mount a data store for VM storage directly to the ESX Server using the following command. It is not possible to use this command to mount CIFS-based shares, however. The mounted file system would be accessible under `/vmfs/volumes/LABEL`. Each mount point in `/vmfs/volumes` also has its own UID associated with it, and ESX uses the UIDs and not the `LABEL` names internally:

```
esxcfg-nas -a -o host -s share LABEL
```

VIC

When accessing an NFS data store from the VIC, there is a handy wizard that will help:

1. Log in to the VIC, either into the VC Server or directly to the host.
2. Select the ESX host in question.
3. Select the *Configuration* tab.
4. Click the *Storage (SCSI, SAN, and NFS)* link.
5. Click the *Add Storage* link opposite in the upper-right corner of the window.
6. Click the *Network File System* button.

7. Click the *Next* button.

8. Specify the server name or IP address, the share to mount, and the label for the data store. It is also possible to mount the share read-only by checking the *Mount NFS Read Only* check box (see Figure 9.45).

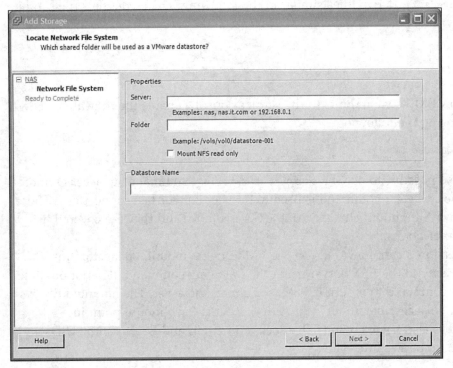

Figure 9.45 VIC specify NFS data store settings

9. Click the *Next* button to review your settings, and then click *Finish*.

Mapping Information

ESX version 3 provides an exciting new feature to the VIC: the mapping feature. The maps enable an administrator to see immediately which ESX Servers or VMs are using which data stores, networks, and hosts. Not only is there the capability to map these relationships, but the elements can also be edited from the map. It is possible to see all the data at once or just a portion of the data corresponding to just the host in question, VM, network, data store, or any combination thereof. The maps provide the pictorial view of the virtual infrastructure that is extremely necessary when dealing with large-scale environments. As they say, "A picture is worth a thousand words." There is *no* command-line version of these maps available.

The mapping feature of the VIC connected to a VC 2.0 server gives a clear understanding of which ESX Servers are connected to which data store and network. In the past, to get a map of these connections, you had to visit each ESX Server independently and then read the data and create a map by hand or use some other tool. Now it is possible to follow some simple steps to produce a handy map to tell you which ESX Servers are connected to which data stores and which networks:

1. Log in to the VIC, either into the VC Server or directly to the host.

2. Select the ESX datacenter, cluster, or folder in question. Selecting a single ESX Server sort of defeats the purpose of the map for data store connectivity.

3. Select the *Map* tab.

4. Select the map options. In the case of Figure 9.46 I selected *Host to Network* and *Host to Datastore*.

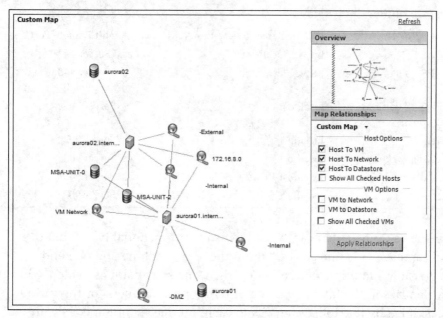

Figure 9.46 VIC use of maps

The use of maps is a great way to verify that all ESX Servers participating in a cluster or VMotion network share the proper data stores and networks. Without this information, VMotion becomes problematic. In addition, it is possible to directly interact with all the icons in the map to either manipulate a data store, network, or host. This interaction opens a menu when you right-click an icon.

Secure Access to Management Interfaces

With later versions of ESX (version 2.5.x and later), it is possible to access the MUI, service console, or VC Servers through a firewall using secure tunnels. SSH can produce such a tunnel and is available for all forms of client machines. For the web interfaces, a client using any operating system can be used. However, for VC or Virtual Infrastructure Client 2.0 (VIC) access, a .NET-enabled Windows operating system is required. Here are the tunnels necessary to create access to ESX management tools remotely through a firewall using secure tunnels. Table 9.4 lists a set of tunnel rules that will apply individually, and Table 9.5 is a set of rules that will allow all tunnels to work at the same time.

Table 9.4

Secure Tunnel Definitions Individual		
Interface	URL or Server to Use to Access	Default Remote Port
MUI	https://localhost	esx2Server:443
Web interface (ESX 3.0 only)	https://localhost	esx3Server:443 or vc2Server:443
Remote console (ESX versions earlier than version 3)	localhost	esxServer:902
VIC (host mode)	localhost	esxServer:902
VIC (remote console web mode)	localhost	esxServer:903
VC1.X	localhost	vc1Server:905
VIC (VC mode)	localhost	vc2Server:902

Table 9.5 shows tunnels that can be created so that functionality will not overlap. A tunnel can have only one start point on the local machine and one endpoint. Table 9.4 shows multiple endpoints for the same start point as evidenced by that last three entries in the table. By using different port numbers for the various web interfaces, it is possible to have access to each interface simultaneously. In addition, by using only VC 2.0, only one tunnel is required for VIC access. VC 2.0 will also integrate with ESX versions earlier than version 3, but access to the MUI

should not be made by clicking the link within the VIC, but via a direct entry of the URL specified (a small gotcha, but easily handled).

Table 9.5

Secure Tunnel Definitions Shared		
Interface	URL or Server to Use to Access	Remote Port
MUI	https://localhost:444	esx25Server:443
Web interface (ESX 3.0 only)	https://localhost:445	esx3Server:443
Web interface remote console	localhost	esx3Server:903
Web interface (VC mode)	https://localhost	vc2Server:443
VIC (VC mode)	localhost	vc2Server:902

Advanced Settings

The FC HBA VMFS section in this chapter touched on how to change appropriate advanced settings and providing mechanisms to do so. However, there are other settings in need of manipulation occasionally. One mentioned in previous chapters is the `ConflictRetries` setting. The setting to modify is `/Scsi/ConflictRetries`.

Best Practice for Advanced Settings

Do not manipulate advance settings unless directed by a VMware support organization or the option is covered in these chapters.

To find the full list of options available to be set from the command line, use the following command:

```
ls -R /proc/vmware/config
```

To see the current settings of an option, from the command line use the following command. Never use an editor to view the contents of any file in `/proc`. Also note that the following command will show a small description of the `config` functionality and possibly the range of values supported:

```
cat /proc/vmware/config/<optionName>
```

To set an option, use either the VIC or the MUI. If it is necessary to use the command line, then, for ESX version 3, use the `esxcfg-advcfg` command. For ESX versions earlier than version 3, there is the two-step process. All these methods to change the advanced settings are described earlier in the "Masking and Max LUN Manipulations" section.

Conclusion

In this chapter, we have gone through the configuration of an ESX Server. Many of these items need to be done prior to creating VMs, specifically anything related to networking and the service console, because these items can require reboots. In addition, a VMFS data store needs to be configured, and we have reviewed the mechanisms to access iSCSI-, SAN-, and NAS-based data stores, and their caveats. Now that this is completed and we have the previous chapters to back us up with necessary information, it is now possible to create a VM on the host.

Chapter 10

Virtual Machines

All the previous chapters have dealt with VMware ESX Server as opposed to virtual machines (VMs). To get to this stage, an understanding of datastores, virtual networking, security, and the hardware is required, which the previous chapters provided. Now we can build on our knowledge and add in some VMs.

Overview of Virtual Hardware

The next step in our progression is to understand what makes up a VM before we start to create them. In essence, what makes up the VM dictates what operating systems and devices the OS can access. As an example, the wrong choice of SCSI adapter could make it very difficult to install or even run Windows XP.

With the multiple versions of VMware ESX Server, there have been subtle but not great changes in the virtual hardware. Some aspects have been made easier to manage, but there is not a lot of difference between what virtual hardware is in use and actually how the physical hardware is used; in some cases, the virtual hardware is emulated, paravirtualized, or fully virtualized in the physical CPUs (pCPUs) of the server in use. There has been quite a bit of talk about which of these concepts are the best, and until now they were not strictly necessary to understand. But they are now:

- **Emulation**

  Emulation is the translation of commands sent to a virtual device to what is acceptable to the physical hardware device. An example is the translation of instructions from a PCNET32 network device to a Broadcom gigabit network adapter. This translation occurs inside the hypervisor.

- **Paravirtualization**

  Paravirtualization is when the OS running inside the VM (guest OS) knows that it is virtualized and is using special drivers specifically designed to work with the virtualization hypervisor. An example of this is the vmxnet network driver provided as part of the VMware Tools to most guest operating systems.

- **Fully virtualized**

  A fully virtualized guest does not have any specialized drivers nor is there any emulation within the hypervisor. This technology actually pushes down into the pCPU any translation activities. Any machine that has a pCPU supporting AMD-V or Intel-VT technology has guests that can be fully virtualized.

Whether emulated, paravirtualized, or fully virtualized, each VM has a limited amount of virtual hardware that can be assigned to it when talking about VMware ESX Server. Granted, although other VMware virtualization products can handle more items, such as USB, sound cards, and serial ports, ESX does not support those workstation-type devices. The following list provides a breakdown of what is supported by ESX and the how the device is supported.

VMs can consist of the following devices:

- **Virtual CPUs (vCPU)**

  Up to four vCPUs are supported under ESX version 3; however, earlier versions of ESX have a limit of two vCPUs. It is possible to overcommit the number of vCPUs in relation to the number of pCPUs. There is one caveat, however; if the VM is to have two or four vCPUs (note that 3 is not a supported number), there must be at least that many threads (in the case of hyperthreaded pCPUs) or cores available to the machine. It is not possible to run a four-vCPU VM on a system with only two cores because each vCPU requires its own core or thread upon which to run.

  Note, however, that more vCPUs does not always imply better performance. Performance depends on whether the guest OS and the application to be used on the VM actually use multiple CPUs. In general, if the application is threaded, it will make use of multiple CPUs. Many applications are not threaded, and adding vCPUs to a VM has an adverse performance impact.

- **PCI Devices**

  Each VM can have up to 6 PCI devices attached at any given time. In essence, there are 5 from which the VM can use as the Display device takes up one slot. Within these 6 slots it is possible to mix and match the other devices up to their maximums.

- **Memory**

  Each VM can have up to 16GB of memory associated with it. However, if the physical memory is below the total used memory of the VMs, the memory for the VMs will start to swap as more is required. This causes performance issues. Note this is used memory, and not necessarily the memory assigned to the VM. For ESX versions earlier than version 3 there is a limit of only 3.6GB of memory no matter the number of vCPUs in use.

- **Virtual IDE drives (vIDE)**

  There is a limit of four vIDE devices. However, all these devices are limited to being only CD/DVD-ROM devices. Like a standard IDE-based system, there are only two IDE controllers available. But unlike them, it is not possible to use IDE-based hard-drives in a VM. All VM hard drives are virtual SCSI devices.

- **Virtual floppy drives (vFloppy)**

  There is a limit of two vFloppy devices. Like most PC-based systems, there is only one floppy controller available, which supports up to two devices.

- **Virtual display (vDisplay, vSVGA)**

  There is only one display available to a VM, which is accessible only via VMware's remote console software (more on this later). Each display can have a depth of 1, 8, 15, 16, or 24 bits. The bit depth of the display tells the virtual super VGA (vSVGA) device how many colors it can display within the remote console. Choose a bit depth that is lower than capability of the display device on which the remote console will be displayed. By default, the depth is set to 1, which lets the remote console decide how many bits to set the vSVGA to.

- **Virtual keyboard and mouse (vKeyboard, vMouse)**

  Like a normal PC-based system, there is only one vKeyboard and one vMouse device. These devices show up as standard PS/2 type devices.

- **Virtual NIC (vNIC)**

  There is a limit of four vNIC adapters available to any VM, and they can either be the standard PCNET32 or vlance device or VMware's vmxnet device. In ESX version 3, the type of device depends entirely on which driver is installed in the VM. On earlier versions of ESX, it was necessary to set the type of vNIC and install the proper driver. This caused no end of confusion and has been changed to make management of the VM easier. The PCNET32 is a simple 10/100-style device, whereas the vmxnet is a 10/100/1000 or GbE device that knows about the virtualization layer and can reach higher speeds. A vmxnet vNIC is a paravirtualized device per our previous definitions and is available only when VMware Tools is installed. VMware Tools is discussed later. It is also possible to use a device type Intel e1000 for some virtual machines, primarily Vista. To select an e1000 driver you need to edit the configuration file after the VM is created.

- **Virtual SCSI controller (vSCSI controller)**

Each VM can support up to four vSCSI controllers. Each controller is either a BusLogic or LSILogic device depending on the OS installed. Older versions of guest operating systems generally support the BusLogic, whereas newer versions support the LSILogic device. The choice of which to use is important because all VMware ESX Server virtual disks are SCSI drives and as such, the guest OS will not find its disk if the wrong type of vSCSI controller is specified. Each vSCSI controller can support up to 16 virtual SCSI devices. vSCSI controllers can have their bus sharing mode for use with shared disk clusters. Bus sharing can be set to nothing (the default), which implies there is no bus sharing or to physical, which implies that a shared disk is shared between two or more VMs or physical machines. In the case of VMs, the VMs reside on different ESX Servers. The last mode is to set bus sharing to virtual, which is used when all the VMs participating in a shared disk cluster are on the same ESX Server. We will delve into setting up clusters later.

- **Virtual SCSI device (vSCSI device)**

A vSCSI device is either a VM disk file (VMDK), system LUN or raw disk map (RDM), or a SCSI pass-thru device. Because each vSCSI controller can handle up to 16 devices, there is a lot of room for disk drives. However, it should be mentioned that depending on the hardware attached and the application suite, there is often a need to put vSCSI devices on multiple controllers. A good case in point is a VMDK used as a quorum drive. Any shared-bus vSCSI controller should not host the C: or root drive for any VM and therefore should be a separate controller. In general, RDMs also use their own controller.

And finally, as mentioned previously, it is possible to also have tape drives or tape robots be part of a VM through a SCSI pass-thru mechanism, where the ESX Server passes all requests from the VM to the locally attached SCSI tape device. It is possible to attach other SCSI devices to a VM using this mechanism. The most common usage is for tape devices, however. An example of this type of device is provided later. Another use of these devices is to present a local SCSI LUN as if it were an RDM. These types of vSCSI devices should have their own vSCSI controller, too.

That is the complete list of all available virtual hardware. When creating a VM, each VM is automatically assigned one device of the following: vCPU, vKeyboard, vMouse, vDisplay, vNIC, vFloppy, and vIDE. The type of vNIC is up to the VM creator but defaults to PCNET32 for versions of ESX earlier than version 3; for version 3, the default is the flexible vNIC. The amount of memory depends on the guest OS to install, and the vSCSI controller does, too. There are by default no vSCSI devices attached to the controller, and that is left up to the VM creator.

Creating VMs

There are three ways to create VMs for ESX versions earlier than version 3, but there are only two ways for ESX version 3. The common methods are to create VMs from the command line or via the Virtual Infrastructure Client (VIC). The alternative way for earlier versions of ESX is via the MUI. In all cases, great care must be made to make sure that the files are placed in the correct locations and that the virtual hardware chosen matches up with the guest OS to use. For various guest operating systems, there are actually a few shortcuts that can be taken. The basic method to create a VM applies to almost all VMs. There are certain differences and considerations during the process, but the process is essentially the same regardless of the guest OS in use. In a subsequent section in this chapter, we review special guest OS cases. This section is all about setting up the virtual hardware or deploying a new server.

Normally, the process of setting up a new server requires a needs analysis, architecture review, purchase order, the wait while the hardware arrives, the time it takes to set up the hardware and configure any connections to storage and network, and then finally the installation of an OS to lead up to the installation of a specific application suite. ESX VMware server alleviates the need for a purchase order, the wait while the hardware arrives, and the time to set up the hardware and configure any connections to storage and network. Although it would be nice to alleviate the other steps, that is not something ESX VMware server can do. Herein, we just cover the steps necessary to create virtual hardware that can have a guest OS installed on it.

There are, however, a few considerations before we begin. Table 10.1 lists the requirements before the virtual hardware can be created.

Table 10.1

Considerations for Virtual Hardware	
Consideration	**Comments**
# of vNICs needed	The number of vNICs depends on whether the VM will be multihomed. A vFW, vRouter, or vGateway will have at least two vNICs. Most other machines only require one vNIC. Do not add a second for failover; that is handled by the VMware ESX Server.
How the VM will be installed	If the VM will be installed via PXEboot or over the web, a network must be connected at boot time of the VM. If the installation mode is via CD-ROM, the CD-ROM must be connected at boot time.
Whether the vSCSI device be a VMDK or system LUN?	If a system LUN or RDM is to be used, is the LUN available to the ESX server? If a VMDK is to be used, what is the base size of the VMDK to use? It is wise to have a standard size in mind for at least the C: or base install drive.
Whether there be more than one vSCSI hard disk in use	If there is more than one vSCSI device in use, what is the SCSI ID mapping? In general, it is suggested that RDMs use a different vSCSI controller than VMDKs, but it is not necessary.
How much memory to assign the VM	More memory is *not* always better. How much memory does the application actually need? It is recommended to use the required memory for the application and not the stated number. An application that requires only 256MB when the documentation calls for 2GB will leave the system with less memory for the creation of other VMs.
The required number of vCPUs?	More vCPU is *not* always better. Be sure the application suite to install is actually a threaded application. If not, use one vCPU. It is easy to add a second or more vCPUs, but it is difficult to go backward.
Whether any generic vSCSI devices will be used	Generic vSCSI devices include tape devices, scanners, and so on (anything that is not a hard drive of some type). In this case, you must know the SCSI LUN number in the service console for the attached device. In addition, there will be a vSCSI controller just for these types of devices.

After we answer these questions, we can begin the VM creation according to one of the three methods depending on the flavor of ESX in use. The following is a Rosetta stone very much like Chapter 8, "Configuring ESX from a Host Connection," was in terms of covering all versions of ESX. However, all the steps are similar, no matter which method is used to create a VM.

Within the VIC, VMs can be created by selecting any of the following:

- **Host**

   A host is a single VMware ESX Server.

- **Cluster**

  A cluster is a collection of VMware ESX Servers participating in either or both of the VMware HA or VMware DRS products. This concept is discussed further in Chapter 11.

- **Resource pool**

  A resource pool is a finite amount of a VMware ESX Server's or cluster's resources, set aside for a subset of VMs. This concept is discussed further in Chapter 11.

In addition, create a VM naming convention that does not include any special characters. Special characters do not include dashes and underlines, but do include periods, question marks, square brackets, curly braces, parenthesis, number signs, less than or greater than symbols, backward/forward slashes, @ symbols, asterisks, pipes or the vertical line, semicolons, quotes of any type, tildes, percent symbols, and ampersands, as well as spaces. Do not include any control characters or multibyte characters. Pretty much only upper- and lowercase characters A to Z, the numerals 0 through 9, and underscores and dashes should be used to create VM names; the rest cause interaction issues when manipulating VMs from the COS.

VM Creation from VIC

When creating a VM from the VIC, it is possible to use either a direct connection to the ESX Server or a connection to the VC Server. It is, however, not possible to use the VIC web interface to create a VM. Yet, it is a useful interface for managing VMs remotely. The steps for creating a VM from the VIC follow:

1. Log in to the VIC.
2. Select the datacenter into which to create the VM.
3. Select the host, datacenter, cluster, or resource pool into which to create the VM.
4. Select the *File > New > Virtual Machine*, and press *Ctrl+N* or right-click the item and select *Virtual Machine* from the menu. You will now see the New Virtual Machine Wizard (see Figure 10.1).
5. Select *Typical* and click Next. Typical is also the default. For some installations, it will be necessary to use *Custom*. We will discuss those in another section.

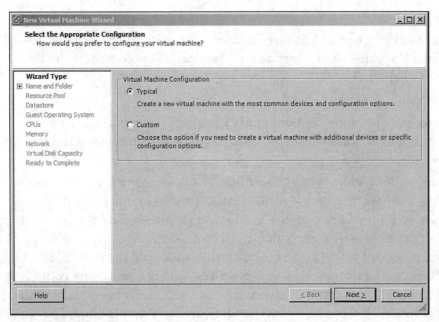

Figure 10.1   New Virtual Machine Wizard

6. Name the VM using a descriptive name with no spaces. Some of the tools do not like spaces or special characters in the name. Use a naming convention; perhaps Department-MachineName-Instance. After the VM is named, select the virtual machine group or folder into which it should go. Figure 10.2 illustrates naming the VM and selecting a folder.

   If at this time there are no folders, choose the default. Click *Next* to continue.

7. Select the host in which to place the VM (see Figure 10.3); this appears only if a resource group, or cluster, is the starting point of the VM creation. Click *Next* to continue.

8. Select the resource pool into which to place the VM (see Figure 10.4). The topmost resource pool is the ESX Server itself. Resource pools are new to ESX version 3. Click Next to continue.

9. Choose where to store the VM and its configuration files. For ESX version 3, the configuration files are usually stored with the VMDK in their own directory, named after the VM, on the datastore chosen (see Figure 10.5). Click Next to continue. Datastores can either be NFS, iSCSI, SAN, or local storage.

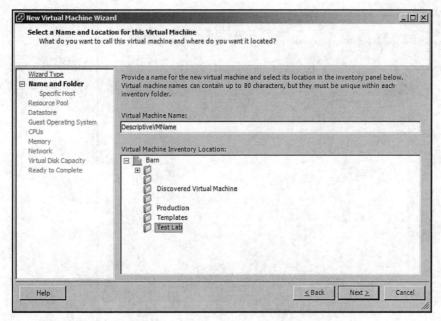

Figure 10.2 Name and Folder

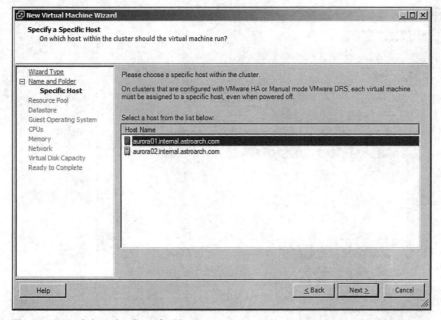

Figure 10.3 Select the Specific Host

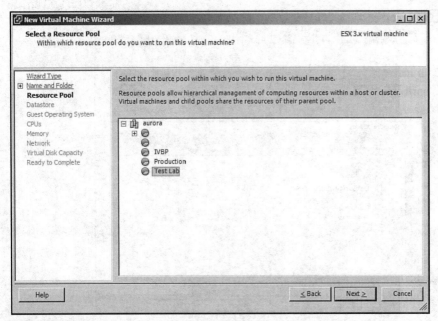

Figure 10.4   Select the Resource Pool where you want to place the VM

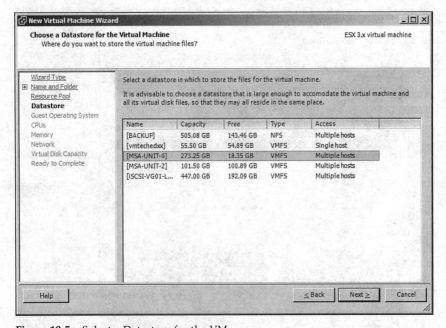

Figure 10.5   Select a Datastore for the VM

10. Select the general type of guest OS to install into the VM (see Figure 10.6). This stage is critical because each guest OS has its own particular setup requirements. The *other* generic type should only be used for unlisted operating systems such as one of the BSD operating systems.

Using the drop-down menu, select the exact version or *Other* if that option is available and the specific version is not mentioned. Use the specific version as often as possible. The *Other* options are only available for the *Other* generic type or for *Linux*. Click Next to continue.

11. Select the number of vCPUs to use (see Figure 10.7). Remember that more vCPUs does not always imply better performance, and although this drop-down will *not* limit to the number of processors, threads, or cores on the system, keep that limitation in mind, too. Unless the application is threaded, the best practice is to select one vCPU and add more as necessary. Click *Next* to continue. Adding additional CPUs comes with a penalty, which will impact the vSMP VM and other VMs running on the same ESX host if the applications installed are not threaded.

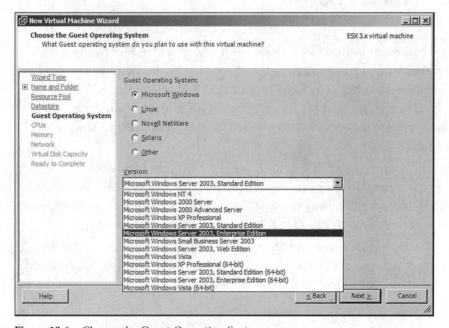

Figure 10.6 Choose the Guest Operating System

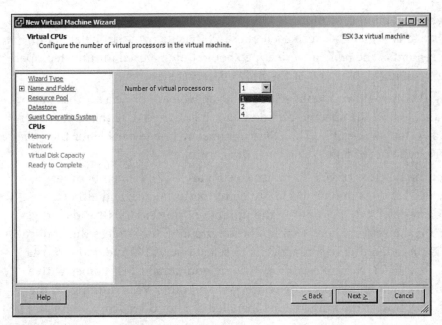

Figure 10.7 Select the number of Virtual CPUs

12. Select the amount of memory to assign to the VM (see Figure 10.8). Remember that more memory is *not* always better. It is quite easy to add memory to a VM, but select an amount that will make sense. Perhaps standardize on a minimum amount per guest OS in use. However, the amount of memory required varies greatly with applications. Click Next to continue.

13. Select the number of vNICs to assign to the VM (see Figure 10.9). In general, there is a need for only one vNIC per VM unless the VM is acting as a vFW, vRouter, or vGateway device. More vNICs will appear or disappear as the number of vNICs to assign to the VM changes.

Select the previously created vSwitch for each vNIC interface from the drop-down list and check the *Connect at Power On* box if the vNIC should be present at boot time. Click Next to continue.

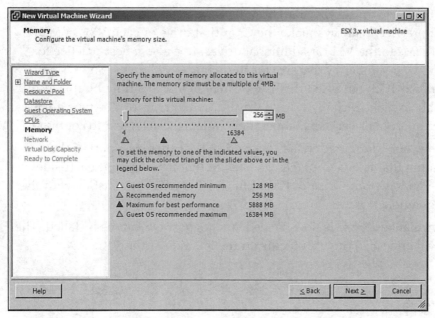

Figure 10.8 Set the amount of Memory for the VM

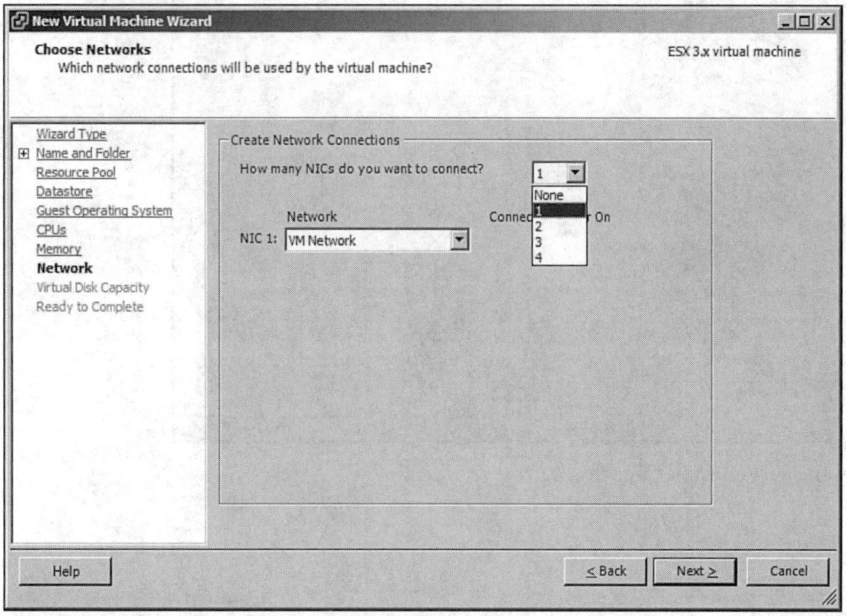

Figure 10.9 Select Network Connections

14. Select the size of the virtual disk (VMDK) to create (see Figure 10.10). It is a best practice to always make the C: or first drive of each VM a VMDK. Add RDMs to the VM for additional drives. It is also a best practice to determine a standard drive size for these initial VM disks. The system defaults to 4GB, but often that is too small to install a full OS. It is also possible to make megabyte-sized drives. Small drives of this type are useful for quorum or very small operating systems. Click Next to continue.

15. Review your configuration (see Figure 10.11). If there is a part of the configuration that is unacceptable, go back to that item using the left-side links window of the wizard. Press Finish when you are satisfied with the configuration.

16. The virtual hardware is now created, and a guest OS can be installed. The VM will appear in the list of VMs on the left side of the VIC.

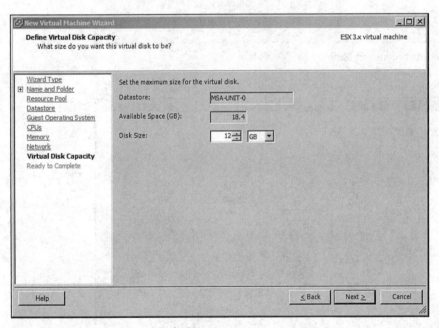

Figure 10.10   Set the Virtual Disk Capacity

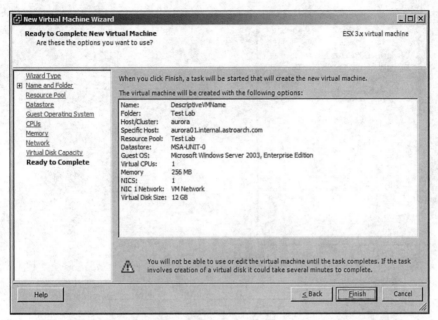

Figure 10.11 Check your configuration over at the Ready to Complete stage

VM Creation from VC1.X

Creating a VM from VC1.X is similar to using the VIC, but in the default mode it has some limitations regarding the setting of the amount of memory to use (there is no way to do this in typical mode) and the adding of multiple vNICs during creation time:

1. Log in to VC1.X.

2. Select an ESX Server host and use *Ctrl+V*, right-click the host name > *New Virtual Machine*, or use *File > New > Virtual Machine* to start the new VM wizard. You will see the greeting window (see Figure 10.12). Click Next to continue.

3. Select the *Typical* setting (see Figure 10.13). This is extremely similar to the VIC example, where the typical setting is generally recommended, except in special cases explained later. Click Next to continue.

4. Select the VM group in which to place the VM (see Figure 10.14). If you do not at this time have VM folders, choose the *Discovered VMs* default folder. Click Next to continue.

Figure 10.12 Welcome to New Virtual Machine Wizard

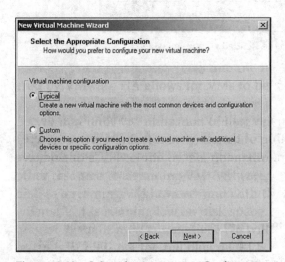

Figure 10.13 Select the Appropriate Configuration

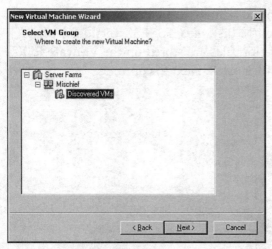

Figure 10.14   Select the VM Group

5. Select the guest operating system to install (see Figure 10.15). First, choose the Guest Operating System type, and then the specific version of the OS. If the OS does not exist in the list, choose Other or the closest version. Click Next to continue.

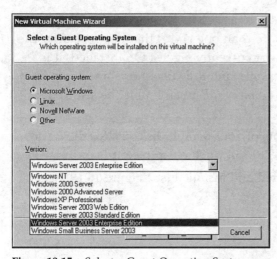

Figure 10.15   Select a Guest Operating System

6. Name the VM using a descriptive *VM name* following a naming convention and the caveat about special characters mentioned at the start of this sec-

tion (see Figure 10.16). In addition to naming the VM, select the datastore or VMFS onto which to store the VM disk files. For ESX versions earlier than version 3, the VM configuration files are stored on the VMware ESX Server and not with the VMDK files. Click Next to continue.

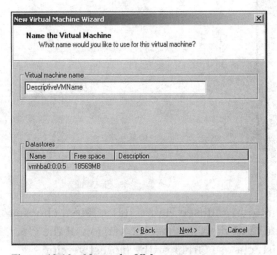

Figure 10.16   Name the VM

7. Select the network to use for the primary vNIC (see Figure 10.17). It is not possible at this time to create more than one vNIC; that happens after the VM is created. Because there is not currently a guest OS installed, it is wise to choose the vlance *adapter type*, and if PXEboot or some other form of network install is to be used, *Connect at Power On* must be selected. Click *Next* to continue.

8. Specify the *disk size* in increments of your default disk size for the C: or root drive for the VM (see Figure 10.18). Click Next to continue.

9. Now the VM is ready to be created and installed (see Figure 10.19). Click *Finish* to continue and create the VM.

Figure 10.17   Select the Network Type

Figure 10.18   Specify Disk Capacity

Figure 10.19 Ready to Submit Task

VM Creation from MUI

Creation of a VM from the MUI is actually rather limited, and has some major caveats if VC is also in use. That caveat is in the directories used to store the configuration files, so it's important to pay close attention to Step 3:

1. Log in to the MUI.
2. Click the *Add Virtual Machine* button.
3. The first dialog, Add Virtual Machine (see Figure 10.20), is one of the more important ones to edit appropriately. Select the type of VM from the *Guest Operating System* drop-down list. Note that there are far fewer choices than on newer versions of ESX and even VC. For the *Display Name*, use a descriptive name for the VM following your VM naming convention with no spaces or special characters within, because some of the tools balk on spaces and special characters. The last bit of information to enter into this dialog is the *location*. The location should be a subdirectory off the /home/vmware directory, because that is the one that VC uses and the subdirectory should be unique for each VM. If the location directories are not unique per VM, there will be performance issues. Click Next to continue.

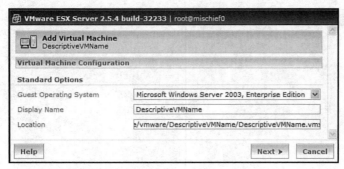

Figure 10.20   Standard options

4. You will now see three settings that you need to configure: Processors, Memory, and Workloads (see Figure 10.21). Select the appropriate number of *Processors* depending on your system licenses. If the VirtualSMP license has not been entered, there will be a limit of one vCPU per VM. Remember that more vCPUs does not always translate to better performance. Set the *Memory* required, and if *Citrix Terminal Services* is to be used, check the appropriate *Workloads* check box. This option presets some Ethernet functionality to improve Citrix performance.

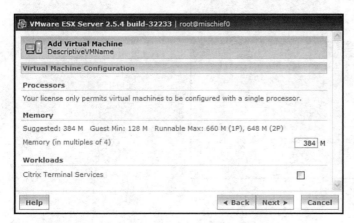

Figure 10.21   Processors, Memory, and Workloads

5. Now wait while the VM is physically created (see Figure 10.22). At this time, the VM will appear in the MUI dashboard, too. However, we are not yet finished with the MUI wizard.

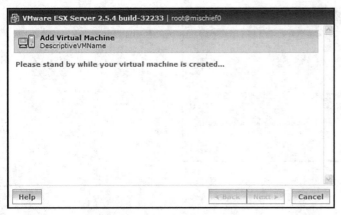

Figure 10.22   VM creation

6. At this point, it is time to choose the type of virtual disk to use: *Blank,* *Existing, or System LUN/Disk (see Figure 10.23). Blank means* a brand new VMDK, *Existing* means a VMDK that already exists on a VMFS, and *System LUN/Disk* means a LUN presented off a SAN. It is possible to use a local LUN, which we discuss later as a special case. For most C: or root drives, the best practice suggests that a VMDK be used. Click the appropriate link to continue.

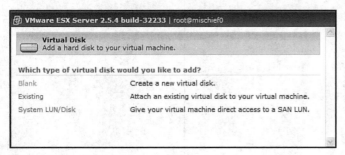

Figure 10.23   Virtual Disk

7. When using a Blank VMDK, it is now the time to set the *Image File Location* to be the VMFS on to which to store the VMDK (see Figure 10.24). Set the *Image File Name* of the VMDK. Use the DescriptiveVMName already chosen because it will help to organize your VMs and map VMDKs to VMs. Set the *Capacity* to your predetermined standard disk size for the guest operating system chosen. The best practice is to not change the *Virtual*

SCSI Node at this time and to use *Persistent Disk Mode*. We discuss disk modes later in this chapter. Click Next to continue.

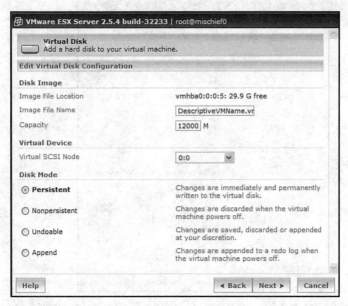

Figure 10.24   Edit Virtual Disk Configuration

8. The VM is now ready to hand off to another to install the guest operating system. It is also possible to add virtual hardware at this time, too. This dialog is the same dialog that appears when the DescriptiveVMName is chosen from the MUI dashboard and the *Hardware* tab is chosen (see Figure 10.25). Click the *Close* link to close this dialog.

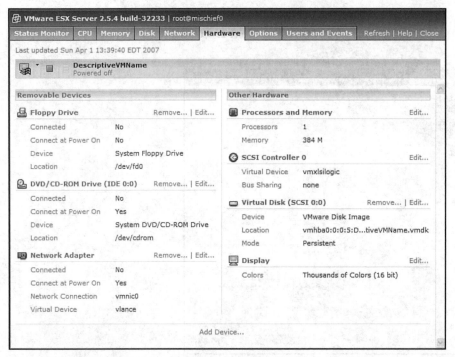

Figure 10.25   Virtual hardware configuration

VM Creation from Command Line

VM creation from the command line provides access to most functionality, but the configuration file is rather cryptic and not easily understood. However, to solve some VM issues, the configuration file must often be edited. What follows in the rest of this section is the configuration file that ends in .vmx for an existing VM. Using an existing VM as a model for future VMs created by the command line is the best practice.

Many files are associated with a VM besides the .vmx file to be discussed. Table 10.2 briefly describes the files associated with a VM and their usage.

Table 10.2

File Association via Extension

Filename Extension	Purpose	Notes
.vmx	Main VM configuration file	Contains all the information necessary to start a VM
.vmdk	VM disk file configuration	Is a short file describing the VM disk
-flat.vmdk	VM disk file	A monolithic file the size of the VMDK in question containing the disk contents
-rdm.vmdk	RDM VM disk file	A hard link to the LUN to which the RDM was linked. This entry takes up one slot on the VMFS metadata but is really a link to the LUN in question. Its size is the size of the LUN.
-delta.vmdk	VM disk file used by snapshots	Each delta represents a specific snapshot
.vswp	The per-VM virtual swap file	Introduced in ESX version 3, this per-VM virtual swap file replaces the monolithic virtual swap of prior versions
.hlog	VMotion log file	Often living long past its use, the .hlog file contains information about a VMotion
.nvram	Nonvolatile RAM file	Each VM has its own NVRAM file containing the VM's BIOS settings
.vmsd	VM snapshot configuration file	Introduced in ESX version 3, contains information about each snapshot
.vmxf	VM foundry configuration file	Introduced in ESX version 3, contains information used by VC
.vzsnp	vRanger virtual snap file	When this extension is seen, an vRanger backup is in use. Every file in the directory will be copied and have this extension.
.log	VM log file	Log of all virtualization actions for the VM
.vmsn	VM memory snapshot	Snapshot of the current memory for use when rebooting a specific snapshot
.vmss	VM sleep state file	Used to store the state of a VM put to sleep

It is not necessary to reproduce every file above when creating a VM by hand. Most of these files are created for you when a VM is used. The steps to create the VM follow:

1. For ESX version 3, create a directory on the datastore in which the VM will reside, by using the following command:

```
cd /vmfs/volumes/dataStoreName; mkdir VMName; cd VMName; vi VMName.vmx
```

For earlier versions of ESX, use the following command:

```
cd /home/vmware; mkdir VMName; cd VMName; vi VMName.vmx
```

2. Then add the following lines:

```
config.version = "8"
virtualHW.version = "4"
```

The first two lines of the configuration file define the configuration and virtual hardware versions used by ESX version 3. For ESX version 2.5.1, the `config.version` will be `6` and the `virtualHW.version` will be `3`. Each version of ESX has its own settings for these variables.

3. Define some information about the VM. Specify the location of the `nvram` file and the action to take on VM power actions. The most important lines in these `config` file options are the `displayName` (how the VM shows up in the VIC), `memsize` (how much memory to allocate to this VM), and the `extendedConfigFile` name, which is used by ESX version 3. Of all these lines, the `memsize` and `displayName` options are required by all versions of ESX:

```
nvram = "W2K3.nvram"
powerType.powerOff = "default"
powerType.powerOn = "default"
powerType.suspend = "default"
powerType.reset = "default"
displayName = "W2K3"
memsize = "512"
extendedConfigFile = "W2K3.vmxf"
```

4. The next chunk of the configuration file, represented in the following listing, shows the configuration of the first vSCSI disk to use. Note that the `scsi0:0.fileName` is specified using the name of the VM. Instead of `lsilogic` for the `virtualDev` type, we could specify `buslogic`. The other lines specify the shared disk cluster bus mode to use with the vSCSI controller (in this case, there is `none`) and the type of the vSCSI device, which is a `scsi-hardDisk` or VMDK. If the `redo` option is set to `true` for ESX version 3, it is possible to create snapshots of the VMDK:

```
scsi0.present = "true"
scsi0.sharedBus = "none"
scsi0.virtualDev = "lsilogic"
scsi0:0.present = "true"
scsi0:0.fileName = "VMName.vmdk"
scsi0:0.redo = "true"
scsi0:0.deviceType = "scsi-hardDisk"
```

5. The following statements define the first IDE CD-ROM-based device and its mode. Alternatively, you can specify the location of an ISO file in the `fileName` field if the filename is accessible on a datastore or in the `/vmimages` folder for ESX version 3. For earlier versions of ESX, the `fileName` can be any location on the system. In addition, this IDE device does not start connected to the VM; set the `startConnected` option to `true` to have the CD-ROM available at boot time:

```
ide0:0.present = "true"
ide0:0.clientDevice = "true"
ide0:0.fileName = ""
ide0:0.deviceType = "cdrom-raw"
ide0:0.startConnected = "false"
```

6. This section adds a vFloppy device to the VM, and like the vIDE CD-ROM device, this device can start connected by setting the `startConnected` option to `true`. The `fileName` will either be a floppy device in the COS or a `.flp` or floppy image file:

```
floppy0.present = "true"
floppy0.startConnected = "false"
floppy0.fileName = "/dev/fd0"
floppy0.clientDevice = "true"
```

7. As with all the other VM creation methods, it is important to have a vNIC device. The following listing defines the network name to use, which should be a defined vNetwork inside the ESX Server. Note that although most premade configuration files will include a `generatedAddress` option, there is no need for one because the MAC address will be generated by the VM when it is registered in the system:

```
ethernet0.present = "true"
ethernet0.allowGuestConnectionControl = "false"
ethernet0.networkName = "VM Network"
ethernet0.addressType = "vpx"
```

8. The final options specify the guest OS installed using `guestOS`, the filename of the log file using `fileName`, and the shares of the CPU to give for this VMs vCPU, and the minimum size of the memory using `minsize` and the shares of memory allocated to the VM. The `uuid.bios` field should be included, but when the VM starts, it will be overwritten with a new value. The location of the log file is quite important and allows you to change the name of the log file from the default. This option is not part of ESX versions earlier than version 3. The `guestOS` option is extremely important because it defines some internal processing:

```
guestOS = "winnetenterprise"
uuid.bios = "50 0f 4b 4d a0 bf 71 a4-20 c5 8e 63 50 f3 b7 b7"
log.fileName = "vmware.log"
sched.cpu.min = "0"
sched.cpu.units = "mhz"
sched.cpu.shares = "normal"
sched.mem.minsize = "0"
sched.mem.shares = "normal"
tools.syncTime = "FALSE"
```

Using Table 10.3, we would use a setting of `linux` for any version of Fedora Core, but because Fedora Core is similar to Red Hat Enterprise Linux, we could use one of `rhel` settings, too. Be careful which setting you select based on the OS, because this tells the virtualization layer how to handle the VM.

Table 10.3

Common Guest OS Definitions	
OS	**Guest OS Setting (Not Case Sensitive)**
Windows NT	winNT
Windows 2000 Server	win2000Serv
Windows 2000 Advanced Server	win2000AdvServ
Windows XP Professional	winXPPro

OS	Guest OS Setting (Not Case Sensitive)
Windows 2003 Standard Edition	winNetStandard
Windows 2003 Enterprise Edition	winNetEnterprise
Windows Small Business Server 2003	winNetBusiness
Windows 2003 Web Edition	winNetWeb
Windows Vista	longhorn
Windows XP Professional 64-bit	winXPPro-64
Windows 2003 Standard Edition 64-bit	winNetStandard-64
Windows 2003 Enterprise Edition 64-bit	winNetEnterprise-64
Windows Vista 64-bit	longhorn-64
Novell NetWare 5.1	netware5
Novell NetWare 6.x	netware6
Sun Solaris 10	solaris10
Sun Solaris 10 64-bit	solaris10-64
SUSE Linux Enterprise Server (SLES 8/9/10)	sles
SUSE Linux Enterprise Server (SLES 8/9/10) 64-bit	sles-64
Red Hat Enterprise Linux 2	rhel2
Red Hat Enterprise Linux 3	rhel3
Red Hat Enterprise Linux 4	rhel4
Red Hat Enterprise Linux 5	rhel5
Open Enterprise Server (OES)	oes
Red Hat Enterprise Linux 3 64-bit	rhel3-64
Red Hat Enterprise Linux four 64-bit	rhel4-64
Other Linux	linux
Other Linux 64-bit	otherlinux-64
Other	other
Other 64-bit	other-64

9. After the VM configuration file is created, it is now possible to create the VM disk file of xx gigabytes and then register the VM:

```
vmkfstools -c XXg /vmfs/volumes/dataStoreName/VMName/VMname.vmdk
vmware-cmd -s register /vmfs/volumes/dataStoreName/VMName/VMName.vmx
```

It is also possible to unregister a VM, which implies that the VIC client, MUI, or VC client will no longer see the VM. To do this, substitute unregister for register in the last command above. The register and unregister functions are very useful when you move VMs by hand.

10. Now the VM is ready to install using any of the installation tools available.

Installing VMs

There are various ways to install VMs within ESX Server. The methods include using the ESX Server's CD-ROM drive, an ISO image stored on the ESX Server, an ISO image stored on a CD-ROM attached to the machine running the VIC, or via some network installation method such as HP Rapid Deployment Pack or Altiris' tool suite. Although the use of remote installation tools is popular, they are beyond the scope of this book, and we instead concentrate on those tools readily available to the VMware ESX Server and its tools.

To install VMs, the remote console must be used, either through the VIC or the web-based tools. Just like a physical console, the remote console enables the use of removable media (CD-ROM and floppy), the capability to disconnect network cables at will, and the capability to power on and off the system. The remote console provides functionality that is not normally available in the physical world, and that is the ability to reach inside the VM and disconnect the CD-ROM and floppy devices while the VM is running.

Using Local to the ESX Server CD-ROMs

The first type of DVD/CD-ROM installation is the type that uses the local ESX Server DVD/CD-ROM device. This option often requires that the installation happen within the datacenter because the DVD/CD-ROM must be placed in the tray. Exceptions to this generalization are the use of remote console tools, such as the HP Remote Insight Lights Out Edition II or newer cards, which have a virtual CD-ROM capability. These devices create a secondary CD-ROM device that can be used in place of the default device, which is /dev/cdrom .

MUI

Installing a VM from the MUI involves the following steps.

1. Log in to the MUI.
2. Select the DescriptiveVMName from the MUI dashboard.
3. Select the *Hardware* tab to display, as we saw earlier (refer to Figure 10.25).
4. Find the CD-ROM device in the list of hardware and click the *Edit* link
5. Ensure the device is set to System DVD/CD-ROM Drive (see Figure 10.26).
6. Ensure that the location is /dev/cdrom or the physical device to use.

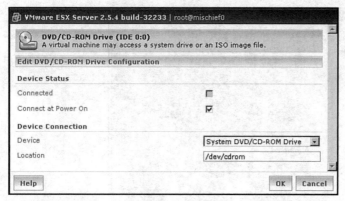

Figure 10.26 DVD/CD-ROM Drive

Command Line

The following are the changes necessary to the VMX configuration file to use the local CD-ROM device:

```
ide0:0.present = "true"
ide0:0.clientDevice = "false"
ide0:0.fileName = "/dev/cdrom"
ide0:0.deviceType = "atapi-cdrom"
ide0:0.startConnected = "true"
```

VC1.x/VIC

Unlike the preceding functions, using the remote console or VIC tools is slightly easier; for one, there is no need to memorize paths to locations of devices or ISO images, because it is possible to use a file dialog to find everything.

1. Log in to the VIC.
2. Select the VM in question to modify.
3. Click the *Edit Settings* link in the middle pane.
4. Select the DVD/CD-ROM virtual device to display the settings for the device (see Figure 10.27).
5. Check the *Connected* and *Connect at Power On* check boxes.
6. Ensure the *Host Device* radio button is selected and that the proper host device is in use.
7. Click OK to continue.

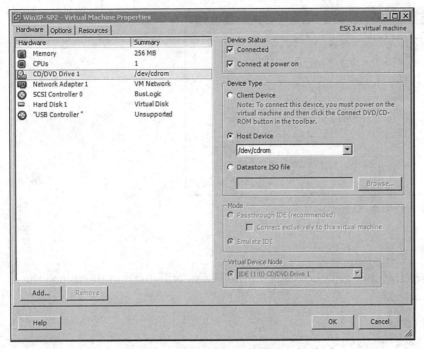

Figure 10.27 The Host Device radio button needs to be checked

Using a Local or Shared ESX Server ISO Image

This option is available to every version of ESX. However, on ESX version 3, all shares or files must reside in the /vmimages directory or any remote datastore to be seen by a VM. This is not the case for earlier versions of ESX.

MUI

To set things up to use a local or shared ESX Server ISO image, do the following:

1. Log in to the MUI.

2. Select the DescriptiveVMName from the MUI dashboard.

3. Select the *Hardware* tab (refer to Figure 10.25).

4. Find the CD-ROM device in the list of hardware and click the *Edit* link.

5. Select the device of "ISO image".

6. Ensure that the device name is the name of the ISO image to use.

Command Line

The following are the changes necessary to the VMX configuration file to use the local ISO image:

```
ide0:0.present = "true"
ide0:0.clientDevice = "false"
ide0:0.fileName = "/vmimages/nameOfISOImage"
ide0:0.deviceType = "cdrom-image"
ide0:0.startConnected = "true"
```

VC1.x/VIC

Again, using the remote console or VIC tools is slightly easier than using the functions just covered. And again, it is because there is no need to memorize paths to locations of devices or ISO images, because it is possible to use a file dialog to find everything.

1. Log in to the VIC.
2. Select the VM in question to modify.
3. Click the *Edit Settings* link in the middle pane.
4. Select the DVD/CD-ROM virtual device to display the settings for the device.
5. Check the *Connected* and *Connect at Power On* check boxes.
6. Ensure the *datastore ISO file* radio button (refer to Figure 10.27) is selected and that the proper file is specified.
7. Click *OK* to continue.

It is possible to specify the name of the ISO file instead of browsing to the file using the *Browse* button. However, it is a best practice to browse to the file in question because not every VC client version will properly pick up the file if it is typed into the dialog box. On ESX versions earlier than version 3, it is possible to browse every file on an ESX Server. The security implications of this capability forced a change in ESX version 3, where it is now only possible to browse to any datastore and anything in the /vmimages directory.

Using Client Device or ISO

This option is only available via ESX version 3 and not any of the earlier versions of ESX. This powerful option enables installation media that reside on the VIC client device to be used during installation of a VM. This option alleviates the need to have enough disk space on the ESX Server for local ISO images, shares mounted on the ESX Server, or even entering the server lab. Everything can be done from any machine that can run the VIC or access the ESX Server command line.

Command Line

Unlike the previous command-line versions, the changes to the file only make sense when the VIC client is actually in use. If the client is not in use, these settings are effectively ignored. Note that the new `clientDevice` option specifies using the filename of the client device. To install from the client, use the following commands:

```
ide0:0.present = "true"
ide0:0.clientDevice = "true"
ide0:0.fileName = "path\to\deviceoriso\on\client\system"
ide0:0.deviceType = "cdrom-raw"
ide0:0.startConnected = "false"
```

VIC

The VIC is the only client that can be used to invoke a `clientDevice` connection, and it can do so only if the remote console is actually in use. These security precautions prevent arbitrary access to a client device from a server and vice versa. The steps to install from the VIC are as follows:

1. Log in to the VIC.
2. Select the VM in question to modify.
3. Click the *Edit Settings* link in the middle pane.
4. Select the DVD/CD-ROM virtual device to display the settings for the device.
5. Ensure the *datastore ISO file* radio button is selected and that the proper file is specified (refer to Figure 10.27).
6. Click *OK* to continue.
7. Click *OK* to close the *Edit Settings* window.
8. Select *Open Console* to open the remote console to the VM.
9. Use Figure 10.28 as a reference and select the *Virtual CD-ROM* menu on the remote console icon bar. Select either the local CD-ROM or an ISO image.

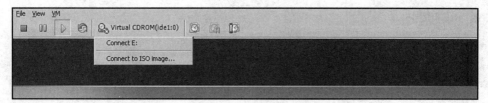

Figure 10.28   Virtual CD-ROM

This is an extremely powerful feature of the VIC because it is no longer necessary to enter the datacenter to access a CD-ROM or even make ISO files. ISO files residing on VMFS or in /vmimages are by far a faster device to use than virtual devices.

Importance of DVD/CD-ROM Devices

DVD/CD-ROM devices and ISO images are important because they allow a much easier installation of many servers without having to physically be in the datacenter. With earlier versions of ESX, what happened at the server console could not happen using the remote console, thereby limiting installation access to the datacenter. In addition, it is possible to restrict access to these features to a limited set of people using roles and permissions. It is also important to note that if a VM is connected to a CD-ROM it is not possible to use VMotion to move the VM from machine to machine. Therefore, it is wise to disconnect the device when finished using it. The exception to this case is the client device type for the VIC, because this connection depends on the VIC host, not an ESX Server host.

Other Installation Options

Each VM can be installed over the network because the base networking device for the virtual hardware has the capability to use PXE (pre-execution) boot commands. If there is a DHCP server and a PXEboot server, it is possible to use a network-based installation. A best practice for network-based installs is to install them within their own vNetwork with no outside access. In this fashion, it is possible to apply patches before the VM is placed out in the wild and offer some protection from zero-day hacks.

Some of the options for a PXEboot environment include Altiris, HP's Rapid Deployment Pack, and a Linux system using a PXEboot setup. These tools are beyond the scope of this book, but they do provide an alternative for installing VMs.

Special Situations

Special situations do arise when putting together the virtual hardware for a VM and when installing a VM with a guest OS. Here are some issues that have occurred when I have discussed this with customers.

Virtual Guest Tagging Driver

When we discussed virtual networking in Chapter 7, "Networking," we discussed the concept of virtual guest tagging (VGT) as a VLAN tagging option for a guest OS. At that time, we mentioned that there needs to be a special driver to allow this behavior. There is no VMware-provided driver to enable VGT; this is a driver that will come from the OS vendor or a third party. In general, this requires access to the networking hardware, and be sure that your vendor-supplied driver understands the Intel e1000, PCNET32, or vmxnet devices, because there is no option to access the ESX Server hardware except through the virtual devices.

Virtual Hardware for Nondisk SCSI Devices

Although connecting a tape device or some other form of nondisk SCSI device (SCSI tape, SCSI scanner, and so on) directly to an ESX Server is never a best practice, there is often a need to do just that. ESX supports a SCSI pass-thru mode that allows a VM to directly access any SCSI device, and this tie between physical and virtual hardware adds quite a bit of power to the VMware ESX Server VMs. To access a non-disk-based SCSI device from a VM is straightforward, but there is a giant caveat: Only one VM can access the device at any time, and this includes the ESX Server. The nature of SCSI locking is not a shared locking system between multiple systems. To handle SCSI locking between shared systems, there needs to be code in each system to handle this behavior. For nondisk SCSI devices, this code does not exist. For disk systems, this is where clustering software comes into play.

Before assigning a physical nondisk SCSI device to a VM, first be sure that the proper hardware is in use on the ESX Server. We discussed this in Chapter 1, "System Considerations." Then, to assign a physical nondisk SCSI device to a VM, there are just a few steps. The first step is to determine the SCSI IDs of the device in question, which are available to the ESX Server by using the following command:

```
# cat /proc/scsi/scsi
Attached devices:
Host: scsi1 Channel: 00 Id: 01 Lun: 00
  Vendor: HP       Model: C7200        Rev: 162D
```

```
  Type:    Medium Changer                ANSI SCSI revision: 03
Host: scsi1 Channel: 00 Id: 02 Lun: 00
  Vendor: QUANTUM  Model: SuperDLT1       Rev: 4949
  Type:    Sequential-Access             ANSI SCSI revision: 02
Host: scsi1 Channel: 00 Id: 03 Lun: 00
  Vendor: QUANTUM  Model: SuperDLT1       Rev: 4949
  Type:    Sequential-Access             ANSI SCSI revision: 02
```

The results will give the SCSI ID for each device in question. These IDs are extremely important when initializing SCSI pass-thru mode. The SCSI ID is the field after the Id: label in the output. Also, note that the output has the vendor and model name of the device. These are also necessary when using the graphical interfaces to choose the appropriate device. When adding the virtual hardware for these devices to a VM, select any unused SCSI adapter number and the same SCSI ID number when selecting the virtual SCSI device. To map the SCSI ID to a device name, use the following command:

```
# dmesg ¦ grep sg
Attached scsi generic sg1 at scsi1, channel 0, id 1, lun 0,  type 8
Attached scsi generic sg2 at scsi1, channel 0, id 2, lun 0,  type 1
Attached scsi generic sg3 at scsi1, channel 0, id 3, lun 0,  type 1
```

The generic device name is important when using the command line to configure the VM.

Command Line

When using the command line, the addition of a SCSI generic device is fairly straightforward. In this example, we are adding in three devices representing a tape changer and two tape drives. First we create a unique virtual SCSI adapter, present it to the VM, and then link a generic SCSI device via its device name (fileName) to a specific SCSI node number, which is composed of the SCSI adapter number and the SCSI ID from the preceding command. In this example, we have nodes 2:1 through 2:3 representing all three devices. Note that deviceType is set to scsi-passthru:

```
scsi2.present = "TRUE"
scsi2:1.present = "TRUE"
scsi2:1.deviceType = "scsi-passthru"
scsi2:1.fileName = "/dev/sg1"
```

```
scsi2:2.present = "TRUE"
scsi2:2.deviceType = "scsi-passthru"
scsi2:2.fileName = "/dev/sg2"
scsi2:3.present = "TRUE"
scsi2:3.deviceType = "scsi-passthru"
scsi2:3.fileName = "/dev/sg3"
```

VIC

The VIC does the same thing as the command line through its graphical interface, as follows:

1. Log in to the VIC.
2. Select the VM in question to modify.
3. Click the *Edit Settings* link in the middle pane.
4. Click the *Add* button at the bottom left of the dialog.
5. Click the *SCSI Device* link to add a generic SCSI device to a VM, and then click Next, as shown in Figure 10.29.

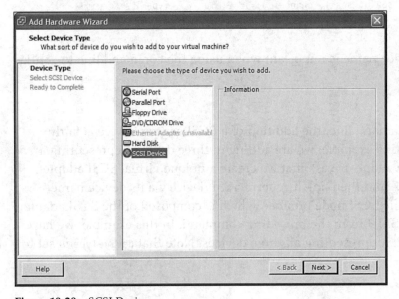

Figure 10.29   SCSI Device

6. Select the *SCSI Device*, in this case a Quantum tape device, and the SCSI device node to use for the device. Note that the Quantum tape device is already prepopulated if the VMware ESX Server sees the device. However, the device node to use can only be determined by the general rule and SCSI adapter number supported and the ID of the device as it is seen by the VMware ESX Server. In this example, the adapter number used is 2, and the SCSI ID is set to 5, for a SCSI node number of 2:5, as shown in Figure 10.30.

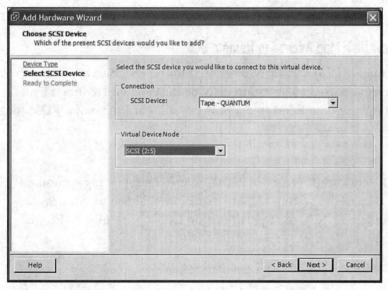

Figure 10.30 SCSI node number

7. Click Next to continue.

8. Click *Finish* to complete the virtual hardware addition to the VM.

MUI

The MUI provides functionality and capability similar to that of the VIC:

1. Log in to the MUI.

2. Select the DescriptiveVMName from the MUI dashboard.

3. Select the *Hardware* tab to display (refer to Figure 10.25).

4. Click the *Add Device* link at the bottom middle of the tab window.

5. Click the *Generic SCSI Device* link.

6. When the passthru dialog appears, select the *Device* to use. This is similar to the SCSI device in Step 6 previously. It is also possible to manually select a device, and that comes in handy sometimes, specifically for tape library robot devices, which do not always appear in the list.

7. Select the *Virtual SCSI Node* to use. Once more, this is similar to Step 6 previously. Be sure to pick a SCSI node that has the same identifier as the device on the system. The identifier is the number after the colon in the list.

8. Click on *OK* to add the SCSI pass-thru device.

Virtual Hardware for Raw Disk Map Access to Remote SCSI

Access to a raw disk map (RDM) of a LUN presented to the ESX Server shows up as a SCSI device that can be used as a system LUN or RDM when creating virtual drives for a VM. Adding a remote RDM to a VM is the standard form of a RDM for VMware ESX Server.

Command Line

To create a RDM in the current directory of a VMFS, use the following command where the X, Y, and Z dictate the system LUN to use. Note that the partition value is 0, implying the complete LUN. Use of partitions on LUNs presented to ESX is never recommended:

```
vmkfstools -r /vmfs/devices/disks/vmhbaX:Y:Z:0 foo-rdm.vmdk
```

After the RDM has been created, add it to the VM configuration file by using the following lines. Note that this maps the RDM to SCSI adapter 0, which is the default adapter. Many times, it is better to use a different adapter for performance reasons:

```
scsi0:0.present = "true"
scsi0:0.fileName = "foo-rdm.vmdk"
scsi0:0.redo = "true"
scsi0:0.deviceType = "scsi-hardDisk"
```

VIC

Because this is the standard mode for handling an RDM in ESX version 3, everything is handled quite easily from the VIC with some slight differences in that the

LUN in question must not have a VMFS installed upon it. Other than that, follow the general path of adding an additional hard disk to the VM:

1. Log in to the VIC.
2. Select the VM in question to modify.
3. Click the *Edit Settings* link in the middle pane.
4. Click the *Add* button at the bottom left of the dialog.
5. Select the *Hard Disk* device type, and then click Next.
6. Toggle *Raw Device Mappings,* and then click Next.
7. Select the system LUN to add to the device, and then click Next.
8. Click Finish to add.

MUI

Adding an RDM via the MUI is similar to adding a SCSI generic device. The main difference is how you get to the list of available LUNs to use:

1. Log in to the MUI.
2. Select the DescriptiveVMName from the MUI dashboard.
3. Select the *Hardware* tab (refer to Figure 10.25).
4. Click the *Add Device* link at the bottom middle of the tab window.
5. Click the *Hard Disk* link.
6. Click the *System LUN/Disk* link.
7. Once the dialog appears, select the *Device* to use.
8. Select the *Virtual SCSI Node* to use.
9. Click *OK* to add the RDM.

Virtual Hardware for RDM-Like Access to Local SCSI

A local hard drive can be mapped as an RDM in quite a different fashion. Instead of using the standard RDM, treat the local SCSI drive as a SCSI generic device and use the command-line method to perform the mapping. Instead of searching for SCSI generic (SG) devices from the `dmesg` command, look for the local SCSI disk device or LUN. In addition, the `fdisk -l` command can be used to see all disks and partitions available to the ESX host. However, it is strongly recommended that you use a LUN. In the following output, there are two identically sized LUNs: `c0d0` and `c0d1`. The one we want to use is `c0d1`, or controller 0, disk 1. Although this output is from an HP system, there will be similar output for other systems, but they will not show the same device naming convention. In general, all /dev/sd? devices in the output of the fdisk command represent SAN or iSCSI-based LUNs, and although useful for other aspects of VM configuration, they do not pertain to this discussion:

```
# fdisk -l
Disk /dev/cciss/c0d0: 91.0 GB, 91020165120 bytes
255 heads, 63 sectors/track, 11065 cylinders
Units = cylinders of 16065 * 512 = 8225280 bytes
```

Device Boot	Start	End	Blocks	Id	System
/dev/cciss/c0d0p1 *	1	13	104391	83	Linux
/dev/cciss/c0d0p2	14	1543	12289725	83	Linux
/dev/cciss/c0d0p3	1544	2053	4096575	83	Linux
/dev/cciss/c0d0p4	2054	11065	72388890	f	Win95 Ext'd (LBA)
/dev/cciss/c0d0p5	2054	2563	4096543+	83	Linux
/dev/cciss/c0d0p6	2564	3200	5116671	83	Linux
/dev/cciss/c0d0p7	3201	10474	58428341	fb	Unknown
/dev/cciss/c0d0p8	10475	10543	554211	82	Linux swap
/dev/cciss/c0d0p9	10544	11052	4088511	83	Linux
/dev/cciss/c0d0p10	11053	11065	104391	fc	Unknown

```
Disk /dev/cciss/c0d1: 91.0 GB, 91020165120 bytes
255 heads, 63 sectors/track, 11065 cylinders
Units = cylinders of 16065 * 512 = 8225280 bytes
```

Device Boot	Start	End	Blocks	Id	System

Do not choose the first LUN (c0d0), because that is the system LUN, and mapping that one would destroy your ESX Server. So, the empty c0d1 is our choice, and the following lines added to the VM configuration file will effectively create a mapping from a local LUN to a VM. Inside the VM, the device shows up as a SCSI generic device that happens to be a disk:

```
scsi2.present = "TRUE"
scsi2:1.present = "TRUE"
```

```
scsi2:1.deviceType = "scsi-passthru"
scsi2:1.fileName = "/dev/cciss/c0d1"
```

To discover which LUNs ESX already knows about as a VMFS or LUN presented to the ESX Server, use the following command for ESX version 3:

```
# esxcfg-vmhbadevs
vmhba0:0:0            /dev/cciss/c0d0
vmhba3:0:1           /dev/sda
vmhba3:0:2           /dev/sdb
vmhba3:0:3           /dev/sdc
```

Or the following for all versions of ESX:

```
# vmkpcidivy -q vmhba_devs
vmhba0:0:0 /dev/cciss/c0d0
vmhba3:0:1 /dev/sda
vmhba3:0:2 /dev/sdb
vmhba3:0:3 /dev/sdc
```

In essence, if the VM HBA to device mapping contains the device you want to use as a SCSI pass-thru device in ESX, use a standard RDM instead, because ESX already knows about the device and has its own mapping. If the device is *not* listed in the mapping, it is safe to map using the generic SCSI device method listed. Our chosen device of /dev/cciss/c0d1 is not listed in the commands, so therefore it is safe to map using this mechanism.

Although all the devices previously listed are for an HP server, it is important to realize that every supported server has its own method for creating a device, and it is important to have a clear understanding of how your hardware appears within a Linux environment.

VM Disk Modes and Snapshots

The old ESX disk modes exist for ESX version 3, and they can be enabled at any time. Unfortunately, enabling these modes will disable the capability to take disk snapshots and instead require the old REDO forms for backups. Before we discuss the disk modes, snapshots need to be expanded upon.

Snapshots are an advanced form of REDO mode that first appeared in Workstation version 5. A snapshot creates a delta disk, memory, and configuration files that are used to keep all the changes since the previous delta of the original

VM. In this way, it is possible to create multiple starting points for a single VM. It is also possible to create a tree of snapshots from a single VM. An example of its use is for testing new patches. It might be necessary to layer multiple patches and, by using snapshots, each patch applied could have what appears to be its own VM image on which to work. Once a patch is accepted, it is possible to merge the snapshot into the main disk image or even remove the snapshot with no change to the parent disk image, whether that is another snapshot or the default VMDK.

There is a little confusion about the control of the snapshot, because deleting a snapshot commits the snapshot to the previous snapshot delta or the parent VMDK, depending on its location in the tree. There is also the capability to revert to the previous snapshot and to go to a specific snapshot in the tree (see Figure 10.31). The Revert to Snapshot option goes to the snapshot immediately to the left of your current position within the snapshot tree, and the Go to Snapshot option moves anywhere within the tree. Judicious use of the Revert to Snapshot and the Go to Snapshot will allow the creation of multiple branches of snapshots. However, use of too many snapshots will slow down a VM considerably. To save a snapshot, you need to power off the VM first. With the snapshot saved, it is possible to create new snapshots or even revert to or go to a specific snapshot and create more branches for the tree of snapshots.

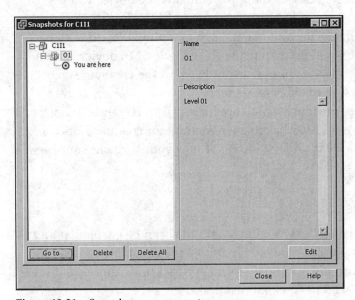

Figure 10.31 Snapshot management

Backup software for ESX version 3 makes quite a bit of use of snapshot functionality because the snapshot will quiesce a VMDK before the delta is created. Once the delta is created, the original VMDK is backed up using your standard backup software. See Chapter 12, "Disaster Recovery and Backup," for more information about backups. However, it is possible to place a VM into a mode where snapshots do not work.

Snapshots of raw disks, RDMs in physical mode, and independent disks are not supported, which includes all ESX versions earlier than version 3. All disks for ESX version 2.x are in independent mode, which provides some other interesting disk modes and requires the old-style REDO mode to create backups. Again, there is more on backups in Chapter 12. Independent mode VMDKs allow the VMDK to be persistent (changes are committed when the VM exits) or nonpersistent (changes are ignored when the VM exits). Earlier versions of ESX throw in two more disk modes: undoable (asks whether changes should be applied when VM exits) and append (changes are appended to the disk on exit). Because undoable and append modes are similar to the nonpersistent and persistent modes, they are no longer available.

The best practice for ESX version 3 is to use VMDKs in the standard mode and not independent mode so that all tools like snapshots and backups work normally. If a disk is in independent mode, backups can be made; you just need to use the old REDO mode defined in detail in Chapter 12.

Previously in this section, there was a mention that it is possible to remove a snapshot. Delete in the snapshot interface will commit all changes to the previous snapshot or original VMDK. To remove the snapshot, you must edit the configuration files by hand and make the necessary edits to remove all references from the deleted VMDK. Here are the steps to do so when you are in the directory that houses the VM in question. The common location is `/vmfs/volumes/VMHBANAME/VMName`. For the sake of brevity of the following, all reference to the `vmware.log` files have been removed because they are unimportant to the task.

1. First get a listing of the directory, because the snapshot VMDK delta file will show up here. In this case, there are at least three snapshots available. Knowing which one to remove depends on how they are labeled:

```
# ls
C1I1-000001-delta.vmdk      C1I1-2cab5a66.vswp      C1I1.vmdk
C1I1-000001.vmdk            C1I1-flat.vmdk          C1I1.vmsd
C1I1-000002-delta.vmdk      C1I1.nvram              C1I1.vmx
```

```
C1I1-000002.vmdk          C1I1-Snapshot1.vmsn   C1I1.vmxf
C1I1-000003-delta.vmdk    C1I1-Snapshot2.vmsn
C1I1-000003.vmdk          C1I1-Snapshot3.vmsn
```

2. The snapshot label is held with the .vmsd file and will equate snapshot name to delta file. For example, if we want to remove the snapshot labeled 02 but leave the rest, we can find the label within the .vmsd file and thus the files associated with the snapshot. Note that the current snapshot is set to snapshot?.uid="3":

```
# cat C1I1.vmsd
snapshot.lastUID = "3"
snapshot.numSnapshots = "3"
snapshot.current = "3"
...

snapshot1.uid = "2"
snapshot1.filename = "C1I1-Snapshot2.vmsn"
snapshot1.parent = "1"
snapshot1.displayName = "02"
snapshot1.description = "Level 02"
snapshot1.type = "1"
snapshot1.createTimeHigh = "274520"
snapshot1.createTimeLow = "-1301417629"
snapshot1.numDisks = "1"
snapshot1.disk0.fileName = "C1I1-000001.vmdk"
snapshot1.disk0.node = "scsi0:0"


...
```

Removing snapshots that are not at the end of the snapshot stream is basically impossible because the running of a VM depends on its disk, and the delta.vmdk file of the right snapshot depends on the previous snapshot's delta file and so forth. Everything is interconnected, and removing a snapshot from the middle of the snapshot levels will make all the levels afterward have a corrupted disk. So, make sure that the snapshot is a leaf node of the snapshot tree. To determine whether this is in the middle of a snapshot branch, look at the snapshot?.parent values, and determine whether any snapshot has as its `snapshot?.parent` value the UID of the snapshot you plan to remove.

If the snapshot is a leaf node, by all means proceed.

3. Note that the `snapshot?.disk0.fileName` in the snapshot stanza of the `.vmsd` represents the delta file upon which this snapshot depends and not the currently used snapshot. The currently used snapshot disk file is the one listed in the `.vmx` file. Because the snapshot disk0 node is `scsi0:0`, look up the `scsi0:0.fileName` line in the `.vmx` file to determine the currently used VMDK file.

4. Shut down the VM if it is running. It is impossible to remove a snapshot while a VM is running. You can use the command `vmware-cmd` `fullPathToVMXFile stop` to shut down a VM. Often, I use the following from the command line. Be sure to use a unique machine name, however:

```
vmware-cmd `vmware-cmd -l¦grep machineName` stop
```

5. Revert the snapshot to the snapshot to the left. Run this command twice:

```
vmware-cmd fullPathToVMXFile revertsnapshot
```

6. Remove the files associated with the original snapshot, the `delta-vmdk`, and the `.vmsn` file.

7. Power on the VM.

Command line

It is also possible to use the command line to manipulate snapshots.

To create a snapshot, use the following:

```
vmware-cmd fullPathToVMXFile createsnapshot name description quiesce memory
```

To remove *all* snapshots, use the following. Note that the last line empties the vmsd file for the VM in question. If the vmsd file is not emptied, snapshot numbers will continue where the file last left off:

```
vmware-cmd fullPathToVMXFile removesnapshots
echo "" > VM.vmsd
```

To move around the snapshot tree, use the following command:

```
vmware-cmd fullPathToVMXFile revertsnapshot
```

OS Installation Peculiarities

When installing a particular OS into an ESX VM, certain hardware and software are required to make it work. Table 10.4 presents a chart with the most common requirements when dealing with each OS type.

Table 10.4

OS Installation Peculiarities		
OS	**ESX v2.x Notes**	**ESX v3.0 Notes**
Windows 2003	Select the LSILogic vSCSI adapter.	None
Windows 2000	None	None
NetWare	Add extra CD-ROMs for all installation CDs to reduce CD-ROM or ISO file switching	Add extra CD-ROMS for all installation CDs to reduce CD-ROM or ISO file switching
OES		
Windows XP	Use the `vmscsi.flp` image provided by VMware and be sure to press F6 at the appropriate time during the install	Select the BUSLogic vSCSI adapter
Vista	Unsupported	None
RHEL 3	None	None
RHEL 4	Select the LSIlogic vSCSI adapter	None
RHEL 5	Select the Buslogic vSCSI adapter	Select the Buslogic vSCSI adapter
SLES 8	None	Select the guest OS type of SUSE Linux Enterprise Server
SLES 9	Select the LSILogic vSCSI adapter	Select the guest OS type of SUSE Linux Enterprise Server
SLES 10	Select the LSILogic vSCSI adapter	Select the guest OS type of SUSE Linux Enterprise Server
Debian Woody	Select the BUSLogic vSCSI adapter and boot using boot compact	Select the BUSLogic vSCSI adapter and boot using boot compact
Debian Sarge	Select the BUSLogic vSCSI adapter and boot using boot compact	Select the BUSLogic vSCSI adapter and boot using boot compact
Debian Edgy	Select the BUSLogic vSCSI adapter and boot using boot compact	Select the BUSLogic vSCSI adapter and boot using boot compact
Solaris 10		None
Netbsd		
Freebsd		
Fedora Core 1	Select the LSILogic vSCSI adapter	Select the LSILogic vSCSI adapter and set the guest OS type to Red Hat Enterprise Linux 3

OS	ESX v2.x Notes	ESX v3.0 Notes
Fedora Core 2–6	Select the LSILogic vSCSI adapter	Select the LSILogic vSCSI adapter and set the guest OS type to Red Hat Enterprise Linux 4
Fedora 7	NA	Select the BusLogic vSCSI adapter and set the guest OS type to Red Hat Enterprise Linux 5

Cloning, Templates, and Deploying VMs

Quite a lot of literature already exists on cloning and deploying VMs, as well as on the fresh installation of a VM. This book will not regurgitate existing sources of information. However, we will discuss the use of the sysprep and the open source Linux tools to customize deployments when using templates.

Templates are fully installed VMs that are used as the basis for the creation of other VMs. This method is faster than reinstalling a VM because a template is generally fully patched and has the applicable application preinstalled and either just waiting for configuration or already configured. Templates can be deployed as if they were being cloned to create a VM within any host, cluster, or resource pool in the VC datacenter. Clusters and resource pools are covered in the Chapter 11 and were introduced in ESX version 3.

The cloning of a VM or deployment of a template will invoke a customization phase during which a predefined customization can be chosen or a new one defined. The customization scripts for Windows invoke sysprep, whereas for Linux they invoke an open source tool that can be used to configure the Linux network and not much else. The storage of predefined customization scripts within VC is new to VC 2.0 and aids in making customizations saved as XML files (for VC 1.0) easy to find.

VM Solutions

There are a number of solutions that we discuss within this book, and most of them require some form of specific VM hardware. Although we will not discuss the installation of the OS in this section, we do discuss the necessary VM and ESX virtual hardware and where some of it should exist. In addition, we also discuss the downloadable virtual appliances and how they fit into the realm of ESX.

Private Lab

A private lab environment does not require much in the way of new virtual hardware. To create a virtual private lab, first create within ESX a vSwitch that is not connected to an external pNIC. After that is done and the vSwitch is properly labeled, to create the private lab environment connect each appropriate VM to the vSwitch using its label. This is as easy as editing the settings for the VM and setting the vNIC network label appropriately.

- **Additional virtual hardware required**

  An additional vSwitch

Firewalled Private Lab

A firewall private lab is slightly different in that there now needs to be a vFW between the virtual lab vSwitch and another vSwitch where the VMs on the second vSwitch need access to the first vSwitch. The second vSwitch could be another virtual private lab or even represent an external connection. This vFW is a specialized VM with two vNICs associated with it. The first vNIC points to the virtual private lab vSwitch, and the second points to the external vSwitch. The vFW can be an existing virtual appliance firewall, Linux, or Windows using ICS. However, the best practice is to use specialized firewall software. In many cases, SmoothWall (www.smoothwall.org) is a very good choice. As of this writing, the SmoothWall 2.0 virtual appliance will not work within ESX because there is no SCSI subsystem in the release. However, the solution is to use SmoothWall 3.0 (which requires the vSCSI Controller of BusLogic to be used), which is not yet a virtual appliance. I have also used Fedora Core 6, SLES9, and various other Linux flavors as firewalls acting as both a vFW and DHCP server.

- **New virtual hardware required**

  An additional vSwitch for the green side of the vFW

  An additional vNIC for the vFW

Firewalled Lab Bench

A firewalled lab bench is one of our examples from Chapter 7, where the firewall was a VM or a vFW. Just as in the previous notes, the vFW requires two vNICs. The first is connected to a vSwitch *not* connected to the lab bench and a vSwitch that represents the lab bench. This often requires more pNICs on a system to create it, and the lab bench will need its own pSwitch or VLAN with a single external connection to the ESX Server hosting the vFW. There might be more cabling needed depending on how many ESX Servers may need to access the lab bench.

- **New virtual hardware required**

  An additional vSwitch for the pNIC attached to the lab bench

  An additional vNIC for the vFW

Cluster in a Box

Cluster in a box refers to a shared disk cluster such as Microsoft Cluster Services. Although we will not discuss how to install Microsoft Cluster, we do delve into the virtual hardware necessary. First, create a VM into which you plan to install Microsoft Windows, preferably 2003 Enterprise edition, because it has an easier Cluster Services setup than Microsoft Windows 2000 Advanced Server. However, either will work. Ensure that the VM's main VMDK is located on some form of local storage and *not* a SAN or iSCSI LUN. After the VM has been created, add a heartbeat vNIC connected to any existing vSwitch or even a private one just for the heartbeat.

Next we need to place the quorum drive and any other shared disk in an appropriate spot. The placement of these shared disks differs greatly in ESX version 3 as compared to its predecessors. With ESX version 2, the shared VMDKs can be placed on a VMFS configured in shared mode. Shared VMFS mode allowed the ESX Server to control locking and not the VMs. Because shared mode no longer exists within ESX version 3, the only available option for the placement of these shared VMDKs is to use some form of RDM mode discussed earlier to contain the data to be shared between the cluster nodes. There should be one RDM or SCSI generic device per shared drive in the cluster.

After the first node has been created, it is now possible to create the other nodes. Be sure to place the primary VMDK onto local storage and not a SAN or iSCSI LUN, and then hook up the secondary vNIC to the same vSwitch as the first node, and attach to the existing RDMs or SCSI generic devices.

ESX version 3 supports clusters with up to eight nodes, whereas ESX version 3's predecessors supported only up to two node clusters.

- **New virtual hardware required**

  An additional vNIC for the heartbeat network

  A local VMFS to store the node boot drives

  An additional RDM or local SCSI generic device for each shared drive, including the small quorum drive

Cluster between ESX Servers

The only difference between this option and the cluster in a box is that the RDMs must live on SAN or iSCSI LUNs and are traditional RDMs. The boot drive for all cluster nodes must be on a local VMFS and not a SAN or iSCSI LUN.

- **New virtual hardware required**

  An additional vNIC for the heartbeat network

  A local VMFS to store the node boot drives

  An additional RDM for each shared drive, including the small quorum drive

Cluster between Virtual and Physical Servers

This is a neat possibility, and because we are using RDMs or LUNs for the preceding options, it is extremely simple to have a physical machine access the same LUNs for its shared drives. The vNIC for the VM will need to be able to reach the physical machine.

- **New virtual hardware required**

  An additional vNIC for the heartbeat network. (Be sure this vNIC is attached to a pNIC that can reach the physical server.)

  A local VMFS to store the node boot drives

  An additional RDM for each shared drive, including the small quorum drive

VC as a VM

VC can be within a VM. If you find yourself in this situation, management of the VC Server becomes difficult. If the ESX Server hosting the VC Server dies, there is no capability for managing VMware HA (but existing VMware HA configurations will still work), nor is there any capability for VMotion or any other VC feature to be of use. To solve this problem, use some other form of monitor tool to move the VM from server to server and reboot the VM on the new host. Downtime is limited to the time it takes to register the VM on a new host and boot up. A number of tools can do this for you. VC and the license manager for ESX 3 are critical to the success of an ESX cluster and therefore should either be run on their own host or have the ESX Server failure case considered.

- **New virtual hardware required**

  None

Virtual Appliances

Not all virtual appliances are created equal. Most virtual appliances were created in VMware Workstation, so importing them into ESX requires the use of the VMware Converter software. However, not all systems behave properly. The SmoothWall example mentioned previously is a prime example. Another is Windows XP Professional SP0 VMs with the workstation VMware Tools installed. In this case, it is important to either update the VM using VMware Workstation or import the VM without updating VMware Tools until you can upgrade the VM to at least SP1. The problem occurs because of a known issue with LSASS, which crashes the machine if VMware Tools are updated. This has been fixed with Windows XP Professional SP1.

Use of VMware Converter is simple. This powerful tool migrates appliances designed for VMware Workstation VMs to ESX; and if VC 2.0 is in use, Converter integrates to become an invaluable VM import tool. Here are the steps for its use:

1. Start VMware Converter.

2. Click the *Import Machine* button and then the *Next* Button twice.

3. Toggle the *Standalone virtual machine* option (see Figure 10.32). At this stage, it is possible to use the tool to import physical computers and convert from an ESX Server to other VMware virtualization engines and back to physical computers. Because P2V and V2P are a science all their own, they are not covered in this book in much detail.

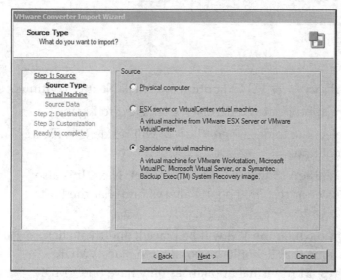

Figure 10.32　VMware Converter

4. Click the *Next* button and browse to the path of the appliance or VM to import and click the *Next* button. The importer will connect to the VM and gather information about its configuration. Sometimes it is necessary to boot the VM using VMware Workstation at least once to get past this stage.

5. Now it is possible to change the size of the disks to import to be smaller or larger as necessary (see Figure 10.33). I always like to make them smaller. Click Next twice to continue.

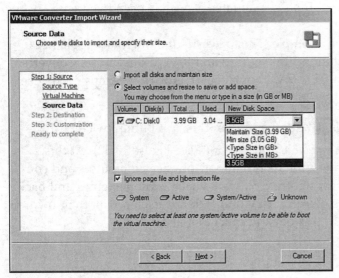

Figure 10.33   VMware Converter disk resize

6. Toggle the *VMware ESX Server or VC VM* option and click Next to continue.

7. Log in to VC using the appropriate credentials; click Next to log in.

8. Name the VM, and select the folder where the VM will reside (see Figure 10.34). Click Next to continue.

9. Select the host in which the VM will live, and then click Next. It is also possible to select a cluster or resource pool. I always find that the host works best.

10. Select the datastore onto which the VM will be placed, and then click Next. It is also at this time that it would be possible to place VMDKs onto multiple datastores. Most virtual appliances only have one VMDK, however. The destination will be checked at this time.

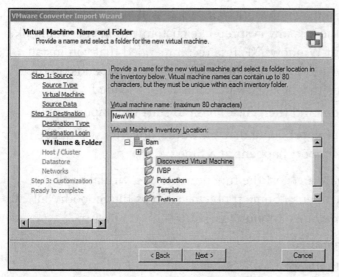

Figure 10.34   VMware Converter VM Name

11. Decide on the VM network to use for each vNIC. Now is the time to create additional vNICs if necessary (see Figure 10.35). For a firewall, at least two are necessary. Once done, click *Next* to continue.

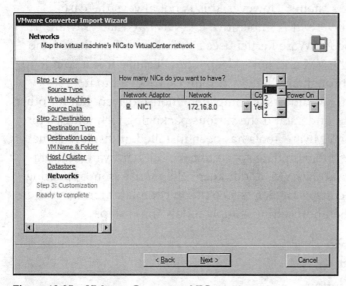

Figure 10.35   VMware Converter vNIC creation

12. Now is the time to decide whether VMware Tools will be installed by default and whether there is any sysprep-like customization you would like to do. For anything but Windows XP, it is recommended that you install VMware Tools. For Windows XP, as stated previously, it depends on the service pack version as to when VMware Tools will be loaded.

13. Review the information, and then click *Finish* to start the import.

14. Set up another VM to import. Note that VMware Converter will queue the VMs so that only one import happens at a time.

It is important to investigate and test the functionality of a virtual appliance and make the necessary adjustments. Some problems such as the SmoothWall 2.0 issue imply that the virtual appliance cannot be used.

- **New virtual hardware required**

   Depends on type of virtual appliance

VMware Tools

After a VM is installed, it is imperative that some form of VMware Tools be installed. VMware Tools provides drivers for the VM that understand virtualization and will make things perform better. Some VMs can live without VMware Tools installed, such as most Linux systems. However, this is not always the case.

The worst offender is NetWare. It is imperative for NetWare that VMware Tools be installed because the NetWare kernel uses a spin loop when there is no processing going on within the VM and not a sleep loop. Because it is a spin loop, it will quietly appear to eat through all the ESX resources assigned to it.

Installing VMware Tools for Windows is completely mouse driven, but for other operating systems you need to understand the various packaging technologies for installation or products. After VMware Tools has been installed, it displays some instructions for changing the screen update speed to have full hardware acceleration. The change is for any Windows VM, and it keeps the mouse from appearing slow when using the remote console, which is a common complaint for many users. To change the hardware acceleration setting, simply follow these steps:

1. Right-click the desktop.

2. Select the Settings tab.

3. Click the Advanced button.

4. Select the Troubleshoot tab.

5. Change the hardware acceleration to Full.

6. Click OK to save the settings.

However, mouse performance for VMs when you access a VMware remote console from within another VM does suffer somewhat. This behavior occurs whether it is via VMware Workstation, Server, or ESX.

For some versions of Linux kernels (versions 2.6.19 and later), VMware does not provide working VMware Tools drivers. However, www.astroarch.com/virtual/patches.html provides patches to the standard ESX VMware Tools for Linux that will fix these deficiencies.

VMX Changes

Every now and then, it will be necessary to modify the VMX file to add new options to solve various issues with the VM. For the predecessors to ESX version 3, this required editing the VMX file directly and adding the options somewhere in the configuration file. For ESX version 3, there is no need to make these changes from the service console, because the VIC has this capability. However, to make the changes from the service console, all you need do is edit the VMX configuration file for the VM in question. Changes to the configuration file should only happen when a VM is powered off. Besides adding hardware, it is possible to set up some specific options for each VM.

The General options (see Figure 10.36) are the virtual machine name and virtual machine type, which we have set above when the VM was created from the command line.

The VMware Tools options (see Figure 10.37) define what to do when the system is powered off, paused, powered on, or reset. In addition, they also include when to run any VMware Tools scripts within the VM. VMware Tools provides a powerful capability to control the exact behavior of a VM with any power-control action.

The Power Management options (see Figure 10.38) for a VM dictate what the VM should do if it is placed in standby mode. There are not many options for this, but the capability to Wake on LAN is similar to the function of many pNICs, and this behavior is now handled by a vNIC.

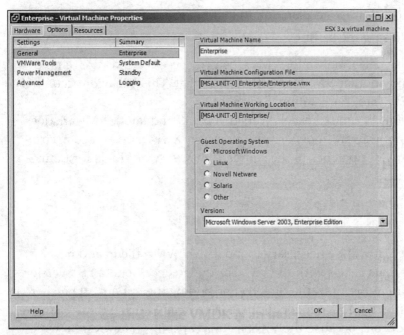

Figure 10.36 VM General options

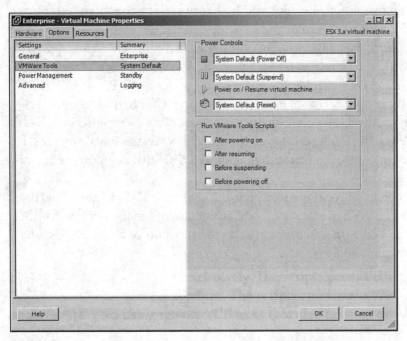

Figure 10.37 VM VMware Tools options

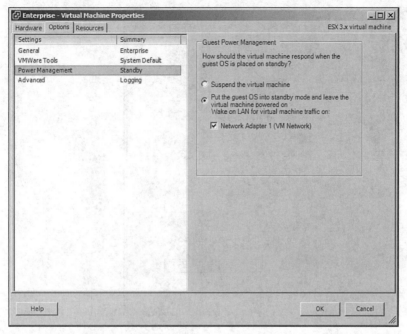

Figure 10.38   VM VMware Power Management options

The most powerful options are the Advanced options (see Figure 10.39), which control the inclusion of debug information in a log, disable any acceleration for the VM, and the capability to enable or disable any logging. In some cases, disabling logging can increase performance. The middle section of the advanced options will increase CPU compatibility for VMotion. By hiding the NxFlag, it is possible to let VMs move between some of the disparate types of hardware in your datacenter. The Advanced button for the CPU identification sets looks at the CPU register set in detail to create specific mappings of CPU capabilities to further reduce or enhance CPU compatibility. Changes to these options are dangerous at best and should be done only when you are told to by your VMware support specialist.

The last section of the Advanced options is the capability to set configuration parameters (see Figure 10.40). These parameters will control the VM and provide the capability to further customize the VM. To manipulate this within the VIC, use the Add Row button, and then enter a name and a value. The OK button will save the results to the VMX configuration file. For all earlier versions of ESX, the file must be edited by hand.

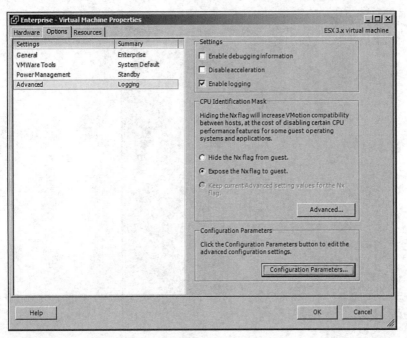

Figure 10.39   VM VMware Advanced options

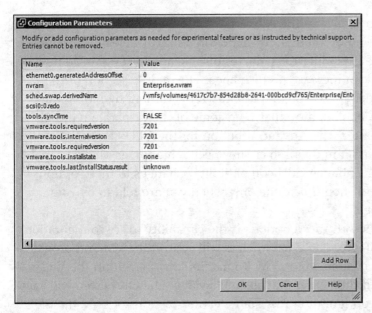

Figure 10.40   VM VMware Configuration Parameters

Here are some popular settings to add. However, there are literally hundreds of other settings undefined by this book. The short list in Table 10.5 is provided to solve specific problems that have been encountered. Any other settings could impact behavior or performance adversely. The full list of VM configuration parameters are at http://sanbarrow.com/vmx.html.

Table 10.5

Configuration Parameters		
Parameter	**Value**	**Notes**
keyboard.typematicMinDelay	200000	For Linux machines, it slows down the auto-repeat within X. Often, I disable auto-repeat entirely using the command `xset r off` in a configuration file. Be sure to place this line at the bottom of the file.
mks.ipc.maxBufferedPackets	0	Prevents the remote console from suddenly going black.
mks.ipc.maxBufferedBytes	0	Prevents the remote console from suddenly going black.
svga.maxWidth	Some integer	Maximum width of the monitor: 640,800,1024,1280,1920, and so on.
svga.maxHeight	Some integer	Maximum height of the monitor: 480,600,768,1024,1200, and so on.
isolation.tools.copy.disable	True	Copy part of copy and paste; there is a security issue (information leakage) with copy and paste to and from a guest using the remote console.
isolation.tools.paste.disable	True	
svga.vramSize	Some integer	`svga.maxWidth * svga.maxHeight * 4`
gui.maxconnection	Some integer	Sets the maximum number of console connections allowed.

Conclusion

This chapter covered many aspects of a VM and how the virtual hardware all fits together. We have not discussed any specific OS. That I leave to you, the reader, but we do discuss those things you need to understand to really work with virtual hardware. In the next chapter, we delve into the concept of dynamic resources and the load balancing of VMs across VMware ESX Servers. Until you understand the way virtual hardware works, it is impossible to discuss how resources can be balanced.

Chapter 11

Dynamic Resource Load Balancing

Dynamic resource load balancing (DRLB) is the automatic balancing of resource usage across multiple ESX Servers. DRLB ranges from simply scripting of VMotion to moving a VM from host to host through the automatic assignment of more resources on-the-fly, while the VM is running. In addition, DRLB is also referred to as business continuity. It is the front line of any disaster prevention and recovery process and the basis for forming an ESX Server cluster. Although DRLB covers a wide range of functionality, it can be broken down into various business continuity processes, some of which require creative scripting to accomplish and others of which exist in various VMware and third-party tools.

Defining DRLB

So let's break down DRLB into various processes with the first one being the simple clustering of ESX hosts. Without the concept of a cluster of ESX Servers, there is no real possibility of pursuing DRLB. In VC parlance, a cluster of ESX Servers is referred to as a farm (ESX Version 2.x) or datacenter (ESX Version 3.x). Even though DRLB can be pursued without VC, a major component is the capability to use VMotion, therefore requiring a VC server to be available, at the very least. Without VMotion, there are other possible tools to use, because DRLB is not just about VMotion. Although VMware VC 2.0 adds the concept of a cluster, it is a specialized subset of this aspect of DRLB.

The second component of DRLB is the capability to monitor ESX Servers and VMs and, based on resource utilization, make changes to where VMs live or to the currently assigned resources (increasing/decreasing memory, adding vCPU, etc). The changes to the currently assigned resources are to either give more resources or take some away as necessary. Dynamic resource allocation is possible with ESX, but is limited to just the migration of VMs to lesser-used hosts but does not allow resource changes on the fly. This would be the ultimate implementation of DRLB. The third component of DRLB is the capability to specify secondary locations for a VM to start up if the VM fails or the ESX Server host fails for some reasons. This ends up being a form of disaster recovery (DR), but only one step on the road to DR. The next chapter covers DR and backup in detail. In essence, this is a major aspect of clustering and is easily applied to ESX either using provided tools or a poor man's approach.

These components are part of the various add-on packages for the VMware ESX Server provided by VMware and other third parties. For the automation aspects of DRLB, there is VMware Dynamic Resource Scheduling (DRS) and the VMware Clustering technology, Virtual Machine Monitors from HP, and IBM as well as other third party add-ons and scripting tools. VMware Clustering also adds VMware High Availability (HA) into the mix. The failover aspects of DRLB are covered by VMware HA allows for VMs to be brought up on new hosts when other hosts fail. And finally, there are resource pools that are part of the VMware ESX Server that limit VM utilization of host resources based on pools of memory and CPU resources. Unfortunately, there are no current ways to change the resources available to a VM on the fly, i.e. no method to add more memory, vCPU, or any other resource to a running VM. VMware has implemented a way to add more disk to a running VM however and with the scripting API it is possible to do this when a VM is running low on disk space. This last aspect of DRLB is the holy grail of virtualization automation. We will discuss further just the DRS and HA features of ESX, not the full blown DRLB.

The Basics

The basic premise behind DRLB is monitoring and the interpretation of what is being monitored. Without some form of understanding about what can be monitored and how to interpret what is monitored, DRLB cannot be pursued with any chance of success. Although the concept of monitoring is not new and is discussed in other chapters of this book, it is important enough to mention once more in detail. The first thing to cover with monitoring is the Virtual Infrastructure Client (VIC).

The VIC provides wonderful graphs by VM and ESX Server host of CPU, memory, disk, and network utilization and will store this data for trend analysis of resources. Trend analysis will enable the careful consideration of existing data to determine whether it is necessary to permanently rebalance the farm nodes or change some of the resources allocated to VMs on a permanent basis. DRLB is not a permanent solution, but is just the automation of resource load balancing to prevent catastrophic failures or to quickly bring up backup VMs if an unexpected failure occurs. Performing an analysis over time and fairly often is the best tool for keeping a well-balanced ESX farm or datacenter.

DRLB uses this data to account for sudden and unexpected behaviors to maintain the peak performance of the datacenter when issues arise. Even so, intelligent decisions must be made in some automated fashion. For example, let's assume that the CPU utilization of a VM goes off the scale and at the same time the ESX host also goes above the defined threshold. It could be that the DRLB tool automatically moves the problem VM to a named host but then that host hits a high in utilization and the VM is once more moved. This cycle could go on forever, with the VM never really finding a home and caught in an endless loop of movements. There needs to be intelligence in the movement of a VM from host to host such that the target host chosen is not or will not also be overloaded. In other words, its thresholds for automatic movement are not met by moving the VM in question. In essence, DRLB must be adaptive and able to make the necessary decisions as a human would. If this cannot be done, DRLB is extremely limited in functionality. It boils down to the tools used for monitoring and how hard it is to get that data into an adaptive tool to prevent such infinite loops of migrations.

The first step in understanding how to apply DRLB is to set some utilization goals for each member of the ESX datacenter. Most, if not all, of my customers look at the utilization goals as no more than 80% utilized at any given time. Most opt for a lot less than this number, but 80% is a nice number because it provides head room for subsequent changes in resource allocation and provides a base number to realize when more ESX Servers are necessary for the entire datacenter. Specifically, 80% CPU utilization is often the target when determining that a new ESX Server is necessary for an ESX datacenter. The other three items on the hit parade—memory, network, and disk utilization—are not as important as utilization goals, but they need to be understood, too.

Memory utilization is how much memory is in use during prime time and is not related to how much is actually assigned to a VM. Memory is generally 100% assigned either to VMs or to a pool of memory waiting for VMs in case of VMotion from another host. The 80% goal really does not apply to memory. However, memory is a finite resource, and in some cases, 80% memory utilization could be realized with only four VMs that use 1GB of memory but with 4GB assigned to each. This implies that on an ESX Server with 16GB of memory, the memory above 5GB is unused and therefore a wasted resource. But there are only four VMs—how do we get to 5GB of used memory? The service console and VMkernel can take the other 1GB of memory. Trend analysis would assist in determining how much memory is used over time for each VM, enabling better utilization of memory.

Network utilization is generally in packets or megabits transferred per second, and although it used to be very hard to have sustained traffic that fills a gigabit pipe with virtualization, this is no longer the case. At most, only seven-tenths of a network is actually used, which translates into 7Mbps for a 10Mbps link, 70Mbps for a 100Mbps link, and 700Mbps for a gigabit link. Full duplex implies that the seven-tenths number is possible when going in both directions at the same time, which implies that transmits and receives both have a seven-tenths rate and if the ESX Server ever hits this limit with all its VMs combined and sustains this rate it's possible that network performance will be a major issue. Because seven-tenths is the most we can expect, we should look at an 80% limit on networking as well, which places the bandwidth limit at slightly higher than one-half the stated rate.

Disk utilization is a number like networking that depends on the data store in use. Fibre uses 2Gbps, whereas NAS is generally 1Gbps, and direct attached SCSI is 320MBps (roughly 2.6Gbps). Each of these have separate sustained rate limits, just like networking speeds, and NAS responds to the same limits as network utilization discussed previously. Although in general SAN currently can handle more data transfer than NAS, there is still a finite limit. Direct attached SCSI, SAS, and SATA still have the best performance for quantity of writes. Once more, the 80% limit can be applied, but this is the sum of all disk accesses, reads, and writes per second over all VMs. That is 1.6Gpbs for Fibre, one-half the network rates for NAS, and 250MBps for direct attached SCSI. In addition, the number of SCSI locks involved increases for the number of hosts attached to a particular device, and that will add delays. For information on SCSI locking, see Chapter 5, "Storage with ESX."

However, does that mean an ESX Server can push these limits without suffering a performance issue? The answer is no. In rare cases, these upper limits can be hit with no impact on performance of ESX, but the utilization goals need to be adjusted for the type of work the VM is performing. Perhaps an ESX Server can burst to these limits, but sustained utilization of these limits would be hard to maintain. The key to determining utilization goals is to understand that the addition of a single VM to the environment will change the overall environment in sometimes radical ways. It is not necessarily possible to assume that adding a 5% utilized VM to the existing VM mix will increase everything by 5%. It could increase by more as the VMkernel now has more work to do, because it does a little bit of the COS, and each VM now has less resources, so the impact could be greater overall.

Creating a baseline will help you understand the utilization of the whole server. Assume our baseline has 20 VMs and shows only 40% utilized for CPU, 1Mbps for network utilization, a few kilobits per second utilization for disk, with an overall memory consumption of 20GB. The assumption will help you realize what is overloaded; we could have a single VM and push this server out of balance with a CPU utilization of 80% while maintaining all else at low-utilization numbers; the packets per second transfer rate is actually fairly high, yet the transfer rate is low. This implies that the VMkernel has to work harder to handle the small size of the packets, thereby increasing the overall utilization.

Hundreds if not thousands of examples display drastic changes in utilization once the behavior of any VM changes. In all these cases, balancing of the VMs should occur. Automating DRLB is a step toward balancing VMs across ESX Servers.

The Advanced Features

An advanced feature of VMware ESX version 3 is the concept of resource pools. A resource pool is a way of limiting the host CPU and memory utilization of a group of VMs. For an ESX Server or cluster of ESX Servers, there is a single limit for the maximum amount of resources available to the host or cluster. In the case of clusters, the maximum amount of resources available is based on adding up the maximum amount of resources available for all the hosts. Granted, the only resources a resource pool will manage are CPU and memory. Resource pools can be layered and thereby further subdivide the maximum amount of resources available to a group or even a single VM. Resource pools, if used properly, will keep a single group of VMs from using all available resources.

The best way to explain this is to look at how resource pools are configured. They can be configured to give a strict limit on the amount of resources or to allow the pool to borrow from a parent pool. A resource pool is very similar to a pool of water. There is a finite amount of water, and if all the water is gone, there is no more. If we further subdivide the pool of water into buckets of water and hand them out, when the bucket of water is gone, there is no more water for the holder of the bucket. However, if the holder of the bucket is allowed to ask for more water, the parent or original pool of water can give more water to the holder of the bucket. If there is no more water in the pool, there is no more water to loan out.

Resource pools are created with the VIC20 client connected to either an ESX Server or when connected to VC. Use of clusters requires VC, and I cover clusters in detail later in this chapter. The important part of creating a resource pool is to determine how many resources are allowed for the group of VMs running within a pool and the behaviors that take place when resources exceed the amount within the pool. To create a resource pool, follow these steps:

1. Log in to VC using the VIC20.

2. Select the host or cluster into which a resource pool will be created. A host within a cluster cannot have a separate resource pool.

3. Select the Create Resource Pool icon.

4. Give the resource pool a name.

5. Set the shares for CPU and memory resources.

6. Set the reserved amount of CPU and memory specific for this pool; this is the memory that is always available to the pool.

7. Check if this is an expandable reservation, one that can borrow from the pool above.

8. Check if this is an unlimited resource limit. This is not recommended except for the topmost resources (see Figure 11.1).

9. Select OK to set the resource pool.

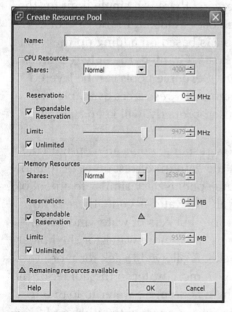

Figure 11.1   Resource Pool

The other advanced concept is the ESX cluster. An ESX cluster is a combination of hosts that will all share a group of resource pools and within which a set of VMs will work. An ESX cluster increases the amount of resources that are available within a resource pool. A cluster is required for VMware DRS. Creation of a cluster is as easy as creating a resource pool. A cluster needs at least two ESX Servers, and is created by following these steps:

1. Log in to VC using the VIC20.
2. Select the datacenter into which to create the cluster.
3. Select the Create Cluster icon.
4. Give the cluster a name and select the options for the cluster. If you have licenses for VMware HA and for VMware DRS, select the appropriate check boxes (see Figure 11.2).

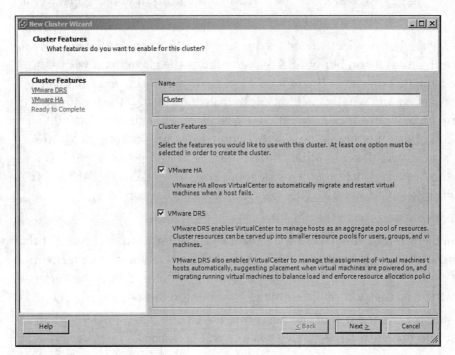

Figure 11.2   Cluster creation

5. If you selected VMware DRS, you will be asked to configure it. The options for VMware DRS include the following:

- **Manual:** This option will allow VC to warn you that balancing should take place but leaves the actually balancing of the VMs across the cluster hosts in your hands.
- **Partially Automated:** This option will, on a VM power on, move the VM to a recommended host. In all other cases, it is like Manual.
- **Fully Automated:** This option will automatically move VMs from overutilized ESX Servers to underutilized ESX Servers. There is a slide bar to set the automated mode from Conservative to Aggressive. Conservative will not move a VM until the server utilization has stayed above the threshold for quite a bit, whereas Aggressive will move the VM when the utilization has gone over a threshold.

6. If VMware HA is selected, you are presented with a screen that allows you to configure the number of ESX Server failures the cluster can withstand. The default is one host. If you have more than two hosts, you can change the number, and what you change it to truly depends on the amount of spare capacity in your cluster. If your hosts are only half utilized and you have six hosts, you might be able to handle three host failures. VMware HA will restart VMs on underutilized hosts. It is also possible per VM to set the host on which it and any dependencies will restart. We talk more about this in Chapter 12, "Disaster Recovery and Backup."

7. Select Finish to create the cluster.

8. Select a host and drag it into the cluster to add a host into a cluster. At that time, any existing resource pools can be included, or you can restart with the cluster. I believe that restarting resource pool allocation is the better way to go as the old pools do not apply with more hosts.

9. Be sure to drag the rest of the hosts into the cluster. Each time you drag a host into the cluster, the cluster services will be started.

Clusters provide for an ever-increasing need of having more resources available for VMs than a single host can provide and the capability to perform DRS or the inclusive capability of DRLB. However, to understand how the scheduling happens and more about scheduling, we need to first understand how the system monitors itself.

Monitoring

There are a myriad of ways to monitor an ESX Server, but few monitoring tools feed into the capability to perform DRLB or have this capability built in. The first is the VC Server (VC). The VC will allow scripts to be called when certain thresholds or actions occur. Another tool with this capability is HP's VMM product, which has similar capabilities to allow scripts to be called when per VM CPU utilization thresholds occur. Each presents, in a different way, the capability to monitor resources. Each has one thing in common, and that is the capability to VMotion a VM to another host. Choosing the new host, however, can be as easy as having the +1 server, of an N+1 configuration, be used as an offload location, or more complex as determining which host has the least amount of utilization and moving a VM there. The first thing to review is the alarm functionality and what can be accomplished with these tools. Then we will look at performance monitoring tools and finally resource shares or how much of a resource a specific VM can use. All these present the background that is ultimately used by DRS, which is a subset of DRLB.

Alarms

Alarms are thrown when a VM or ESX Server has issues and show up as different colored triangles on a VM or host on the left-side panel of the VIC20. Alarms can also be accessed on the *Alarm* tab of the right-side panel. These alarms can be used to trigger DRLB actions. Besides the default alarms, quite a few other alarms are available. The alarms can have actions associated with them, such as the capability to send e-mail, run a script on the VC server, send an SNMP trap, or perform a power operation on a VM. Given these options, alarms have an incredible power. The alarms trigger when VMs or hosts change state. All changes in state act as triggers and are defined by the administrator except for some predefined basics. The basic alarms trigger when a host loses connectivity to the VC Server; the CPU utilization of a VM or host is greater than 75%; or memory utilization of a VM or host is greater than 75%. The basic alarms would need to be duplicated to trigger any action besides the default, which is to just show the alarm in VC.

Some useful state changes are when VMotion is started or completed; the VM power state changes; a VM is created or destroyed; and CPU, disk, memory, or network usage goes above a certain percentage or specific amount. It is also possible to set a warning (yellow), all clear (green), or problem (red) alarm within VC. In addition, it is possible to set a tolerance range in which an alarm will not trigger unless it goes above or below the specified range. It is also possible to set the frequency of an alarm. For example, you can set things such that the system does not report a new alarm of this type until a time limit specified has expired.

Virtual Center Alarms have increased in functionality from early generations of VC, unfortunately much more tuning needs to be done to the alarm subsystem in order to make it useful and practical. VC alarms have the following weaknesses:

1. The inability to configure how long an alarm threshold needs to be crossed in order to generate an alarm. The result, excessive alarms are generated typically resulting in an overage of nuisance email alerts.

2. The inability to configure specific time periods alarms should and should not be armed. For instance, VM and host resource usage tends to skyrocket after hours when virus scans and network backups are performed. This causes CPU, disk I/O, and network utilization thresholds to be crossed for an extended period of time after hours. The result, excessive alarms are generated typically resulting in an overage of nuisance email alerts.

There is, however, one caveat. If network issues exist between the VC Server and the ESX Servers or VMs, it is possible to get false positives on some alarms, specifically those dealing with host availability or power settings. Setting alarms within the VC is fairly straightforward and is a great way to monitor the utilization of VMs and ESX Servers. Here are the steps to set up CPU and memory utilization alarms. The default setups are to warn when the utilization goes above 75% and to notify that there is a problem when the utilization is above 90%. Because the default alarms cannot be modified, here is how you have create alarms that can perform other actions:

1. Log in to the VIC20.
2. Select the host or VM on which to set the alarm.
3. Select the Alarm tab.
4. Select the Definitions button.
5. Right-click in the blank space in the right hand frame and select the New Alarm menu option.
6. Give the alarm a name (see Figure 11.3) and a description, and choose whether to monitor a VM or a host. If you select a VM on which to add an alarm, it will automatically set it to monitor a VM, and the same holds true for a host. To get the choice, choose a cluster, datacenter, or so forth.
7. Enter the trigger priority of Red or Green. Red triggers an alarm by default, but you can set this alarm to trigger when it changes to green.

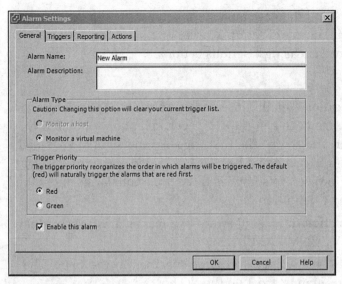

Figure 11.3   New Alarm

8. Enable the alarm.

9. Select the *Triggers* tab and *add* a trigger. The default chosen will be a VM CPU Usage or Host CPU Usage depending on where you are setting the alarm (VM or host) from. This is the default alarm setting you already see under definitions. If the VM CPU usage is above 75%, the system will give a yellow warning, and if it is above 90%, it will give a red problem report. Add as many alarms as necessary.

10. Select the *Reporting* tab.

11. Choose the tolerance (or how many percentage points above and below the limit until the alarm triggers). For example, you could use the default and set the tolerance to 5%, which means the alarm will not trigger yellow until the VM CPU usage is > 80%.

12. Choose the frequency in minutes. In other words, do not report any change to this alarm for the time limit set. You could, for example, set this to 10 minutes, which will imply that if the VM CPU usage drops below and raises once more above 80% (75% + 5% tolerance) within 10 minutes, there will not be a report. This allows a single report, and, assuming there is a spike, it may just go away and not go off again. This is a good way to tell whether the alarm you have is really vital. If the frequency is low enough, you could see whether there is a trend over a set time limit.

13. Select the *Actions* tab, and then add an action. You can have more than one action for each alarm. You could set up a series of alarms that, depending on the alarm, perform increasingly serious actions.

14. Select an action:

- **Send a notification e-mail:** This sends an e-mail to the value entered. An e-mail can be sent to a pager, cell phone, e-mail list, logging server, and so on. The first trigger could send to an e-mail list, the second trigger could be sent to a pager, and a third trigger could page. However, this implies three different alarms and not all within the same definition.

- **Send a notification trap:** Send a trap to a management server that understands VC SNMPD MIBS.

- **Run a script:** Run a script or program specified by the value. The script or program must exist on the VC host.

- **Power on a VM:** Power on a VM, which is useful when an alarm triggers that the VM has powered off for some reason.

- **Power off a VM:** Power off a VM, which is useful when a VM that perhaps competes for resources powers on.

- **Suspend a VM:** Suspends a VM, which is useful if utilization perhaps jumps too high and you need a temporary reprieve. This type of trigger can free up resources temporarily.

- **Reset a VM:** Reset a VM will reboot the VM and thereby clean up memory utilization. This could be a useful action if an application has a known memory leak and you want to reboot the VM automatically before there is a catastrophic failure.

15. Select a direction:

- **From green to yellow:** Alarm triggered as a warning.
- **From yellow to red:** Alarm triggered as a problem.
- **From red to yellow:** Alarm notifies that the problem is no longer vital but there is still a warning.
- **From yellow to green:** The all clear alarm.

16. Select OK to set the alarm.

Useful alarms include the default, but there are some others that would be nice to have. If VMware DRS is in automated mode, or perhaps more than one person can perform VMotions, it is possible to trigger alarms for every VMotion completed or started. At the very least, you can get an e-mail that will tell you when the VMotion happened, and you can then investigate why it happened to better understand how VMware DRS triggers itself.

Another extremely useful alarm is one that is triggered when the VM network usage goes above a certain percent. This alarm will help pinpoint VMs that are overusing network resources. The default alarms do not handle network utilization, but this type of alarm can be created. I set up this alarm to let me know when a VM or even a network is overloaded. If it remains consistently overloaded, there is need for more network bandwidth for the ESX host. However this type of alarm may not be practical when network backups are running due to the number of alarms that can be generated.

The last useful alarm is VM or host disk usage. If the disk usage consistently goes above the alarm state, it may be necessary to increase the amount of storage. Perhaps you can solve the problem by adding a new LUN, perhaps from a different SAN, to offset the load. Once more, these are not default alarms or actions, but they are extremely useful for determining when more resources are required for your ESX host or cluster.

Alarms are powerful, and they give you trigger points to let you know when a system is overloaded or an unexpected action occurs. If you never expect a VM to power down or crash, it would be useful to set an alarm. Perhaps set up one per VM. This way you get a timestamp as to when the problem occurred, which gives you a leg up on analysis of the issue. Time is the one thing you need to know when reviewing log files and performance. When something happened is just as important as what happened as we will see from the next section.

Performance Analysis

Another tool for monitoring is to review the performance of the ESX Server hosts, clusters, resource pools, and VMs by using the Performance tab on the right-side panel of the VIC20. There are also tools such as vCharter from Vizioncore, and the Performance Management Pack plug-in for the HPSIM product. All these tools provide quite a bit of extremely useful information when there is a need to look at performance. Some people constantly review the performance graphs from these tools, and others wait for an alarm to trigger a problem.

Performance analysis inside ESX in many ways is an art form, but there are simple rules to understand before beginning.

- The performance within a VM does not always map to the real performance for the VM inside ESX. The only time that there is a legitimate mapping of what the VM states to the real performance is when there is a one to one mapping between vCPUs to pCPUs. In most cases, this almost never happens. Tools that gather performance data from within a VM are useful for determining whether there was a change, but not the exact values. Tools such as Windows Task Manager's Performance tab, HP OpenView, and so forth are great for seeing what has changed within a VM but not the exact value of a change. I have seen situations within a VM where the vCPU utilization was around 80%, yet the real utilization using ESX-based tools was only 15% for the VM. If the descheduler VMware Tool is in use, there is a closer mapping between what ESX shows and what the VM will show. ESX is the final arbiter of performance values, not the VM.

A common question concerns why a VM does not internally show the proper performance numbers. The answer is that it is mainly due to the use of a vCPU rather than a pCPU. A vCPU uses only a part of the pCPU, the time slice allotted for the VM. Because the program counters used by the performance tools look at the total speed of a full CPU and the number of cycles of the CPU, the calculations are based on a pCPU and not the reduced cycles and speed allocated as a vCPU. So, the numbers can be off by quite a bit. For example, a pCPU of 2.4GHz may only give 32MHz for the vCPU time slice for a VM. Although on a full 2.4GHz the pCPU utilization could be 15% but with a 32MHz vCPU, the performance is 80% as there are reduced cycles and speed available to the vCPU. Is there a formula for determining the difference? Not that I have found. After you have a baseline of performance, the internal measurements become a gauge telling you whether things are better or worse.

- The addition of a new VM to a virtualization host will affect the performance of every VM. I have seen customers who will only look at the performance of the single VM that has an issue instead of the performance of the whole ESX Server. The two are not unrelated.

- The addition of vSwitches to a VMware ESX Server will also affect the performance of every VM. Increasing network paths will increase the amount of pCPU and memory that the VMkernel uses and allow for a new balancing act across physical networks.

- There is a theoretical limit of 16 vCPUs per pCPU core with ESX version 3. Earlier versions had a theoretical limit of eight vCPUs per pCPU core.

Because most dual-core pCPUs share the same L2 Cache, it is wise to look at the number of cores as one less than the actual number.

- When memory is overcommitted and the in use memory exceeds the physical memory of an ESX Server, performance is adversely affected. Swapping in any form adversely affects performance. Although memory can be overcommitted, the best practice is to keep used memory within the bounds of the available physical memory.

- The use of mixed operating systems within an ESX Server will affect performance. ESX caches common blocks of code for a VM; in this way, the memory needed for the code segments of a guest operating system is shared between multiple VMs using the same guest (see Figure 11.4). This allows less memory to be shared for like VMs. Consider this an advanced form of shared libraries. In a shared library, the nonvolatile code or instructions to issue for a given function are shared, but the volatile and private memory of the same function used by multiple applications is not shared.

  However, when there are disparate guest operating systems, the code sharing does not happen as often.

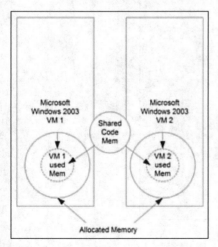

Figure 11.4   Multiple guest OS caching

- Mixing VMs with different vCPUs on a host will cause performance problems. When there are VMs with single, dual, and quad vCPUs on the same ESX Server, the scheduler has to work quite a bit harder than it does if all the VMs have the same number of vCPUs. Because a vCPU is mapped to a pCPU when the VM is running, consider the following example. The example shown in Figure 11.5 takes a four-core host and we will try to fit into those four cores all the vCPUs to run three VMs with single vCPUs, two VMs with dual vCPUs, and one VM with a quad vCPU. Each set of lines represents when a vCPU will run. The first time the solid lines will run; the next time the dashed lines of the dual vCPU VM and a single vCPU VM will run, and one of the existing single vCPU VMs is not swapped out. Lastly, the dotted lines of the quad vCPU VM will run.

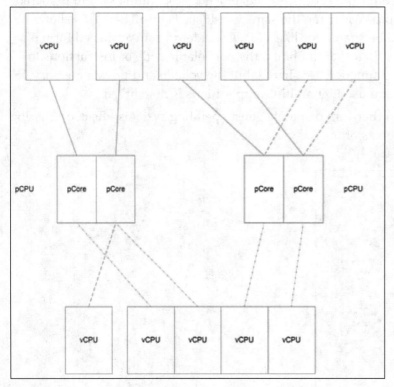

Figure 11.5 Multiple vCPU scheduling

- Use of RDMs for large file shares will change performance, and there is one less layer to go through the share. However, this could also impact performance adversely because more storage network bandwidth could be used.
- After deploying any VMs, always get a new baseline to assist with future performance analysis, either from within the VM or without.

Now that we have the basics of what will affect performance, how do we monitor performance to determine the cause of any problem? Table 11.1 outlines the available tools and some notes about them. Also note that the nine items listed previously are not the end all and be all of performance, but merely some considerations when looking at performance.

Table 11.1

Performance-Monitoring Tools			
Tool	**ESX v2.x**	**ESX v3.x**	**Notes**
Virtual Center	V1.0 and V2.x	V2.x	V1.0 is prone to misinformation in native mode. For very accurate information, most people use vmkusage. V2.0 has a resolution of up to 5 minutes, whereas V1.0 has a resolution of every 5 minutes, but is only displayed every half hour.
vmkusage	Yes	N/A	Provided as an add-on to the MUI that allowed the user to drill down into the host and VMs. Data was gathered every 5 minutes. vmkusagectl install was used to initialize vmkusage.
vCharter from Vizioncore	Yes	Yes	Provides a single pane to see all utilizations for a server or VM. The resolution is once a minute. In addition, it provides a graphical way to manage all VM processes.
esxtop	Yes	Yes	Used when a problem occurs as its resolution is as low as 10 seconds.

Each tool has its own uses. However, we shall discuss mainly esxtop and VC2.x analysis. vmkusage is similar to VC2, in that the data is taken every 5 minutes. Although the drilldown is different, the results are similar. vCharter is a useful tool for looking at a finer resolution without having to resort to the CLI and esxtop. To view performance in VC 2.x, select the host, cluster, or VM to review, and then select the Performance tab. In the following discussion, we have the normal alarms and noticed that we got a yellow or warning alarm, and want to know what gave the alarm and why. It is easier to explain performance analysis by looking at a real problem.

The chart in Figure 11.6 shows a change in performance of the VM, which occurred at 12:38:04 p.m. on June 10, 2007. The system went from less than 10% CPU usage to 81.78% and finally to an average value below 50%. That is a large swing in performance, which caused a yellow or warning alarm to trigger when the CPU usage went over 75%. However, the alarm did not trigger again as the performance was below 50%. So the question to ask is, what happened at 12:38 PM? When we look at the logs for the application on the VM, we will notice that a backup was occurring, which explains the large CPU utilization and then the steady state. However, this is not the only performance chart to look at. We should also look at the chart for the complete system. Isolating just a single VM does not show the complete performance implication.

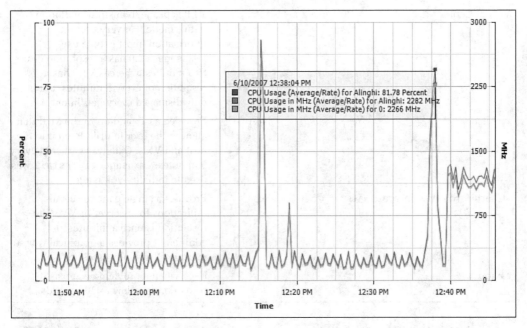

Figure 11.6 VC2.x VM performance chart

When we look at the host performance chart (see Figure 11.7) for that same time frame we notice that the CPU usage for the host goes to 74.58% and stays there for the duration of the backup, and that a single CPU stays at roughly 89% or just under our red or problem trigger. However, the yellow warning trigger on the host already fired. There are five lines on this chart; the topmost gray line represents the overall performance of the system and the other four lines represent the four physical CPUs in the system. One CPU is running extremely high, and the others are not. The overall performance of the host is also high. Because the system backup makes use of an NFS/NAS datastore, this is to be expected, because there is a lot of VMkernel CPU being used to transfer packets from one datastore to another.

Understanding performance is not just about the graphs. You need to understand how your applications work, how tools work inside ESX, and how they interact with each other. The backup tool being used here is VizionCore vRanger.

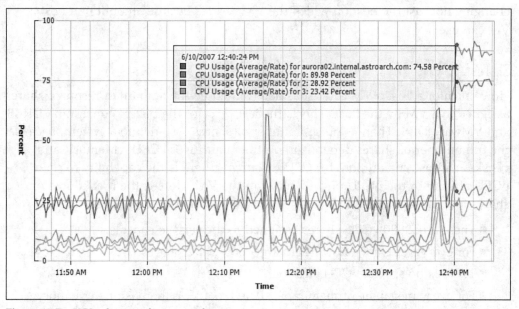

6/10/2007 12:40:24 PM
■ CPU Usage (Average/Rate) for aurora02.internal.astroarch.com: 74.58 Percent
■ CPU Usage (Average/Rate) for 0: 89.98 Percent
■ CPU Usage (Average/Rate) for 2: 28.92 Percent
■ CPU Usage (Average/Rate) for 3: 23.42 Percent

Figure 11.7 VC2.x host performance chart

There are similar graphs for disk I/O, memory usage, network usage, and system usage given in real time (updated every 20 seconds) or historically for the past day, week, month, or year. The one caveat of this system is that the system time of the VC server needs to be kept synchronized with the time on the ESX Servers.

Best Practice for Performance Monitoring
Keep the VC Server and ESX Servers synchronized using an NTP or external clock service.

Although VMware DRS uses CPU usage to determine which VMs to move from host to host, there is more to the balancing act besides this simple yet vital approach. This is one reason why VMware DRS is only a small part of DRLB, which encompasses all of the available resources and would do more than just move VMs from host to host. Unfortunately, to realize full DRLB requires quite a bit of scripting and knowledge of your hardware environment and requires changing not just the host on which the VM resides but the amount of a host a VM can use.

Shares

How much of a host a VM can use is determined by the amount of resource shares assigned to a VM by the host. This is the last piece of the puzzle concerning DRLB and VMware DRS. There is no set number of shares assigned to a system, because the full number of shares depends upon the quantity of vCPU, vMemory, and vDisk on a host. In addition, for CPU resources, there is the capability to set a pCPU affinity or the pCPU on which to run the VM. Here is the breakdown of shares for a host or cluster. Network sharing is defined in the next section.

- There are 2,000 vCPU shares assigned to the service console.
- For every vCPU on a host, there are 1,000 vCPU shares.
- There is no special pCPU affinity.
- For every megabyte of memory assigned to a VM, there is one vMemory share.
- For every vDisk on a host, there are 1,000 vDisk shares.
- There are no shares associated with a vNIC.

Given the preceding rules, consider an example of eight VMs on a single host with two dual-core 3.1GHz CPUs and 16GB of memory. Although the speed and memory of the system is relatively unimportant to the conversation, it will help to point out an important feature. Four of the VMs have a single vCPU, vDisk, and 1GB of memory assigned to each; one has four vCPUs, two vDisks, and 2GB of memory assigned; the last three have two vCPUs, 512MB of memory, and one vDisk each. In addition, the service console is using 384MB of memory. Using the previously defined rules, the host has how many shares?

- **CPU shares:** (4 * 1 vCPU + 4 vCPU + 3 * 2 vCPU + 2 SC) * 1,000 = 16,000
- **Memory shares:** (4 * 1024MB + 2048MB + 3 * 512MB + 1 SC * 384) = 8064
- **Disk shares:** (4 * 1 vDisk + 1 * 2 vDisk + 3 * 1 vDisk + 2 * 1 vDisk) * 1,000 = 11,000

Therefore, the answer is

- 16,000 CPU shares, 8,064 memory shares, and 11,000 disk shares

How are these shares applied to how the VMkernel manages each VM? In the preceding example, the four-vCPU machine is the most interesting because it uses the most resources when it runs. It uses the resources outline in Table 11.2.

Table 11.2

Example Resource Utilization			
VM	CPU Shares	Memory Shares	Disk Shares
Single vCPU VMs	1,000 / 16,000	1,024 / 8,064	1,000 / 11,000
4 vCPU VMs	4,000 / 16,000	2,048 / 8,064	2,000 / 11,000
2 vCPU VMs	2,000 / 16,000	512 / 8,064	1,000 / 11,000

These numbers define how much CPU, memory, and disk each VM gets when that VM runs only when there is host resource contention. So, a four-vCPU machine would get 4x the CPU of a single vCPU machine. In addition, a four-vCPU machine can only run on a host with at least four cores, thereby possibly limiting where the VM can be moved with VMware DRS. This is a very important concept. Just as important to performance is the amount of disk and memory used by each VM. However, in many cases these are overlooked as CPU usage is the main telling point for performance. But let's say that the four-vCPU machine is also a database server with quite a lot of disk I/O. Would it not be prudent to increase its disk shares so that it can get more disk I/O done when it runs? Suppose we want to increase its disk shares by 1,000 shares per disk, giving it a total of 4,000 shares. If that is the case, the total number of disk shares also increases by 2,000.

- **Disk shares:** (4 * 1 vDisk + 2 * 2 vDisk + 3 * 1 vDisk + 2 * 1 vDisk) * 1,000 = 13,000
- **4 vCPU VM disk shares:** 4,000 / 13,000
- **All other (7) VM disk shares:** 1,000 / 13,000

As can be seen from continuing the discussion of shares, while the number of disk shares for the VM have doubled, there is a subsequent increase in the total number of shares available to the host or cluster. This increase in shares is the basic design of ESX resources. The more VMs you run, the less resources per VM the system grants. However, the number of resource shares available increase as VMs are added or when resources are modified by hand. However, remember that the service console also has resources associated with it in the realm of 2x normal resources, except for memory.

In addition to the capability to change resources at will, it is possible to set limits on resources and reservations. Limits are the maximum resources a VM can use, and reservations are the amount of resources reserved just for this VM. If the reserved amount of resources is not available, a VM will not start.

The changes to resources, whether CPU, disk, or memory, affect the performance of a VM and may not always trigger a VMware DRS VMotion to occur. If a VM is I/O bound, it would use less CPU but wait longer to finish its disk I/O, and therefore have an overall lower chance of being moved to a less-utilized server. However, if a VM is CPU bound, it would definitely be a candidate for ESX to suggest it be moved, or automatically move it, to a less-used host using VMware DRS.

Resource Pool Addendum

With the explanation of shares, we can further enhance the usage of resource pools. A resource pool takes the total available CPU and memory resources and allows them to be divided up into groups or smaller chunks of available resources. The split in resources for resource pools can be used to ensure that the selected VMs only use at maximum the resources that are available in the pool. Each resource pool can be further subdivided to grant even less resources to each group. This advancement in resource management can guarantee that a VM cannot take over all the resources of an ESX Server. Just like a VM, a resource pool can have a reservation and a hard limit on the amount of resources it can use. But, unlike a VM, it can also borrow resources from the parent resource pool as necessary.

Because resources are the monetary unit in a virtual environment, it is possible to reduce resources based on how much a VM owner is willing to pay for the use of the VM. This can translate into something billable to the VMware ESX Server VM owners. Because this is the monetary unit of a virtualization host, it might not be wise, unless a customer pays for the resources, to allow a resource pool to borrow from a parent pool. But then again, it depends on the billing. However, this still does not explain how to split up network usage.

Network resources are handled differently in ESX version 3 than in earlier versions. In earlier versions, each VM could have its own traffic shaping controls, which could lead to quite a bit of illogical setups where each VM was assigned more resources than was physically possible. Now with ESX version 3, each vSwitch can have traffic shaping applied and then from the amount of traffic available further apply traffic shaping to each port group off a vSwitch. Traffic shaping is discussed in Chapter 7, "Networking." However, let's reiterate, traffic shaping allows the administrator to set the average bandwidth a vSwitch or port group can attain, its peak bandwidth, and burst transmission packets. These numbers will, like resources, allow the vSwitch to control how much of the network a VM can use. If traffic shaping is enabled, like resource shares, the VM can be limited on the bandwidth it could use, and this could lead to a VM being I/O bound while it waits on the network. I/O bound does not necessarily translate to CPU usage for a VM, but because traffic shaping happens in the vSwitch, the overall system CPU usage can increase as this is handled. vSwitch utilization has a direct impact on the amount of CPU the VMkernel will use.

Putting It All Together

Because resources and utilization govern DRLB and its subset encompassed within VMware DRS, it is first important to realize how the resource and utilization tools within ESX interact. The preceding description now allows us to visit how to automate the load balancing of VMs across hosts. But, first we need to expand our rules for load balancing and how they relate to CPU utilization.

- CPU-bound VMs will impact overall CPU usage and trigger VC CPU alarms, and possibly VMware DRS migration.
- Disk I/O-bound VMs may not impact overall CPU usage, may not trigger VC CPU alarms, and most likely will not trigger a VMware DRS migration.
- Network I/O-bound VMs will impact overall CPU usage of the VMkernel, may not trigger VC alarms, and most likely will not trigger a VMware DRS migration.
- High overall network usage will impact overall CPU usage, may trigger a VC CPU alarm, and most likely will trigger a VMware DRS migration.
- High overall disk usage will impact overall CPU usage, may trigger a VC CPU alarm, and most likely will trigger a VMware DRS migration.
- High overall memory usage may not impact overall CPU usage, may trigger a VC memory alarm, and most likely will not trigger a VMware DRS migration.

As can be seen, CPU usage is the main trigger for a VMware DRS migration. The use of VMotion is only one tool in the toolbox for load balancing the virtual environment. The HP VMM product can also trigger scripts when CPU usage of a VM hits a certain level, too, but that is still only one piece of the puzzle.

The other pieces of the puzzle are the capability to change CPU, disk, and memory shares on-the-fly and adjust traffic shaping to reduce network utilization of VMs. All these adjustments can happen on-the-fly. Changes to the resource shares and traffic-shaping settings take place at once. These changes, plus the capability to VMotion, can better balance VM utilization across the host, cluster, and datacenter. Currently implemented as a product is the capability to migrate running machines on-the-fly (VMware DRS or other automated VMotion). All other methods of resource management are purely a by-hand mechanism. Resource pools are a step toward automation of this behavior by limiting a group of VMs to a certain amount of resources.

Now, how do you manipulate the other settings? Unfortunately, there is no automated way to do this yet and no easy answer. You can use the VMware SDK, VIPerl, and `vimsh` to read the options, but to set them requires a bit more logic than what is available. However, there is some hope in using alarms for disk and network usage. High usage could force a VMotion of the VMs from host to host, thereby complementing the existing VMware DRS CPU usage constraints with increased capabilities.

Conclusion

VMware DRS automates the movement of VMs from host to host and is just a subset of the real DRLB. More functionality will be necessary within ESX for the full DRLB to be available, but VMware DRS is the current batch of tools for balancing out your ESX based data centers. The VMware SDK, VIPerl, and `vimsh` interfaces are a great step in the direction of enabling full DRLB at some point or a subset of the functionality for your datacenter. The other aspect of DRLB is disaster recovery and business continuity, and that is discussed in Chapter 12.

Chapter 12

Disaster Recovery and Backup

Disaster recovery (DR) takes many forms, and the preceding chapter on DRLB covers a small part of DR. Actually, DRLB is more a preventative measure than a prelude to DR. However, although being able to prevent the need for DR is a great goal, too many disasters happen to rely on any one mechanism. In this chapter, we categorize disasters and provide solutions for each one. You will see that the backup tool to use will not dictate how to perform DR, but it's the other way around. In addition to DR, there is the concept of business continuity (BC) or the need to keep things running even if a disaster happens. Some of what we discuss in this chapter is BC and not truly DR. However, the two go hand in hand because BC plans are often tied to DR plans and handle a subset of the disasters.

What Is the Goal of Disaster Recovery?
The goal of DR is to either prevent or reduce downtime caused by either man or nature.

Disaster Types

There are various forms of well-defined disasters and ways to prevent or workaround these to meet the defined goal. There is no one way to get around disasters, but knowing they exist is the first step in planning for them. Having a DR or BC plan is the first step toward prevention, implementation, and reduction in downtime. At a conference presentation, I asked a room of 200 customers if any of them had a DR or BC plan. Only two people stated they had a DR or BC plan, which was disconcerting but by no means unexpected.

Best Practice for DR and BC
Create a written DR and BC plan.

Stating in writing the DR and BC plan will, in the case that it is needed, help immensely because there will be absolutely no confusion about it in an emergency situation. For one customer, the author was requested to make a DR plan to cover all possible disasters. Never in the customer's wildest dreams did they think it would need to be used. Unfortunately, the "wildest dream" scenario occurred, and the written DR plan enabled the customer to restore the environment in an orderly fashion extremely quickly. It is in your best interest to have a written DR plan that covers all possible disasters to minimize confusion and reduce downtime when, and not if, a disaster occurs.

Best Practice for DR and BC
Plan for failure; do not fail to plan.

Yes, this last best practice sounds like so many other truisms in life, but it is definitely worth considering around DR and BC, because failures will occur with surprising frequency, and it is better to have a plan than everyone running around trying to do everything at once. So what should be in a DR and BC plan? First, we should understand the types of disasters possible and use these as a basis for a DR and BC plan template. Granted, some of the following examples are scary and unthinkable, but they are not improbable. It is suggested that you use the following list and add to it items that are common to your region of the world as a first step to understanding what you may face when you start a DR or BC plan. A customer I consulted for asked for a DR plan, and we did one considering all of these possibilities. When finished, we were told that a regional disaster was not possible and that it did not need to be considered. Unfortunately, Katrina happened, which goes to show that if we can think it up, it is possible. Perhaps a disaster is improbable, but nature is surprising.

Disasters take many forms. The following list is undoubtedly not exhaustive, but it includes many different types of potential disasters.

- **Application failure**

  An application failure is the sudden death of a necessary application, which can be caused by poorly coded applications and are exploited by denial-of-service (DoS) attacks that force an application to crash.

- **VM failure**

  A VM failure could be man-made, by nature, or both. Consider the man-made possibilities such as where a security patch needs to be applied or software is to be added to the VM. By nature could be the failure of the VM due to an OS bug, an unimplemented procedure within the virtualization layer, or an application issue that used up enough resources to cause the VM to crash. In general, VM failures are unrelated to hardware because the virtualization layer removes the hardware from the equation. But it does not remove OS bugs from the equation.

- **ESX Server failure**

  A machine failure can be man-made, by nature, or even both. For example, a man-made failure could be the planned outage to upgrade firmware, hardware, the ESX OS, or the possible occurrence of a hardware failure of some sort that causes a crash. Another example is if power is inadvertently shut off to the server.

- **Communication failure**

  A communication failure is unrelated to ESX, but will affect ESX nonetheless. Communication can be either via Fibre Channel or Ethernet. The errors could be related to a communication card, cable, switch, or a device at the non-ESX side of the communication. An example of this type of failure is a Fibre or network cable being pulled from the box or a switch is powered off or rebooted.

- **Rack disaster**

  Rack failures are extremely bad and are often caused by the rack being moved around or even toppling over. Not only will such an incident cause failures to the systems or communications, but it could cause physical injury to someone caught by the rack when it topples. Another rack failure could be the removal of power to fans of and around the whole rack, causing a massive overheat situation where all the servers in the rack fail simultaneously.

- **Datacenter disaster**

  Datacenter disasters include air conditioning failures that cause overheating, power spikes, lack of power, earthquakes, floods, fire, and anything else imaginable that could render the datacenter unavailable. An example of this type of disaster is the inadvertent triggering of a sprinkler system or a sprinkler tank bursting and flooding the datacenter below. It may seem odd, but some datacenters still use water and no other flame prevention system. Use of halon and other gasses can be dangerous to human life and therefore may not be used.

- **Building disaster**

  Like datacenter disasters, these disasters cause the building to become untenable. These include loss of power or some form of massive physical destruction. An example of this type of disaster is what happened to the World Trade Center.

- **Campus disaster**

  Campus disasters include a host of natural and man-made disasters where destruction is total. An example of this type of disaster are tornados, which will strike one place and skip others but will render anything in its path rubble.

- **Citywide disaster**

  Citywide disasters are campus disasters on a much larger scale. In some cases, the town is the campus (as is the case for larger universities). Examples range from earthquakes, to hurricanes, to atomic bombs.

- **Regional disaster**

  Regional disasters include massive power outages similar to the blackout in the New England area in the 2003 and hurricanes such as Katrina that cover well over 200 miles of coastline.

■ **National disasters**

For small countries such as Singapore or Luxembourg, a national disaster is equivalent to a citywide disaster and could equate to a regional disaster. National disasters in larger countries may be unthinkable, but it is not impossible.

■ **Multinational disaster**

Again because most countries touch other countries and there are myriad small countries all connected, this must be a consideration for planning. Tsunamis, earthquakes, and other massive natural disasters are occurring around us. Another option is a massive planned terrorist attack on a single multinational company.

■ **World disaster**

This sort of disaster is unthinkable and way out of scope!

Recovery Methods

Now that the different levels of disasters are defined, a set of tools and skills necessary to recover from each one can be determined. The tools and skills will be specific to ESX and will outline physical, operational, and backup methodologies that will reduce downtime or prevent a disaster:

■ **Application failure**

The recovery mechanism for a failed application is to have some form of watchdog that will launch the application anew if it was detected to be down. Multiple VMs running the same application connected to a network load balancer will also help in this situation by reducing the traffic to any one VM, and hence the application, and will remove application from the list of possible targets if it is down. Many of these types of clusters also come with ways of restarting applications if they are down. Use of shared data disk clustering à la Microsoft clusters is also a possible solution.

■ **VM failure**

Recovery from a VM failure can be as simple as rebooting the VM in question via some form of watchdog. However, if the VM dies, it is necessary to determine why the problem occurred, and therefore this type of failure often needs debugging. In this case, the setup of some form of shared data disk cluster à la Microsoft clusters will allow a secondary VM to take over the duties of the failed VM. Any VM failure should be investigated to determine the cause. Another mechanism is to have a secondary VM ready and waiting to take over duties if necessary. If the data of the primary VM is necessary to continue, consider placing the data on a second VMDK and have both VMs pointing to the second disk. Just make sure that only one is booted at the same time. Use DRLB tools to automatically launch this secondary VM if necessary.

■ **Machine failure**

Hardware often has issues. To alleviate machine failures have a second machine running and ready to take on the load of the first machine. Use VMware High Availability (HA) or other high-availability tools to automatically specify a host on which to launch the VMs if a host fails. In addition, if you know the host will fail due to a software or hardware upgrade, first VMotion all the VMs to the secondary host. VMware HA can be set up when you create a VMware cluster or even after the fact. We discussed the creation of VMware clusters in Chapter 11, "Dynamic Resource Load Balancing." VMware HA makes use of the Legato Automated Availability Management (Legato AAM) suite to manage the ESX Server cluster failover. There is more on HA later in this chapter in the section "Business Continuity."

■ **Communication failure**

Everyone knows that Fibre and network connections fail, so ensure that multiple switches and paths are available for the communications to and from the ESX Server. In addition, make local copies of the most important VMs so that they can be launched using a local disk in the case of a SAN failure. This often requires more local disk for the host and the avoidance of booting from SAN.

■ **Rack disaster**

To avoid a rack disaster, make sure racks are on earthquake-proof stands, are locked in place, and perhaps have stabilizers deployed. But also be sure that your ESX host and switches are located in separate racks in different locations on the datacenter floor, so that there is no catastrophic failure and that if a rack does fail, everything can be brought back up on the secondary server.

■ **Datacenter disaster**

To avoid datacenter disasters, add more hosts to a secondary datacenter either in the same building or elsewhere on the campus. Often this is referred to as a hot site and requires an investment in new SAN and

ESX hosts. Also ensure there are adequate backups to tape secured in a vault. In addition, it is possible with ESX version 3 to VMotion VMs across subnets via routers. In this way, if a datacenter was planned to go down, it would be possible to move running VMs to another datacenter where other hosts reside.

- **Building disaster**

  The use of a hot site and offsite tape backups will get around building disasters. Just be sure the hot site is not located in the same building.

- **Campus disaster**

  Just like a building disaster, just be sure the other location is off the campus.

- **Citywide disaster**

  Similar to campus disasters, just be sure the hot site or backup location is outside the city.

- **Regional disaster**

  Similar to campus disasters, just be sure the hot site or backup location is outside the region.

- **National disasters**

  Similar to campus disasters, just be sure the hot site or backup location is outside the country, or if the countries are small, in another country far away.

- **Multinational disasters**

  Because this could be considered a regional disaster in many cases, see the national DR strategy.

- **World disasters**

  We can dream some here and place a datacenter on another astronomical body or space station.

Best Practices

Now that the actions to take for each disaster are outlines, a list of best practices can be developed to define a DR or BC plan to use. The following list considers an ESX Server from a single host to enterprisewide with the thought of DR and BC in mind. The list covers mainly ESX, not all the other parts to creating a successful and highly redundant network. The list is divided between local practices and remote practices. This way the growth of an implementation can be seen. The idea behind these best practices is to look at our list of possible failures and to have a response to each one and the knowledge that many eggs are being placed into one basket. On average for larger machines, ESX Servers can house 20+ VMs. That is a lot of service that could go down if a disaster happens.

First we need to consider the local practices around DR:

- Implement ESX using N+1 hosts where N is the necessary number of hosts to run the VMs required. The extra host is used for DR.
- When racking the hosts, ensure that hosts are stored in different racks in different parts of the datacenter.
- Be sure there are at least two Fibre Channel cards using different PCI buses if possible.
- Be sure there are at least two NIC ports for each network to be attached to the host using different PCI buses if possible.
- When cabling the hosts, ensure that redundant cables go to different switches and that no redundant path uses the same PCI card.
- Be sure that all racks are stabilized.
- Be sure that there is enough cable available so that machines can be fully extended from the rack as necessary.
- Ensure there is enough local disk space to store exported versions of the VMs and to run the most important VMs if necessary.
- Ensure HA is configured so that VMs running on a failed host are automatically started on another host.
- Create DRLB scripts to start VMs locally if SAN connectivity is lost.
- Create DRLB scripts or enable VMware DRS to move VMs when CPU load is too high on a single host.

Second, we need to consider the remote practices around DR:

- When creating DR backups, ensure there is safe storage for tapes onsite and offsite.
- Follow all the local items listed above at all remote sites.
- Create a list of tasks necessary to be completed if there is a massive site failure. This list should include who does what and the necessary dependencies for each task.

The suggestions translate into more physical hardware to create a redundant and safe installation of ESX. It also translates into more software and licenses, too.

Before going down the path of hot sites and offsite tape storage, the local DR plan needs to be fully understood from a software perspective, specifically the methods for producing backups, and there are plenty of methods. Some methods adversely impact performance; others that do not. Some methods lend themselves to expansion to hot sites, and others that will take sneaker nets and other mechanisms to get the data from one site to the other.

Backup and Business Continuity

The simplest approach to DR is to make a good backup of everything so that restoration is simplified when the time comes, but backups can happen in two distinctly different ways with ESX. In some cases, some of these suggestions do not make sense because the application in use can govern how things go. As an example, we were asked to look at DR backup for an application with its own built-in DR capabilities with a DR plan that the machine be reinstalled on new hardware if an issue occurred. The time to redeploy in their current environment was approximately an hour, and it took the same amount of time for a full DR backup through ESX. Because of this, the customer decided not to go with full DR backups.

Backup

But what is a full DR backup? As stated previously, there are two major backup styles. The first in terms of ESX is referred to as a backup for individual file restoration or a backup made from within the VM. The second is a DR-level backup of the full VM disk image and configuration file. The difference is the restoration method. A standard backup, using agents running within the VM, usually follows these steps for restoration:

1. Install OS onto machine.
2. Install restoration tools.
3. Test restoration tools.
4. Restore system.
5. Test restoration.

A full DR-level backup has the following restoration process:

1. Restore VMDK and configuration file.
2. Register VM into ESX.
3. Boot VM.

As can be seen, the restoration process for a full DR backup is much faster than the normal method, which in many cases makes a DR backup more acceptable, but it generally requires more hardware. But what hardware is really the question, and one that needs to be considered for ESX. A standard ESX stand-alone ESX Server consists of lots of memory and as much disk as can be placed into the server. A standard remote data store–attached ESX Server consists of lots of memory and very little local disk space, and a boot from SAN (BFS) ESX Server usually has no local disk space, which is not a best practice, as outlined in Chapter 3, "Installation." Our best practice for installing ESX outlines a need for a very large /vmimages directory and a local VMFS partition, and the main reason for this is to perform safe backups. Figure 12.1 presents backup steps from the point of view of a simple ESX Server connected to an entry-level SAN. Entry-level remote data stores are missing the BC or copy features available on larger remote data stores.

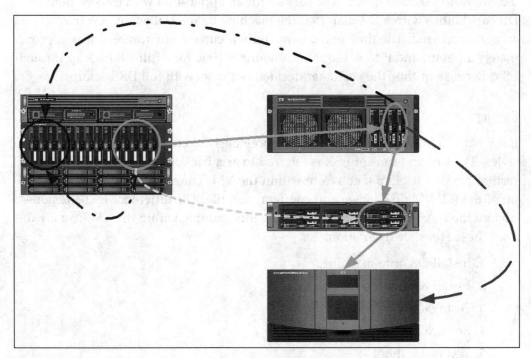

Figure 12.1 Entry-level backup options
Visio templates for image courtesy of Hewlett-Packard.

Whether there is an entry-level remote data store, SCSI-attached storage, or local storage, the steps are similar for creating backups and for DR. There are few ways to create backups, and the methods are similar no matter where the data will eventually reside. DR backups can be made many ways using an equally different number of tools. Built into ESX is the first method, the second is to use VMware Consolidated Backup (VCB), and one of the other tools is to use Vizioncore's ESXRanger. All can be used to eventually place the data on a tape device, local storage, remote storage, or a remote hot site. File restore backups can be made using VCB and other third-party backup agents.

The simplest form of backup is the single ESX Server approach, as outlined in Figure 12.1. Now it does not matter whether the VMFS data stores are SAN, iSCSI, or even local SCSI for this method. This method works quite well with low-cost, no-frills data store solutions like an entry-level SAN without BC features.

In Figure 12.1, there are several backup paths and destinations shown that are intrinsic within the ESX version 3 software. All but one of these paths exist in earlier versions of ESX. In addition, some third-party backup solutions provide the same functionality as the intrinsic tools but in a more graphical function.

Backup Paths

Path 1, designated by the solid gray lines, represents a common backup approach for earlier versions of ESX. This approach still provides a level of redundancy that protects a system from catastrophic remote storage failures. This is a full DR-level backup:

- VMs are exported from the remote or local VMFS datastores to a placeholder on the local machine. This placeholder is usually an ext3 file system, but should be another VMFS designated as a special repository just in case the SAN fails. It would not be available for normal usage.

- The exported VM files are in turn sent to a remote backup server through a secure network copy mechanism.

- All but the *most important* VM files are then deleted from the ESX Server. By keeping the *most important* VM files locally, we have taken a simple and useful precaution in the event of failed remote storage.

- The remote backup server sends the data to tape storage.

Path 2 is very similar to Path 1, designated by the short-dash light-gray line. This patch is only available with ESX version 3 and represents the use of the VCB. This can either be a full DR-level backup or per-file backup if the VCB proxy server, Windows 2003, understands the file system to be mounted by the VCB tools:

- The remote storage data stores are mounted onto a VCB proxy server.

- The VCB proxy server will mount the VM from the remote datastore and either export the VM to another location on the VCB in a monolithic full DR backup, or provide a means to access the VMDKs for a per-file backup. (Once more, per-file backup is only available if the VCB Proxy understands the underlying file system of the VMDK.)
- When the VMDK is exported or the per-file backup is finished, the proxy server unmounts the VMDKs of the VM.
- The data is then sent to tape or a tape server from the VCB proxy.

Path 3 has two branches designated by the dash-dot black lines, and is used to clone VMs from one remote storage location to another; this is a poor man's BC copy that more expensive SANs can perform automatically. The branches can be explained as follows:

- **Upper path:** VMs are exported to a local file system.
- **Upper path:** VMs are imported or copied to a new file system on the remote storage.
- **Upper path:** All but the *most important* VMs are deleted from the local file system.
- **Lower path:** VMs are exported from one file system of the remote storage directly to another file system on the remote storage using service console-based VCB or other service console-based backup tools, including Vizioncore's ESXRanger Pro product.

Path 4 is designated by the long-dash, dark-gray line and is not a recommended path but is there for use in rare cases. This is an alternative to Path 1 in that instead of sending the files to a remote backup server, the data would be sent directly to a tape library using the service console. This path is never recommended because there is a need for an Adaptec SCSI HBA, and when the SCSI HBA has issues, the entire ESX Server may need to be rebooted and may crash.

Modification to Path 3

As can be seen, even for a single-server ESX Server, there are a myriad of paths for backup and BC. Now let's look at a slightly different configuration. This configuration, outlined in Figure 12.2, describes a system where the remote storage has the capability of doing a business copy or LUN snapshot.

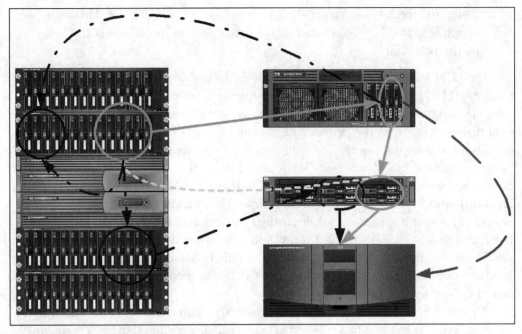

Figure 12.2 Enterprise class SAN backup options
Visio templates for image courtesy of Hewlett-Packard.

Figure 12.2 gives us a change to one of our existing backup paths described previously. Specifically, that change is a modification of Path 3.

Path 3 has two branches designated by the dash-dot black lines and is used to clone VMs from one remote storage location to another; a poor man's BC copy that the more expensive SANs can perform automatically. Path 3 and the modification (essentially creating Path 5) work this way:

- **Upper path:** VMs are exported to a local file system.
- **Upper path:** VMs are imported or copied to a new file system on the remote storage.
- **Upper path:** All but the *most important* VMs are deleted from the local file system.
- **Middle path (previously lower path):** VMs are exported from one file system of the remote storage directly to another file system on the remote storage using service console-based VCB or other service console-based backup tools, including Vizioncore's ESXRanger Pro product.
- **Lower path (this is the new path or Path 5):** If a SAN is capable of doing a LUN snap or LUN-to-LUN copy, it is now possible to copy the complete LUN

443

using just the SAN software. ESX is unaware of this behavior. However, the caveat is that this produces a crash-consistent backup, whereas the other methods do not.

The LUN snap or LUN-to-LUN copy procedure starts by mirroring the data from one LUN to another LUN, when the mirror is fully built and consistent, creating an instantaneous copy of a LUN with no impact on the ESX Server that would snap it off from the primary LUN. The LUN-to-LUN copy would be crash consistent and happen while VMs are running. Now here is the tricky part; because the new LUN houses a VMFS, and thus all the VMDKs, another ESX Server is required to access the new LUN so that the VMDKs can be exported to a local disk and from there be dropped to tape. This backup processing ESX Server would in general not be used for anything else and may belong to its own farm. For ESX versions earlier than 3.0, a method to transfer the VM configuration files would need to be added, too, but that is a small chunk of data to transfer off the production ESX Servers compared to the VMDKs and could be set up to be transferred only when the files change.

A crash-consistent backup is one in which the data written to the VMDKs has been halted as if the VM has crashed. Therefore, all backups that are crash consistent have the same chance of being rebooted as if the VM has crashed. One solution to this problem is to quiesce the VMDKs prior to the LUN mirror copy being completed, which would require some way to communicate from the SAN to the ESX Servers. The creation of a snapshot, which VCB does, will quiesce the VMDK so that it is safe to copy. Unfortunately, disk quiescing only happens in Windows, NetWare, and a few other types of VMs, but not necessarily Linux. It also requires VMware Tools to be installed. It is possible, however, to write your own quiescing tools to be run when the VM is placed into snapshot mode.

Additional Hot Site Backup Paths

Figure 12.3 demonstrates multiple methods to create a hot site from the original ESX environment. A hot site is limited in distance by the technology used to copy data from one location to another. There are three methods to copy data from site to site: via Fibre, via network, and via sneaker. In addition to the four existing paths, we can now add the paths covered in this section.

Path 6, depicted by the leftmost dash-dot-dot gray line, is the copying of local remote storage to similar remote storage at a hot site. Path 6 picks up where Path 3 ends and adds on the transfer of a full LUN from one remote storage device to another remote storage device using Dark Fibre, Fibre Channel over IP, or standard networking methods. After the LUN has been copied to the remote storage, Path 2 or Path 3 could once more be put into use at the hot site to create more backups.

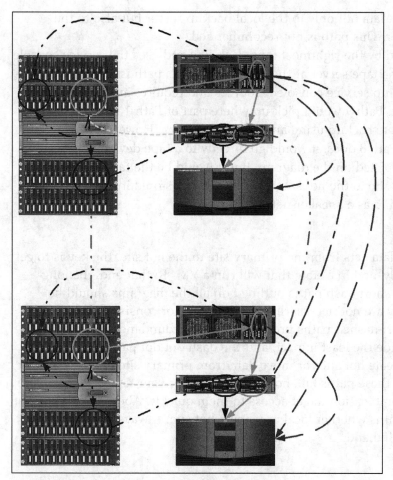

Figure 12.3   Enterprise class SAN hot site and remote backup options
Visio templates for image courtesy of Hewlett-Packard.

Path 7, depicted by the rightmost dash-dot-dot gray line, is the copying of the local ESX storage to a remote location using a secure network copy mechanism. Path 7 picks up where Path 1, 2, or even 3 leave off and uses standard network protocols to get the data onto a backup server on the hot site. From the backup server at the hot site, the VMs could then be restored to the hot site datastores waiting to be enabled in case of failure. Or from there they could be sent to a remote tape device.

Path 8 is depicted by the long-dash, short-dash line and uses the service console of the ESX Server to create the backup described in Path 7. This is not recommended because you do not want to tie up service console resources with a lengthy network traversal. Path 8 picks up where part of Path 1 finishes and would initiate a copy of the data not only to the local backup server but also to the remote backup server. This path is not recommended.

Path 9 is depicted by the rightmost long-dash line and uses the service console to write directly to the tape server at the remote site. This path is not recommended because it will tie up service console resources and requires an IP-based tape device at the hot site. Path 9 would pick up where part of Path 1 finishes and would initiate a remote backup using an IP-based network. However, instead of going to a disk like Path 8 does, it would go directly to a tape device.

Path 10 is not depicted on the diagram, but it would be the taking of backup tapes from the main site to the hot site to be restored or stored in secure storage. This is often referred to as a sneaker-net approach.

Summary of Backup

No matter how the data gets from the primary site to the hot site, the key is to get it there quickly, safely, and in a state that will run a VM. To that end, the long-dash and long-dash, short-dash paths outlined on all the diagrams should be avoided because they are not necessarily very fast, safe, or consistent. The green or solid line and short-dashed paths provide the most redundancy, whereas the dash-dot paths provide the least impact, and the dash-dot-dot paths provide the better methods to create hot sites or move data from primary site to hot site short of sneaker net. If all these paths fail, however, remember your tapes sitting offsite in a vault and the combination to get access to them quickly. Above all, *always* test your backups and paths whether local or using a hot site. Always remember, backup and DR go hand in hand.

Business Continuity

BC with ESX can be accomplished in several fashions. Just like backups, BC has multiple paths that it can take. Some of these paths are automated, whereas others require human intervention. One of the ideas behind BC is to provide a way for the business to continue uninterrupted and the VMware cluster technology provides a part of this by the implementation of VMware DRS and VMware HA. Where DR-level backups are generally geared toward the re-creation of the environment, BC is the application of clustering technology to prevent the need for such time-consuming restoration. This is achieved using VMware HA but also through the use of preconfigured hot sites that can come online in a fraction of the full restoration time. Our methods discussed earlier implement hot sites by using backup means. However, hot servers or servers in the datacenter that do not do anything until they are needed are other options. VMware HA covers the latter case. VMware HA is a high-availability-based solution that will, when an ESX

Server crashes, boot the VMs running there onto other ESX Servers either randomly (according to VMware DRS rules) or by using defined placement and boot order rules. The HPSIM VMM plug-in module also provides a similar HA capability by specifying an alternative host on which to run the VMs. Although VMware HA is only available for ESX 3, all versions can benefit from the HPSIM VMM alternative host method.

Outside of VMware HA, a myriad of other BC options are available. These include having as many redundant components as possible in different places within the datacenter, building, or campus, and there are multiple paths to all these devices from the ESX Servers. This leads to a much higher cost in and availability of hardware, but it will be the difference between a short service interruption and an absolute disaster. Consider the case of an ESX Server crashing with smoke pouring out of a vent. If you had invested in VMware HA, the software would automatically boot the VMs on another system. However, if you purchased a HP C-class blade in a RAID blade configuration, the ESX Server would fail over using a complete hardware solution. This leads to the question of which is better, hardware or software solutions. And the answer is, as always, it depends on the cost benefit. This same HP C-class blade has one limitation, the designated RAID blade must be in the same chassis of the failing node, and they must both share disks on a disk blade. This limits the amount of processing power to the blade chassis; and what happens if the chassis itself fails?

Many sites keep identical preinstalled hardware locked in a closet to solve some of these problems. However, it is your disaster to recover from, so think of all the solutions and draft the plan for both DR and BC appropriate for you.

The Tools

Now that the theory is explained, what tools are available for performing the tasks? Although each family of enterprise class remote storage has its own names for the capability to make LUN-to-LUN copies, refer to the SAN compatibility documentation to determine what is and is not supported, because it might turn out that the hot-copy mechanism for your SAN is not supported by any version of ESX. For example, HP SANs Business Copy and Continuous Access are supported, as is EMC SANs Hot Copy.

Beyond the remote storage–to–remote storage copies, many other tools are available from VMware and various vendors. These, in most cases, require some form of agent to be used to create the backup and place it on a data store associated with the tool. All these tools must first place a running VM in a delta mode (snapshot or REDO), which changes the file to which disk writes occur so that the backup software can make a copy of the primary VMDK, as in Figure 12.4. When the backup finishes, the delta is committed, and once more the primary VMDK is now used. The delta file grows over time as more data is written to it and grows in 15MB chunks to reduce SCSI-2 Reservation conflicts. However, because the delta file is really a FIFO and not a true VMDK, it is much slower and therefore dictates that a backup should occur when the VM is relatively inactive. And finally, the longer a VM is in a delta mode, the slower it will run, and the larger the delta file, which implies more locks. Each SCSI disk associated with a VMDK should be backed up separately to reduce the overall time spent in delta mode. Now, because we discussed with snapshots in Chapter 8, "Configuring ESX from a Host Connection," it is possible to have a tree of delta files for every VM. In this case, most tools will not work, including VMware Consolidated Backup and Vizioncore's ESXRanger Pro products. They require all deltas or snapshots to be deleted first. These situations may require a specialized backup script to be used. In addition, these tools will not back up templates, and those also require a specialized backup script.

Figure 12.4 depicts delta mode processing for ESX version 3 and earlier versions. In previous versions, delta mode was really REDO mode. Deltas in ESX 3 are now created by the snapshot mechanism.

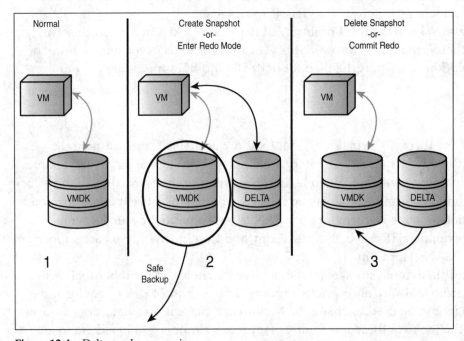

Figure 12.4 Delta mode processing

Once in delta mode, if the disk was not quiesced, a crash-consistent backup is created, which implies that a boot of a restored VMDK will boot as if the VM had crashed. Quiescing disks is limited to Windows VMs and only those that have snapshots. In addition, LUN-to-LUN or remote storage–to–remote storage copies also produce crash-consistent backups. A crash-consistent backup, depending on how it was achieved, should not be restored to anything other than a VMFS because the VMDKs are sparse files or monolithic files that have a beginning marker, some data, and an end marker and not much else. Restoration of such files to non-VMFS can result in loss of data. However, if the VM is first exported, resides on an NFS data store, or is in 2Gb sparse disk format, it can be restored to any file system and imported back into ESX with no possibility of data loss. With Fibre connections, it is not even necessary for the host that places the VM into delta mode to be the host that actually does the backup. This generally requires extra scripting, but it is possible for a host that is running the VM to place the VM into delta mode and then signal a backup host that the backup can be made. When the backup is completed, another signal is made to the running host to commit the backup. In this way, the backup host offloads the work from the running ESX Server. The signals could even be reversed so that the backup host does all the work and calls the running host only as necessary. Following here is an example script of this behavior for version 2.5. As for ESX version 3, this script is necessary only when the VMware Consolidated Backup proxy server is not in use or other tools such as Vizioncore's ESXRanger Pro or HPSIM's VMM are not in use.

Simple Backup Scripts

The following are by far the simplest backup scripts that can be written using the tools intrinsic to ESX. For ESX version 3, the script uses VCB, and for ESX version 2, the script uses vmsnap.pl. Although the latter script exists in ESX 3, it points the user to the VCB functionality and does nothing else. Some VM configurations, however, will still need similar functionality. These are for those VMs that have snapshots disabled.

ESX version 3

The VCB tool has a command-line component for the ESX service console and a Windows 2003 Enterprise server. The VCB command-line tools will export VMs, create snapshots, and access the contents of and complete virtual disks for a VM. VCB provides a way to access and backup all VMs in an organized fashion for all ESX Servers and VMs using the VCB proxy server and any version 3 ESX Server.

In addition to implementing VCB, ESX version 3 implements a form of VMware Workstation version 5 snapshot capability. VCB makes exclusive use of the snapshot functionality to make copies of VMDKs before a backup of the snapshot occurs. Under the hood, this keeps delta mode to a minimum and results in a copy of the VMDK that can then be exported or mounted to produce a valuable backup from what is now referred to as a proxy server. The proxy server in the preceding figures is not only the backup server but also forwards the backup images to another server, which talks to a tape or hot site. For example, in Figure 12.1, the proxy server is the second machine from the top on the right side of the image. This proxy server is a Windows machine or another ESX Server that has access to any of the storage devices used by ESX so that it can use the VCB commands to either mount the VMDK to the proxy server to aid in backup or export the VMDK to another location to create a backup.

If the VMDK is a physical mode raw disk map (RDM), a snapshot cannot be made, and the only method of backup of the RDM is to use the traditional methods available: backup from within the host or SAN copies. A virtual mode RDM still works as expected. If the VMDK is an independent disk, snapshots will not work, and the traditional methods to make backups must be used. ESX version 2.5.x and earlier use the independent disk VMDK format, which requires the REDO mode capabilities provided by `vmsnap.pl`. Because snapshots are used by VCB, the disabling of the snapshot features will keep VCB from working.

ESX version 3 also includes a method of scheduling automatic snapshots to make a point-in-time backup of the guest that can then be explicitly exported using VCB, and then dropped to tape, media, or copied across to a hot site after the snapshot is fully built. This functionality will work with running and stopped VMs, which is an advance over ESX version 2.5.x. Automating a snapshot offers a method to save old data from being overwritten until the snapshot is deleted or merged with the previous snapshot. Currently, VCB-based backup tools will not work if there are existing snapshots, so this functionality has limited usage, except perhaps to automatically trigger an action to occur. No alarm will trigger when a snapshot is made, but using the open source VI Perl interface it is possible to poll for this state and take an appropriate action. It is a complex method that most tools that hook into VCB already do for you.

The other option is to use VCB with the provided scripts or write your own to back up the VMs using VCB exclusively. The scripts provided are for TSM and Veritas Networker and BackupExec. The scripts run from a Windows proxy server to access the VMs using remote VCB tools that also exist on every ESX Server. The VCB scripts provide pre- and post-backup work to be done in relation to the backup of the VM in question. However, these scripts are not useful if the VM's VMDKs are in independent mode.

VCB consolidates the need for licenses to just the proxy server. That way, if there are 300 VMs running, there is no need for 300 VM or 10 or so ESX Server licenses of the backup client. This cost savings can be significant, and the single location to produce backups, the proxy server, aids in operational issues by placing the burden of backup there so that backups no longer impact the performance of the VM or ESX Server and cuts down locking to a minimum.

The following script works from the ESX 3 service console. This code locks the BACKUP volume, and if the lock exists, does not perform the backup. When the lock exists, it uses the service console vcbMounter command to run the backup:

```
#!/bin/sh

PATH=/usr/sbin:/bin:/usr/bin
export PATH

BACKUP=/vmfs/volumes/BACKUP/vcb

if [ -e $BACKUP/.lock ]
then
        exit
fi
for x in `/usr/bin/vmware-cmd -l ¦ sort -r`
do
        /bin/touch $BACKUP/.lock
        y=`/bin/basename $x .vmx`
        #### Keep two backups, uncomment the following two lines
        #/bin/rm -rf $BACKUP/${y}.bak
        #/bin/mv $BACKUP/$y $BACKUP/${y}.bak
        /usr/sbin/vcbMounter -a name:$y -r $BACKUP/$y
done
/bin/touch $BACKUP/.done
```

By uncommenting the two lines inside the for loop, it is possible to keep two copies of the backups. This is a simplistic approach to backups using two common ESX commands (vmware-cmd, vcbMounter). Note that normally the vcbMounter command takes a host, username, and password, but these are hard-coded into the /etc/vmware/backuptools.conf file, which for security reasons should just have read-only permissions for the root user.

ESX Version 2

The vmsnap_all and vmsnap.pl scripts provide a scripted mechanism to create a crash-consistent backup image that can be placed on any file system, because the process followed is to place the VM into REDO mode, export the VM, and commit the REDO. Because the VM was exported and not just copied, any file system will work. Many vendor tools make use of the vmsap.pl functionality local to the ESX Server to make backups. However, vmsnap_all and vmsnap.pl will not work on non-running VMs, and those need to be exported and backed up using a traditional script.

The only change to the ESX v3 script presented above for earlier versions is to change the vcbMounter command to use vmsnap.pl with the appropriate arguments to send backups to local storage.

However, if the backup of a nonrunning VM is made to look the same as the ones produced by vmsnap.pl, the vmres.pl script can be used to restore them. The following script produces an ESX v2.5 backup of a nonrunning VM that will work with vmres.pl:

```
#!/bin/sh
VMX=$1
if [ -f $VMX ]
then
        vmd=`dirname $VMX`
      vmp=`basename $vmd`
      mkdir /vmimages/localbackup/$vmp
      cp $VMX /vmimages/localbackup/$vmp
      cp $vmd/nvram /vmimages/localbackup/$vmp/$vmp.nvram
      cp $vmd/vmware.log.* /vmimages/localbackup/$vmp/
      # Get list of SCSI devices
      for x in `grep scsi $VMX¦grep : ¦grep present¦ grep TRUE ¦ awk
'{print $1}'`
    do
            y=`basename $x .present`
            z=`grep $y.name $VMX ¦ awk '{print $3}'`
```

```
          vmkfstools -e $vmp.$vmp.vmdk $z
      done
fi
```

ESX Version Earlier Than 2.5.0

Before ESX version 2.5.0, users and vendors had to create their own scripts. These scripts would place a running VM in REDO mode and either copy the data to another VMFS or export to another file system. Often, these VMs were backed up to tape directly from the VMFS, which will produce a tape image that can only be restored to another VMFS, which limits its functionality.

Local Tape Devices

Other than these methods, ESX does not have the tools necessary to directly control tape libraries or tapes installed by default. Therefore, these are not recommended to be used. Local tape devices and libraries require two things: a specific Adaptec SCSI HBA and software to control the robot or tape. The software is extremely easy to find, but once installed is not really supported by VMware or other support organizations. Either way, when there is a problem with the local tape or tape library device, the ESX Server often has to be rebooted, and although it is possible to remove and reload the appropriate kernel module, some devices are not fully reconfigured unless they are seen at boot time. This is a failing in the COS version, the drivers used, and how the device or devices are allocated. On ESX version 3, all devices are assigned to the VMkernel, which implies a failure of the device for some reason could still require a reboot of the ESX Server. Using tape devices and libraries attached to remote archive servers is the recommended choice if possible.

In Chapter 4, it is suggested that you install `mtx`, which is a tool to manipulate tape libraries. MTX is vital to manipulate tape libraries from within ESX. But it often requires some form of scripting to use it properly. Specifically, there is a combination of tools necessary to properly manipulate tapes and the robotics of the libraries. The combination is MT and MTX. MT is found on the ESX media. Both of these tools use SCSI protocols to communicate with the tape and robot, respectively. Included is a simple script that can be used to manipulate a robot and tape device to flip tapes as necessary. If you *must* roll your own backup solution that uses a local tape device, this is invaluable and is often an inherent part of other solutions.

> **Caution**
>
> Do not use this script unless you absolutely have to do backups from the ESX service console.
>
> Using tape devices from the ESX service console could result in the need to reboot the ESX server if there are tape device errors, and the same holds true if using tape devices via pass-thru mode from a VM.

The following script takes two arguments, one to specify the tape device to use and the second is the tape volume to use. This is exactly the arguments the Linux dump command issues to a tape-changing script when dump is given the -F option. Before proceeding, it is best to become familiar with dump and other backup tools. There are several references available in the "References" element at the end of this book. In addition to taking arguments, the script uses three files to define its actions, all of which are located in /usr/local/etc. Table 12.1 provides the names of the files and what they do.

Table 12.1

Filenames for MTX Script	
Filename	**Usage**
/usr/local/etc/slot	Defines the current tape library slot being used
/usr/local/etc/maxslot	Defines the maximum slots available in the tape library
/usr/local/etc/history	A log file that lists the history of tapes used

The basic use of the following script is to rewind a given tape, eject it if necessary, and then use the robot to unload the current tape, store it in the proper slot, and reload the tape device with a new tape. When the new tape is loaded into the tape device, the script waits until it is available for write before returning to whatever program called it, which could be another script, a tool such as dump, or something else:

```ksh
#!/bin/ksh -x
# Manipulate Tape Library and Tape device.


# Get args
dev=$1
```

```
vol=$2
echo "$dev $vol"

# read slot files
SLOT=/usr/local/etc/slot
MAXS=/usr/local/etc/maxslot
HIST=/usr/local/etc/history
mslo=`/bin/cat $MAXS`
slot=`/bin/cat $SLOT`

# Find the device number
d=`echo $dev¦ /usr/bin/wc -c¦/bin/sed 's/[\t ]//g'`
let d=$d-1
dnum=`echo $dev ¦ /usr/bin/cut -c $d`
# let dnum=$dnum-1

# force rewind device
# Rewind and unload tape:
skiptape=1
while [ $skiptape -eq 1 ]
do
        st=`echo $dev¦/bin/sed 's/n//'`
        /bin/mt -f $st rewind
#        /bin/mt -f $st offline
        /usr/local/sbin/mtx unload $slot $dnum
        let slot=$slot+1

        # wrap for now. Be sure we are on even borders however!
        if [ $slot -gt $mslo ]
        then
                if [ $vol -eq 0 ]
                then
                        slot=1
                else
                        # if in a volume 'abort'
                        echo 0 > $SLOT
```

```
        exit 2
    fi
fi


# keep track of where we are
echo $slot > $SLOT
if [ ! -z "$TAPELABEL" ]
then
    echo "$slot      $TAPELABEL      $vol" >> $HIST
fi


# load tape.
/usr/local/sbin/mtx load $slot $dnum


# only release when tape is available for write
rc="false"
i=0
while [ Z"$rc" != Z"true" ]
do
    let i=$i+1
    /bin/sleep 10
    msg=`/bin/mt -f $st status | /usr/bin/tail -1`
    rc=`echo $msg | /usr/bin/awk '/WR_PROT/ {print "skip"}'`
    if [ Z"$rc" = Z"skip" ]
    then
        rc = "true";
    else
        rc=`echo $msg | /usr/bin/awk '/ONLINE/ {print "true"}'`
    fi
    # reached timeout of 120 seconds
    if [ $i -gt 24 ]
    then
        exit 2
    fi
done
rc=`echo $msg | /usr/bin/awk '/WR_PROT/ {print "skip"}'`
```

```
    if [ Z"$rc" != Z"skip" ]
    then
          skiptape=0;
    fi
done

# this is goodness
sleep 20
exit 0
```

In addition to being able to roll your own via the service console, it is also possible to connect a VM to a local tape device. In this case, a VM is attached to a local tape device using the SCSI generic devices available when building a VM. The virtual SCSI device ID must match the physical SCSI device ID in these cases, and the device needs to be multitarget and not multi-LUN; in other words, multiple device IDs should be present and not multiple LUNs for the same device ID. The latter is not supported under any version of ESX. However, a VM attached to the local SCSI tape or tape library should have its SCSI HBA assigned to the VMs, as is the case with ESX version 3, so that there is no contention on the device.

Best Practices for Local Tape Devices
Do not use local tape devices; if it becomes absolutely necessary, be sure to understand the impact on the local ESX Server and plan VM deployments accordingly.

Vendor Tools

A small number of vendors produce backup tools specifically for ESX. Some are designed specifically for ESX, whereas others can be used with ESX. Pretty much any current backup tool that has a Linux client will work with ESX in some form. However, tools such as VizionCore vRanger and HPSIM VMM have specific code for use with ESX. No matter which tool is chosen, there is a first step for all the backup tools. See Chapter 5, "Storage with ESX," and open up the firewall to allow the appropriate ports to be used before performing any backup and installing any necessary agents. The next step is to install the appropriate agents, if any, and then to perform a test backup to verify everything is set up properly.

ESXRanger

ESXRanger has a graphical mechanism for creating backups and a series of dialog boxes to use when scheduling backups to run. It can also make multiple versions of backups so that different VM states can be restored as necessary. For ESX versions earlier than version 3, ESXRanger uses the vmsnap.pl functionality to perform all backups. For ESX version 3, ESXRanger (see Figure 12.5) uses snapshots and implements its own form of VCB. However, it will work with the legitimate VCB.

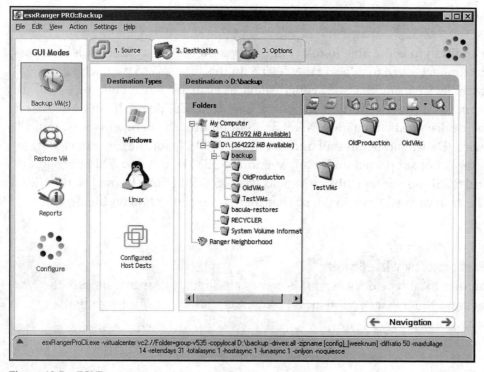

Figure 12.5 ESXRanger

HPSIM VMM

In addition to being able to schedule backups of a VM, it is possible to set up a failover host for when an ESX Server that is a part of DRLB dies. This functionality, discussed in the preceding chapter, makes this web-based tool extremely powerful. To use VMM, the ESX Server must be registered in HPSIM (see Figure 12.6) and the VMM component properly licensed and available. Without this, HPSIM only monitors the hardware of the ESX Server.

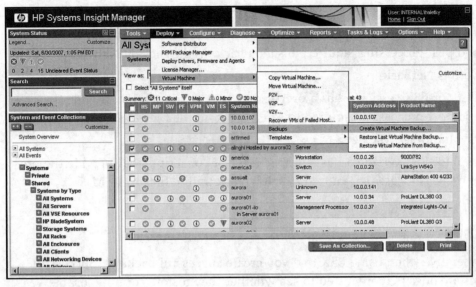

Figure 12.6   HPSIMM VMM

Other Tools

Another set of tools requires additions to make them work; unfortunately, the specific scripts for the tools may not exist prepackaged by VMware or any other vendor. VMware and vendors offer suggestions on their use, but the final scripting could be left to the implementer. Each of these tools has a method to schedule a backup that is initiated via an agent running on the backup client (VCB proxy server), and these agents will make a call out to a local script to do anything that is necessary to do prior to the backup occurring. In these cases, it is best to use the VMware-provided scripts to create a safe backup of the VMDK before letting the agent transfer the data to the backup server. And finally, the backup agents call another local script to complete any tasks necessary after the backup has occurred. In addition to often requiring specific scripting, these tools require different versions of the application to be used for different versions of ESX. All of these tools work from within the VM, and most will work from the service console if they are at the proper version of the tool for the version of ESX, and all will work with VCB given proper pre- and post-backup processing scripts. Examples of these other tools include the following:

- **HP Data Protector**

   There are no prepackaged VCB scripts for use by HP Data Protector.

- **Legato Networker**

  VCB for ESX version 3 has a prepackaged set of scripts that provide the pre- and post-processing required to safely back up the files by Networker.

- **Veritas NetBackup**

  VCB for ESX version 3 has a prepackaged set of scripts that provide the pre- and post-processing required to safely back up the files by NetBackup.

- **Tivoli Storage Manager**

  VCB for ESX version 3 has a prepackaged set of scripts that provide the pre- and post-processing required to safely back up the files by TSM.

Conclusion

It is imperative when using ESX that you create successful backups. Successful backups are ones that are tested to see whether they restore running, usable VMs. The goal of this chapter was to present what is available to the users of ESX and the advanced capabilities of VMware clusters in terms of BC. I may have used ESXRanger and HPSIM VMM to create backups in addition to the intrinsic tools, but they are by no means the only methods available. Just be sure that a good DR and BC plan exists that covers all the possible disasters and that the plan is implemented and tested as often as necessary.

Epilogue

The Future of Virtualization

Closing a book of this type is nearly impossible because the nature of virtualization is changing almost daily. VMware is releasing version 3.5 of their premier virtualization product, VMware Virtual Infrastructure, with updates for new hardware and software packages. The virtualization news is full of new add-on products, partnerships, and competing products such as VirtualIron and XenEnterprise Server. There is also news in the security arena; for instance, the Black Hat conference spent many hours discussing how to escape from a VM to the host OS. There currently exists at least one virtualization product for every type of hardware available. The field is changing rapidly.

But let's look at some specifics. Processor makers currently have plans to produce eight core processors, and there are already quad-core processors available. A simple 2-CPU machine can now theoretically handle eight VMs per core, which implies that an 8-core, 2-CPU machine can theoretically handle 128 VMs. Imagine the power available with an 8-core 8-CPU system? That is more pure power than ever imagined before, and our discussions on cache and hardware in Chapter 1, "System Considerations," will prove to be invaluable. With eight cores per CPU, shared cache would be necessary to keep costs down, yet would not be desirable in the virtualized world. Shared hardware code caches, may now be necessary as opposed to a pure instruction/memory cache. This would move ESX's existing abilities down into the hardware. Hardware Virtual Machines are now available but this lowers the hypervisor into the hardware, not the caching mechanisms.

Throughout this book, I have mentioned that we should consider each VMware ESX Server to be a datacenter. With the advent of eight-core two-, four-, and eight-CPU systems, each VMware ESX Server and cluster can contain all the current processing power of most small business datacenters today, and just a few of these massive machines could be the datacenters of even larger businesses. Once I was asked to design a virtualization system to condense as many machines as possible within an extremely large datacenter.

Outside of a few specific UNIX machines, the resultant design would have had five full racks of systems and five full racks of storage in a datacenter half the size of a football field. That was over a year ago. Today, those same five full racks of systems with the latest hardware would be serious overkill for the same uses. And with judicious use of UNIX virtualization products such as Sun Containers and HP VM, it is even possible to condense those systems to single racks of computers. However, would the cost be worth it in the short term? Would everyone want all those eggs in very few baskets?

The business needs that dictate virtualization is necessary will not change; however, the use of virtualization will become the norm. As more hardware failover solutions are created (HP C Class blades with RAID blade functionality) virtualization will also get a boost. However, even though the hardware changes, virtualization security and software will also change.

Black Hat 2007 discussed how to "Escape the VM" and access the host OS. Granted, all their tests were run on VMware Server, and VMware Workstation, but the concepts of how to do this will apply to the datacenter, too. Was the virtualization software actually broken to escape the VM? No. The escapees made use of existing errors in the underlying host OS that were propagated to the VM using file-sharing technology. A properly configured virtualization server then should not serve up files to the VMs, which is the default setting. In other words, someone found a way to take advantage of an improperly configured system. Is this the only security risk? Absolutely not; you must be ever vigilant and check for new issues constantly.

Security for VMware will improve, as will other features. For example, the advent of VMware 3i will once more change the face of virtualization but not the basics discussed in this book. Although 3i does away with the full service console, it still has a CLI for setting up various aspects of the virtualization server.

In addition to new virtualization products, there are new limits to virtualization appearing. For example, the number of files per VMFS has been measured at 30,710 files before the VMFS fails to write files. Could a hacker use this to create a denial-of-service attack? Do we do it ourselves by not properly removing older log files as the monitoring recipe suggests in Chapter 4, "Auditing, Monitoring, and Securing"?

The virtualization community is growing, too. The VMware and Xen community forums are widely used to ask questions from newbies and experts alike concerning problems with virtualization. As an alternative to long holdtimes for support, the forums provide quick answers that are searchable. It also gives administrators an opportunity to find out that someone else has had the same issue and there is a solution or workaround. I am very active in the Security and Compliance forums.

The advent of the latest versions of Xen, Virtual Iron, and Oracle VM, gives the virtualization marketplace more choices, too. Although VMware is by far the leader, Xen has an ardent following, too, and that is growing daily. Should you look into Xen as an option when thinking about virtualization? I think so. Although some of the specifics in this book do not apply to Xen, the concepts do. The theory and subsystems are the same between VMware and Xen. There are only so many ways to do the same thing. The choice of which to use, however, depends on the application mix you use and the tests that can be run against each.

VMware now has a performance suite that is independent of VMware or Xen and can be used on either virtualizations system. It simulates a known load of applications in any environment. Although it might not simulate your exact application mix, it provides enough that performance can finally be listed in specifications for virtualization. This is a big win; however, be careful, because the application mix in use by your site should still be tested.

If there is anything to take from this book, take away the following: With planning and understanding of all the different subsystems that affect virtualization, it is easy to be successful with virtualization within the datacenter. Plan ahead, run the appropriate tests, and go forward and virtualize!

Appendix A

Security Script

Listing A.1 is a shell script that can be used to increase the security of an ESX Server such that the CISscan and Bastille assessment tools will score higher and the system will be more secure. The script will increase security such that normal users will not be able to adversely affect the system, and many unnecessary and insecure system protocols are completely disabled. Note that USERNAME must be replaced with an administrative user of your choice.

Listing A.1

A Script That Will Work for ESX Version 3

```
# sudo
/bin/cat "%wheel ALL=  /*bin/*,/usr/*bin/*,!/bin/*sh,!/bin/vi /etc/sudoers" >>
➥/etc/sudoers
# cis-scan
# Initial score is: 6.30/10.00
#
# Download cis-secure and install in /opt/cis once installed uncomment the
# following lines:
#echo "/usr/lib/vmware/bin/vmkload_app" >> /opt/cis/cis_ruler_suid_programs_redhat_RHEL3
#echo "/usr/lib/vmware/bin-debug/vmware-vmx" >>
➥/opt/cis/cis_ruler_suid_programs_redhat_RHEL3
#echo "/usr/lib/vmware/bin/vmware-vmx" >> /opt/cis/cis_ruler_suid_programs_redhat_RHEL3
#echo "/usr/lib/vmware/bin-debug/vmkload_app" >>
➥/opt/cis/cis_ruler_suid_programs_redhat_RHEL3
#echo "/usr/lib/vmware/bin/vmkping" >> /opt/cis/cis_ruler_suid_programs_redhat_RHEL3
```

```
#echo "/usr/sbin/vmware-authd" >> /opt/cis/cis_ruler_suid_programs_redhat_RHEL3
#
# Start of script
/bin/cat >> /etc/ssh/sshd_config << EOF
Protocol 2
Banner /etc/motd
EOF
/bin/sed 's/#.*Host \*/Host \*/' </etc/ssh/ssh_config > /tmp/ssh_config
mv /tmp/ssh_config /etc/ssh/ssh_config
/sbin/chkconfig telnet off
/sbin/chkconfig ftp off
/bin/sed '2s/^/umask 077/' </etc/rc.d/init.d/microcode_ctl> /tmp/microcode_ctl
/bin/mv /tmp/microcode_ctl /etc/rc.d/init.d/microcode_ctl
/usr/sbin/usermod -G wheel elh
/sbin/chkconfig —level 0123456 gpm off
/bin/cat >> /etc/sysctl.conf << EOF
net.ipv4.conf.default.secure_redirects=0
net.ipv4.conf.all.secure_redirects=0
net.ipv4.conf.all.rp_filter=1
net.ipv4.icmp_echo_ignore_broadcasts=1
net.ipv4.conf.all.accept_redirects=0
net.ipv4.conf.default.accept_source_route=0
net.ipv4.tcp_syncookies=1
net.ipv4.conf.default.accept_redirects=0
net.ipv4.tcp_max_syn_backlog=4096
net.ipv4.conf.all.send_redirects=0
net.ipv4.conf.default.send_redirects=0
EOF
/bin/chmod 600 /etc/sysctl.conf
/sbin/sysctl -p
/bin/sed '/boot/s/defaults/defaults,nodev/' < /etc/fstab > /tmp/fstab
/bin/sed '/vmimages/s/defaults/defaults,nodev/' < /tmp/fstab > /etc/fstab
/bin/sed '/var\/log/s/defaults/defaults,nodev/' < /etc/fstab > /tmp/fstab
/bin/sed '/cdrom/s/kudzu/kudzu,nosuid,nodev/' < /tmp/fstab > /etc/fstab
/bin/sed '/floppy/s/kudzu/kudzu,nosuid,nodev/' < /etc/fstab > /tmp/fstab
/bin/mv /tmp/fstab /etc/fstab
```

```
/bin/sed '/0660 <floppy>/s/^/#/' < /etc/security/console.perms > /tmp/console.perms
/bin/sed '/0600 <cdrom>/s/^/#/' < /tmp/console.perms > /etc/security/console.perms
/bin/sed '/0600 <pilot>/s/^/#/' < /etc/security/console.perms > /tmp/console.perms
/bin/sed '/0600 <jaz>/s/^/#/' < /tmp/console.perms > /etc/security/console.perms
/bin/sed '/0600 <zip>/s/^/#/' < /etc/security/console.perms > /tmp/console.perms
/bin/sed '/0600 <ls120>/s/^/#/' < /tmp/console.perms > /etc/security/console.perms
/bin/sed '/0600 <camera>/s/^/#/' < /etc/security/console.perms > /tmp/console.perms
/bin/sed '/0600 <memstick>/s/^/#/' < /tmp/console.perms > /etc/security/console.perms
/bin/sed '/0600 <flash>/s/^/#/' < /etc/security/console.perms > /tmp/console.perms
/bin/sed '/0600 <diskonkey>/s/^/#/' < /tmp/console.perms > /etc/security/console.perms
/bin/sed '/0600 <rem_ide>/s/^/#/' < /etc/security/console.perms > /tmp/console.perms
/bin/sed '/0600 <rio500>/s/^/#/' < /tmp/console.perms > /etc/security/console.perms
#/bin/sed '/server_args/s/-l -a/-l -a -d/' < /etc/xinetd.d/wu-ftpd > /tmp/wu-ftpd
#/bin/mv /tmp/wu-ftpd /etc/xinetd.d
#/bin/sed '/vpxuser/s/0:99999/7:90/' < /etc/shadow > /tmp/shadow
#/bin/mv /tmp/shadow /etc/shadow
#/bin/mkdir -p /home/vpxuser
#/bin/chmod 750 /home/vpxuser
#/bin/chown vpxuser /home/vpxuser
#/usr/sbin/usermod -d /home/vpxuser vpxuser
/bin/rpm -e —nodeps hotplug
echo 'root' > /etc/cron.allow
echo 'root' > /etc/at.allow
/bin/chmod 600 /etc/crontab
/bin/sed 's/}/     only_from          = 10.0.0.0\n}/' < /etc/xinetd.conf >
/tmp/xinetd.conf
/bin/mv /tmp/xinetd.conf /etc/xinetd.conf
grep -v 'tty7' /etc/securetty¦ grep -v 'tty8' ¦ grep -v 'tty9' ¦ grep -v 'tty10' ¦ grep
➥-v 'tty11' > /tmp/securetty
mv /tmp/securetty /etc/securetty
/bin/sed  '22s/^/~:S:wait:\/sbin\/sulogin/' < /etc/inittab > /tmp/inittab
mv /tmp/inittab /etc/inittab
/bin/sed '/nologin/d' < /etc/shells > /tmp/shells
/bin/mv /tmp/shells /etc/shells
#/bin/sed 's/PASS_MAX_DAYS     99999/PASS_MAX_DAYS     90/' < /etc/login.defs >
➥ /tmp/login.defs
```

```
/bin/sed 's/PASS_MIN_DAYS.*0/PASS_MIN_DAYS     7/' < /etc/login.defs > /tmp/login.defs
#/bin/sed 's/PASS_MIN_LEN    5/PASS_MIN_LEN    6/' < /etc/login.defs >
➤ /tmp/login.defs
/bin/mv /tmp/login.defs /etc/login.defs
/usr/sbin/usermod -s /sbin/nologin news
#/usr/sbin/usermod -s /sbin/nologin rpm
/bin/sed 's/umask 002/umask 077/' < /etc/bashrc > /tmp/bashrc
/bin/sed 's/umask 002/umask 077/' < /etc/csh.cshrc > /tmp/csh.cshrc
/bin/sed 's/umask 022/umask 077/' < /tmp/bashrc > /etc/bashrc
/bin/sed 's/umask 022/umask 077/' < /tmp/csh.cshrc > /etc/csh.cshrc
#/bin/sed '/ctrlaltdel/s/^/#/' < /etc/inittab > /tmp/inittab
/bin/sed '/pam_wheel.so use_uid/s/^#//' < /etc/pam.d/su > /tmp/su
/bin/mv /tmp/su /etc/pam.d/su
echo '*     soft     core     0' >> /etc/security/limits.conf
/bin/cat > /etc/motd << EOF
*****************************************************************************
                         NOTICE TO USERS
```

This computer system is the private property of its owner, whether
individual, corporate or government. It is for authorized use only.
Users (AUTHORIZED or UNAUTHORIZED) have no explicit or implicit
expectation of privacy.

Any or all uses of this system and all files on this system may be
intercepted, monitored, recorded, copied, audited, inspected, and
disclosed to your employer, to authorized site, government, and law
enforcement personnel, as well as authorized officials of government
agencies, both domestic and foreign.

By using this system, the user consents to such interception, monitoring,
recording, copying, auditing, inspection, and disclosure at the
discretion of such personnel or officials. Unauthorized or improper use
of this system may result in civil and criminal penalties and
administrative or disciplinary action, as appropriate. By continuing to
use this system you indicate your awareness of and consent to these terms

and conditions of use. LOG OFF IMMEDIATELY if you do not agree to the
conditions stated in this warning.

```
****************************************************************************
EOF
echo "AUTHORIZED USE ONLY" > /etc/issue
/bin/chmod o-w /opt/LGTOaam512/config/vmware-sites /opt/LGTOaam512/bin/dbwork.dbd
➥ /opt/LGTOaam512/bin/dbm_records51.dbd
#
# To increase security even more:
#     Password protect Grub — uncomment and fill in the proper MD5 password
#     created running grub-md5-crypt
#/bin/sed '/default=/s/^/password —md5 $1$lL.J51$2MlAp5n6aVSgzLLTiVikh0\n/' <
➥ /boot/grub/grub.conf > /tmp/grub.conf
#/bin/mv /tmp/grub.conf /boot/grub/grub.conf
#     Install sysstat
#     Install Bastille
# Finale score with EVERYTHING done: 9.45/10.00
# Bastille
# Initial score: 8.11/10.00
# Initial score after CIS Security: 8.68/10.00
echo "ALL: 10.0.0." >> /etc/hosts.allow
echo "ALL: ALL" >> /etc/hosts.deny
/bin/sed '5s/^/umask 077/' < /etc/profile > /tmp/profile
/bin/mv /tmp/profile /etc/profile
echo "umask 077" >> /etc/zprofile
/bin/sed '4s/^/umask 077/' < /etc/csh.login > /tmp/csh.login
/bin/mv /tmp/csh.login /etc/csh.login
/bin/sed '2s/^/umask 077/' < /root/.bash_profile > /tmp/.bash_profile
/bin/mv /tmp/.bash_profile /root/.bash_profile
/usr/sbin/userdel gopher
/usr/sbin/userdel games
/bin/chmod 600 /boot/grub/grub.conf
echo "console" > /etc/securetty
for x in /usr/sbin/ping6 /usr/sbin/traceroute /usr/sbin/traceroute6
➥/usr/sbin/usernetctl
```

```
 /usr/bin/rcp /usr/bin/rlogin /usr/bin/rsh /usr/bin/rdist /usr/bin/rexec
➥/usr/bin/rcp
 /usr/bin/at /bin/ping /bin/umount /usr/bin/smbmnt
do
     if [ -e $x ]
     then
          chmod u-s $x
     fi
done
for x in /bin/mt /bin/setserial /sbin/badblocks /sbin/ctrlaltdel /sbin/chkconfig
➥ /sbin/debugfs /sbin/depmod /sbin/dumpe2fs /sbin/fdisk /sbin/fsck
➥/sbin/fsck.minix
 /sbin/fsck.ext2 /sbin/halt /sbin/hdparm /sbin/hwclock /sbin/ifconfig
➥/sbin/ifdown
 /sbin/ifup /sbin/init /sbin/insmod /sbin/killall5 /sbin/mingetty
➥/sbin/mkbootdisk
 /sbin/mke2fs /sbin/mkfs /sbin/lilo /sbin/mkfs.minix
do
     if [ -e $x ]
     then
          chmod 750 $x
     fi
done
for x in /sbin/mkfs.ext2 /sbin/mkfs.msdos /sbin/mkinitrd /sbin/mkraid
➥/sbin/mkswap
 /sbin/modinfo /sbin/modprobe /sbin/portmap /sbin/quotaon /sbin/runlevel
➥/sbin/swapon
 /sbin/tune2fs /usr/bin/eject /usr/bin/minicom /usr/sbin/atd /usr/sbin/atrun
➥ /usr/sbin/crond /usr/sbin/edquota /usr/sbin/exportfs /usr/sbin/groupadd
➥ /usr/sbin/groupdel
do
     if [ -e $x ]
     then
          chmod 750 $x
     fi
done
```

```
for x in /usr/sbin/grpck /usr/sbin/grpconv /usr/sbin/grpunconv /usr/sbin/imapd
➥ /usr/sbin/ipop2d /usr/sbin/ipop3d /usr/sbin/logrotate
➥/usr/sbin/mouseconfig
 /usr/sbin/newusers /usr/sbin/nmbd /usr/sbin/ntpdate /usr/sbin/ntpq
➥/usr/sbin/ntptime
 /usr/sbin/ntptrace /usr/sbin/ntsysv /usr/sbin/pppd /usr/sbin/pwck
➥/usr/sbin/pwconv
 /usr/sbin/pwunconv /usr/sbin/in.telnetd
do
     if [ -e $x ]
     then
          chmod 750 $x
     fi
done
for x in /usr/sbin/rdev /usr/sbin/rotatelogs /usr/sbin/rpc.mountd
➥/usr/sbin/rpc.nfsd
 /usr/sbin/rpc.rquotad /usr/sbin/rpcinfo /usr/sbin/setup /usr/sbin/showmount
➥ /usr/sbin/smbd /sbin/syslogd /usr/sbin/tcpd /usr/sbin/tcpdump
/usr/sbin/timeconfig
➥ /usr/sbin/tmpwatch /usr/sbin/useradd /usr/sbin/userdel /usr/sbin/usermod
/usr/sbin/vipw
➥ /sbin/stinit /usr/sbin/groupmod
do
     if [ -e $x ]
     then
          chmod 750 $x
     fi
done
for x in /sbin/klogd /usr/sbin/lpc /sbin/rpc.statd /usr/sbin/squid /usr/sbin/tunelp
do
     if [ -e $x ]
     then
          chmod 750 $x
     fi
done
for x in /sbin/dump /sbin/restore
```

```
do
      if [ -e $x ]
      then
            chmod 770 $x
      fi
done
for x in /usr/bin/gpasswd /sbin/netreport /usr/sbin/userhelper /usr/sbin/usernetctl
do
      if [ -e $x ]
      then
            chmod o-rwx $x
      fi
done
for x in /usr/sbin/makemap /usr/sbin/quotastats /usr/sbin/repquota
do
      if [ -e $x ]
      then
            chmod 550 $x
      fi
done
/bin/sed "s/'rexec', 'rlogin', 'rsh','login','shell'/'rexec', 'rlogin', 'rsh'/"
➥< /usr/lib/Bastille/test_AccountSecurity.pm > /tmp/test_AccountSecurity.pm
/bin/mv /tmp/test_AccountSecurity.pm /usr/lib/Bastille/test_AccountSecurity.pm
/bin/chmod 755 /usr/lib/Bastille/test_AccountSecurity.pm
#
# install psacct RPM and enable
#
/usr/sbin/bastille -n —assessnobrowser
/bin/rm /tmp/bashrc /tmp/console.perms /tmp/csh.cshrc /tmp/t


# When finished without psacct: 9.81/10.00
# When finished with psacct: 10.00/10.00
The following script will work for ESX v2.x.y
# cis-scan
# vpxuser is special user with /tmp as a homedir.
exec >> /var/log/post.log
```

```
set -x
echo "Red Hat Linux release 7.2" > /etc/redhat-release
/bin/cat >> /etc/ssh/sshd_config << EOF
Protocol 2
Banner /etc/motd
EOF
echo '     Protocol 2' >> /etc/ssh/ssh_config
/sbin/chkconfig telnet off
/sbin/chkconfig ftp off
/bin/sed '2s/^/umask 077/' </etc/rc.d/init.d/vmkhalt> /tmp/vmkhalt
/bin/mv /tmp/vmkhalt /etc/rc.d/init.d/vmkhalt
/usr/sbin/useradd USERNAME
/usr/sbin/usermod -G wheel USERNAME
/sbin/chkconfig xfs off
/sbin/chkconfig —level 0123456 gpm off
/sbin/chkconfig nfslock off
/sbin/chkconfig —level 0123456 sendmail off
/sbin/chkconfig nfs off
/sbin/chkconfig autofs off
/sbin/chkconfig smb off
/sbin/chkconfig portmap off
/bin/cat >> /etc/sysctl.conf << EOF
net.ipv4.conf.default.secure_redirects=0
net.ipv4.conf.all.secure_redirects=0
net.ipv4.conf.all.rp_filter=1
net.ipv4.icmp_echo_ignore_broadcasts=1
net.ipv4.conf.all.accept_redirects=0
net.ipv4.conf.default.accept_source_route=0
net.ipv4.tcp_syncookies=1
net.ipv4.conf.default.accept_redirects=0
net.ipv4.tcp_max_syn_backlog=4096
net.ipv4.conf.all.send_redirects=0
net.ipv4.conf.default.send_redirects=0
EOF
/bin/chmod 600 /etc/sysctl.conf
/usr/sbin/sysctl -p
```

```
/bin/sed '/boot/s/defaults/defaults,nodev/' < /etc/fstab > /tmp/fstab
/bin/sed '/vmimages/s/defaults/defaults,nodev/' < /tmp/fstab > /etc/fstab
/bin/sed '/cdrom/s/kudzu/kudzu,nosuid,nodev/' < /etc/fstab > /tmp/fstab
/bin/sed '/floppy/s/kudzu/kudzu,nosuid,nodev/' < /tmp/fstab > /etc/fstab
/bin/sed '/0660 <floppy>/s/^/#/' < /etc/security/console.perms > /tmp/console.perms
/bin/sed '/0600 <cdrom>/s/^/#/' < /tmp/console.perms > /etc/security/console.perms
/bin/sed '/0600 <pilot>/s/^/#/' < /etc/security/console.perms > /tmp/console.perms
/bin/sed '/0600 <jaz>/s/^/#/' < /tmp/console.perms > /etc/security/console.perms
/bin/sed '/0600 <zip>/s/^/#/' < /etc/security/console.perms > /tmp/console.perms
/bin/sed '/0600 <ls120>/s/^/#/' < /tmp/console.perms > /etc/security/console.perms
/bin/sed '/0600 <camera>/s/^/#/' < /etc/security/console.perms > /tmp/console.perms
/bin/sed '/0600 <memstick>/s/^/#/' < /tmp/console.perms > /etc/security/console.perms
/bin/sed '/0600 <flash>/s/^/#/' < /etc/security/console.perms > /tmp/console.perms
/bin/sed '/0600 <diskonkey>/s/^/#/' < /tmp/console.perms > /etc/security/console.perms
/bin/sed '/0600 <rem_ide>/s/^/#/' < /etc/security/console.perms > /tmp/console.perms
/bin/sed '/0600 <rio500>/s/^/#/' < /tmp/console.perms > /etc/security/console.perms
/bin/sed '/server_args/s/-l -a/-l -a -d/' < /etc/xinetd.d/wu-ftpd > /tmp/wu-ftpd
/bin/mv /tmp/wu-ftpd /etc/xinetd.d
/bin/sed '/vpxuser/s/0:99999/7:90/' < /etc/shadow > /tmp/shadow
/bin/mv /tmp/shadow /etc/shadow
/bin/mkdir -p /home/vpxuser
/bin/chmod 750 /home/vpxuser
/bin/chown vpxuser /home/vpxuser
/usr/sbin/usermod -d /home/vpxuser vpxuser
/bin/rpm -e —nodeps hotplug
echo 'root' > /etc/cron.allow
echo 'root' > /etc/at.allow
/bin/chmod 600 /etc/crontab
/bin/sed '/nologin/d' < /etc/shells > /tmp/shells
/bin/mv /tmp/shells /etc/shells
/bin/sed 's/PASS_MAX_DAYS     99999/PASS_MAX_DAYS     90/' < /etc/login.defs >
➥ /tmp/login.defs
/bin/sed 's/PASS_MIN_DAYS     0/PASS_MIN_DAYS     7/' < /tmp/login.defs >
➥ /etc/login.defs
/bin/sed 's/PASS_MIN_LEN     5/PASS_MIN_LEN     6/' < /etc/login.defs >
➥ /tmp/login.defs
```

```
/bin/mv /tmp/login.defs /etc/login.defs
/usr/sbin/usermod -s /sbin/nologin news
/usr/sbin/usermod -s /sbin/nologin rpm
grep -v 'tty7' /etc/securetty¦ grep -v 'tty8' ¦ grep -v 'tty9' ¦ grep -v 'tty10' ¦ grep
➡ -v 'tty11' > /tmp/securetty
mv /tmp/securetty /etc/securetty
/bin/sed 's/}/        only_from            = 10.0.0.0\n}/' < /etc/xinetd.conf >
/tmp/xinetd.conf
/bin/mv /tmp/xinetd.conf /etc/xinetd.conf
/bin/sed 's/umask 002/umask 077/' < /etc/bashrc > /tmp/bashrc
/bin/sed 's/umask 002/umask 077/' < /etc/csh.cshrc > /tmp/csh.cshrc
/bin/sed 's/umask 022/umask 077/' < /tmp/bashrc > /etc/bashrc
/bin/sed 's/umask 022/umask 077/' < /tmp/csh.cshrc > /etc/csh.cshrc
/bin/sed '/ctrlaltdel/s/^/#/' < /etc/inittab > /tmp/inittab
/bin/sed '22s/^/~:S:wait:\/sbin\/sulogin/' < /tmp/inittab > /etc/inittab
/bin/cat > /etc/motd << EOF
*****************************************************************************
                                NOTICE TO USERS


This computer system is the private property of its owner, whether individual, corporate
or government. It is for authorized use only. Users (AUTHORIZED or UNAUTHORIZED) have no
explicit or implicit expectation of privacy.


Any or all uses of this system and all files on this system may be intercepted, moni-
tored, recorded, copied, audited, inspected, and disclosed to your employer, to author-
ized site, government, and law enforcement personnel, as well as authorized officials of
government agencies, both domestic and foreign.


By using this system, the user consents to such interception, monitoring, recording,
copying, auditing, inspection, and disclosure at the discretion of such personnel or
officials. Unauthorized or improper use of this system may result in civil and criminal
penalties and administrative or disciplinary action, as appropriate. By continuing to use
this system you indicate your awareness of and consent to these terms and conditions of
use. LOG OFF IMMEDIATELY if you do not agree to the conditions stated in this warning.


*****************************************************************************
EOF
echo "AUTHORIZED USE ONLY" > /etc/issue
```

```
/bin/sed '/pam_wheel.so use_uid/s/^#//' < /etc/pam.d/su > /tmp/su
/bin/mv /tmp/su /etc/pam.d/su
echo '*       soft      core      0' >>  /etc/security/limits.conf

# Bastille
echo "ALL: 10.0.0." >> /etc/hosts.allow
echo "ALL: ALL" >> /etc/hosts.deny
/bin/sed '5s/^/umask 077/' < /etc/profile > /tmp/profile
/bin/mv /tmp/profile /etc/profile
echo "umask 077" >> /etc/zprofile
/bin/sed '4s/^/umask 077/' < /etc/csh.login > /tmp/csh.login
/bin/mv /tmp/csh.login /etc/csh.login
/bin/sed '2s/^/umask 077/' < /root/.bash_profile > /tmp/.bash_profile
/bin/mv /tmp/.bash_profile /root/.bash_profile
/bin/chmod u-s /usr/sbin/ping6
/bin/chmod u-s /usr/sbin/traceroute
/bin/chmod u-s /usr/sbin/traceroute6
/bin/chmod u-s /usr/sbin/usernetctl
/bin/chmod u-s /usr/bin/rcp
/bin/chmod u-s /usr/bin/rlogin
/bin/chmod u-s /usr/bin/rsh
/bin/chmod u-s /usr/bin/rdist
/bin/chmod u-s /usr/bin/rexec
/bin/chmod u-s /usr/bin/rcp
/bin/chmod u-s /usr/bin/at
/bin/chmod u-s /bin/ping
/bin/chmod u-s /bin/mount
/bin/chmod u-s /bin/umount
/bin/chmod u-s /usr/bin/smbmnt

for x in /bin/mt /bin/setserial /sbin/badblocks /sbin/ctrlaltdel /sbin/chkconfig
➥ /sbin/debugfs /sbin/depmod /sbin/dumpe2fs /sbin/fdisk /sbin/fsck
/sbin/fsck.minix
➥ /sbin/fsck.ext2 /sbin/halt /sbin/hdparm /sbin/hwclock /sbin/ifconfig
/sbin/ifdown
➥ /sbin/ifup /sbin/init /sbin/insmod /sbin/killall5 /sbin/mingetty
```

```
/sbin/mkbootdisk
➥ /sbin/mke2fs /sbin/mkfs /sbin/lilo /sbin/mkfs.minix
do
     if [ -e $x ]
     then
          chmod 750 $x
     fi
done
for x in /sbin/mkfs.ext2 /sbin/mkfs.msdos /sbin/mkinitrd /sbin/mkraid /sbin/mkswap
➥ /sbin/modinfo /sbin/modprobe /sbin/portmap /sbin/quotaon /sbin/runlevel
➥ /sbin/swapon /sbin/tune2fs /usr/bin/eject /usr/bin/minicom /usr/sbin/atd
➥ /usr/sbin/atrun /usr/sbin/crond /usr/sbin/edquota /usr/sbin/exportfs
➥ /usr/sbin/groupadd/usr/sbin/groupdel
do
     if [ -e $x ]
     then
          chmod 750 $x
     fi
done
for x in /usr/sbin/grpck /usr/sbin/grpconv /usr/sbin/grpunconv /usr/sbin/imapd
➥ /usr/sbin/ipop2d /usr/sbin/ipop3d /usr/sbin/logrotate /usr/sbin/mouseconfig
➥ /usr/sbin/newusers /usr/sbin/nmbd /usr/sbin/ntpdate /usr/sbin/ntpq
➥ /usr/sbin/ntptime /usr/sbin/ntptrace /usr/sbin/ntsysv /usr/sbin/pppd
➥ /usr/sbin/pwck /usr/sbin/pwconv
➥ /usr/sbin/pwunconv /usr/sbin/in.telnetd
do
     if [ -e $x ]
     then
          chmod 750 $x
     fi
done
for x in /usr/sbin/rdev /usr/sbin/rotatelogs /usr/sbin/rpc.mountd /usr/sbin/rpc.nfsd
➥ /usr/sbin/rpc.rquotad /usr/sbin/rpcinfo /usr/sbin/setup /usr/sbin/showmount
➥ /usr/sbin/smbd /sbin/syslogd /usr/sbin/tcpd /usr/sbin/tcpdump
➥ /usr/sbin/timeconfig /usr/sbin/tmpwatch
➥ /usr/sbin/useradd /usr/sbin/userdel /usr/sbin/usermod /usr/sbin/vipw
```

```
➥ /sbin/stinit /usr/sbin/groupmod
do
      if [ -e $x ]
      then
            chmod 750 $x
      fi
done
for x in /sbin/klogd /usr/sbin/lpc /sbin/rpc.statd /usr/sbin/squid /usr/sbin/tunelp
do
      if [ -e $x ]
      then
            chmod 750 $x
      fi
done
/bin/chmod o-rwx /usr/bin/gpasswd /sbin/netreport /usr/sbin/userhelper
/usr/sbin/usernetctl
/bin/chmod 770 /sbin/dump /sbin/restore
/bin/chmod 550 /usr/sbin/makemap /usr/sbin/quotastats /usr/sbin/repquota
/bin/sed "s/'rexec', 'rlogin', 'rsh','login','shell'/'rexec', 'rlogin', 'rsh'/"
➥ < /usr/lib/Bastille/test_AccountSecurity.pm > /tmp/test_AccountSecurity.pm
/bin/mv /tmp/test_AccountSecurity.pm /usr/lib/Bastille/test_AccountSecurity.pm
/bin/chmod 755 /usr/lib/Bastille/test_AccountSecurity.pm
#/bin/sed 's/Options FollowSymLinks/Options None/' < /etc/httpd/conf/httpd.conf
➥> /tmp/httpd.conf
#/bin/sed 's/FollowSymLinks//' < /tmp/httpd.conf > /etc/httpd/conf/httpd.conf
/bin/chmod 400 /etc/shadow
/usr/sbin/bastille -n —assessnobrowser
/bin/rm /tmp/bashrc /tmp/console.perms /tmp/csh.cshrc /tmp/fstab /tmp/inittab
➥ /tmp/t /tmp/httpd.conf
IPTables Script for ESX v3
IPTABLES=/sbin/iptables
AdminIP="10.0.0.18 10.0.0.9" # change to include all administrative and ESX nodes

# Standard Rules
for x in 902 80 443 2050:5000 8042:8045 427 22 5989 5988
do
```

```
          rulenum=`$IPTABLES —line-numbers -L INPUT -n ¦ grep "tcp" ¦ grep
➡ "$x state NEW" ¦ awk '{print $1}'`
              # Replace original rule to DROP everything from all other hosts
          $IPTABLES -R INPUT $rulenum -m state —state NEW -m tcp -p tcp —dport $x
➡ -j DROP
          for y in $AdminIP
          do
                  $IPTABLES -I INPUT $rulenum -m state —state NEW -s $y -m tcp -p tcp
➡ —dport $x -j ACCEPT
          done
done
# Added to allow HPSIM/HPSMH access
for x in 2381
do
          rulenum=`$IPTABLES —line-numbers -L INPUT -n ¦ grep "tcp" ¦ grep "$x" ¦
➡ awk '{print $1}'`
              # Replace original rule to DROP everything from all other hosts
          $IPTABLES -R INPUT $rulenum -m tcp -p tcp —dport $x -j DROP
          for y in $AdminIP
          do
                  $IPTABLES -I INPUT $rulenum -s $y -m tcp -p tcp —dport $x -j ACCEPT
          done
done
#Standard Rules
for x in 2050:5000 8042:8045
do
          rulenum=`$IPTABLES —line-numbers -L INPUT -n ¦ grep udp ¦ grep "$x state NEW" ¦
awk
'{print $1}'`
              # Replace original rule to DROP everything from all other hosts
          $IPTABLES -R INPUT $rulenum -m state —state NEW -m udp -p udp —dport $x
➡ -j DROP
          for y in $AdminIP
          do
                  $IPTABLES -I INPUT $rulenum -m state —state NEW -s $y -m udp -p udp
➡ —dport $x -j ACCEPT
```

```
        done
done
# Standard rules
for x in 427
do
     rulenum=`$IPTABLES —line-numbers -L INPUT -n ¦ grep "udp" ¦ grep "$x" ¦
➡ awk '{print $1}'`
        # Replace original rule to DROP everything from all other hosts
     $IPTABLES -R INPUT $rulenum -m udp -p udp —dport $x -j DROP
     for y in $AdminIP
     do
          $IPTABLES -I INPUT $rulenum -s $y -m udp -p udp —dport $x -j ACCEPT
     done
done
```

Appendix B

ESX Version 3
Text Installation

This first section of this appendix covers the steps common to both a clean installation and an upgrade or reinstall. The second section then focuses on all the steps to complete the installation but highlights those that are distinctly different between the two processes.

Steps Common to Clean Installations and Reinstalls/Upgrades

To run a text-based install, enter esx text at the main installation page (see Figure B.1) and then press Return. If nothing is typed, a graphical install will begin.

Use the media test selection to verify a downloaded ISO image either used to install via a virtual media device or a freshly created CD-ROM. All other times, it is safe to skip the verification process. When using some form of virtual media device, it could take awhile to run the verification step. To skip the media test, press Return. To test, press the Tab key, and then press Return (see Figure B.2).

Next you will see the welcome screen (see Figure B.3). Press Return to continue.

Select the appropriate type of keyboard (see Figure B.4). Press the Tab key, and then press Return to continue.

Select the appropriate mouse. In our case, a generic two-button PS/2-style mouse is appropriate (see Figure B.5). Press the Tab key twice, and then press Return to Continue.

In a fresh install, the Installation Type screen does not appear. The image in Figure B.6 only appears when the installer detects an earlier version of ESX. If this occurs, select Install using the down-arrow key, press Tab, and then press Return to continue.

Figure B.1   Main ESX Server 3 installation

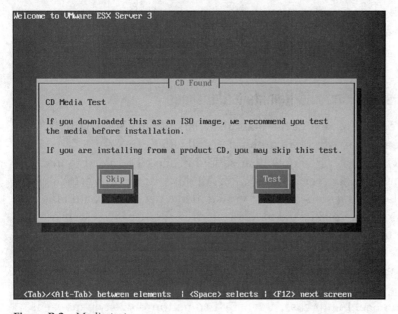

Figure B.2   Media test screen

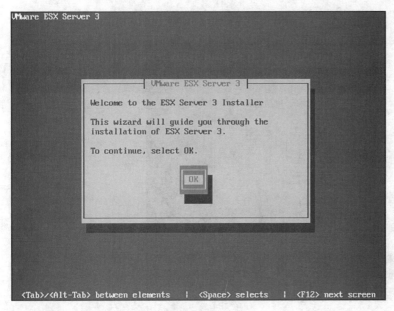

Figure B.3 Welcome to ESX Server 3 installer

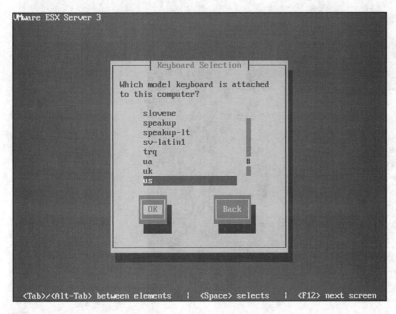

Figure B.4 Select keyboard

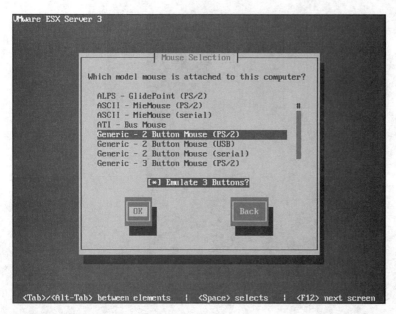

Figure B.5 Mouse configuration

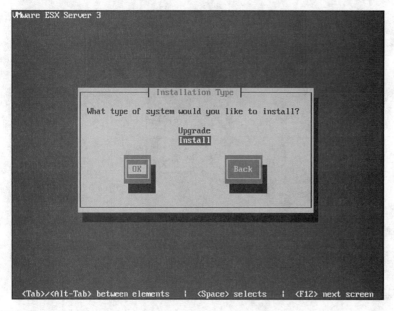

Figure B.6 Select the installation type

Clean Install and Reinstallation/Upgrade Steps

The steps for a clean install and for reinstallation or upgrading differ a bit. Both situations are covered in this section and the differences noted.

Read the EULA (see Figure B.7). After you have done so, use the spacebar to select your acceptance, press Tab, then press Return to continue.

Because this is a clean install, it is paramount that you start with a fresh disk. Press Return to continue.

Note that if a SAN is connected, zoned, and presented to the ESX server, the message shown in Figure B.8 can occur for each LUN depending on whether ESX can interpret the partition table. In some cases, ESX cannot interpret the partition table, and this could be catastrophic, so read and select Yes with care. In this case, it is best to leave a SAN disconnected or unpresented until after the installation.

Choose the default by pressing Tab three times, and then press Return to continue. If there exists a local VMFS to preserve, use the spacebar when at the appropriate location to select Keep Existing VMFS Partitions, and then continue with pressing the Tab until OK is highlighted (see Figure B.9).

For a clean install, just press the Tab key, and then press Return to continue, which selects the Yes button. If you are not doing a clean install, you will see something like Figure B.10.

Use the down-arrow button to select /var/log, and then press the Tab key twice, and then press Return when Edit is highlighted (see Figure B.11).

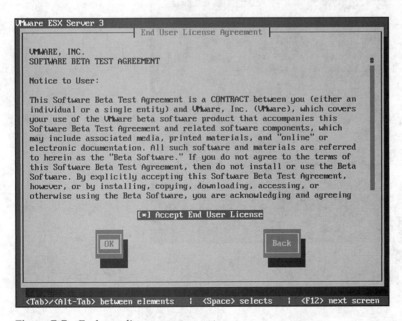

Figure B.7   End-user license agreement

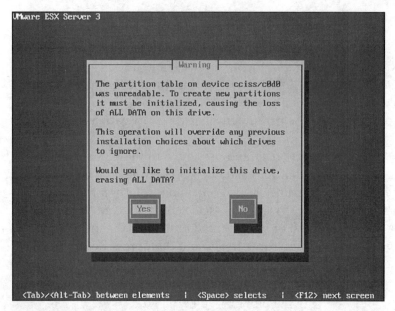

Figure B.8   Unreadable partition table warning

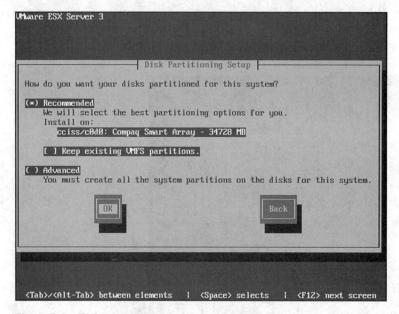

Figure B.9   Disk partitioning setup

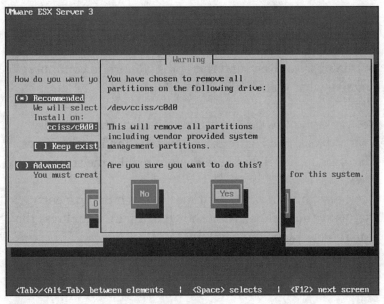

Figure B.10   Disk partitioning warning

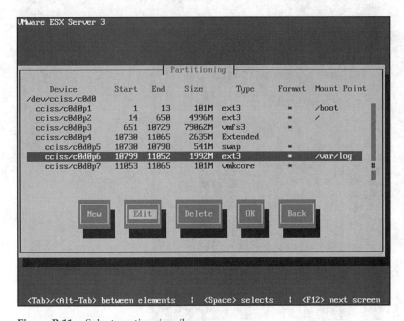

Figure B.11   Select partion /var/log

Press the Tab key six times and change the Fill Maximum Size of (MB) value of 2000 to 4000 (see Figure B.12). Press the Tab key two more times, and then press the Return key to continue.

Use the left-arrow button to select New, and then press Return to continue. You should see something like what is shown in Figure B.13.

Press Return to continue.

Type in /var, and then press the Tab key three times to reach the size entry. Type 4000. Your screen should look like Figure B.14. Press the Tab key five times, and then press Return to continue. You should see something like the screen shown in Figure B.15. Press Tab again.

Type in /tmp, and then press the Tab key three times to reach the size entry. Type 4000. You should see something like what is shown in Figure B.16. Press the Tab key five times, and press Return to continue.

You should see a screen like that shown in Figure B.17. Press Return to continue.

Type in /vmimages, and then press the Tab key three times to reach the size entry. Type 12000. You should see a screen that looks like Figure B.18. Press the Tab key five times, and then press Return to continue.

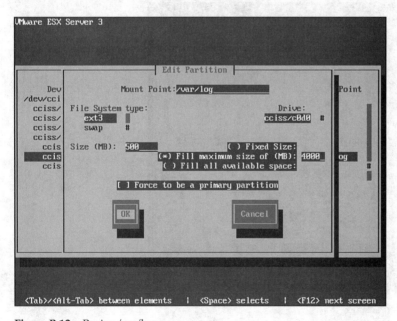

Figure B.12　Resize /var/log

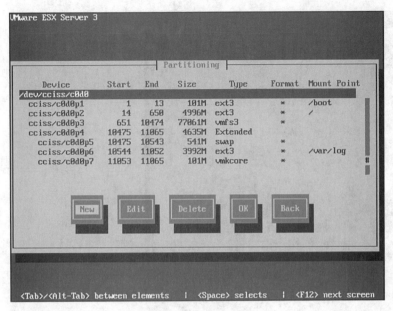

Figure B.13 Partition disk after resize of /var/log

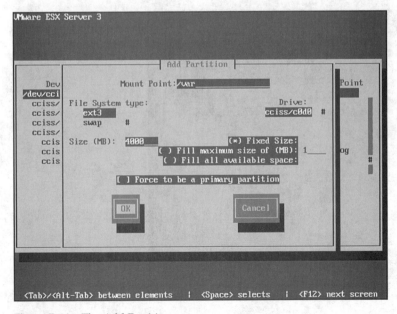

Figure B.14 The Add Partition screen

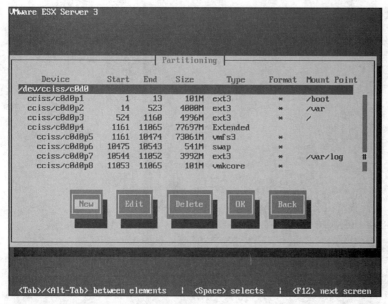

Figure B.15 Partition disk after add /var

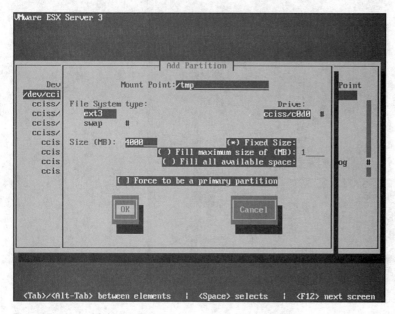

Figure B.16 Add /tmp

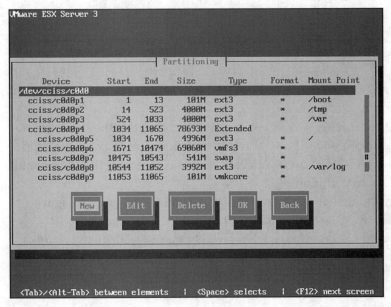

Figure B.17   Partition disk after add /tmp

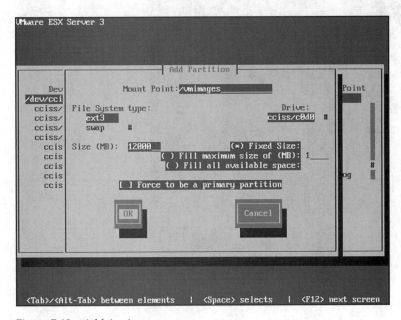

Figure B.18   Add /vmimages

You should see a screen like that in Figure B.19. Press the Tab key three times, and then press Return to continue.

Press Return to continue. You should see the Boot Loader Configuration screen (see Figure B.20).

You should see a second Boot Loader Configuration screen, as shown in Figure B.21. Simply press Return to continue.

In the Console Ethernet Selection screen (see Figure B.22) use the down-arrow button to select the second on-board NIC. Press Tab and Return to continue. We did this because the first NIC was not connected. If it is connected, this step could be just a Tab and Return to continue.

Next you will find yourself at the Network Configuration screen (see Figure B.23). Use the spacebar to deselect Use bootp/dhcp, and then enter in the IP address, netmask, gateway, and primary DNS given to you by your network folks. Use Tab to proceed from field to field. After the DNS is entered, press Tab until the Create Virtual Machine Network option is selected, and use the spacebar to disable this feature. Press Tab and then Return to continue.

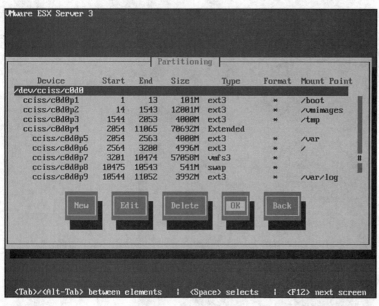

Figure B.19   Partition disk after add /vmimages

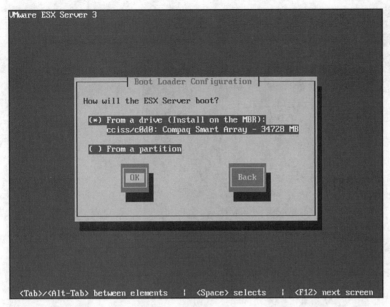

Figure B. 20   Boot Loader Configuration screen

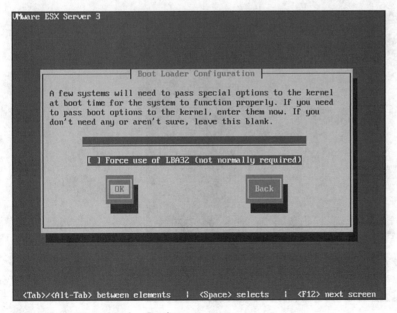

Figure B.21   Boot Loader Configuration screen

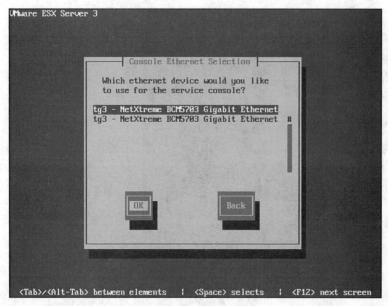

Figure B.22   Console Ethernet Selection screen

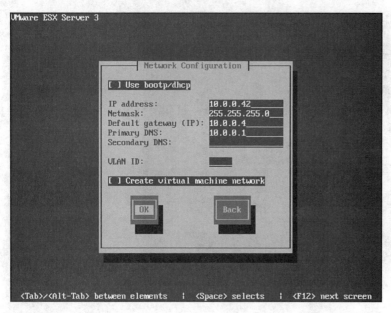

Figure B.23   Network configuration

At the Hostname Configuration screen shown in Figure B.24, enter in the fully qualified domain name (FQDN) for this server. Press Tab and Return to continue. Failure to use the FQDN will result in VMware HA failing to work.

You will now see the Time Zone Selection screen (see Figure B.25). Use the up-arrow key to find and select the appropriate time zone, which is Chicago for this server. Press Tab and Return to continue.

As in Figure B.26, set the root password twice using Tab to go between fields. Then Tab to highlight OK, and press Return to continue.

Figure B.27 shows the setup for a clean install. Review the installation setup. Press Page Down to review, or press OK to continue. Move on to Figure B.31.

Figures B.28 through B.30 show the setup screens for the reinstallation/upgrade scenario. Review the installation setup.

Press OK to continue.

Figure B.31 shows installation starting.

Figure B.32 shows the Perl programming language starting to install.

Finally, you get a screen indicating installation is complete (see Figure B.33).

Press Return to eject the media and reboot the server to run ESX version 3.

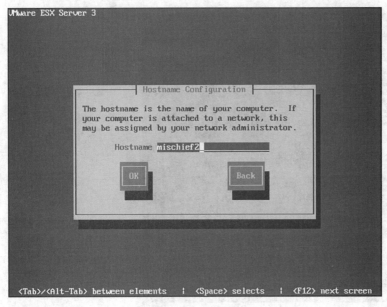

Figure B.24 Hostname Configuration screen

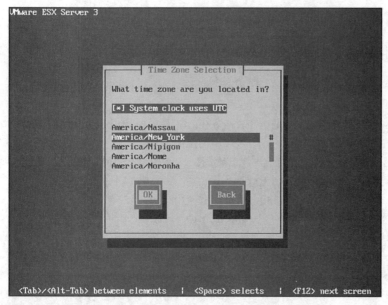

Figure B.25 Time Zone Selection screen

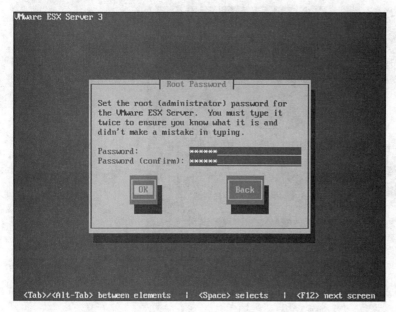

Figure B.26 Set root password

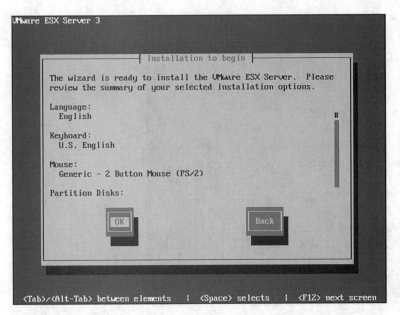

Figure B.27 About to install

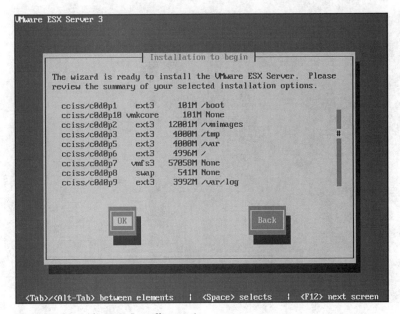

Figure B.28 About to Install page 1

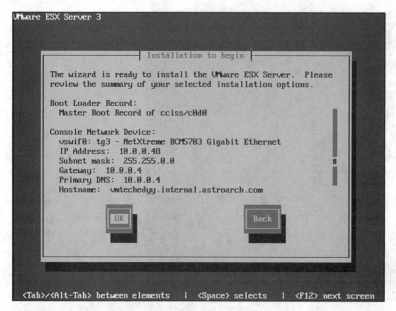

Figure B.29 About to Install page 2

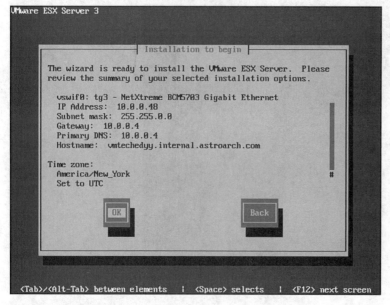

Figure B.30 About to Install page 3

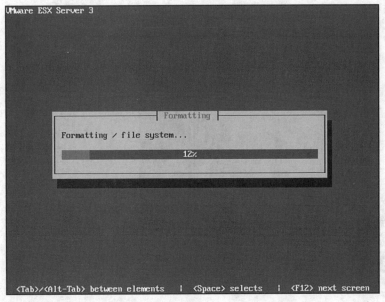

Figure B.31 The installation beginning to format the file system

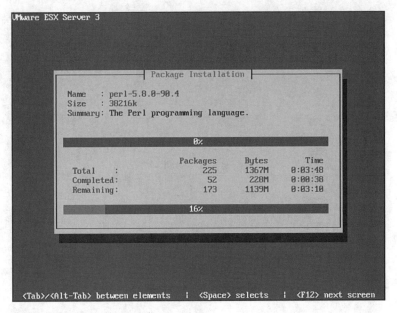

Figure B.32 Installing packages

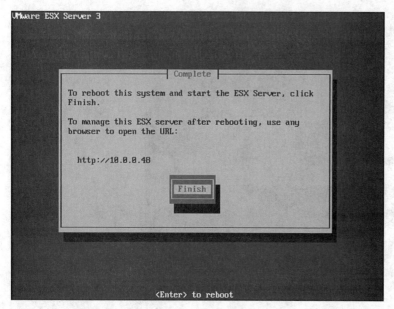

Figure B.33   ESX Server 3 installer complete

Appendix C

ESX Version 3 Graphical Installation

This appendix covers both clean installations and reinstallations/upgrades. The first installation screen is shown in Figure C.1.

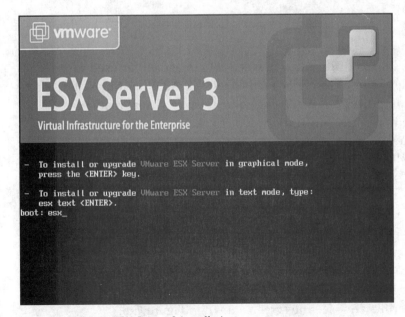

Figure C.1 Main ESX Server 3 installation

To run a text based install, enter esx text and then press Return. If nothing is typed, a graphical install will begin. However, the first screen, as shown in Figure C.2, is actually text based.

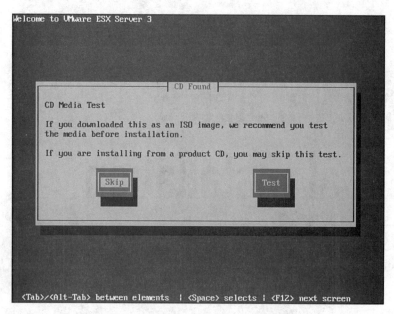

Figure C.2 Media test screen

Use the media test selection to verify a downloaded ISO image either used to install via a virtual media device or a freshly created CD-ROM. All other times, it is safe to skip the verification process. When using some form of virtual media device, it could take awhile to run the verification step. To skip, press Return; otherwise, press Tab then Return to test.

The first graphical installation screen will appear, a welcome screen (see Figure C.3).

Click next to continue.

At the next screen, you must select your keyboard type (see Figure C.4).

Select the appropriate keyboard, then click Next to continue. You should now see the Mouse Configuration screen (see Figure C.5).

Select the appropriate mouse. In our case, a generic two-button PS/2-style mouse is appropriate. Click Next to continue.

At this point, you may or may not see the screen shown in Figure C.6.

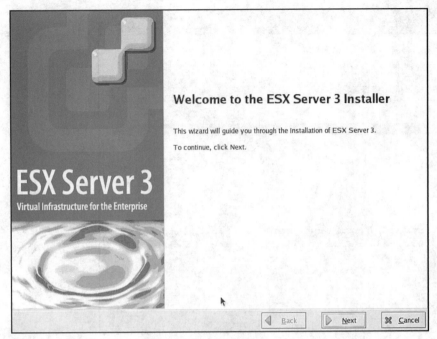

Figure C.3 Welcome to ESX Server 3 Installer screen

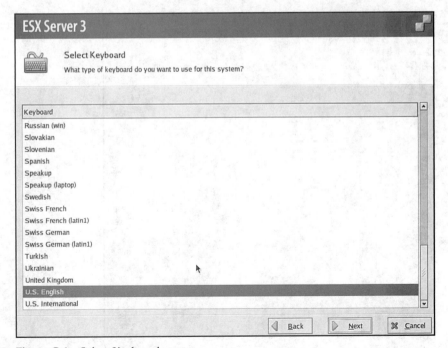

Figure C.4 Select Keyboard screen

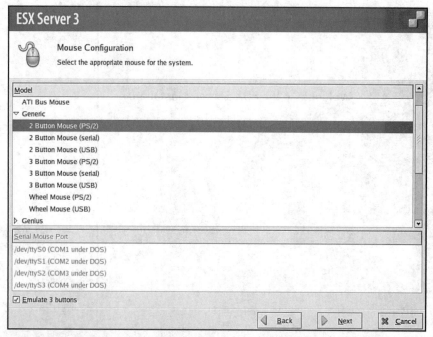

Figure C.5   Mouse Configuration screen

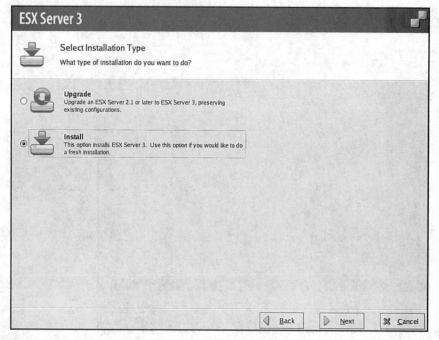

Figure C.6   Select Installation Type screen

In a fresh install, the Select Installation Type screen does not appear. It only appears when a previous version of ESX is detected. If this occurs, select Install, and then click Next to continue. This should take you to the End User License Agreement page (see Figure C.7)

Read the EULA. Once completed, check the check box to select your acceptance and click Next to continue.

Assuming you are attempting a reinstall or upgrade, you will see the warning screen shown in Figure C.8.

Because this is a clean install, it is paramount that you start with a fresh disk. Press Return to continue. Note that if a SAN is connected, zoned, and presented to the ESX Server, this message can occur for each LUN depending on whether or not ESX can interpret the partition table. In some cases, ESX cannot interpret the partition table, and this could be catastrophic, so read and select Yes with care. In this case, it is best to leave a SAN disconnected or unpresented until after the installation.

Figure C.9 shows the Partitioning Options screen.

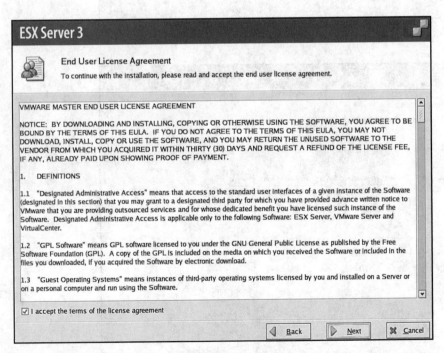

Figure C.7   End User License Agreement page

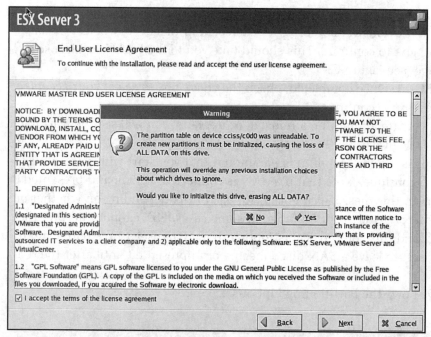

Figure C.8 Unreadable Partition Table Warning screen

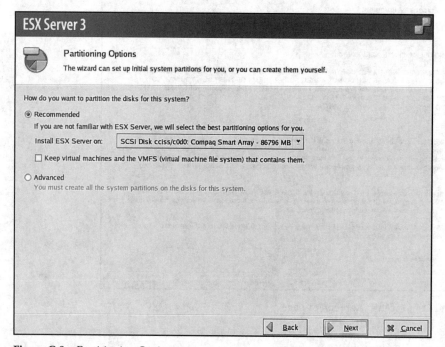

Figure C.9 Partitioning Options screen

Choose the recommended partitioning. If there exists a local VMFS to preserve, check the "Keep virtual machines and the VMFS (virtual machine files system) that contains them" box and click Next to continue.

You should see a warning like that shown in Figure C.10.

For a clean install, select Yes to continue. Next you will see the Partition Disks screen (see Figure C.11).

Select /var/log, and then select Edit to continue. As shown in Figure C.12, change the 2000 value to 4000. Then click OK to continue.

You should see all the Partition Disks page again (see Figure C.13). The size of the partition should have changed.

Now let's add a partition. Select New to continue. At the Add Partition dialog, type in /var, and then type 4000 in the Size entry, as shown in Figure C.14. Click OK to continue.

Figure C.15 shows the result of adding /var.

Select New to continue. The Add Partition dialog appears again. Type in /tmp and then type 4000 in the Size entry, as shown in Figure C.16. Click OK to continue.

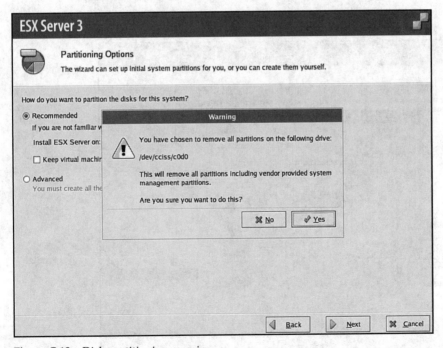

Figure C.10 Disk partitioning warning

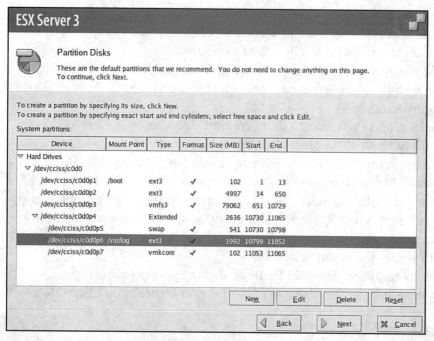

Figure C.11   Select partion /var/log

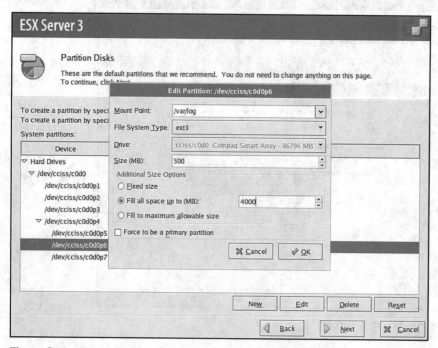

Figure C.12   Resize /var/log

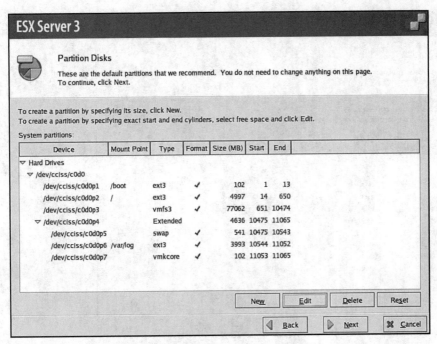

Figure C.13 Partition disk after resize of /var/log

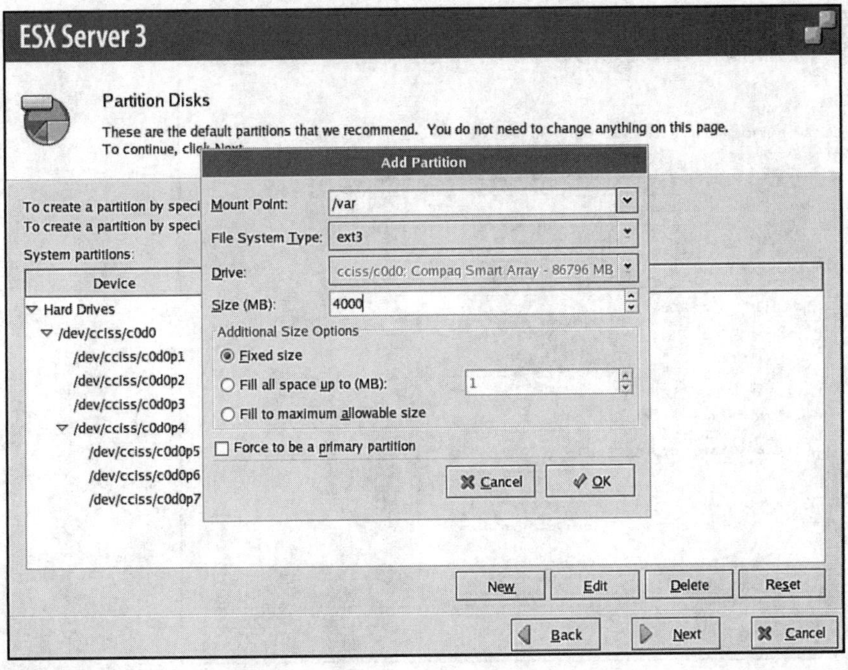

Figure C.14 The Add Partition dialog

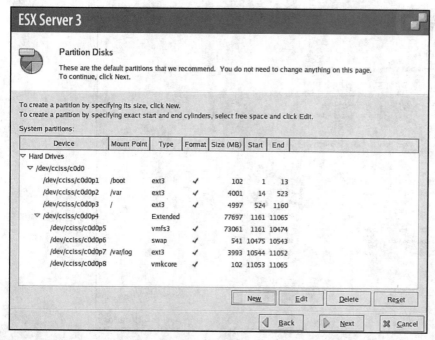

Figure C.15 Partition disk after adding /var

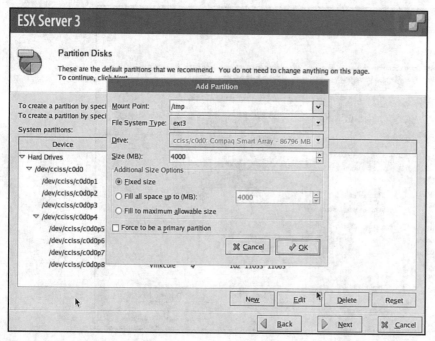

Figure C.16 Add /tmp

Figure C.17 shows the result of adding /tmp.

Let's add another partition. Select New to continue. Type in /vmimages, and then type 12000 in the Size entry, as in Figure C.18. Click OK to continue.

Figure C.19 shows the result of adding /vimages.

Click Next to continue to the Advanced Options screen. Figure C.20 shows the Advanced Options screen.

Click Next to continue. You should now be at the Network Configuration screen (see Figure C.21).

Select the second NIC in the drop-down list. This is because the first NIC is not connected.

Select the non-DHCP dialog button, and then enter in the IP address (A), net-mask (B), gateway (C), and primary DNS (D) given to you by your network folks. You can use Tab to proceed from field to field or select them with your mouse. After the DNS has been entered, deselect "Create a default network for virtual machines." Enter in the fully qualified domain name (FQDN) (F) for this server. Click Next to continue. Failure to use the FQDN will result in VMware HA failing to work.

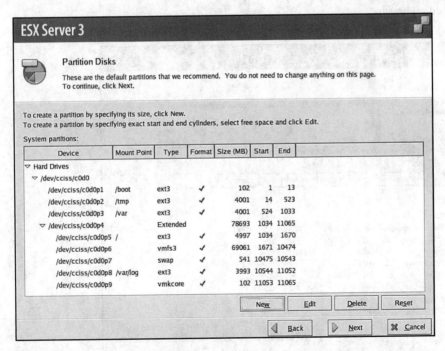

Figure C.17 Partition disk after adding /tmp

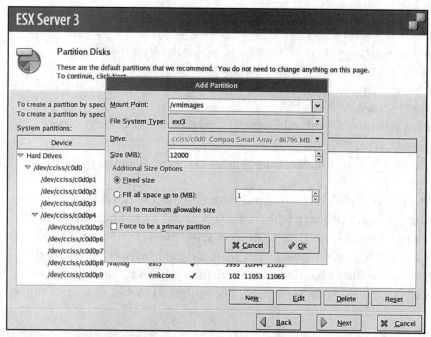

Figure C.18 Add /vmimages

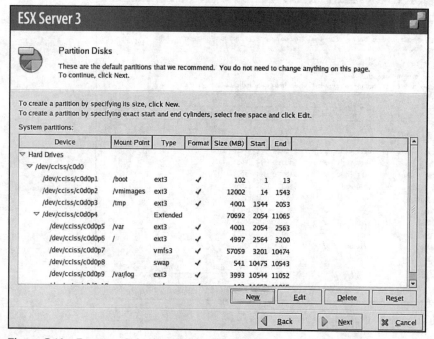

Figure C.19 Partition disk after adding /vmimages

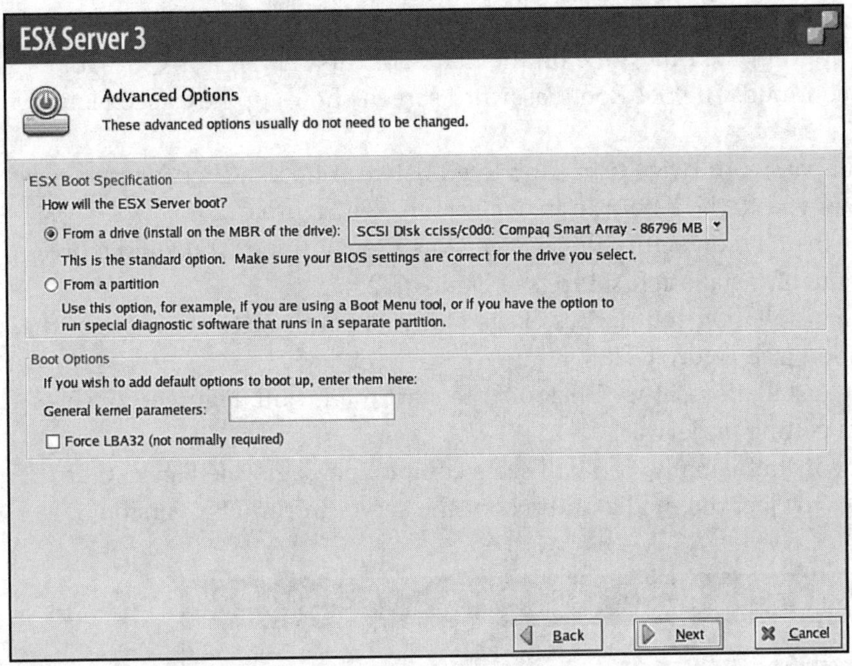

Figure C.20   Advanced Options screen

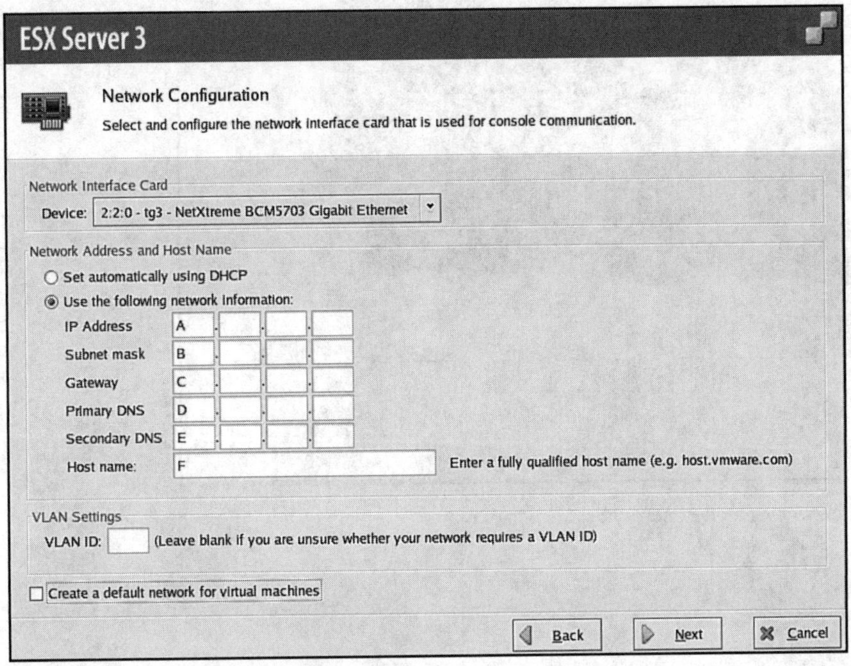

Figure C.21   Network Configuration screen

The Time Zone Selection screen is next (see Figure C.22).

Select the appropriate time zone on the map. For this server, it is Chicago. Click Next to continue. The Set Root Password screen shows up next (see Figure C.23)

Set the root password twice using Tab to go between fields. Click Next to continue. This takes you to the About to Install screen (see Figure C.24)

Review the installation setup. Press Page Down to continue. You will be presented with more of installation setup (see Figure C.25).

Review the installation setup. Press Page Down to continue to see more of the setup information (see Figure C.26).

Review the installation setup. Click next to start the install. Figure C.27 show the installation getting underway.

Monitor the install. Finally, you will see a completion page (see Figure C.28).

Click Finish to eject the media and reboot the server to run ESX version 3.

Figure C.22   Time Zone Selection screen

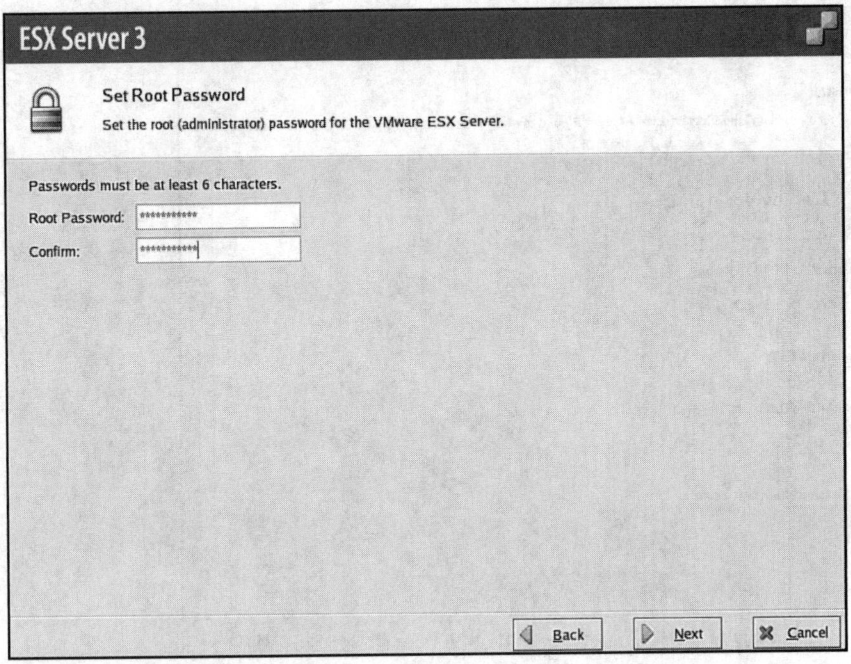

Figure C.23 Set Root Password screen

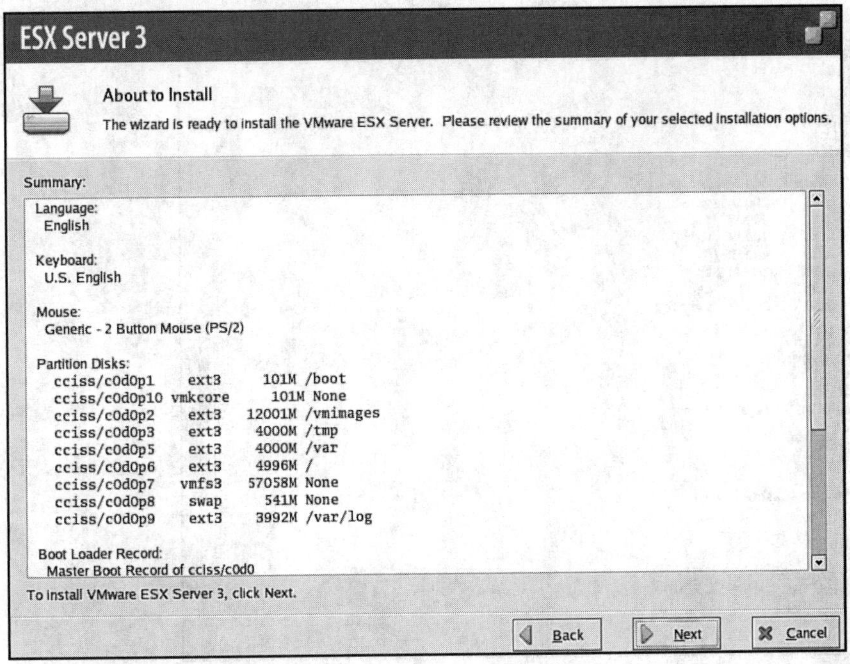

Figure C.24 About to Install screen

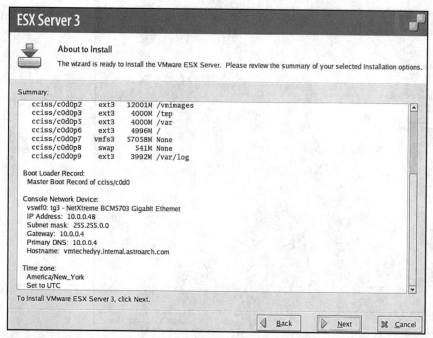

Figure C.25   About to Install screen

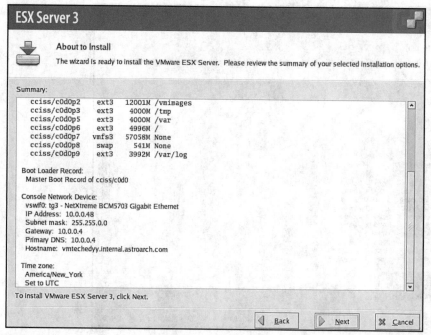

Figure C.26   About to Install screen

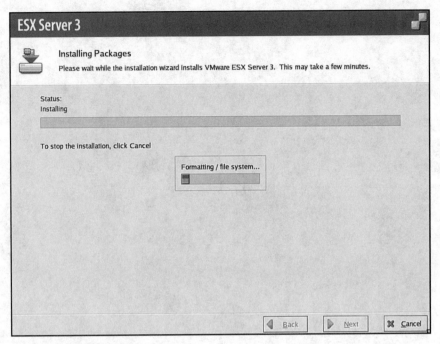

Figure C.27 Installing Packages screen

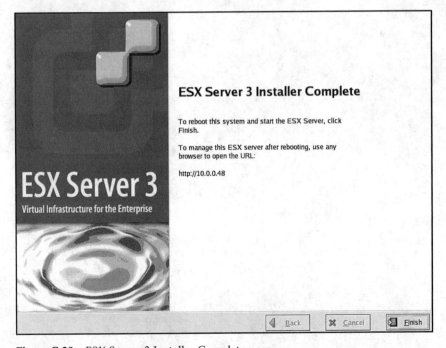

Figure C.28 ESX Server 3 Installer Complete page

References

Benvenuti, Christian. *Understanding LINUX Network Internals.* Sebastopol, CA.: O'Reilly Media, Inc., 2006.

Bovet, David and Cesati, Marco. *Understanding the LINUX Kernel.* Sebastopol, CA: O'Reilly Media, 2001.

Kroah-Hartman, Greg. *Linux Kernel in a Nutshell.* Sebastopol, CA: O'Reilly Media, 2007.

Massed VMware links: www.vmware-land.com/Vmware_Links.html.

Oglesby, Ron, et al. *VMware ESX Server: Advanced Technical Design Guide.* Bethel Park, PA: The Brian Madden Company, 2005.

Preston, W. Curtis. *UNIX Backup and Recovery.* Sebastopol, CA: O'Reilly Media, 2007.

Processor information: www.sandpile.org.

Purdy, Gregor N. *Linux iptables Pocket Reference.* Sebastopol, CA: O'Reilly Media, 2004.

Siever, Ellen, et al. *LINUX in a Nutshell, 5th Edition.* Sebastopol, CA.: O'Reilly Media, 2005.

Terpstra, John H. *Samba-3 By Example.* Upper Saddle River, NJ: Prentice Hall, 2004.

VMware community forums: http://communities.vmware.com/index.jspa.

VMware Professional: www.vmprofessional.com.

VMware Virtual Infrastructure documentation: www.vmware.com/support/pubs/vi_pubs.html.

VMware Virtual Infrastructure IO HCL: www.vmware.com/pdf/vi3_io_guide.pdf.

VMware Virtual Infrastructure SAN HCL: www.vmware.com/pdf/vi3_san_guide.pdf.

VMware Virtual Infrastructure Systems HCL: www.vmware.com/pdf/vi3_systems_guide.pdf.

XtraVirt: www.xtravirt.com.

Index

Safari®
BOOKS ONLINE
ENABLED

THIS BOOK IS SAFARI ENABLED

INCLUDES FREE 45-DAY ACCESS TO THE ONLINE EDITION

The Safari® Enabled icon on the cover of your favorite technology book means the book is available through Safari Bookshelf. When you buy this book, you get free access to the online edition for 45 days.

Safari Bookshelf is an electronic reference library that lets you easily search thousands of technical books, find code samples, download chapters, and access technical information whenever and wherever you need it.

TO GAIN 45-DAY SAFARI ENABLED ACCESS TO THIS BOOK:

- Go to **informit.com/safarienabled**
- Complete the brief registration form
- Enter the coupon code found in the front of this book on the "Copyright" page

If you have difficulty registering on Safari Bookshelf or accessing the online edition, please e-mail customer-service@safaribooksonline.com.